T0272123

PROCEEDINGS

OF THE

HARVARD CELTIC COLLOQUIUM

Volume 41, 2022

Edited by

Lorena Alessandrini
Colin Brady
Rachel Martin
Oisín Ó Muirthile
Graham O'Toole

Published by
The Department of Celtic Languages and Literatures
Faculty of Arts and Sciences, Harvard University

Distributed by
Harvard University Press
Cambridge and London

ISBN: 978-0-674-29578-0

The cover design is based on the medallion of an
Early Christian belt shrine from Moylough, Co. Sligo.
Drawing by Margo Granfors

Designed and typeset by the Fenway Group
Boston, Massachusetts

CONTENTS

PREFACE

The annual Harvard Celtic Colloquium originated in a graduate student conference convened in 1980 by students in the Harvard University Department of Celtic Languages and Literatures. Since then the conference has developed into an internationally recognized event drawing together scholars and students from around the world to present papers on all facets of Celtic Studies. The Colloquium is the oldest graduate-run conference in the field of Celtic Studies, and, true to its origins, it remains entirely run and organized by the graduate students of the Harvard Celtic Department. The principal organizers of the Colloquium then become the editorial board for the publication of its Colloquium proceedings.

Papers given at the Colloquium may be submitted for publication following peer review in the journal, *The Proceedings of the Harvard Celtic Colloquium* (*PHCC*). The journal is distributed by Harvard University Press, which also handles subscriptions and single volume orders. Information on the Colloquium and *PHCC* may be fount through the Harvard University Department of Celtic Languages and Literatures web site. The managing editor for *PHCC* may be contacted directly at phcc@fas.harvard.edu.

Acknowledgements

The editors are indebted to Professor Catherine McKenna for her advice and encouragement, and to the Celtic department staff, Ms. Mary Violette, and Mr. Steven Duede, for their help with the Colloquium and administrative matters. We also wish to thank the managing editor of *PHCC*, and the staff of Fenway Group for their help with the publication of this volume.

Lorena Alessandrini
Colin Brady
Rachel Martin
Oisín Ó Muirthile
Graham O'Toole

Organizers of the Harvard Celtic Colloquium 2022, and Editors of *PHCC* volume 41

Trapped and Transported:
The Fianna from the *Bruíon* to Boston

Natasha Sumner

Fionn and his Fianna have had an enduring presence across all eras of Gaelic literature, and the extant body of story and song about these long-embattled heroes is sizable. Several loose categories serve to organize the vast Fenian corpus and aid comparative analysis, one of which centres upon the theme of the Fianna's entrapment in a hostile supernatural abode, or *bruíon*. In what follows, I will first re-examine the bruíon tale category to establish a definitive structural pattern. I will then provide an overview of the literary and oral corpus that demonstrates the structural cohesion of the category. Finally, I will explore the bruíon tales that Irish and Scottish immigrants carried with them to the so-called 'new' world, documenting a treasure trove of previously unknown or understudied copies in North American manuscripts and a much smaller body of collected folklore. By enabling a better understanding of the composition and breadth of this category of Fenian narrative, it is my hope that this article will stimulate new work on bruíon tales at home and abroad.

The Fenian Bruíon Tale

The bruíon tale category has a fairly lengthy critical history. It was described by William Alexander Craigie as far back as the 1890s, then by Reider Thoralf Christiansen and Cormac Ó Cadhlaigh in the 1930s, Gerard Murphy in the 1950s, and Alan Bruford in the 1960s. These descriptions preceded more thorough discussions by Seosamh Watson in the 1970s, Joseph F. Nagy and Dáithí Ó hÓgáin in the 1980s, and Breandán Ó Cróinín more recently.[1] The following examination of the category builds on their scholarship.

---

[1] W.C. Craigie, "Three Tales of the Fiann," *The Scottish Review* 24 (1894): 270-97; Reidar Thoralf Christiansen, *The Vikings and the Viking Wars in Irish and Gaelic Tradition* (Oslo: I Kommisjon Hos J. Dybwad, 1931), 28, 30-32; Cormac Ó Cadhlaigh, *An*

1

The word appears as *bruiden* in Old and Middle Irish, *bruidhean* in Early Modern Gaelic and modern Scottish Gaelic, and *bruíon* in Modern Irish. Lexicographers of both medieval and modern forms of the Gaelic languages agree that bruíon is a homonym with the following two distinct meanings:

A.) Hostel, large banqueting-hall; house, mansion (also of similar hall in otherworld) (eDIL). Hostel, fairy dwelling (Ó Dónaill).

B.) Fight, contest, quarrel (eDIL). Strife, quarrel (Ó Dónaill).[2]

In usage (A.) it denotes a building intended for hospitality—a hostel, banqueting hall, house, or mansion—that may be of an otherworldly nature. In usage (B.) it means a fight or quarrel. The first meaning is primary in the categorization of bruíon tales: the protagonists of the tale enter a banqueting hall or

---

Fhiannuidheacht (Dublin: Oifig an tSoláthair, 1936), 83; Gerard Murphy, ed. and trans., *Duanaire Finn: The Book of the Lays of Fionn,* vol. 3, Irish Texts Society 43 (London: Irish Texts Society, 1953), 26 n.1; Gerard Murphy, *The Ossianic Lore and Romantic Tales of Medieval Ireland: Fianaíocht agus Rómánsaíocht,* Irish Life and Culture 11 (Dublin: Cultural Relations Committee, 1955), 52-54; Alan Bruford, *Gaelic Folk-Tales and Mediaeval Romances: A Study of the Early Modern Irish 'Romantic Tales' and their Oral Derivatives* (Dublin: An Cumann le Béaloideas Éireann, 1969), 9, 115; Seosamh Watson, *Mac na Míchomhairle* (Dublin: An Clóchomhar, 1979), 56-74; Joseph F. Nagy, "Shamanic Aspects of the Bruidhean Tale," *History of Religions* 20 (1981): 302-22 at 306; Dáithí Ó hÓgáin, *Fionn Mac Cumhaill: Images of the Gaelic Hero* (Dublin: Gill and Macmillan, 1988), 202-16; Breandán Ó Cróinín, "Bruíonta na Féinne" in *Séimhfhear Suairc: Aistí in Ómós don Ollamh Breandán Ó Conchúir,* ed. Seán Ó Coileáin, Liam P. Ó Murchú, and Pádraigín Riggs (Dingle: An Sagart, 2013), 480-501; Breandán Ó Cróinín, "Bruidhean Chaorthainnón Lámhscríbhinn is Sine i Leabharlann Náisiúnta na hAlban," unpublished MA thesis (National University of Ireland, Maynooth, 1995), 69-89.

[2] *Electronic Dictionary of the Irish Language* (eDIL), s.v. bruiden, accessed 24 September 2022; Niall Ó Dónaill, ed., *Foclóir Gaeilge-Béarla* (Dublin: An Gúm, 1977), s.v. bruíon; cf. Ó Cróinín, "Bruidhean Chaorthainn," 48.

dwelling suitable for hospitality. In these tales, moreover, the protagonists are verifiably human, and the dwelling is invariably supernatural or otherworldly.[3]

The first criterion of the Fenian bruíon tale category–that the human protagonists of a story will enter a supernatural abode–is not a scenario unique to Fenian literature. Characters enter dwellings in supernatural realms in numerous cultural traditions, and the applicable international motif for such expeditions is F370: Visit to fairyland.[4] The motif is widely used in Gaelic literature,[5] and a little over a century ago, T.F.

---

[3] Cf. Ó Cróinín, "Bruíonta," 481-82; Ó Cróinín, "Bruidhean Chaorthainn," 48, 91. It is worth noting, as others have done (e.g. Ó Cróinín, "Bruíonta," 482; Ó Cróinín, "Bruidhean Chaorthainn," 48; Nagy, "Shamanic Aspects," 306 n.16), that many (but not all) bruíon tales also portray a battle, either inside or near this structure. We could therefore read a double meaning into the category heading in some cases. That said, tales in which 'fight' or 'quarrel' seems to be the primary meaning of bruíon–such as *Bruidhean Bheag na hAlmhaine* (The Little Brawl at Allen)–are not necessarily bruíon tales. Although Ó Cróinín ("Bruíonta," 480) includes Bruidhean Bheag na hAlmhaine in a title-dependent thematic categorization of bruíon tales, it does not meet other structural criteria of the category. Following Murphy and Bruford, and with reference to current folkloristic approaches, I employ a strictly structural categorization that necessarily excludes this tale; c.f. Murphy, *Ossianic Lore*, 53; Bruford, *Gaelic Folk-Tales*, 115, 120. See also Standish Hayes O'Grady's note on the use of the word in this tale in *Silva Gadelica (I–XXXI): A Collection of Tales in Irish*, vol. 2 (London: Williams and Norgate, 1892), xvi-xvii, n.1.
[4] Stith Thompson, *Motif-Index of Folk-Literature*, revised edition. (Bloomington: Indiana University Press, 1956), 75; Tom Peete Cross, *Motif-Index of Early Irish Literature*, Folklore Series 7 (Bloomington: Indiana University Press, 1952), 264; Arthur A. Wachsler, "The 'Elaborate Ruse': A Motif of Deception in Early Celtic Historical Variant of the Journey to the Otherworld," *Journal of the Folklore Institute* 12.1 (1975): 29-46 at 29.
[5] For a detailed account of the bruíon motif in early Irish literature, see Ó Cróinín, "Bruidhean Chaorthainn," 46-93. Regarding comparable encounters with the otherworld in modern fairy lore, see *e.g.* Alan Bruford, "Oral and Literary Fenian Tales," in *Fiannaíocht:*

O'Rahilly produced a list of three reasons a human might be enticed into a supernatural bruíon in medieval Irish tales:

    i.   As the love interest of a supernatural or otherworldly person.

    ii.   As an ally against an enemy.

    iii.   To get revenge on the human.[6]

Somewhat more recently, Arthur A. Wachsler identified an additional reason:

    iv.   "As the recipient of some apparently vital information."[7]

Of course, as Nagy has so well elucidated, Fionn and his companions regularly frequent those remote regions in which the boundary between this world and the other is most penetrable, and they are therefore more prone to otherworldly encounters than other mortal Gaelic heroes.[8] Taking the Fenian corpus as a whole, we can observe that the Fianna are enticed into supernatural dwellings for all of these reasons. Indeed, O'Rahilly cites two illustrative medieval Fenian tales, one in which the Fianna are brought into the home of a large otherworldly man so that Fionn can meet and marry the man's daughter, which he does;[9] and another in which the sons of a Tuatha Dé Danann lord (Midhir son of the Daghda) seek the

---

Essays on the Fenian Tradition of Ireland and Scotland, ed. Bo Almqvist, Séamas Ó Catháin, and Pádraig Ó Héalaí (Dublin: An Cumann le Béaloideas Éireann, 1987), 25-56 at 31.

[6] Thomas F. O'Rahilly, "Díthreabhach Ghlinne an Pheice," *Gadelica: A Journal of Modern-Irish Studies* 1 (1912-13): 279-83 at 283; Watson, *Mac na Míchomhairle*, 47-48.

[7] Wachsler, "Elaborate Ruse," 29, 42; *cf.* Nagy, "Shamanic Aspects," 306. Nagy views such bruíon journeys as "shamanic."

[8] Joseph F. Nagy, *The Wisdom of the Outlaw: The Boyhood Deeds of Finn in Gaelic Narrative Tradition* (Berkeley, Los Angeles, and London: University of California Press, 1985), 20-21, 37; *cf.* Nagy, "Shamanic Aspects," 302.

[9] O'Rahilly, "*Díthreabhach*," 283. See *Laoidh Síthil Caoilti* (The Lay of Caoilte's Dipper) in Eoin Mac Neill, ed. and trans., *Duanaire Finn: The Book of the Lays of Fionn*, vol. 1, Irish Texts Society 7 (London: Irish Texts Society, 1908), 38-45.

Fianna so that the heroes can help defeat an otherworldly enemy, which also comes to pass.[10] In the Fenian bruíon tale category, specifically, the third reason is most common, the first and fourth are occasional, and the second is not found.

The reason the Fianna's presence is wanted by the inhabitants of the bruíon is not initially apparent to Fionn and his men. This, too, is not unique to the bruíon tale category. As Wachsler further observed, in most medieval Irish tales concerning supernatural dwellings, the human seems to need to enter the dwelling willingly, and so a deceptive ruse is often employed to accomplish this.[11] In the Fianna's case, the ruse tends to be fairly simple; our peripatetic heroes' principal leisure activity–hunting–leads them far into the liminal wilderness, where, as nightfall approaches, or after being surrounded by a magic mist, they become vulnerable to disingenuous offers of food, drink, and lodging. They may even be lured to the bruíon by a shapeshifter in animal form–a sure tactic, given the Fianna's penchant for the chase. On other occasions, an emissary might be sent to the Fianna to formally issue a deceptive offer of hospitality, such as an invitation to a feast in the fateful bruíon. In these cases, a complex explanation for the invitation may be given.[12]

Simply being enticed into a bruíon does not make a story a bruíon tale, however. The above criteria are common to many Irish tales that employ international motif F370. The most important criterion that distinguishes Fenian bruíon tales– besides the fact that they are necessarily about the Fianna–is that

---

[10] O'Rahilly, "Díthreabhach," 283. This is one of the many stories told by Caoilte in *Acallam na Senórach*; see Whitley Stokes, ed., "Acallamh na Senórach" in *Irische Texte,* vol. 4.1, ed. Whitley Stokes and Ernst Windisch (Leipzig: Verlag Von S. Hirzel, 1900), 136-47, ll. 5005-264; *cf.* Ann Dooley and Harry Roe, trans., *Tales of the Elders of Ireland: Acallam na Senórach* (Oxford: Oxford University Press, 1999), 139-46.

[11] Wachsler, "Elaborate Ruse," 31.

[12] Ó Cróinín, "Bruidhean Chaorthainn," 86, 91; *cf.* Ó Cadhlaigh, *An Fhiannuidheacht,* 83.

our heroes become trapped in the bruíon.[13] As Seosamh Watson has noted, supernatural individuals–be they fairies, members of the Tuatha Dé Danann, or similar otherworldly or quasi-otherworldly people–frequently torment humans who venture into their realm, and the inhabitants of the bruíonta in question in this tale category are no exception.[14] In fact, Dáithí Ó hÓgáin observes that an otherworldly abode assigned this appellation is, more often than not, "a hostile and macabre underworld."[15] The bulk of a Fenian bruíon tale frequently concerns the torments endured, and the Fianna's escape from them (for which, see below).[16] The trap may be accomplished by magical incapacitation, whether by enervating music, magically sticky surfaces, or charmed drinks.[17] Or, other strange and potentially life-threatening occurrences can serve to stymy the Fianna, often while they are surrounded by the powerful and unpredictable inhabitants of the bruíon, and perhaps also the inhabitants' equally intimidating allies. For instance, in several bruíon tales, the Fianna are presented with an enchanted livestock animal that they are unable to catch, cook, or serve, try as they might.

But the Fianna, being the heroes of these tales, always escape in the end.[18] Depending on the tale, they may be rescued by one or more comrades who have learned of their plight; or, they successfully convince one of the inhabitants of the bruíon to help them; or, occasionally, their supernatural captor simply chooses to free them. The latter scenario might occur if, for

---

[13] Bruford, *Gaelic Folk-Tales*, 115; Ó hÓgáin, *Fionn Mac Cumhaill*, 202; Ó Cróinín, "Bruidhean Chaorthainn," 46.

[14] Watson, *Mac na Míchomhairle*, 56-74. Watson compares this motif in medieval Irish literature with popular folklore in which fairies torment humans for their own amusement (48).

[15] Ó hÓgáin, *Fionn Mac Cumhaill*, 202.

[16] Bruford, *Gaelic Folk-Tales*, 115.

[17] *Cf.* Ó Cróinín, "Bruidhean Chaorthainn," 87.

[18] Minor characters (the 'bit parts' in these stories) do not always survive, but members of the *gnáthfhiann* 'standing fían' always do; *cf.* Ó Cróinín, *Bruidhean Chaorthainn*, 88, 91-92. For the term *gnáthfhiann*, see *e.g.* Stokes, "Acallamh," 181, l. 6538 and 182, l. 6563; *cf.* Dooley and Roe, *Tales of the Elders*, 183, 184.

instance, the captor's aim was to communicate pertinent information to the Fianna in order to teach them a life lesson. Alternatively, the captor may have tired of his or her antics. That this means of release is often accompanied by the motif of the disappearing phantom house suggests influence from popular fairy stories in which humans who, unwisely roaming at dusk, stumble into otherworldly dwellings and form the subject of the inhabitants' entertainment until the fairy fort and its lavish trappings disappear at daybreak, leaving the disoriented human alone on barren ground.[19] More often than not, however, the Fianna's release is violent, and it may be accompanied by a battle initiated either by the trapped heroes themselves or by those who have come to rescue them. If a battle takes place, the Fianna will successfully defeat their captor and his allies, resulting in a satisfying–and crowd-pleasing–resolution to the bruíon tale.

These criteria are reflected in the structural map below and the following overview of the Fenian bruíon tale corpus.[20]

Structure of a Fenian Bruíon Tale

A.   One or more Fenian heroes are wanted by a supernatural/otherworldly person:

    1.   To get revenge on the heroes.

    2.   As the recipients of some apparently vital information.

    3.   As the love interest of a supernatural/otherworldly person.

B.   Because the heroes usually need to enter the supernatural/ otherworldly person's bruíon willingly, a deceptive ruse is required, e.g.:

---

[19] The motif is F771.6. Phantom house: disappears at dawn: Thompson, *Motif-Index*, 210; Cross, *Motif-Index*, 298; *cf.* Ó Cróinín, "Bruidhean Chaorthainn," 88.

[20] Compare the structural map developed by Ó Cróinín ("Bruidhean Chaorthainn," 86-89), which provided a starting point for this exploration.

1. Having gone astray, generally while hunting, the heroes receive a disingenuous offer of hospitality.

2. The heroes are formally issued a deceptive offer of hospitality, such as an invitation to a feast.

C. The heroes are trapped in the bruíon and subjected to magical torments:

1. Incapacitating device(s), e.g.: enervating music; magically sticky surfaces; charmed drinks.

2. Confounding trickery, e.g.: an enchanted livestock animal that cannot be caught/cooked/served; numerous other strange and threatening occurrences.

D. The heroes are released from the bruíon:

1. By an external rescuer.

2. By turning an inhabitant of the bruíon to their cause.

3. By their captor, sometimes via the motif of the disappearing phantom house.

E. If a battle was initiated to release the heroes, they will defeat their captor.

The Fenian Bruíon Tale Corpus

The bruíon tale category encompasses both prose stories and poetic lays. Fenian prose and poetry differ considerably in style: while the lengthy early modern prose stories spare no detail, the events celebrated in lays tend to be more sparsely narrated, and contextual details may be lacking. It is likely that the same authors composed in both forms, however.[21] They

---

[21] Fenian poetry and prose are generally not ascribed to named authors, but the composition of both likely fell under the purview of *filí*; see Marc Caball and Kaarina Hollo, "The Literature of Later Medieval Ireland, 1200–1600: From the Normans to the Tudors," *The Cambridge History of Irish Literature*, vol. 1, ed. Margaret

drew inspiration from the same topical wells, and both the tales and the lays are narrative, i.e. they tell stories.[22] Despite stylistic differences, therefore, Fenian stories and lays are complementary forms that are most appropriately considered alongside one another, as they are here.

Brief summaries highlight the structural features that identify these thirteen stories and lays as Fenian bruíon tales. It should be noted that some of the stories and lays in the bruíon tale category are complex and may fit concurrently into other common Fenian thematic categories, such as foreign invasion or overseas adventure. Space does not allow me to examine overlapping categories here, and the summaries' focus is limited to structural features of bruíon tales.

The number of known manuscript and orally collected versions is given for each story or lay. Manuscript circulation data for the prose texts is taken from Bruford's index in *Gaelic Folk-Tales and Mediaeval Romances*, unless a more recent study has been completed.[23] I am reliant on studies of individual lays, when available, for poetry circulation data. Information about the oral corpus comes from the Fionn Folklore Database. It will be observed that there are generally more individual tellings in the database than the number of unique versions given here. This is because sometimes a particular tradition bearer's version was collected two or more times, resulting in multiple tellings of the same version of the tale.

Kelleher and Philip O'Leary (Cambridge: Cambridge University Press, 2006), 74-139 at 94, 111.

[22] Because the lay form came to incorporate elements of lyric, lament, and panegyric as it developed, several late medieval and early modern Fenian texts classed as lays are not strictly narrative verse; see Joseph Flahive, *The Fenian Cycle in Irish and Scots-Gaelic Literature*, Cork Studies in Celtic Literatures 1 (Cork: Cork Studies in Celtic Literatures, 2017), 32. The lays in the bruíon tale category are narrative, however.

[23] Bruford's index, while useful, is outdated and insufficient. Whenever one of the texts he examined is re-edited, additional manuscript copies are uncovered that were not well documented around the midpoint of the last century when he was doing his research.

While most of the tales extant in early modern and modern Gaelic languages found their way into oral circulation, there are no orally collected versions of the earliest tale. This is typical of Fenian texts in Old and Middle Irish, which are not nearly as well preserved as later texts. Because more manuscript copies of the latter are generally extant, many of them circulating in very late manuscripts, there is consequently a much stronger relationship between post-twelfth-century literature and modern Fenian folklore. The availability of nineteenth- and twentieth-century print editions likely further supported the transmission of those texts that were already circulating orally. Nearly all of the Fenian bruíon tales have been published, and the dates of the earliest editions are given. Academic editions, generally the most recent, are footnoted after each summary.

Óenach indiu luid in rí (Today the king went to a fair)

> Oisín, Fionn, and Caoilte unwittingly seek hospitality in an unfriendly otherworldly dwelling not while hunting, but after an impromptu horse race carries them far from their comrades. The experience becomes increasing strange and hostile; they are surrounded by people with more (or fewer) heads and eyes than one might expect, who sing unharmoniously, and flay and try to feed them their own horses, but the meat will not cook. A battle erupts, which ends at daybreak when a mist descends, the strange combatants fall dead, the house disappears, and the horses re-appear, alive and well. We then learn that the occupants of the dwelling were seeking vengeance from the Fianna.[24]
> A1-B1-C2-D3

---

[24] Marieke van Kranenburg, "'Oenach indiu luid in rí': An Edition of the Three Known Version of 'Today the King Went to a Fair' or 'Finn and the Phantoms' with Translation and Textual Notes," unpublished MA thesis (University of Utrecht, 2008), 27-81.

The earliest bruíon tale is relatively rare in the manuscript record. It is found first in a circa eleventh-century prose version known as *Echtra Finn* (Fionn's Adventure), which is extant in a single manuscript copy. This is clearly related to an eleventh- or early twelfth-century lay preserved in the Book of Leinster and a few later witnesses, which opens "Óenach indiu luid in rí," but which Whitley Stokes dubbed "Fionn and the Phantoms."[25] No orally-collected versions exist. The lay was first edited from manuscript in 1886 and the prose version in 1892.[26]

***Teach Cuanna* (Cuanna's House) /**
***An Óige, an Saol, agus An Bás* (Youth, the World, and Death)**

> A group of Fianna are out hunting when they are surrounded by a magical mist. When the mist clears, they see an unfamiliar dwelling and enter it, whereupon the inhabitants subject them to trickery in the guise of hospitality, such as having them fetch and consume water that turns bitter, or try to catch a talking ram that mysteriously eludes them. After several trying incidents, a member of the household proceeds to share wisdom with the Fianna through allegorical explanations of the trials they have just faced, and explains that they were lured to the dwelling to receive this wisdom. They then

[25] Van Kranenburg," Oenach indiu," 4, 9-10; Kevin Murray, *The Early Fenian Corpus* (Cork: Cork Studies in Celtic Literatures, 2021), 20-21, 23-26. Later adaptations of the lay can be found in *Acallam na Senórach, Duanaire Finn*, the late *Agallamh na Seanórach*, and a handful of eighteenth- and nineteenth-century manuscripts. For the *Acallam* adaptation, see Stokes "Acallam," 45-46, ll. 1595-1618; Dooley and Roe, *Tales of the Elders*, 50.
[26] Whitley Stokes, ed. and trans., "Find and the Phantoms," *Revue Celtique* 7 (1886): 289-307; Ludwig Christian Stern, ed. and trans., "Le Manuscrit Irlandais de Leide," *Revue Celtique* 13 (1892): 1-30 at 5-7, 12-17.

sleep and awaken to find that the otherworldly
dwelling has disappeared.[27]
A2-B1-C2-D3

This prose story first appears in the fourteenth- or fifteenth-
century *Feis Tighe Chonáin* (The Feast at Conán's House), a
composite text, perhaps loosely modeled on the *Acallam*, in
which two of the Fianna lodge at the house of Conán Chinn
tSléibhe and share a series of episodic stories in response to their
host's questions. The narrative frame itself approximates a
bruíon tale insofar as the otherworldly host has a grievance with
Fionn.[28] Although Conán's demand that Fionn answer his
queries is hostile and Fionn must be placed under *geasa* (a
quasi-magical charm) to respond, however, Fionn clearly has
the upper hand in the exchange. In fact, Fionn goes so far as to
torment Conán, forcing the otherworldly man to give his
daughter in marriage to the Fenian leader, despite the fact that
she is already betrothed to a highly eligible suitor. When the rest
of the Fianna arrive, they find that their companions hardly need
rescuing. If the frame tale in *Feis Tighe Chonáin* is not truly a
bruíon tale, however, the *Teach Cuanna* episode unequivocally
is, as we can see from its structural pattern.

The *Feis Tighe Chonáin* compilation, and the *Teach
Cúanna* episode in particular, were very popular. There are at
least fifty-seven known manuscript copies of the early modern
text,[29] and seventy-three unique orally-collected versions of the
episode, which is known in modern Irish as *An Óige, an Saol,*

---

[27] Maud Joynt, ed. *Feis Tighe Chonáin*, Mediaeval and Modern Irish
Series 7 (Dublin: The Stationary Office, 1936), 14-20 ll. 471-659.
See also Ó hÓgáin, *Fionn Mac Cumhaill*, 234-36, 238-41; Bruford,
Gaelic Folk-Tales, 118, 261; Christiansen, *Vikings*, 30-33.
[28] Fionn was responsible for the deaths of multiple members of
Conán Chinn tSléibhe's family (Joynt, *Feis Tighe Chonáin*, 3).
[29] Bruford (*Gaelic Folk-Tales*, 261) only lists fifty-six manuscript
copies; he was unaware of a North American copy, regarding which
see below. Some manuscript copies are fragmentary and do not
contain the *Teach Cuanna* episode. I have not consulted every
manuscript.

agus An Bás (Youth, the World, and Death).[30] It was first edited from manuscript in 1855.[31]

Cliabhán cuill cía do-róine (Who made a hazel bird trap)

> A magic mist surrounds some of the Fianna. A large man carrying a bird trap approaches and invites them to feast at his fortress. He locks them in for seven days intending to starve them to death, but Fionn makes a bird trap modeled on that of their captor so they can sustain themselves by catching birds. When the big man returns, Fionn demonstrates clemency by preventing the Fianna from killing him.[32]
> A2*-B1-C1*-D2*

The otherworldly nature of the captor in this circa fifteenth-century lay is signaled first by the magic mist preceding his arrival and later by a reference to his *draoithacht* 'magic'.[33] That his motivation to harm the Fianna is left untold is a consequence of the abbreviated narrative style of some lays. The structural pattern of this highly condensed text is also somewhat modified. Thus, the Fianna are not physically incapacitated, their captor assuming that merely locking them in the bruíon will suffice. The big man does not need to be convinced to help them, moreover, since he has already unintentionally shown them the secret to surviving his trap. They therefore receive valuable knowledge from the encounter, apparently in spite of the intentions of their captor.

---

[30] Eighty-eight total tellings are currently recorded: https://fionnfolklore.org/#/lays/tc.

[31] Nicholas O'Kearney, ed. and trans., *Feis Tighe Chonain Chinn-Shleibhe or The Festivities at the House of Conan of Cenn Sleibhe*, Transactions of the Ossianic Society 2 (Dublin: John O'Daly, 1855), 116-99.

[32] Gerard Murphy, ed. and trans., *Duanaire Finn: The Book of the Lays of Fionn,* vol. 2, Irish Texts Society 28 (London: Irish Texts Society, 1933), 60-65; see also Ó Cróinín, *Bruidhean Chaorthainn,* 75.

[33] Murphy *Duanaire Finn*, vol. 2, 64.

The number of extant manuscript copies of this lay, which Murphy dubbed "The Bird-Crib," is not presently known, but it is likely rare. No orally-transmitted versions have been collected.

Bruidhean Chéise Corainn (The Enchanted Hall at Keshcorann)

Several of the Fianna come upon a bruion at Keshcorann while hunting. They are magically incapacitated and bound by the three monstrous daughters of the Tuatha Dé Danann lord of the bruíon, who has a grievance against them. On the brink of death, they are eventually rescued by Goll mac Morna, who defeats the three monstrous women.[34]

A1-B1-C1-D1-E

This prose story was probably composed in the fourteenth to the sixteenth centuries.[35] It was quite popular in manuscripts, with sixty-seven known copies, and moderately popular in the oral sphere, with twenty-five unique orally collected versions in the Fionn Folklore Database.[36] It was first edited from manuscript in 1892.[37]

---

[34] Ní Shéaghdha, Nessa, ed., "Bruighion Chéisi Coruin[n]" in *Trí Bruidhne*, ed. Nessa Ní Shéaghdha and Máire Ní Mhuirgheasa (Dublin: Oifig an tSoláthair, 1941), 3-15. See also Ó Cróinín, "Bruíonta," 483-86; Ó hÓgáin, *Fionn Mac Cumhaill*, 204-5; Bruford, *Gaelic Folk-Tales*, 116-17, 252; Christiansen, *Vikings*, 30.

[35] Ó Cróinín posits that *Bruidhean Chéise Corainn* may have been composed as early as the turn of the fourteenth century, given that the thirteenth- or fourteenth-century lay beginning *Uathadh damh sa coirthe-so* (Alone am I on this crag) appears to reference the story: Ó Cróinín, "Bruíonta," 486; Mac Neill, *Duanaire Finn*, 91-92. We do not know whether the poet's referend was this literary romance or an earlier version of the tale, however, and others have dated the romance later; see *e.g.* Ó hÓgáin, *Fionn Mac Cumhaill*, 204.

[36] Bruford (*Gaelic Folk-Tales*, 252) lists sixty-six manuscript copies; see below. Twenty-seven total tellings are currently recorded: https://fionnfolklore.org /#/lays/bcc.

[37] Standish Hayes O'Grady ed., *Silva Gadelica (I–XXXI): a collection of tales in Irish*, vol. 1 (London: Williams and Norgate, 1892), 306-10.

Bruidhean Chaorthainn **(The Enchanted Hall of the Rowan Tree)**

A disgruntled Lochlanner invites a group of Fianna under false pretenses to a feast in a hostile bruíon. They become magically fastened to either the ground or their seats and must get word of their situation, and the means of their rescue, to their Fenian comrades. The rescuers free them using the blood of three enemy kings, but it runs out and Conán mac Morna must be pulled free, leaving his backside *maol* 'bare' (and giving him his nickname, Conán Maol). The Fianna then battle and defeat their captors.[38]

A1-B2-C1-D1-E

Probably the most well-known bruíon tale today, this prose story dates to the fifteenth or sixteenth century.[39] There are ninety-one known manuscript copies and ninety-eight unique

---

[38] Ó Cróinín, *Bruidhean Chaorthainn*, 163-78. See also Ó Cróinín, "Bruíonta," 487-94; Ó hÓgáin, *Fionn Mac Cumhaill*, 212-16; Bruford, *Gaelic Folk-Tales*, 115-16, 251-52.

[39] Ó Cróinín would date the text as early as 1400, while Caoimhín Breatnach has suggested that it post-dates *Tóraíocht Dhiarmada agus Ghráinne* (The Pursuit of Diarmaid and Gráinne), which he would place perhaps as late as the sixteenth century: Ó Cróinín, *Bruidhean Chaorthainn*, 121-22; Caoimhín Breatnach, "*Bruidhean Chaorthainn*: A Parody of In-Tales in *Tóruigheacht Dhiarmada agus Ghráinne*?," conference presentation, *Fíanaigecht*: 4th International Finn Cycle Conference, 23-25 June 2022, Limerick. Murphy thought the story was probably composed in the sixteenth century: *Ossianic Lore*, 53. The earliest manuscript witness dates to the early seventeenth century.

oral versions, making this the most popular bruíon tale in the oral sphere.[40] It was first edited from manuscript in 1889.[41]

It may be observed that the captor here is Scandinavian rather than otherworldly. In Fenian narrative, invading or visiting foreigners–especially Scandinavians and Greeks, but others as well–typically exhibit supernatural qualities, and there is considerable overlap in the portrayal of foreigners and of otherworldly people like the Tuatha Dé Danann. I therefore draw no distinction between supernatural and otherworldly aggressors.

Bruidhean Eochaidh Bhig Dheirg (Little Red Eochaidh's Enchanted Hall)

> Eochaidh Beag Dearg lures several of the Fianna to his bruíon with a deceptive invitation to feast and lodge there. Upon arrival, they are surrounded by a hostile otherworldly force and subjected to near-deadly trickery in the guise of hospitality: e.g. Eochaidh gives them caustic washing-water that burns off Conán's toe, and tasks them to cook an immovable boar that reanimates upon the application of fire.

---

[40] Ó Cróinín (Bruidhean Chaorthainn, 16-33) lists ninety manuscript copies; see below. One hundred and sixteen total oral tellings are currently recorded: https://fionnfolklore.org/#/lays/bch. Several of these are combined with other Fenian tales, as commonly happens in the oral corpus. One such oral compilation misled Gerard Murphy to categorize the Fenian helper tale *Lorcán mac Luirc* as a bruíon tale due to the incorporation of a *Bruidhean Chaorthainn*-like episode in the version he consulted: Murphy, *Duanaire Finn*, vol. 3, xxiv-xl, 26 n.1.

[41] D. Maignéar [Daniel Magner] (?), ed., "Bruighean Caorthainn an Oileain," *Irish-American* 41.42 (12 Oct. 1889): 3; 41.43 (19 Oct. 1889): 3; 41.44 (25 Oct. 1889): 3; 41.45 (2 Nov. 1889): 3; 41.47 (16 Nov. 1889): 3; 41.48 (23 Nov. 1889): 3.

Another group of Fianna ultimately rescues
them and helps them defeat their captors.[42]
A1-B2-C2-D1-E

This somewhat popular prose story dates to the sixteenth
or seventeenth century. There are at least thirty-three extant
manuscript copies and twenty-six unique orally-collected
versions.[43] It was first edited from manuscript in 1893.[44]

***Laoidh Chruimlinn na gCath* (The Lay of Cruimlinn of the
Battles) / *Turas Fhinn do Lochlann* (Fionn's Journey to
Lochlann) / *Suirghe Fhinn go Críocha Lochlann* (Fionn's Wooing
in Lochlann)**

A vengeful foreigner arrives with the purported
aim of making a match between Fionn and the
daughter of the king of Lochlann. The marriage
proposal is a pretense to entice the Fianna to a
hostile bruíon. They are required to surrender
their weapons before entry, the doors are shut,
and each member of the Fianna is seated
between two armed Lochlanners. One or more
of the Fianna are carrying concealed knives,
however, and in some versions an absent
member of the Fianna also arrives in disguise

---

[42] Máire Ní Mhuirgheasa, ed. "Bruighean Eochaidh Bhig Dheirg" in
Trí Bruidhne, ed. Nessa Ní Shéaghdha and Máire Ní Mhuirgheasa
(Dublin: Oifig an tSoláthair, 1941), 40-91. See also Ó Cróinín,
"Bruíonta," 494-97; Ó hÓgáin, *Fionn Mac Cumhaill*, 207-12, 288-
89; Bruford, *Gaelic Folk-Tales*, 117-18, 257-58.
[43] Bruford (*Gaelic Folk-Tales*, 257-58) lists thirty-two manuscript
copies; see below. Thirty-two total oral tellings are currently
recorded: https://fionnfolklore.org/#/lays/ebd.
[44] Padruig Ó Briain, ed., *Bláithfhleasg de Mhílseáinibh na
Gaoidheilge* (Dublin: Patrick O'Brien, 1893), 129-57.

to help free them. They defeat their captors in
battle.[45]
A1-B2-C1*/2*-D1*-E

Although the Fianna are not physically incapacitated, they
are rendered defenseless by other means–or so their captors
think, for here it is the Fianna who engage in trickery by
concealing their knives.

There are both Irish and Scottish versions of this lay, the
former titled *Laoidh Chruimlinn na gCath* and the latter *Turas
Fhinn do Lochlann*. An adapted account in the Book of Howth
dates the plot at least as early as the sixteenth century, and the
lay is known to have been circulating in the seventeenth century.
An expanded eighteenth-century version titled *Suirghe Fhinn
go Críocha Lochlann* also exists.[46] The lay is preserved in at
least ten extant manuscript copies and was first edited from
manuscript in 1829.[47] Seventy-one unique orally-collected
prose and poetic versions have also been identified.[48]

Eachtra Lomnochtáin (The Adventures of Lomnochtán)

Lomnochtán arrives from overseas and invites
the Fianna to a feast on a faraway island. When
they arrive, he serves them a drink that saps

[45] Christiansen, *Vikings*, 183-85, 195-96, 335-44. See also Máirtín Ó
Briain, "Suirghe Fhinn" in *An Fhiannaíocht*, ed. Pádraig Ó
Fiannachta, Léachtaí Cholm Cille 25 (Maynooth: An Sagart, 1995),
69-95 at 77-78.
[46] J.S. Brewer, ed., "The Book of Howth," *Calendar of the Carew
Manuscripts Preserved in the Archiepiscopal Library at Lambeth*,
vol. 5 (London: Longman and Co. and Trübner and Co., 1871), 1-
260 at 9-10; Ó Briain, "Suirghe Fhinn," 70-72.
[47] Ó Briain, "Suirghe Fhinn," 91; Connellan, Thaddaeus, ed., *An
Duanaire. Fiannaigheacht, Danta, agus Ranna le'r tTeanga Mhin
Bhinn Mhilis a Léigheadh. A Selection of Irish Poems and Moral
Epigrams* (Dublin: M. Goodwin, 1829), 6-8. Connellan's edition is
of the expanded version. The earlier version was first edited in John
Francis Campbell, ed., *Leabhar na Féinne* (London: Spottiswoode,
1872), 83-86.
[48] Eighty-one total oral tellings are currently recorded: https://
fionnfolklore.org/#/lays/ftl.

them of their strength, and reveals his intention to avenge a grievance. The Fianna escape with the help of the daughter of the local king, who falls in love with Diarmaid and reveals Lomnochtán's weakness. Conán, who was left behind on the Fianna's ship, arrives and defeats Lomnochtán in battle.

A1-B2-C1-D1/2-E

This prose story has been dated to the seventeenth century.[49] It was popular in manuscripts, but not in the oral sphere; there are at least fifty-three manuscript copies, but I know of only one orally collected version.[50] It was first edited from manuscript in 1893.[51]

Seilg Ghleanna an Smóil (The Chase in Glenasmole) / Laoidh na Mná Móire thar Lear (The Lay of the Big Woman Overseas)

Several of the Fianna are invited to a bruíon by a shapeshifting deer-woman who is actually the gigantic daughter of the king of Greece. They are given a feast, after which the woman demands to marry an unwilling Fionn. They are then incapacitated by sleep music. While Goll battles the woman and her forces from without, a female guard falls in love with Diarmaid and agrees to release them.[52]

A3-B2-C1-D1/2-E

---

[49] Ó hÓgáin, *Fionn Mac Cumhaill*, 261.

[50] Bruford (*Gaelic Folk-Tales*, 262) lists fifty-two manuscript copies; see below. For the oral version, see: https://fionnfolklore.org/#/lays/lsr.

[51] Thomas D. Norris, ed., "Eachtradh Lomnochtain Sléibe Riffi," *Irish-American* 45.47 (20 Nov. 1893): 8; 45.48 (27 Nov. 1893): 8; 45.48 [sic] (4 Dec. 1893): 10; 45.45 [sic] (11 Dec. 1893): 8; 45.50 [sic] (18 Dec. 1893): 8.

[52] Pádraig Ó Siochfhradha [An Seabhac], ed., *Laoithe na Féinne* (Dublin: An Cumann le Béaloideas Éireann, 1941), 137-45. See also Ó hÓgáin, *Fionn Mac Cumhaill*, 266-27.

This lay, which is known by two different names, has been dated to the seventeenth or eighteenth century.[53] It was quite popular, and around ninety manuscript copies are known to exist.[54] Several oral versions have also been collected, but because they tend to omit the bruíon motif and follow a more straightforward foreign invasion structural pattern, they are not particularly relevant to an exploration of the bruíon tale corpus.[55] The lay was first edited from manuscript in 1861.[56]

Seilg Sléibhe Fuaid (The Chase on Sliabh Fuaid)

> A vengeful foreigner uses strange, sleep-inducing music to capture the Fianna while hunting. They are bound and imprisoned in a nearby fortress. (They do not, in this case, enter willingly.) Conán begs for their captor's mercy, only to deceive him at the moment of their immanent execution. Oscar then kills their captor.[57]
>
> A1-B1*-C1-D2-E

---

[53] Ó hÓgáin suggests two different dates for this lay, without explanation: see Ó hÓgáin, *Fionn Mac Cumhaill*, 265-66; Dáithí Ó hÓgáin, "Magic Attributes of the Hero in Fenian Lore." *Béaloideas* 54/55 (1986-87): 207-42 at 228.

[54] Duane Long, email correspondence, 4 Jan. 2023; Duane Long, "The Loathly Lady and *Bruidheann* Aspects of *Laoi Na Mná Móire*," conference presentation, XIV International Congress of Celtic Studies, 22-26 July 2019, Bangor, Wales.

[55] Fifty-six total oral tellings are currently recorded: https://fionnfolklore.org/#/lays/mtl.

[56] John O'Daly, ed. and trans., *Laoithe Fiannuigheachta; or, Fenian Poems,* second series, Transactions of the Ossianic Society 6 (Dublin: John O'Daly, 1861), 74-101. An earlier translation appeared in William Hamilton Drummond, *Ancient Irish Minstrelsy* (Dublin: Hodges and Smith, 1852), 61-79.

[57] Ó Siochfhradha, *Laoithe*, 93-110. See also Ó hÓgáin, *Fionn Mac Cumhaill*, 266.

This text is part of the popular *Agallamh Oisín agus Phádraig* compilation of lays, the earliest copy of which was written between 1775-81.[58] It never appears outside of the *Agallamh Oisín agus Phádraig* compilation in manuscripts, although Síle Ní Mhurchú posits that the lay may have circulated orally before that point.[59] While this is possible, I am not aware of any orally collected versions. The oral collection record is somewhat happenstance, however, particularly when lays more common to Ireland than Scotland are concerned. *Seilg Sléibhe Fuaid* was first edited from manuscript in 1861.[60]

Cath na Suiridhe (The Courting Battle)

> A beautiful woman approaches the Fianna while hunting and invites them to her fortress. They become magically fastened to their seats and the ground, and she says they will remain stuck until her husband arrives. They summon their blacksmith, who comes from Allen and frees Conán, but both are subsequently captured. The woman then frees Conán, Fionn, and the blacksmith so that they can fight an approaching warrior, but Fionn divines that he can overcome her magic and free them all by illicitly kissing her, which he does. Several warriors approach, there is a battle, and the Fianna are victorious.[61]
> B2-C1-D1/3-E

The captors' motivation is not revealed in this lay, but comparative examination with other bruíon tales might suggest that the magic-wielding woman's husband has contrived with her to lure and entrap the Fianna in order to exact vengeance for

---

[58] Síle Ní Mhurchú, "Agallamh Oisín agus Phádraig: Téacs agus Tráchtaireacht," unpublished PhD thesis (National University of Ireland, Galway, 2012), 203.

[59] Ní Mhurchú, "Agallamh," 203.

[60] O'Daly, *Laoithe*, 20-75. An earlier translation appeared in John Hawkins Simpson, *Poems of Oisin, Bard of Erin* (London: Bosworth and Harrison; Dublin: M'Glashan and Gill, 1857), 152-85.

[61] Ó Briain, *Bláithfhleasg*, 163-75.

TRAPPED AND TRANSPORTED

an offense. The captors may, however, simply wish to test whether the Fianna's renown is justified.

The lay probably dates to the eighteenth century.[62] The number of extant manuscript copies is not presently known, but it may be rare. To my knowledge, it has not been edited since its first appearance in print in 1893, and I am not aware of any orally-collected versions.

Cuireadh Mhaoil Uí Mhanannáin (Maol Ó Manannán's Invitation)

> An otherworldly man called Maol Ó Manannáin invites the Fianna to a feast in his dwelling. There they are subjected to trickery, including a pig that they need help catching and killing, which cooks but comes back to life. We eventually learn that Maol needs the Fianna's assistance to verify the fidelity of his wife. This goal is achieved via a magical truth test, after which they feast. Diarmaid and Fionn then try to reach the faithful woman during the night, but are thwarted through more trickery. The house disappears at dawn, leaving the Fianna safe and sound.[63]
> A2*-B2-C2-D3

The captor's motivation in this prose story is an inversion of the normative desire to communicate vital information to the Fianna; here, the captor requires the Fianna's presence in order to obtain information.

The story dates to the eighteenth century and does not appear to have been popular; there are only two known

---

[62] Ó Cróinín, *Bruidhean Chaorthainn*, 84-5; Murphy, *Duanaire Finn*, vol. 3, 26 n.1.
[63] Douglas Hyde and Tomás Ó Caomhánaigh, ed., "Cuireadh Mhaoil uí Mhananáin ar Fionn mac Cumhaill agus Fiannaibh Éirionn," *Lia Fáil* 3 (1930): 87-114. See also Ó hÓgáin, *Fionn Mac Cumhaill*, 270-72; Bruford, *Gaelic Folk-Tales*, 50, 262.

22

manuscript copies and four unique orally-collected versions.[64] It has only been edited from manuscript once in 1930.

Laoidh Chab an Dosáin (The Lay of Cab an Dosáin)

> Conán and Diarmaid are invited to feast in an otherworldly dwelling, where Conán is subjected to a series of magical hallucinations as punishment for attempting to assault a woman in the dwelling during the night. Once Conán has been taught his lesson, Goll arrives to rescue him and Diarmaid.[65]
> A2-B2-C2-D1

This lay, which dates to the late seventeenth or eighteenth-century, engages with the theme of lustful Fenian entitlement more critically than *Cuireadh Mhaoil Uí Mhanannáin* does. There are approximately twenty manuscript copies and eleven unique oral versions.[66] Only adapted translations have been published; these date to the 1850s and 60s.[67]

One final lay merits mentioning. While *Duan na Ceàrdaich* (The Lay of the Smithy) contains some elements of the structure outlined above, I would not classify it as a bruíon tale.[68] In this lay, the Fianna are enticed into a Lochlanner's smithy, where Caoilte joins in the labour of forging the Fianna's

---

[64] Bruford, *Gaelic Folk-Tales*, 262. Six total oral tellings are currently recorded: https://fionnfolklore.org/#/lays/mom.

[65] James McCann, "Laoidh Chab an Dosáin," unpublished MA thesis (University of Aberystwyth, 2012), 32-62. See also Ó hÓgáin, *Fionn Mac Cumhaill*, 272-73. Conán's sexual offense and reciprocal punishment is omitted from oral versions.

[66] McCann, "Laoidh Chab an Dosáin," 1; *cf.* Seosamh Watson, "Laoi Chab an Dosáin: Background to a Late Ossianic Ballad," *Eighteenth-Century Ireland / Iris an Dá Chultúr* 5 (1990): 37-44 at 37. Thirteen total oral tellings are currently recorded: https://fionnfolklore.org/#/lays/ecd.

[67] Patrick Kennedy, *Legendary Fictions of the Irish Celts* (London: Macmillan and Co., 1866), 232-35; Simpson, *Poems of Oisin*, 217-20.

[68] Christiansen, *Vikings*, 198-200, 345-58; Murphy, *Duanaire Finn*, vol. 2, 2-15.

magically endowed swords and receives his name. The most crucial element of the bruíon tale structure is missing here: the Fianna do not appear to be trapped in the smithy. While some versions do have a violent end, moreover, the violence comes about not in the Fianna's effort to escape, but because Fionn callously causes the smith to kill his own mother, then kills the smith, then leads the Fianna to the king of Lochlann where they provoke a battle. Thus, like numerous other Gaelic tales, *Duan na Ceàrdaich* employs the bruíon motif, but it does so differently than the Fenian bruíon tales described above.

Bruíon Tales in North America

The recent publication of Neil Buttimer's *Catalogue of Irish Manuscripts in Houghton Library, Harvard University* presents an opportunity to examine the transmission of Fenian bruíon tales among Irish and Scottish Gaelic-speaking immigrants and their descendants in North America.[69] The presence of Scottish Gaels on the continent is well documented. The tens of thousands of Gaelic speakers along North Carolina's Cape Fear River in the mid-eighteenth century composed sermons and poetry and printed the first Gaelic book in North America. After the American War of Independence, when Scottish emigration largely shifted to Canada, sizable regions within the Maritime provinces came to be dominated by people who maintained Gaelic as their first language for several generations, socializing, worshipping, versifying, and publishing in the language.[70] The story of the Irish language in North America is somewhat less well recognized, even though the massive influx of Irish immigrants in the mid- to late nineteenth century is well known. While accurate linguistic data cannot be derived from contemporary census records, however,

---

[69] Cornelius G. Buttimer, *Catalogue of Irish Manuscripts in Houghton Library, Harvard University* (Notre Dame: University of Notre Dame Press, 2022.

[70] Natasha Sumner and Aidan Doyle, "North American Gaels" in *North American Gaels: Speech, Story, and Song in the Diaspora*, ed. Natasha Sumner and Aidan Doyle (Montreal and Kingston: McGill-Queen's University Press, 2020), 3-36 at 12-18. Substantial numbers of Scottish Gaelic speakers settled in other regions in Canada as well.

many of those who arrived must have been Irish speakers, given their regions of origin. In fact, it has been estimated that by the 1890s the United States was home to as many as four hundred thousand Irish speakers.[71]

Not only did Irish speakers arrive in large numbers, the mementos of home that they carried with them included manuscripts written in their native tongue.[72] Since the period of mass immigration encompassed both the long Ossianic controversy and the Irish language revival movement–which produced many of the first print editions of Fenian tales–we might expect to find Fenian material among the numerous Irish manuscripts circulating in North America by the turn of the twentieth century. And indeed, a perusal of manuscript indices (and associated manuscripts) alongside American Irish periodicals (in which material edited from manuscripts appeared) reveals numerous copies of Fenian bruíon tales in North American circulation.[73] (See Appendix)

Fenian bruíon tales were clearly popular among Irish immigrants, some of whom went so far as to copy them into

---

[71] Sumner and Doyle, "North American Gaels," 4, 7-9; Kenneth E. Nilsen, "The Irish Language in New York, 1850-1900" in *The New York Irish*, ed. Ronald H. Bayor and Timothy J. Meagher (Baltimore: Johns Hopkins University Press, 1996), 252-74 at 254.

[72] Kenneth E. Nilsen, "Three Irish Manuscripts in Massachusetts," *Proceedings of the Harvard Celtic Colloquium* 5 (1985): 1-21 at 1-2; Sumner and Doyle, "North American Gaels," 9. While most Irish-speaking immigrants would not have been literate, given the state of Irish-language education prior to the late nineteenth-century revival movement, some clearly were.

[73] I have reviewed all available indices of North American manuscripts. I have also consulted indices of Gaelic columns in American newspapers in search of bruíon tales edited from manuscripts. As above, folklore data comes from the Fionn Folklore Database. Although the manuscript and print sources noted here were not well known when Bruford compiled his index in *Gaelic Folk-Tales and Mediaeval Romances* and he therefore overlooked them, they are included in the counts of known manuscript versions above. The catalogue of Irish manuscripts in North American locations currently being completed by Breandán Ó Conchúir may reveal further copies of bruíon tales that circulated in North America.

their own commonplace books and to edit them for publication in North American print media. While individual opinions must certainly have varied, the bruíon tales' prominent liberation theme may have resonated strongly with those who chose to leave their homelands due to personal hardship, as was the case for many Irish immigrants. Some of those engaging with the texts in North America were likely also motivated by Ossianism and language revivalism. For instance, the *Irish Echo* text of *Bruidhean Chéise Corainn* can be squarely situated within revivalist activity in Boston. As Matthew Knight has pointed out, it appeared one issue after the *Irish Echo* printed a partial translation of Ernst Windisch's "L'Ancienne Légende Irlandaise et les Poésies Ossianiques," or "Ancient Irish Legendary Literature and Ossianic Poetry," which originally appeared in *Revue Celtique*. The edition was printed with an accompanying vocabulary and would have been intended as reading material for students in Irish language classes, whose interest in the Fenian text would presumably have been piqued by the recent Windisch essay.[74]

The editions of bruíon tales in North American print media, drawn from manuscripts circulating on this continent, are further notable in that some of them are the first ever print editions of these tales. *Eachtra Lomnochtáin an tSléibhe Riffe* had never been published prior to the edition by New York Philo-Celtic Society (NYPCS) member Thomas D. Norris (Tomás D. de Norradh) in the *Irish-American* in 1893. In the case of *Bruidhean Chaorthainn*, moreover, although the credit for the first full edition has elsewhere been given to Patrick Pearse (Pádraic Mac Piarais), who edited the text for the Gaelic League in 1908, the edition in the *Irish-American* in 1889, which was likely edited by Daniel Magner (Domhnall Maignéar) of the NYPCS, precedes Pearse's by nearly twenty years.[75]

---

[74] Knight, "Our Gaelic Department," 182.
[75] Norris, "Eachtradh Lomnochtain"; Maignéar, "Bruighean Caorthainn"; Pádraic Mac Piarais, ed., *Bruidhean Chaorthainn: Sgéal Fiannaidheachta* (Dublin: Conradh na Gaeilge, 1908); Ó

The Oral Tradition

Where there are manuscript copies of Fenian tales, there are often oral versions circulating too. Given Irish and Scottish immigration data, it would be reasonable to assume that many Fenian bruíon tales were told or sung in North America. Unfortunately, folklore collecting was nowhere near as robust as it was in Ireland and Scotland. In the late nineteenth and early twentieth centuries, Irish language revivalists encouraged the collection of stories and songs from the oral tradition, much like their counterparts in Ireland were doing, but the amount of North American Irish folklore to find its way into journals and archives is not great.[76] While no large-scale, systematic folklore collecting ever took place among Irish speakers in North America, however, every now and then a highly proficient immigrant storyteller would fortuitously return to Ireland at just the right time for the Irish Folklore Commission to record their tales. The efforts of Ken Nilsen to collect Irish-language folklore among the small number of regular speakers still present in Portland, Maine in the 1980s and 90s are also noteworthy. Nilsen found one storyteller at that late date who had Fenian tales, including a prose version of *Suirghe Fhinn go*

Cróinín, *Bruidhean Chaorthainn*, 8; Knight, "Our Gaelic Department," 159, 204, 223-24, 301-3. Credit for the first partial publication of *Bruidhean Chaorthainn* goes to John Francis Campbell, who published an excerpt from a Scottish manuscript in *Leabhar na Féinne* in 1872 (86-88). Regarding Thomas D. Norris and Danel Magner, see Knight, "Champions."

[76] Sumner and Doyle, "North American Gaels," 12. More Irish songs were collected in North America than stories, but I am not aware of any bruíon lays among them. Regarding one prolific song collection, see Deirdre Ní Chonghaile, "Mapping Song Through Time and Space: Rev. Daniel J. Murphy Collects Sean-Nós Song in Pennsylvania, 1884-1935," unpublished lecture in *Culture Unconfined: An Online Festival Celebrating Film, Drama, Music, and Poetry* (University of Liverpool, 11-15 May 2020), https://www.liverpool.ac.uk/irish-studies/events/culture-unconfined/cultures-unconfined-deirdre-ni-chonghaile/, accessed 15 Jan. 2023.

Críocha Lochlann. This was collected from Pat Malone of Portland, Maine (originally from Casla, Co. Galway).[77]

The situation with Scottish Gaelic folklore is somewhat better. Cultural organizations and periodicals encouraged folklore collecting in the nineteenth century, and a number of leading Scottish and North American folklorists made collecting trips to Nova Scotia in the mid-twentieth century. But the most important initiative undertaken was the Gaelic Language and Folklore Project, under the auspices of which John Shaw recorded over two thousand items of oral narrative from 1977 to 1982 that now form the Cape Breton Folklore Collection at St. Francis Xavier University.[78] While this effort was belated and small in comparison to folklore collecting in the language's country of origin, it was more than was done for Irish, and the resultant collection gives us a sense of the rich vein of tradition that surely existed among both language communities.

It is to the Gaelic Language and Folklore Project that we owe the only other Fenian bruíon tales I know to have been orally collected in North America: two versions of *Bruidhean Chaorthainn* and one version of *Bruidhean Eochaidh Bhig Dheirg*, all told by Joe Neil MacNeil of Middle Cape, Cape Breton in 1978.[79] That other bruíon tales did not turn up in the

---

[77] Nilsen published a short excerpt from this tale in Kenneth E. Nilsen, "Collecting Celtic Folklore in the United States" in *Proceedings of the First North American Congress of Celtic Studies*, ed. Gordon MacLennan (Ottawa: University of Ottawa, 1988), 55-74 at 72-73; *cf.* https://fionnfolklore.org/#/item/1500). Nilsen's folklore collection is soon to be transferred to Harvard University, where it will be publicly accessible.

[78] Sumner and Doyle, "North American Gaels," 18.

[79] Both versions of *Bruidhean Chaorthainn* are fragmentary: "Ìseadal Mac Rìgh nan Sealg, Dalta Fhìnn," Cape Breton Folklore Collection, recording 038.A04-39.A01, collected 16 Mar. 1978 (Joe Neil MacNeil, *Tales Until Dawn / Sgeul gu Latha*, ed. and trans. John Shaw [Montreal and Kingston: McGill-Queen's University Press, 1987], 60-63; *cf.* https://fionnfolklore.org/#/item/124); and "Diarmaid agus Bean Chaol a' Chòta Uaine," Cape Breton Folklore

Nova Scotian corpus is interesting, but not particularly surprising upon closer examination. Collection data shows that almost all of the remaining tales were found exclusively in Ireland, suggesting that the bruíon category was most productive there. If folklore collecting among Irish speakers in North America had been more robust in the nineteenth and twentieth centuries, it is likely that versions of several additional bruíon tales would have been gathered.

Conclusion

I have sought here to delineate the structure of the Fenian bruíon tale category more clearly, building on the work of those scholars who preceded me; to outline the literary and oral composition of the corpus; and to highlight the hitherto largely overlooked North American aspect of the corpus. The thirteen stories and lays that I have described clearly share more than the thematic similarity of a bruíon *locus*. As we have seen, there is a definitive overarching structure to tales in which our heroes find themselves trapped in a supernatural or otherworldly abode. The affinity that Irish and, to a lesser extent, Scottish immigrants appear to have had for this category of Fenian narrative may also be linked to thematic and structural factors. The Fianna's ability, time and again, to overcome adversity and escape from the once-welcoming halls where they find themselves imprisoned may have resonated well among those who journeyed overseas to escape hardship. Alternatively, those for whom America had come to resemble a lustre-less bruíon may have longed to follow in their heroes' footsteps and return home. For us, as for our forebears, there is much to appreciate in these complex tales. There is also much work yet to be done, and I hope this contribution can serve as a new departure.

Collection, recording 145.A04, collected 24 Nov. 1978 (MacNeil, *Tales*, 68-71; *cf.* https://fionnfolklore.org/#/item/123). Regarding *Bruidhean Eochaidh Bhig Dheirg*, see "Fionn ann an Taigh a Bhlàir Bhuidhe," Cape Breton Folklore Collection, recording 160.A02 - 161.A01, collected 28 Nov. 1978 (*cf.* https://fionnfolklore.org/#/item/855).

Acknowledgements

I wish to thank the conference organizers for inviting me to speak at the 41st Harvard Celtic Colloquium, and I greatly appreciate those whose comments on the presentation helped to improve this article. Thanks are also due to Matthew Knight for providing scans of texts in the *Irish-American*, to Andrew Isidoro and Rachel Brody for helping to locate manuscript material in the John J. Burns Library at Boston College, and to Jay Moschella and Claire Drone-Silvers for answering queries, sending images of the table of contents, and facilitating my visit to consult the relevant manuscript in the Boston Public Library.

APPENDIX

Bruíon Tales in North American Manuscripts

Feis Tighe Chonáin

- Harvard MS Ir 9, pp. 23-45. Scribe: Tomás Ó Conchubhair, 19th century (?).[80]
- Boston College (hereafter BC) MS 2012-005, pp. 1- 64. Scribe: Tearlach Ó Gallachobhair (Charles Gallagher), New York, NY, 1787.[81]
- New York Public Library MssCol 1774, between pp. 94-95 (photostat pp. 40b-41a). Note: Acephelous and fragmentary. Possibly not original to this MS. Teach Cuanna episode not included in extant text.[82]

Bruidhean Chéise Corainn

- BC, MS 1986.085.002, pp. 62-68, 73-76. Scribe: Seághan Ó Domhnail, 1780. Note: MS disassembled and pp. 65-68 and 73-76 torn and separated; p. 75 is the bottom of p. 65, p. 76 is the bottom of p. 66, p. 73 is the bottom of p. 67, and p. 74 is the bottom of p. 68.[83]

---

[80] Buttimer, *Catalogue,* 153.

[81] "Handlist of Irish Gaelic Manuscripts at the John J. Burns Library, Boston College," June 23, 2016, digitized as: https://library.bc.edu/iiif/view/MS2012_005_112767.

[82] Elliott Lash, "An Eighteenth-Century Irish Manuscript in New York (NYPL, MssCol 1774)," *North American Journal of Celtic Studies* 6.2 (2022): 193-215 at 206.

[83] "Handlist."

- BC, MS 2012-005, pp. 210-222. Scribe: Tearlach Ó Gallachobhair (Charles Gallagher), New York, NY, 1793.[84]
- New York Public Library MssCol 1774, pp. 195-205 (photostat pp. 82b-87b). Scribe: Seághan Ó Muláin, Co. Cork, 1790.[85] Edition: *Irish Echo* (Boston), 1893.[86]
- MS missing. Edition: *Irish-American* (New York), 1894.[87]

Bruidhean Chaorthainn

- Harvard, MS *66M-91 (Buttimer #42), pp. 262-305. Scribe: Dáth a Cearailt (David Fitzgerald), Co. Kerry and New York (?), 19th-century.[88]
- MS missing. Edition: *Irish-American* (New York), 1889.[89]

Bruidhean Eochaidh Bhig Dheirg

- BC, MS 1986.085.002, pp. 50-61. Scribe: Seághan Ó Domhnail, 1780. Note: MS disassembled, pp. 59-60 damaged.[90]

Eachtra Lomnochtáin

- BC, MS 1986.085.007, pp. 187-210. Scribe: Padruic Mac a Bhaird, 1823.[91]

---

[84] "Handlist," digitized as: https://library.bc.edu/iiif/view/MS2012_005_112767.
[85] Lash, "Eighteenth-Century," 198-99, 208. Bruford overlooked the *Irish Echo* edition, despite its inclusion in a list of recent editions in W.R. Craigie, "Three Tales," 275.
[86] "Bruighean Chéise Chorrain," *Irish Echo* 4.2 (1893): 18-27.
[87] Thomas D. Norris, ed., "Bruigheann Chéise an Corruinn," *Irish-American* 46.10 (5 Mar. 1894): 8; 46.11 (12 Mar. 1894): 8; Matthew Knight, "Champions of the Irish Language in America: Daniel Magner, Thomas D. Norris, and their Contributions to 'Our Gaelic Department' in the *Irish-American*, 1878-1900," *Proceedings of the Harvard Celtic Colloquium* 40 (2023): 236-65 at 264. Regarding the manuscript, see Matthew Knight, "'Our Gaelic Department': The Irish-Language Column in the New York *Irish-American*, 1857-1896," unpublished PhD thesis (Harvard University, 2020), 302.
[88] Buttimer, *Catalogue*, 263.
[89] Maignéar, "Bruighean Caorthainn"; Knight, "Champions," 264.
[90] "Handlist. "
[91] Nilsen, "Three Irish Manuscripts," 10, digitized as: https://library.bc.edu/iiif/view/MS1986_085_007_ref3.

- MS missing. Edition: *Irish-American* (New York), 1893.[92]

Seilg Ghleanna an Smóil / Laoidh na Mná Móire thar Lear[93]

- Harvard MS Ir 19, pp. 33-32 (text inverted). 19th century (?).[94] Note: MS disassembled.

- Harvard, MS Ir 22, II, pp. 297-322. Scribe: Seagan Ó Dulane, 19th century.[95]

- BC, MS 86-85, #8 (formerly MS 1986.085.08), pp. 120-21 (?).[96] Note: MS disassembled and some page numbers obscure. Poem incomplete.

  o (copy) BC, MS 86-85, #9 (formerly MS 1986.085.09), 3 pages (unpaginated). Scribe: Séamus Bunbuire, 1817.[97] Note: Poem incomplete.

- Boston Public Library MS q.Eng.484, pp. 97-100 [#61]. Scribe: Patrick O'Mahony, Co. Cork, 1824-25 (?).[98]

- Dublin Institute for Advanced Studies, School of Celtic Studies (hereafter DIAS) Dunnington MS 1, pp. 127-40. Scribe: Uilliam Breathnach, Co. Waterford, 1813-18.[99]

---

[92] Norris, "Eachtradh Lomnochtain"; Knight, "Champions," 264. Regarding the ms, see Knight, "Our Gaelic Department, "302.

[93] In 1861 the *Irish-American* also printed an advance copy of John O'Daly's edition and translation of this lay from the forthcoming second volume of his *Laoithe Fiannuigheachta* (74-101): John O'Daly, ed. and trans., "Seilg Ghleanna an Smóil, nó Eachtra na Mná Moire tar Lear," *Irish-American* 13.46 (16 Nov. 1861): 2, 4; 13.47 (23 Nov. 1861): 4; 13.48 (30 Nov. 1861): 4; 13.49 (7 Dec. 1861): 4.

[94] Buttimer, *Catalogue*, 197.

[95] Buttimer, *Catalogue*, 213.

[96] "Handlist."

[97] "Handlist."

[98] This ms was purchased from the Jenkins Company (Austin, TX) in March 1973. Its prior circulation history is not presently known: email correspondence, Claire Drone-Silvers, Rare Books and Manuscripts Librarian, Boston Public Library, 17 Jan. 2023.

[99] Edgar M. Slotkin, "Two Irish Literary Manuscripts in the Mid-West," *Éigse* 25 (1991), at 59, digitized as: https://www.isos.dias.ie/DIAS/DIAS_Dunnington_MS_1.html. The ms was formerly in the possession of the Holy Cross Fathers in Ohio and Kentucky.

Seilg Sléibhe Fuaid

- Harvard, MS Ir 10, pp. 174-211. Scribe: Míchael Ó Haragáin, 1800.[100]
- Harvard, MS Ir 22, I, pp. 192-245. Scribe: Saoghan Luchidh, 19th-century.[101]
- Harvard, MS *66M-91 (Buttimer #40), pp. 117-30. Scribe: Fínighin H. Hallúráin (?), Co. Cork (?), 19th-century.[102]
- Harvard, MS *66M-91 (Buttimer #42), pp. 211-45. Scribe: Dáth a Cearailt (David Fitzgerald), Co. Kerry and New York (?), 19th-century.[103]
- BC, MS 86-85, #8 (formerly MS 1986.085.08), pp. 234-67.[104] Note: MS disassembled and some page numbers obscure.
  - o (copy) BC, MS 86-85, #9 (formerly MS 1986.085.09), 36 pages (unpaginated, beginning shortly after heading "Teacht Draoigheantóir ag Díoghailt Bháis Meargaigh 's a Muintire"). Scribe: Séamus Bunbuire, 1817.[105]
- BC, MS 1986.085.011, verses 797-947 (unpaginated, incomplete). Note: MS disassembled and pages out of order. The final page of the MS is approximately forty quatrains before the typical end of the lay, and is damaged.
- Boston Athenaeum, MS S22, pp. 143-59. Scribe: Seumas Muilsineach, Co. Cork, 1820-25.[106]
- Villanova University (hereafter VU) MS PB1397.M3 (Mahon #2), pp. 87-126. Scribe: Míachael O Chinnéde, Co. Limerick, 1811.[107]

---

[100] Buttimer, *Catalogue*, 155. A modern edition of this text can be found in Ní Mhurchú, *Agallamh*, 337-60.
[101] Buttimer, *Catalogue*, 212.
[102] Buttimer, *Catalogue*, 249.
[103] Buttimer, *Catalogue*, 263.
[104] "Handlist."
[105] "Handlist."
[106] Cornelius G. Buttimer, "A Catalogue of Irish Manuscripts in the Boston Athenaeum," in *Folia Gadelica*, ed. R.A. Breatnach (Cork: Cork University Press, 1983), 105-23 at 112.
[107] William Mahon, *Catalogue of Irish Manuscripts in Villanova University Pennsylvania* (Dublin: Dublin Institute for Advanced Studies, 2007), 26-27, digitized as: https://digital.library.villanova.edu/Item/vudl:68806.

- VU, MS PB1397.F407 (Mahon #3), pp. 114-141. Scribe: Conchúbhar Ua Máille (Cornelius O'Mealy), 1816-17.[108]

  o (copy) VU, MS PB1397.G8.v.2 (Mahon #10), pp. 223 ff. Scribe: Tomás Ua Griomhtha (Thomas Griffin), Lawrence, MA, 1890.[109]

Cath na Suiridhe

- DIAS, Dunnington MS 1, pp. 159-202. Scribe: Uilliam Breathnach, Co. Waterford, 1813-18.[110]

Laoidh Chab an Dosáin

- BC, MS 1986.085.010, pp. 191-208. Scribe: Aindriú Ó Murchughadh, Co. Cork, 1835.[111]

- VU, Art Curiosa PB1397.G18 (Mahon #1), pp. 189-202. Scribe: Seán Gaillieghe (John Galwey), Co. Cork, 18th-century. [112]

  o (copy) VU, MS PB1397.G8.v.2 (Mahon #10), pp. 115 ff. Scribe: Tomás Ua Griomhtha (Thomas Griffin), Lawrence, MA, 1890.[113]

  o (copy) VU, MS PB1397.G8.v.4 (Mahon #12), pp. 214-26. Scribe: Tomás Ua Griomhtha (Thomas Griffin), Lawrence, MA, 1891-92.[114]

- VU, MS PB1397.C8.v.2 (Mahon #7), pp. 3-10. Scribe: Aodh Ó Crónaoin (Hugh Cronin), 1830.[115] Note: Acephelous.

- DIAS, Dunnington MS 1, pp. 1-11. Scribe: Uilliam Breathnach, Co. Waterford, 1813-18.[116]

---

[108] Mahon, *Catalogue*, 29, digitized as https://digital.library.villanova.edu/Item/vudl:68938.

[109] Mahon, *Catalogue,* 63, 101.

[110] Slotkin, "Two Irish Literary Manuscripts," 59, digitized as: https://www.isos.dias.ie/DIAS/DIAS_Dunnington_MS_1.html. Pages 169-89 correspond most closely with the published edition of *Cath na Suiridhe.*

[111] "Handlist."

[112] Mahon, *Catalogue*, 25.

[113] Mahon, *Catalogue*, 63, 94.

[114] Mahon, *Catalogue*, 71, 94.

[115] Mahon, *Catalogue*, 52, digitized as: https://digital.library.villanova.edu/Item/vudl:69492.

[116] Slotkin, "Two Irish Literary Manuscripts," 58, digitized as https://www.isos.dias.ie/DIAS/DIAS_Dunnington_MS_1.html.

Modeling Impairment and Disability in
Early Irish Literature

Matthieu Boyd

This paper is concerned with disability, in a corpus of text–early Irish saga literature–that is, I argue, unusually attentive to it.[1] Focusing here on physical conditions,[2] I find that the early Irish vernacular sagas

---

[1] Aspects of this topic have previously been examined by Patrick K. Ford, "The Blind, the Dumb, and the Ugly: Aspects of Poets and their Craft in Medieval Ireland and Wales," *CMCS* 19 (1990): 27-40; Lois Bragg, "From the Mute God to the Lesser God: Disability in Medieval Celtic and Old Norse Literature." *Disability & Society* 12.2 (1997): 165-77; William Sayers, "Kingship and the Hero's Flaw: Disfigurement as Ideological Vehicle in Early Irish Narrative," *Disability Studies Quarterly* 17 (1997): 263-267, "Portraits of the Ulster Hero *Conall Cernach*: a Case for Waardenburg's Syndrome?" *Emania* 20 (2006): 75-80, and "The Laconic Scar in Early Irish Literature," in *Wounds and Wound Repair in Medieval Culture*, ed. Larissa Tracy and Kelly DeVries (Leiden and Boston: Brill, 205), 473-495; Amy C. Mulligan (formerly Eichhorn-Mulligan), "*Togail Bruidne Da Derga* and the Politics of Anatomy," *CMCS* 49 (2005): 1-19, "The Anatomy of Power and the Miracle of Kingship: The Female Body of Sovereignty in a Medieval Irish Kingship Tale," *Speculum* 81.4 (2006): 1014-1054, and "'The satire of the poet is a pregnancy': Pregnant Poets, Body Metaphors, and Cultural Production in Medieval Ireland." *Journal of English and Germanic Philology* 108.4 (2009): 481-505; Sarah Sheehan, "Losing Face: Heroic Discourse and Inscription in Flesh in *Scéla Muicce Meic Dathó*," in *The Ends of the Body: Identity and Community in Medieval Culture*, ed. Suzanne Conklin Akbari and Jill Ross (University of Toronto Press, 2013), 132-152; and Sarah Künzler, *Flesh and Word: Reading Bodies in Old Norse-Icelandic and Early Irish Literature* (Berlin: De Gruyter, 2016).

[2] Early Irish law has a reasonably sophisticated grasp of mental states and mental disability: see Fergus Kelly, *A Guide to Early Irish Law* (Dublin: Dublin Institute for Advanced Studies 1988), 91-94. While many of the conclusions I reach here will be applicable to mental conditions, I expect to focus on them in a sequel to the present essay. Examples such as *Aided Muirchertaig mac Erca*, "The (Violent) Death of Muirchertach mac Erca" (trans. Whitley Stokes, "The Death of Muirchertach mac Erca," *Revue*

35

have several distinct paradigms for disability, some of which correspond imperfectly to the prevailing paradigms in medieval Christian Europe as a whole: that is, the Irish sagas are doing something special. These Irish paradigms are:

(1) impairment as the result of shame,

(2) impairment as the "before" condition of a transformation,

(3) impairment as the price of power (or knowledge or art), and, paradoxically,

(4) impairment as the result of honor, and non-impairment as the result of shame.

It also seems that in applying these paradigms, the sagas understand that disability is socially determined, or at least socially ratified, and are interested in exploring that process rather than taking it for granted.

The latter insight is one that the sagas share with the contemporary field of Disability Studies, which has grown very large and very diverse.[3] Its founding assumption is that disability is, by

---

Celtique 23 [1902]: 395-437, with corrigenda in *Revue Celtique* 24 [1903]: 349) and *Buile Shuibne*, and figures such as the *drúth* 'developmentally disabled person; jester' (see Matthieu Boyd, "Competing assumptions about the *drúth* in *Orgain Denna Ríg*," *Ériu* 59 [2009]: 37-47) are obvious candidates for this investigation. Irina Metzler, *Fools and Idiots?: Intellectual Disability in the Middle Ages* (Manchester University Press, 2016) now deals in a general way with intellectual disability in the Middle Ages.

[3] See, e.g., Rosemary Garland Thomson, *Extraordinary Bodies: Figuring Physical Disability in American Culture and Literature* (New York: Columbia University Press, 1997); Simi Linton, *Claiming Disability: Knowledge and Identity* (New York: NYU Press, 1998) and "What is Disability Studies?" *PMLA* 120 (2005): 518-22; Robert McRuer, *Crip Theory: Cultural Signs of Queerness and Disability* (New York: NYU Press 2006); Michael Davidson, *Concerto for the Left Hand: Disability and the Defamiliar Body* (Ann Arbor, MI: University of Michigan Press, 2008); *Rethinking Normalcy: A Disability Studies Reader*, ed. Tanya Titchkosky and Rod Michalko (Toronto: Canadian Scholars' Press, 2009); and Nirmala

MATTHIEU BOYD

Erevelles, "Thinking with Disability Studies," *Disability Studies Quarterly*
34.2 (2014), online at http://dsq-sds.org/article/view/4248. Intersectionality
is a major theme of recent research, as in Alison Kafer, *Feminist, Queer,
Crip* (Bloomington: Indiana University Press, 2013). I have personally
appreciated the writing of Dave Hingsburger (at davehingsburger.
blogspot.com). On the application of Disability Studies to the Middle Ages,
see Irina Metzler, *Disability in Medieval Europe: Thinking about Physical
Impairment during the High Middle Ages, c.1100-c.1400* (New York:
Routledge, 2006), "Disability in the Middle Ages: Impairment at the
Intersection of Historical Inquiry and Disability Studies." *History Compass*
9.1 (2011): 45-60, *A Social History of Disability in the Middle Ages:
Cultural Considerations of Physical Impairment* (Routledge, 2013), and
*Fools and Idiots? Disability in the Middle Ages: Reconsiderations and
Reverberations*, ed. Joshua R. Eyler (Burlington, VT: Ashgate, 2010);
Edward Wheatley, *Stumbling Blocks before the Blind: Medieval
Constructions of a Disability*. (University of Michigan Press, 2010) and
"Monsters, Saints, and Sinners: Disability in Medieval Literature" in *The
Cambridge Companion to Literature and Disability*, ed. Clare Barker and
Stuart Murray (Cambridge University Press, 2018), 17-31; Wendy J.
Turner, "Past, Present, and Future of Medieval Disability Studies" (2016),
online at https://massmedieval.com/2016/02/29/past-present-and-future-of-
medieval-disability-studies-wendy-j-turner/; and *Medieval Disability
Sourcebook: Western Europe*, ed. Cameron Hunt McNabb (Punctum Books,
2020), online at https://library.oapen.org/handle/20.500.12657/22299;
and note the bibliographies at https://premoderndisability. com/ medieval-
post-classical-disability-studies-500-1500/ and https://
medievaldisabilityglossary.hcommons.org/bibliography- future-of-
medieval-disability-studies/ (also https://medievaldisabilityglossary.
hcommons.org/disability-in-the-global-middle-ages/). *Medieval Disability
Sourcebook*, ed. McNabb, is a noteworthy recent example of how Ireland
has been mostly left out of the discourse on medieval disability. Non-
normative bodies have also been approached in medieval studies through
the lens of "the monstrous," which has been heavily theorized: see, e.g.,
John Block Friedman, *The Monstrous Races in Medieval Art and Thought*
(Cambridge, MA: Harvard University Press, 1981); David Williams,
*Deformed Discourse: The Function of the Monster in Mediaeval Thought
and Literature* (Montreal: McGill-Queen's University Press, 1996); Jeffrey
Jerome Cohen, *Monster Theory: Reading Culture* (Minneapolis: University
of Minnesota Press, 1996), *Of Giants: Sex, Monsters, and the Middle Ages*
(Minneapolis: University of Minnesota Press, 1999), and *Hybridity,*

definition, socially determined. Disability is society's failure to fully accommodate mental and physical difference–that is, a failure of equal opportunit–or an active process of othering. Rosemary Garland Thomson, in an often-cited passage, explains that "[t]he 'physically disabled' are produced by way of legal, medical, political, cultural, and literary narratives that comprise an exclusionary discourse. [. . .] Disability [. . .] is the attribution of corporal deviance–not so much a product of bodies as a product of cultural rules about what bodies should be or do."[4] Since there have been spoken or unspoken cultural rules (or norms) about bodies in every society since the dawn of time, a Disability Studies perspective invites us to go back and look for them. It is precisely as "legal, medical, political, cultural, and literary narratives that comprise an exclusionary discourse" that I am looking at the sagas here.[5]

I am certainly not claiming that a Disability Studies lens can be imported wholesale to investigate material from early Ireland in an anachronistic way. For example, an aspect of contemporary Disability Studies that the sagas manifestly do *not* share is a sense of "the disabled" as a self-reflective group or movement. A great deal of the disability scholarship affirms that disability has become an identity one can assert, with solidarity and pride. Robert McRuer writes of

---

Identity, and Monstrosity in Medieval Britain: On Difficult Middles (New York: Palgrave Macmillan, 2006); *The Monstrous Middle Ages*, ed. Bettina Bildhauer and Robert Mills (Toronto: University of Toronto Press, 2nd ed., 2004); Asa Simon Mittman, *Maps and Monsters in Medieval England* (New York: Routledge, 2006); and, for early Irish literature, Jacqueline Borsje, *From Chaos to Enemy: Encounters with Monsters in Early Irish Texts* (Turnhout: Brepols, 1996) and "Evil and the Changing Nature of Monsters in Early Irish Texts," in *Monsters and the Monstrous in Medieval Northwest Europe*, ed. K.E. Olsen and L.A.J.R. Houwen (Leuven/Paris/Sterling, VA: Peeters, 2001), 59-77. As Wheatley's title "Monsters, Saints, and Sinners" indicates, these separate lines of inquiry can inform each other, inasmuch as some medieval people's "visible differences could be considered a physical ailment or impairment, or they could be considered part of a race of monsters and not entirely human" (Kara Larson Maloney on dwarfism, in McNabb, 365).

[4] Thomson, *Extraordinary Bodies*, 6.

[5] The sagas are literary, but they operate in all these other registers as well: they showcase legal concepts, function as political propaganda, and so on.

"coming out crip," and Michael Davidson of effectively "becoming disabled" by writing about disability, as he "became aware of cultural meanings associated with hemophilia and deafness, conditions with which I have lived my entire life but seldom acknowledged."[6] "Increasingly," Davidson adds, "claiming disability means claiming intersectional alliances with communities formed around queer, raced, gendered, classed, and [. . .] subaltern identities."[7]

Where the idea of "claiming disability" becomes useful for working with early Irish literature is in the underlying realization that "becoming disabled," the way Davidson meant it, involves putting a particular spin on a particular set of biological facts. It becomes possible to imagine a world in which, depending on the frame of reference, "No one is disabled. Everyone is disabled."[8] Within Disability Studies there is debate about whether it makes sense to distinguish between disability and impairment, which is a feature of the "social model" of disability.[9] Those who argue that this is a valid

---

[6] Davidson, *Concerto*, 223.

[7] Davidson, *Concerto*, 224. Or as Simi Linton writes: "We are everywhere these days, wheeling and loping down the street, tapping our canes, sucking on our breathing tubes, following our guide dogs, puffing and sipping on the mouth sticks that propel our motorized chairs. We may drool, hear voices, speak in staccato syllables, wear catheters to collect our urine, or live with a compromised immune system. We are all bound together, not by this list of our collective symptoms but by the social and political circumstances that have forged us a group" (*Claiming Disability*, 4). By contrast, William Sayers says of early Ireland that "[I]n a society where a majority of people bore the traces of accident, disease, injury, maltreatment, or malnourishment, the notion of disability, as conceived in today's discourse of public policy, could not have been an operative category. Nor would the demographic slice of the impaired have been sufficiently narrow for stigmatization to occur. Compared to battle wounds, simple physical incapacitation might have been borne socially much more easily" ("The Laconic Scar," 494). (Sayers adds "and, consequently, does not figure in literature," which seems over-broad.)

[8] Davidson, *Concerto*, xiii.

[9] Various models are conveniently summarized by McNabb (15): medical model, religious model (both focused on diagnosis, correction, and control); social model (distinguishes biological impairment from socially constructed

distinction take 'impairment' to mean a biological fact, while 'disability' refers to how that fact is socially and morally defined. (Thus impairment is to disability roughly as sex is to gender.[10]) The alternative 'cultural model' is to think of disability as always already socially constructed.

I find the distinction useful. Biological conditions can be socially interpreted in different ways. In strictly biological terms, it might be an advantage to have three arms, as in the Scottish Gaelic song *Sgeir an Òir*, "The Cave of Gold": "I wish I had three arms, two for the bagpipes and one for the sword . . . ."[11] But in most communities throughout history, the social disadvantages (reactions of pity, fear, disgust, Kristevan abjection, the label 'monster' or 'freak' etc.) might outweigh the biological advantage. By contrast, the biological condition of losing a hand one was born with is an impairment

---

disability); cultural model (disability always already socially constructed); critical realist model (socially constructed, but also biological, plus "universal impairment": we all are or will be disabled somehow at some point). Metzler, *Disability in Medieval Europe,* finds the social model's distinction useful, whereas Joshua Eyler suggests that "it may benefit our field more if we remove the term 'impairment' from the discussion altogether and think of disability in the Middle Ages as something that is constructed by both bodily difference and social perception at the same time" (*Disability in the Middle Ages,* 5-8). He notes that this suggestion "runs at odds" with the approach taken by some of the contributors to his edited collection, but says that contrasting approaches are "expected and, in fact, welcome" as we strive to "construct a model for understanding medieval disabilities based on the evidence of our sources rather than applying a pre-fabricated model backward" (8).
[10] This is meant to be a helpful analogy, but while the sex/gender distinction may be useful, it is also far from simple; one only needs to glance at the evolving views of a theorist like Judith Butler (*Gender Trouble* [New York: Routledge, 1990], *Bodies that Matter* [Routledge, 1993], *Undoing Gender* [Routledge, 2004].) to see how complex the situation is.
[11] Likewise, in *Táin bó Cúailnge* the hero Cú Chulainn has seven fingers and seven toes, and this is presented as something quite wonderful. See *Táin bó Cúailnge, Recension I,* ed. and trans. Cecile O'Rahilly (Dublin: Dublin Institute for Advanced Studies, 1976), 205.

however you slice it; how a one-handed person functions in society is the basis for describing it as a disability.[12]

Irina Metzler, whose work is now a common starting point for thinking about disability in the Middle Ages, finds the impairment-disability distinction useful too. I am in dialogue with her work and will continue to use it throughout this essay. Using mainly medical treatises and saints' lives, Metzler found that there were two main paradigms of disability in the European Middle Ages overall, and that these "existed in an ambivalent tension." In Metzler's words, these two paradigms are (1) "notions of impairment (and, in a way, *all* illness) as the result of sin," and (2) "impairment as something that required healing [e.g. by saints performing miraculous cures]."[13]

Metzler's paradigms for disability in medieval Christian Europe

Paradigm (1), "impairment as the result of sin," assumes that the state of one's body mirrors the state of one's soul. To this way of thinking, a blind person is blind because they cannot 'see' God's truth. The twelfth-century Cambro-Norman Gerald of Wales[14] was thinking this way when he wrote about the Irish:

> I have never seen among any other people so many blind by birth, so many lame, so many maimed in body, and so many suffering from some natural

---

[12] In Cú Chulainn's death-tale, when Conall Cernach confronts Lugaid mac Con Roí to avenge Cú Chulainn's death, he agrees to fight with one arm tied down because Lugaid has lost a hand/arm. See Bettina Kimpton, *The Death of Cú Chulainn: A Critical Edition of the Earliest Version of* Brislech Mór Maige Muirthemni *with Introduction, Translation, Notes, Bibliography and Vocabulary* (Maynooth: School of Celtic Studies, National University of Ireland, Maynooth, 2009), 26-27, trans. 45. The accommodation is explicitly identified as an application of *fír fer*, literally 'truth of men,' the rules of fair play in combat. See Philip O'Leary, *"Fír fer*: an internalized ethical concept in early Irish literature?" *Éigse 22 (1987): 1-14,* for general discussion of this concept.

[13] Metzler, *Disability in Medieval Europe*, 187.

[14] On Gerald's ethnographic project, see Laura Ashe, *Fiction and History in England, 1066-1200* (Cambridge University Press, 2007), 166-179, and Shirin Khanmohamadi, In *Light of Another's Word: European Ethnography in the Middle Ages.* Philadelphia: University of Pennsylvania Press, 2013), ch. 2.

defect. Just as those that are well formed are magnificent and second to none, so those that are badly formed have not their like elsewhere. And just as those who are kindly fashioned by nature turn out fine, so those that are without nature's blessing turn out in a horrible way.

And it is not surprising if nature sometimes produces such beings contrary to her ordinary laws when dealing with a people that is adulterous, incestuous, unlawfully conceived and born, outside the law, and shamefully abusing nature herself in spiteful and horrible practices. It seems a just punishment from God that those who do not look to him with the interior light of the mind, should often grieve in being deprived of the gift of the light that is bodily and external.[15]

"Impairment as the result of sin" is not just a paradigm for explaining physical difference; it is an invitation to treat physical difference as a basis for moral conclusions. Gerald invites his reader to treat Irish bodies as crime scenes, filled with evidence of sin and vice.[16]

---

[15] §109; trans. John O'Meara, *Gerald of Wales: The History and Topography of Ireland* (London: Penguin, rev. ed., 1982), 117-118. To keep this essay to a reasonable length, the original Latin and Irish are quoted only to highlight key terms or when a translation might be debatable.

[16] See James D. Cain, "Unnatural History: Gender and Genealogy in Gerald of Wales's *Topographia Hibernica*," *Essays in Medieval Studies* 19 (2002): 29-43, at 34, for an analysis of this passage in terms of the concepts of positive and natural justice that existed in Gerald's intellectual milieu. Mittman, *Maps and Monsters*, responding specifically to this passage, writes that, in general, "medieval viewers [...] made a direct connection between deformity and sin" (89). Citing Katherine O'Brien O'Keeffe, "Body and Law in Late Anglo-Saxon England," *Anglo-Saxon England* 27 (1998): 209-232, he says that in early English law this was expressed by the mutilation of criminals, which was primarily "evidentiary" rather than punitive: "[g]uilt was [made] manifest, visible and legible on the body, through mutilation" (91). Cf. Jeffrey Jerome Cohen, "Hybrids, Monsters,

Metzler's paradigm (2), by contrast, can be imagined as the "before" photo in the kind of before-and-after montage used to advertise cosmetic surgery and weight-loss drugs. To this way of thinking, a blind person is blind not because of any personal failing but because it serves the purposes of God or of the narrative to miraculously grant them sight–you cannot have miraculous healing without someone to heal.

Metzler's two paradigms are good generalizations but not all-encompassing.[17] For one thing, they are explicitly Christian.[18] What we might call traditional Irish thinking[19] seems to have emerged before and later also outside of Christianity in Ireland. It turns out, though, that Metzler's paradigms have close secular counterparts in Irish saga. For paradigm (1), impairment as the result of sin, the counterpart is impairment as the result of shame. For paradigm (2), impairment as the "before" condition in miraculous healing, the counterpart is impairment as the "before" condition in transformations that reveal the essential nature.

Borderlands: The Bodies of Gerald of Wales," in *The Postcolonial Middle Ages*, ed. Jeffrey Jerome Cohen (New York: St. Martin's Press, 2000), 85–104, on Gerald's depiction of Welsh bodies. Mittman additionally discusses a manuscript image of "a genuine deformed Irishman, whom [readers] are then to personally condemn as wicked" (90).

[17] Joshua Eyler, for example, has responded that "[w]hile it is certainly accurate to say that *some* people in the Middle Ages believed disability to be God's punishment for sin, this way of understanding medieval disability has only a limited viability. In truth, there were many lenses through which medieval societies viewed disability, as current research is beginning to demonstrate" (*Disability in the Middle Ages*, 3).

[18] On disability in medieval Islam, see now Kristina Richardson, *Difference and Disability in the Medieval Islamic World: Blighted Bodies* (Edinburgh University Press, 2012).

[19] To borrow a phrase from Margaret Clunies-Ross in another context ("traditional Norse thinking"). Of course, we can expect to see Metzler's Christian paradigms reflected in Irish saints' lives. In general, saints' lives are outside the scope of this essay. I do cite one example involving St. Brigit.

MODELING IMPAIRMENT AND DISABILITY

Irish counterparts to Metzler's paradigm (1): impairment as the result of shame

In anthropological terms, the social world of early Irish saga is a 'shame' rather than a 'guilt' culture. Public honor is essential.[20] This is thought of concretely in terms of 'saving face': the word for honor, status, reputation (*DIL*, s.v. *1 enech II*[21]) is literally the same as the word for cheeks or face (s.v. *1 enech I*). *Lóg n-enech*, conventionally translated 'honor-price,' the variable (status-based) compensation a person is entitled to receive from someone who causes them public embarrassment, literally means 'the price of one's cheeks.' Poetic satire (*áer, glám,* etc.) was thought to raise blisters or boils (*DIL*, s.v. nescóit and s.v.1 on) on the face as a sign that the target's honor was besmirched. Early Irish 'satire' is not a mocking parody, but a formal direct attack, a weaponization of language that works like a curse or a magic spell. The two verbs "to satirize," *áeraid* and *rindaid*, have the primary meanings 'cut' and 'gouge.' As a matter of law, being the target of justified satire makes a king unfit to rule, while in the sagas there are severe physical effects, up to and including death.[22]

---

[20] Bibliography on this topic is extensive. Philip O'Leary has a number of relevant studies: "*Fír fer*," "The Honour of Women in Early Irish Literature," *Ériu* 38 (1987): 27-44, "Honour-bound: the social context of early Irish heroic *geis*," *Celtica* 20 (1988), 85-107, "Jeers and judgments: laughter in early Irish literature," *CMCS* 22 (1991): 15-29, and "Magnanimous conduct in Irish heroic literature," *Éigse* 25 (1991): 28-44.

[21] *DIL* indicates an entry from the Royal Irish Academy *Dictionary of the Irish Language* (originally published 1913-76 and now online at http://edil.qub.ac.uk/dictionary/search.php).

[22] Kelly, *Guide*, 43-44, 137-138; Jacqueline Borsje, "Approaching Danger: *Togail Bruidne Da Derga and the Motif of Being One-Eyed*," in *CSANA Yearbook 2: Identifying the Celtic*, ed. Joseph Falaky Nagy (Dublin: Four Courts Press, 2002), 75-99, at 92-96. On early Irish satire in general, see Liam Breatnach, "On satire and the poet's circuit," in *Unity in Diversity: Studies in Irish and Scottish Gaelic language, literature and history*, 1, ed. Cathal G. Ó Háinle, and Donald E. Meek (Dublin: School of Irish, Trinity College Dublin, 2004), 25-35, "Satire, praise and the early Irish poet," *Ériu* 56 (2006): 63-84, and "*Araile felmac féig don Mumain*: unruly pupils and the limitations of satire," *Ériu* 59 (2009): 111-137; Roisin McLaughlin, *Early Irish Satire* (Dublin: Dublin Institute for Advanced Studies, 2008);

There is a general principle that any physical impairment or 'blemish' (generally *ainim* or *on*; see Appendix for other vocabulary used to communicate impairment), not just facial blisters, makes a king unfit to rule.[23] While in early Irish law, injuries causing impairment were not always necessarily considered a matter of honor,[24] in the sagas it appears that honor is generally associated with "the public perception of bodily integrity,"[25] while violations of honor, social norms, supernatural taboos, or the sanctity of the Otherworld (*síd*) invariably result in physical defects. Here are some examples:

> In his death-tale, the hero Cú Chulainn, whose name means "The Hound of Culann," is put in a situation where it seems he must violate a personal taboo (*geis*) against eating dog: in a partial violation of the geis, he takes a piece of dog-meat with his left hand and tucks it under his left thigh, and both his hand and thigh immediately lose their strength.[26]

---

and Tomás Ó Cathasaigh, *Coire Sois, The Cauldron of Knowledge: A Companion to Early Irish Saga*, ed. Matthieu Boyd (University of Notre Dame Press, 2014), 95-100, 140-142, 263-264.

[23] The king was proverbially supposed to be 'cen ainim cen on' or 'cen locht cen ainim'. See Kelly, *Guide*, 19; Robin Chapman Stacey, *Dark Speech: The Performance of Law in Early Ireland* (Philadelphia: University of Pennsylvania Press, 2007), 42-43; and Sheehan, "Losing Face," 135-136.

[24] Charlene Eska, "The Mutilation of Derbforgaill," in *Wounds and Wound Repair in Medieval Culture*, ed. Larissa Tracy and Kelly DeVries (Leiden and Boston: Brill, 2015), 252-266, at 260-261, explains that according to the law-text *Bretha Éitgid*, "if a man is deprived of his hand, foot, eye, or tongue, he is to be paid his full or half his *éraic* fine, which is the body-fine fixed for homicide [and] additional fines are added if the maiming is intentional." That is, the compensation is *not* based on the victim's honor-price. Whether the implication is that severe impairment is then akin to social "death" is debatable. As Sayers puts it, "post-traumatic competencies would have varied and been recognized in terms of longer-term outcomes. The one-legged warrior might just succeed as a well-married, propertied farmer" ("The Laconic Scar," 494).

[25] Sheehan, "Losing Face," 134.

[26] See Kimpton, *The Death of Cú Chulainn*, 39. I discuss the geis against eating dog in "On Not Eating Dog," in *Ollam: Studies in Gaelic and*

King Ailill Ólomm of Munster, whose epithet Ólomm is understood to mean 'Bare-Ear,' has his ear sucked off by a fairy-woman as he rapes her; she promises that she will leave no land in his possession when they part, a statement that reflects her role as a sovereignty-figure and tutelary goddess of the land, and means that she will strip him of his kingship.[27]

In the epic *Táin bó Cúailnge,* "The cattle-raid of Cooley," the armies of Queen Medb of Connacht invade the northern province of Ulster during the winter months when the Ulstermen are subject to a paralyzing 'debility,' (c*es noínden*). One interpretation of this mysterious paralysis or torpor is as a reflection of seasonal myth, a winter sleep. But in the literature it is presented as a punishment inflicted by the horse-goddess Macha, after the king of Ulster, Conchobor, forces her to run a race against his horses while she is pregnant, denying her the legal protection of *turbaid* 'postponement.'[28] She wins; gives birth to twins on the finish line (the name of the Ulster royal seat at Emain Macha is thus reinterpreted as meaning "the Twins of Macha"); and curses the Ulstermen to be as defenseless in their hour of need as a woman giving birth, a severe impairment that directly corresponds to how they exploited her. Or it is the impropriety of gazing on her naked during her delivery, or her agonized screams, that has this effect: another literary explanation of this imposed *ces* attributes it to a different Otherworld woman who

---

Related Traditions in Honor of Tomás Ó Cathasaigh, ed. Matthieu Boyd (Madison, NJ: Fairleigh Dickinson University Press, 2016), 35-46.
[27] In Ó Cathasaigh, *Coire Sois,* see Ch. 2 on the contractual and potentially adverse relationship between humans and the Otherworld (*síd*), and Ch. 23 on the text *Cath Maige Mucrama,* "The Battle of Mag Mucrama" (ed. and trans. Máirín O Daly, *Cath Maige Mucrama* [Dublin: Irish Texts Society, 1975]), and its recurring theme of 'stripping' or 'laying bare' that includes Ailill's ear.
[28] Text ed. and trans. Vernam Hull, "Noínden Ulad: The Debility of the Ulidians," *Celtica* 8 (1968), 1-42; discussed by Gregory Toner, "Macha and the Invention of Myth," *Ériu* 60 (2010): 81-109, at 90-94.

exposes herself to the Ulstermen after Cú Chulainn mutilates her husband and claims her as a prize.[29]

> In *Togail bruidne Da Derga*, "The Destruction of Da Derga's Hostel," the otherwise exemplary king Conaire delivers an unjust judgment that violates the conditions of his support by the Otherworld, and causes the social and natural order of his kingdom to collapse. In the titular hostel, where he dies, he is surrounded by characters whose impaired or atypical bodies express, in Amy Mulligan's analysis,[30] the breakdown of the body politic.

These and other examples suggest that the state of one's body was understood to express the state of one's honor, i.e. reflecting one's good standing (or otherwise) with human society or the supernatural Otherworld.

The Irish counterpart to Metzler's paradigm (2): impairment as a "before" condition

Metzler's paradigm has to do with miraculous cures, caused by some external agent like a saint. There would obviously be examples of this in Irish hagiography, although perhaps not as many as in other

---

[29] Text ed. and trans. Vernam Hull, "*Ces Ulad*: The Affliction of the Ulstermen," *Zeitschrift für Celtische Philologie* 29 (1962-64): 305-314. Also translated in John T. Koch with John Carey, eds. and trans., *The Celtic Heroic Age* (Aberystwyth: Celtic Studies Publications, fourth ed., 2004), 67-68. Discussed by Toner, "Macha," 94.

[30] Eichhorn-Mulligan, "Togail Bruidne Da Derga and the Politics of Anatomy"; cf. Ralph O'Connor, *The Destruction of Da Derga's Hostel: Kingship & Narrative Artistry in a Mediaeval Irish Saga* (Oxford University Press, 2014).

European literatures.[31] Its secular counterparts,[32] like the "Ash-Lad" scenario for heroic warriors, have to do with transformation that is innate and reveals aspects of one's essential self. Thus impairment is the "before" condition of poets whose "eloquence is born of dumbness, vision of blindness, and radiance of loathsomeness."[33] In the various examples discussed by Patrick Ford, poets like Amairgen of Ulster, and even the Spirit of Poetry, first appear disabled–mute, blind, bloated and unable to move, or so physically loathsome that society shuns them–before transforming into beings of radiant eloquence. The glory of the "after" condition is emphasized by the contrast.[34]

A similar situation exists with the female personification of the Sovereignty of Ireland in *Echtra mac nEchdach Muigmedóin*, "The Adventures of the Sons of Eochaid Mugmedón."[35] The future king, Niall, meets a hag in the forest who demands a kiss in exchange for water from the well that she is guarding. The hag is characterized as decrepit and truly loathsome: she has a huge belly speckled with

---

[31] On this point, see Wendy Davies, "The Place of Healing in Early Irish Society," in *Sages, Saints and Storytellers: Celtic Studies in Honour of Professor James Carney*, Donnchadh Ó Corráin, Liam Breatnach, and Kim R. McCone (Maynooth: An Sagart, 1989), 43-55. Helen Oxenham, *Perceptions of Femininity in Early Irish Society* (Woodbridge, Suffolk: D.S. Brewer, 2016), 138-140, comments on the extent to which the miracles of Irish saints might be gendered. Because the details of Irish healing miracles would not seem to call Metzler's paradigms broadly into question, and above all for reasons of space, it would not be opportune to explore them in any detail here. But see below for Donn Bó in *Cath Almaine*.

[32] Admittedly the line between hagiography and heroic literature is not clear-cut: see Dorothy Bray, "Heroic Tradition in the Lives of the Early Irish Saints: a Study in Hagio-Biographical Patterning," in *Proceedings of the First North American Congress of Celtic Studies*, ed. G. W. MacLennan (Ottawa: Chair of Celtic Studies, University of Ottawa, 1988), 261-271, for a classic study of the affinities.

[33] Ford, "The Blind, the Dumb," 27.

[34] Ford, "The Blind, the Dumb"; and for more on this, see Mulligan, "The Satire of the Poet."

[35] Whitley Stokes, "The Death of Crimthann son of Fidach, and the Adventures of the Sons of Eochaid Muigmedón," *Revue Celtique* 24 (1903): 172-207, 446; trans. in Koch and Carey, *The Celtic Heroic Age*, 203-208.

disease, green teeth, shins broad as shovels, and so on. But when Niall agrees to lie with her, she is transformed into a woman of great beauty, who explains that her condition mirrors the daunting prospect of gaining the sovereignty by force, followed by the pleasure of possessing it: "as you have seen me at first fearsome, wolfish, terrifying, and at last beautiful, thus is the sovereignty: for it is not obtained without battle and conflicts; but at last it is fair and gracious to anyone."[36]

Context effects: impairment does not have to equal disability

Even the adjusted versions of Metzler's paradigms are not a complete picture of how impairment is handled in Irish sagas, however. That is, I have shown two ways impairment can translate to disability. But, and this is where the insight that disability is socially constructed begins to have a more substantial role, this translation does not *have* to happen as such. Context and perspective are essential. A story about Saint Brigit of Kildare will do to illustrate the point:

> [A] certain man of honourable birth came to Dubthach [Brigit's father] to seek his daughter in marriage, which pleased her father and brothers. Brigit however turned him down. And when they began to put great pressure on her to marry the man, saint Brigit asked God to afflict her body with some deformity in order that men might stop paying suit to her. Thereupon one of her eyes burst and liquefied in her head. For she preferred to lose her bodily eye than the eye of her soul and loved beauty of soul more than that of the body. When her father saw this he allowed her to take the veil and her eye was restored and she was healed on taking the veil[.][37]

---

[36] Trans. Koch and Carey, *The Celtic Heroic Age*, 208. For more on this, see Eichhorn-Mulligan, "The Anatomy of Power."

[37] Trans. Seán Connolly, "Vita Prima Sanctae Brigitae: Background and Historical Value," *Journal of the Royal Society of Antiquaries of Ireland* 19 (1989): 5-49, anthologized in *The Field Day of Irish Writing, Vol. IV: Irish Women's Writing and Traditions*, ed. Angela Bourke et al. (Cork University

At the time when Brigit is missing an eye, she is physically impaired. In the eyes of the world, especially her father and prospective suitors, she is also disabled, since she is less attractive as a potential wife and might seem to have less value as a woman: this is the circumstance that Derbforgaill experienced as profoundly shameful. But the liquefaction of Brigit's eye actually shows her special standing with God and allows her to escape the expectation that she marry; it is empowering. The conflict of interpretations here also demonstrates the principle in 1 Corinthians 3:18-19: "If any of you think you are wise by the standards of this age, you should become 'fools' so that you may become wise. For the wisdom of this world is foolishness in God's sight."[38]

In a Middle Irish homily, the same physical condition is used to express quite different things when Brigit does it to herself and when God does it to her brother:

> Shortly after that came a certain nobleman unto Dubthach to ask for his daughter (in marriage). Dubthach and his sons were willing, but Brigit refused. [One of her brothers] named Beccán [said] unto her: "Idle is the fair eye that is in thy head not to be on a pillow near a husband." "The Son of the Virgin knoweth," said Brigit, "it is not lively[39] for us if it brings harm upon us." Then Brigit put her finger under her eye, and drew it out of her head till it was on her cheek; and she said: "Lo, here for thee is thy

---

Press/New York University Press, 2002), 67. Brigit's eye is discussed in detail by Victoria Simmons, "Saint Brigit and the Modular Eye," *Studi Celtici* 3 (2004): 181-205, and Máire Johnson, "In the Bursting of an Eye: Blinding and Blindness in Ireland's Medieval Hagiography," in *Wounds and Wound Repair in Medieval Culture*, ed. Larissa Tracy and Kelly DeVries (Leiden and Boston: Brill, 2015), 448-471.

[38] One observes a similar principle in Irish archaeology: objects recovered from lakes and bogs are often found damaged, perhaps because they have been ritually slighted to consecrate them to the use of the gods. Translation from the New International Version.

[39] *beoda* (*DIL*, s.v. béodai): although the basic meaning of this word is 'living, animate; alive, active, vigorous,' it also has the meaning 'lucky, auspicious,' which would be a more appropriate translation here.

delightful eye, O Beccán!" Then *his* eye burst forthwith. When Dubthach and her brethren beheld that, they promised that she should never be told to go unto a husband. Then she put her palm to her eye and it was quite whole at once. But Beccán's eye was not whole till his death.[40]

The consequence for Beccán fits Metzler's paradigm (1): he loses an eye because he has failed to look at his sister in a way that appreciates her spiritual calling; his comment on her eye is an indication of his inward blindness, and his eye-loss reflects this. Brigit's eye-loss, since it wins her the right to live as a nun, is something rather different. We might call this new paradigm "impairment as the price of power."[41]

The same paradigm applies to the speaker's decrepitude in the famous "Lament of the Old Woman of Beare," specifically when she says: "My right eye has been taken from me to be sold for a land that will be for ever mine; the left eye has been taken also, to make my claim to that land more secure."[42] While presumably this refers to the effects of age on her eyesight, it also makes a recognized allusion to Matthew 5:29 ("If your right eye causes you to stumble, gouge it out and throw it away. It is better for you to lose one part of your body

---

[40] Trans. Whitley Stokes, in *Three Middle-Irish Homilies on the Lives of Saints Patrick, Brigit, and Columba* (Calcutta, 1877), 65. This passage was adduced by C. H. Tawney in *The Kathá Sarit Ságara, or Ocean of the Streams of Story, translated from the original Sanskrit. Volume I* (Calcutta: J. W. Thomas, at the Baptist Mission Press, 1880), 247-248, as a parallel for an episode in the eleventh-century *Katha-saritsagara* "Ocean of Rivers of Stories" by the Sanskrit writer Somadeva: a prince who goes about as a beggar in an exercise of contempt for the world meets a merchant's wife who admires his eyes. He responds by tearing out one eye and presenting it to her.

[41] I make no claim that this paradigm is *uniquely* Irish. Without leaving medieval Europe, we can compare Óðinn's sacrifice of an eye at Mimir's Well in exchange for wisdom, or Julian of Norwich's prayer to suffer bodily sickness and three wounds along with insight into Christ's Passion (see *The Writings of Julian of Norwich*, ed. Nicholas Watson and Jacqueline Jenkins [University Park, PA: Pennsylvania State University Press, 2006], 63).

[42] Trans. Gerard Murphy in *Early Irish Lyrics: Eighth to Twelfth Century* (Oxford University Press, 1956), 81.

than for your whole body to be thrown into hell," *(NIV)*, but reframes this as a trade for a higher reward: one's eyesight for a claim to paradise.

Brigit's eye is restored when she becomes a nun. Even the *Cailleach Bhéara* can look forward to having her eyesight fully restored in heaven: the Bible says the faithful will receive a heavenly body that is like Christ's body (1 Corinthians 15:35-58,[43] 2 Corinthians 5:1-10, Philippians 3:21; compare 1 Corinthians 13:12 specifically for unimpaired sight). In this Christian context, no impairment is permanent: there is temporary sacrifice for eternal reward. And everyone on earth is temporarily impaired in the sense that the earthly body falls short of the heavenly body. These factors combine to make Brigit's eye interpretable in line with Metzler's paradigm (2), the "before" photo. Such complications are largely absent from the sagas, where impairment pays for power within the secular sphere.[44]

Paradigm (3): impairment as the price of power

A good example of this third paradigm is the god Lug's demonic grandfather Balor in the mythological saga *Cath Maige Tuired*, (The (Second) Battle of Mag Tuired)."[45] Balor has a magic eye with the power to overthrow a host of enemies: "The host which looked at that

---

[43] For example, 1 Corinthians 15:44, on the post-resurrection body, is quoted by the seventh-century Augustinus Hibernicus, *On the Miracles of Holy Scripture*, trans. John Carey, *King of Mysteries: Early Irish Religious Writings* (Dublin: Four Courts Press, 2000), 73.

[44] At the 42nd Harvard Celtic Colloquium in 2023, Dylan Bailey presented on an episode from the life of St. Ruadán, arguably derivative of the episode with Brigit's eye, in which a one-eyed king tears out his own remaining eye to give to a druid who has threatened to satirize him, and the saint restores both of the king's eyes by blinding the druid. (See Appendix 1 to Betha Ruadhain, ed. and trans. Charles Plummer in *Bethada Náem nÉrenn: Lives of the Irish Saints* [Oxford: Clarendon Press, 1922; repr. 1968], Volume 1, 317-329, and Volume 2, 308-320, trans. online at https://celt.ucc.ie/published/T201000G/text016.html.) This presents an interesting combination of the paradigms I present in this essay, and hopefully Bailey's incisive analysis will find its way into *PHCC* 42.

[45] Ed. and trans. Elizabeth Gray, *Cath Maige Tuired: The Second Battle of Mag Tuired* (Dublin: Irish Texts Society, 1982).

eye, even if they were many thousands in number, would offer no resistance to warriors" (§133). The eye "had that poisonous power for this reason: once [Balor's] father's druids were brewing magic. He came and looked over the window, and the fumes of the concoction affected the eye and the venomous power of the brew settled in it." This experience, like the mutations that turn ordinary people into comic-book supervillains, cannot have been pleasant–and at a minimum, its destructive power means that Balor cannot use his contaminated eye for purposes of ordinary sight. The eye "was never opened except on a battlefield. Four men would raise the lid of the eye by a polished ring in its lid" (§133).[46]

A similar situation arises in the Ulster Cycle with Cú Chulainn's death-tale.[47] Characters seeking revenge on the hero are trained in sorcery and then blinded in their left eye "[so] that their fury (i.e. their pain or longing) might be great to avenge their father by means of that

---

[46] Balor has a long-standing popular reputation as "the Fomorian cyclops-god with one eye" (e.g. Lewis Spence, *The Magic Arts in Celtic Britain* [New York: Rider, 1945], 35), but *Cath Maige Tuired* never says that he is a cyclops. Before he encounters Lug he succeeds in killing Núadu in battle with his magic eye closed, so perhaps he is still partially sighted, in which case the classic line "Lift up my eyelid, lad [. . .] so I may see the talkative fellow who is conversing with me" (Gray, *Cath Maige Tuired*, §134) is just a trick to subject Lug to his baleful gaze, and not actually required to see him, unless Lug is standing in his blind spot.

[47] Cú Chulainn's *ríastrad*, his 'warp-spasm,' is a special case, because it is not an example of realistic physical impairment; it is obviously a manifestation of superhuman power, and is so regarded by everyone who deals with it. Some of the conclusions I draw may relate to it, but it is not in the main line of my analysis. There are useful discussions by Ralph O'Connor, "Monsters of the Tribe: Berserk Fury, Shapeshifting and Social Dysfunction in *Táin bó Cúailnge, Egils saga* and *Hrólfs saga kraka*," in *Kings and Warriors in Early North-West Europe*, ed. Jan Erik Rekdal and Charles Doherty (Dublin: Four Courts Press, 2016), 180-236; Amy Mulligan, "The Erasure of a Warrior's Body: Cú Chulainn, Isidore of Seville, and Irish Independence," in *From Enlightenment to Rebellion: Essays in Honor of Christopher Fox*, ed. James G. Buickerood (Lewisburg: Bucknell University Press, 2018), 33-46; and Ron J. Popenhagen, "Cú Chulainn Unbound," in *The Medieval Cultures of the Irish Sea and the North Sea: Manannán and his Neighbors*, ed. Joseph Falaky Nagy and Charles W. MacQuarrie (Amsterdam University Press, 2019), 59-78.

craft they had learned."[48] The blinding may have directly enhanced their occult power, or it may have been a badge of shame (like the eye-gouging inflicted on Israelite captives by Nahash the Ammonite in 1 Samuel 11:2) which meant they had to compensate with even greater feats; either way, this impairment was ultimately supposed to empower rather than disable them in their efforts to destroy Cú Chulainn.[49] The characters involved here are the sons *and* daughters of the warrior Calatín Dána, killed by Cú Chulainn in the *Táin*, so this is evidently a gender-neutral paradigm.

In the birth-tale of the Leinster king Fiachu Muillethan (Fiachu Broad-Forehead) or Muinlethan (Broad-Nape), his mother has been told by a druid that if she gives birth on a certain day, her son will be a great king, but if he is born a day earlier, he will be the *ríg-drúth* (royal jester) of Ireland. When she goes into labor, she squats over a flat rock to hold her baby in until the second day. He avoids being born a jester, but his head or neck flattens out against the stone, leaving him with a permanent physical mark and an accompanying epithet.[50]

Arguably, "impairment as the price of power" is also the paradigm in play with the Ulster women of *Serglige Con Culainn*, "The Wasting-Sickness of Cú Chulainn," who express their devotion to the heroes Cú Chulainn, Conall Cernach, and Cúscraid Menn

---

[48] Kimpton, *The Death of Cú Chulainn*, 35.

[49] Some survivors of sexual violence seem to be understood as similarly empowered or motivated by that fact. See my discussion of Clothru and Medb in "Aspects of Sexual Violence in Early Irish Literature," *PHCC* 39 (2019): 72-90, at 79-87.

[50] See O Daly, *Cath Maige Mucrama*, 64-65, and Tomás Ó Cathasaigh, *The Heroic Biography of Cormac mac Airt* (Dublin: Dublin Institute for Advanced Studies, 1977), 107-111. This is Stith Thompson's motif T589.8, "woman strives to delay birth until auspicious day"; see Tom Peete Cross, *Motif-Index of Early Irish Literature* (Bloomington, IN: Indiana University Press, 1952), for other Irish examples, which do not specify what alternative the delayed birth is avoiding. In saints' lives, the baby's head, instead of being flattened, puts a dent in the stone, which suggests that in an overt Christian context even Irish narratives may be more constrained by Metzler's paradigms. (The dented stones are then also used to point out the veracity of the story, as "proof" that the incident occurred.) On the *drúth* 'jester,' a word that is also used to refer to people with developmental disabilities, see Boyd, "Competing Assumptions about the *drúth*."

Machae (Cúscraid the Stammerer of Macha) by gouging out one eye, crooking their necks, and stuttering, respectively, to mimic aspects of the heroes themselves, and presumably to win their favor.[51] At the very least, the groupies find solidarity with one another through the manifestation of these 'blemishes,' and perhaps a sense of superiority over women who are not prepared to take such drastic action.

In all these cases, impairment suggests disability (these characters cannot see out of one eye, etc.) but expresses ability on a deeper level (their destructive power or social stature is enhanced). Finn mac Cumaill's blistered thumb of knowledge also fits this paradigm, since he has to bite it to the marrow to gain its insights. Saint Brigit has a "blind lad" who could "memorise instantly whatever he heard,"[52] enabling him to learn the liturgy of the undersea community of Plea while all his traveling-companions forget the liturgy they learned in Rome.[53] In the following case, amazing ability is the manifestation of an impairment whose negative aspects are left to the imagination.

Several texts relate how the "brain of forgetfulness" (*inchinn dermait*) was:

---

[51] Trans. Jeffrey Gantz, *Early Irish Myths and Sagas* (Harmondsworth: Penguin, 1981); discussion in Sayers, "Kingship and the Hero's Flaw" and "The Laconic Scar," 487. Cú Chulainn is not actually blind in one eye, but this impairment mimics his warrior state of *ríastrad*, in which one of his eyes bulges and the other shrinks and retracts. In the *Táin* it is said that "Cú Chulainn had seven pupils in his royal eyes, two of which were asquint," but that "this was more an adornment than a disfigurement to Cú Chulainn," and another warrior's attempt to taunt him with being a squinter is not convincing for this reason (O'Rahilly, *TBC I*, 206). Sayers, "Portraits of the Ulster Hero Conall Cernach," discusses Conall Cernach's allegedly misshapen head. Cúscraid's stammering, apparently caused by a wound to the throat, is discussed below along with *The Story of Mac Da Thó's Pig*. Crucially, the imitation of Cúscraid requires only the *performance* of an impairment, not the permanent fact of one. Arguably, this is also how the episode with Brigit's eye works, since it is later restored. Exploring the applicability of a concept of "disability as performance" is a planned follow-up to my paper here.

[52] Trans. John Carey, *King of Mysteries*, 165.

[53] For discussion, see Dorothy Bray, "The Story of *Plea*," *North American Journal of Celtic Studies* 2:1 (2018): 56-78.

beaten out of the head of Cenn Fáelad son of Ailell, after it had been cloven in two in the battle of Mag Rath. [. . .] This battle ha[d] three distinctive qualities [. . . but] the beating of his brain of forgetfulness out of the head of Cenn Fáelad in the battle of Mag Rath was not the distinctive quality, but rather all that he has left of well-composed books behind him in Ireland.[54] And his treatment was done in Túaim nDrecan at the meeting of three streets between the houses of three scholars, namely a scholar of traditional Irish law, and a scholar of poetry, and a scholar of Latin learning; and all that the three schools would recite each day, he would have through the sharpness of his intellect each night, and all of it that he deemed worthy of expounding, he would bring it into a poetical form, and it was written by him into parchment books.[55]

---

[54] In listing the other "distinctive qualities" of the battle, the text corrects itself with equal care, stating, for example, that the madness of Suibne Geilt was notable not for its own sake, but for "what he has left behind of tales and of songs, entertaining everyone from then until now." Suibne's experience can be analyzed in the same way as Cenn Fáelad's: see Feargal Ó Béarra, "*Buile Shuibhne: vox insaniae* from Medieval Ireland," in *Mental Health, Spirituality, and Religion in the Middle Ages and Early Modern Age*, ed. Albrecht Classen (Berlin: de Gruyter, 2014), 242-289.

[55] Trans. David Stifter, online at https://listserv.heanet.ie/cgi-bin/wa?A3 =ind0406&L=OLD-IRISH-L&E=Quoted-printable&P=87678&B=-- &T=text%2Fplain;%20charset=ISO-8859-1, from the preface to the law-text *Bretha Éitgid*. On the different versions of the story, see David Georgi, "A Stunning Blow on the Head: Literacy and the Anxiety of Memory in the Legend of Cenn Faelad's Brain of Forgetting," *PHCC* 16/17 (1996-97): 195-205, at 198-202, and also Proinsias Mac Cana, "The Three Languages and the Three Laws," *Studia Celtica* 5 (1970): 62-78; and Hildegard L.C. Tristram, "Why James Joyce also Lost His 'Brain of Forgetting': Patterns of Memory and Media in Irish Writing," in *Anglistentag 1988 Gottingen: Vortrage*, ed. Heinz-Joachim Mullenbrock and Renate Noll-Wiemann (Tubingen: Niemeyer, 1989), 220-233, and "Warum Cenn Faelad sein 'Gehirn des Vergessens verlor': Wort und Schrift in der älteren irischen

This is a famous passage. It has been read as "a metaphor for the very process of transition from the oral to the written": "[h]owever retentive a culture's oral *memoria*," writes Hildegard Tristram, "some of it is bound to be lost through prolonged use, by accident, or by inadvertent transformation. This is the *brain of forgetting* Cenn Faelad lost when he fixed what he knew on vellum."[56] David Georgi modifies this by proposing that Cenn Fáelad lends his authority to the oral tradition at the moment of transition: "the reader can trust the book because he would trust Cenn Faelad," the man of "infallible memory."[57] But "[t]he essential fact" remains, as Georgi puts it, that "the acquisition of exhaustive memory is figured as a loss or mutilation [of] a natural trait, something inborn"[58]–that is, as impairment.[59] In Cenn Fáelad's case it is a highly productive impairment, since it expresses itself in the profusion of well-composed books that he leaves behind. But the creative product masks what is likely to have been a difficult condition. We can imagine him suffering. His impairment, while rare, is not unheard of; in the modern psychiatric literature the inability to forget anything is known as hyperthymestic syndrome.[60] People with this syndrome seldom feel wholly positive about it. Losing his brain of forgetting would mean, at the very least, that Cenn Fáelad's mind would fill with a constant stream of wrong information and meaningless trivia; and he would never be able to dull the force of the awful sights and sounds he

---

Literatur," in *Deutsche, Kelten und Iren: 150 Jahre deutsche Keltologie: Gearóid Mac Eoin zum 60. Geburtstag gewidmet*, ed. Hildegard L. C. Tristram (Hamburg: Buske, 1990), 207-248.

[56] Tristram, "Why James Joyce," 227.

[57] Georgi, "A Stunning Blow," 203.

[58] Georgi, "A Stunning Blow," 202.

[59] According to Edgar Slotkin, medically speaking "it does not seem unlikely that Cenn Faelad [actually] suffered some sort of specialized aphasia [. . .] which made it impossible for him to retain for any length of time oral instruction [...] He *had* to write it down" (Edgar M. Slotkin, "Medieval Irish Scribes and Fixed Texts," *Éigse* 17 [1977-79]: 437-450, at 438-440; cf. Georgi, "A Stunning Blow," 197). But Slotkin is only speculating. The texts are unanimous in saying that the brain of forgetfulness was lost.

[60] See Elisabeth S. Parker, Larry Cahill, and James L. McGaugh, "A Case of Unusual Autobiographical Remembering," *Neurocase* 12 (2006): 35-49.

experienced in battle. To quote the description of the battle in *Cath Maige Ratha*, "The Battle of Mag Rath":

> Great the havoc and slaughter of heroes that took place there throughout those three whole days. [. . .] [M]any were the streams of blood upon the fair skin of a delicate youth rushing into danger [. . .] Frightful also the turmoil all over the battlefield, the din and crashing of the bright shields, the swish of the swords and sabres, the clatter and rattling of the quivers and reins, the whirring of arrows and the crashing strokes of the weapons. And as they were felling one another, the points of their fingers and their feet almost met, so that they were falling from their standing owing to the slipperiness of the blood under their feet, and their heads were struck off them sitting. [It was a] gory, wound-inflicting, sharp, bloody battle [. . .][61]

Complications in the Irish counterpart of paradigm (1): impairment alone as insufficient evidence of shame

Metzler's paradigm (1), impairment as a result of sin, and its Irish counterpart, impairment as a result of shame, lend themselves to being reverse-engineered: one concludes sin or shame from impairment, as though it were forensic evidence. Gerald of Wales does this in the passage quoted earlier. This kind of reasoning, left unchecked, leads to a blanket assumption that people with physical impairments must somehow deserve them.[62]

---

[61] Trans. Carl Marstrander, "A New Version of the Battle of Mag Rath," *Ériu* 5 (1911): 226-247, online at http://www.ucd.ie/tlh/trans/cm.eriu. 5.002.t.text.html, at 238-239.

[62] Of course, this is bad logic, unless the state of the body cannot be accounted for in any other way. Consider this joke:
"A disheveled man, who was obviously drunk and reeked with the smell of booze, sat down on a subway seat next to a priest. The man's shirt was stained, his face was plastered with red lipstick, and a half empty bottle of gin was sticking out of his torn coat pocket.
He opened his newspaper and began reading. After a few minutes the man turned to the priest and asked, 'Say, Father, what causes arthritis?'

The mutilation of Derbforgaill[63] by the women of Ulster, in the face of the threat they think she poses with her sex appeal, goes further: it *inflicts* impairment in order to *produce* shame. While the women's action is "unjustified," "excessive," "illegitimate," and "transgressive," "not a punishment for sexual transgression but a response to their own fear and jealousy,"[64] it succeeds in making Derbforgaill feel such shame that she refuses to be seen by anyone, and it might be the shame rather than the injuries themselves that kills her. The fact that Cú Chulainn avenges her on the women has no bearing on this. Unlike in some of the cases discussed below, there seems to be no room to negotiate the social construction of her impairment, perhaps because she has so thoroughly internalized the connection with shame.[65] To the extent that women's beauty is one of

---

'My son, it's caused by loose living, being with cheap, wicked women, too much alcohol and a contempt for your fellow man, sleeping around with prostitutes and a lack of bathing.'

'Well, I'll be damned,' the drunk muttered, returning to his paper.

The priest, thinking about what he had said, nudged the man and apologized. 'I'm very sorry. I didn't mean to come on so strong. How long have you had arthritis?' 'I don't have it, Father. I was just reading here that the Pope does.'" (Fred Neil, *A Funny Thing Happened . . . on the Way to the Health Fair* [College Station, TX: Virtualbookworm.com Publishing, 2002], 51)

[63] This is told in her death-tale *Aided Derbforgaill,* ed. and trans. Kicki Ingridsdotter, "*Aided Derbforgaill* 'The Violent Death of Derbforgaill': A Critical Edition with Introduction, Translation and Textual Notes" (Ph.D. dissertation, Uppsala University, 2009), and discussed in detail by Charlene Eska, "The Mutilation of Derbforgaill."

[64] Eska, "The Mutilation of Derbforgaill," 258, 262.

[65] Incidentally, I think I can answer the note by Eska, "The Mutilation of Derbforgaill," that "[n]o explanation is given in the text as to the significance of snow being on [Derforgaill's] house" (254n10), when this is what tips off Cú Chulainn and his foster-son Lugaid that something is wrong with her. Derbforgaill's sex appeal expresses itself as literal hotness, as demonstrated by the pissing-contest in the snow (Derbforgaill's urine melts more snow than other women's): presumably she would also radiate heat that would melt snow around or above her. Snow on her house is a sign that her hotness is gone, clearly the result of some catastrophe. To the extent

their major currencies in this culture, and there is no particular context outside Christian self-mortification that would call for them to bear honorable wounds, it might be harder for them to resist this connection than it is for men.[66]

Early Irish law broadly rejects concluding shame from impairment. However, the law expects that people will indulge in it anyway, and so imposes a heavy fine for mocking someone with a physical impairment.[67] In other words, while dishonor may result in bodily impairment, no one is invited to see impairment and conclude dishonor; impairment alone is not sufficient evidence to shame a person. Rather, in that case the impairment should not even be acknowledged.

This is illustrated in a subtle way by the otherwise wildly unsubtle Ulster Cycle tale *Scéla Mucce Meic Dathó*, "The story of Mac Da Thó's pig," where injuries received in battle play a key role. Sarah

---

that this text makes sex appeal seem like a matter of objective physical fact rather than social convention or personal preference, it makes it harder to avoid the same approach to shame–not as a feeling one has, but as something that simply exists.

[66] A classic discussion of women's honor in early Irish literature is O'Leary, "The Honour of Women." Sayers, "The Laconic Scar," now comments in his discussion of epic heroes that "[w]omen, too, might be subject to blows in early Ireland," but his summary of the issue is that "women warriors, with more than a touch of the preternatural, may trade blows with men but invariably treat for peace under threat of death" (he cites *Tochmarc Emire,* "The Wooing of Emer," but the same could be said of Medb's encounter with Cú Chulainn at the end of the *Táin*) and that "[s]ome few sorceresses, in the guise of aged women [. . .] are killed, often by non-martial means, such as being hurled off a cliff. This is because the hero can win glory only in a conventional battle with conventional weapons between peers. A disparity in sex, age, or social status puts the hero at risk of gaining nothing but losing a great deal" (482). This seems broadly plausible but not exceptionless: in the *Táin*, Cethern seems no more disgraced by being wounded by Medb than by anyone else; and Cú Chulainn's encounters with Scáthach and Aífe and with the Morrígan (see Sayers, "The Laconic Scar," 479) are clearly supposed to enhance his reputation.

[67] Kelly, *Guide*, 94-95; Sheehan, "Losing Face," 134-135. This is an offence described as *nóad ainmne*, 'making known a blemish,' or *ainmed*, '[the] act of drawing attention to a blemish (esp. by satire)' (*DIL*, s.vv.)

Sheehan has claimed that this saga's "masculine, honour-based hierarchy is grounded in the public perception of bodily integrity; mere association with a deficient body renders a warrior ineligible for heroic privilege. Yet the vulnerability of the body upon which this external honour depends makes shame an imminent threat to identity."[68] Her article is theoretically rich and full of insight, but I do not think that this conclusion is entirely correct. "The public perception of bodily integrity" and "mere association with a deficient body" mean disability, i.e. a socially-constructed state (the key words in Sheehan are "public perception," "association"–in other words, "bodily integrity" and "deficient body" are socially determined). However, the saga actually makes it clear that any wound or damage to a body (its "vulnerability") does not automatically register as disability; it has to be made to register as such. To see how this is so, I will review the crucial sequence of the saga in full:

> Ailill and Medb, the king and queen of Connacht, and Conchobor, the king of Ulster, have both asked the Leinster king Mac Da Thó to let them have his wonderful dog, which protects the entire province of Leinster. Mac Da Thó, taking his wife's advice, invites both the Connachtmen and the Ulstermen to a feast at which he hopes that they will sort the issue out among themselves. At this feast he serves his enormous pig. By custom, the best warrior present is entitled to divide up the pig and claim the "champion's portion" of it for himself. The Connacht warrior Cet mac Magach goes and sits by the pig, and threatens to carve it unless a warrior is found to match him. Conchobor urges the Ulster champion Lóegaire to reply. A pattern is established whereby:
>
> i. Cet demands that the contest continue, or he will carve the pig;
> ii. an Ulsterman stands up, and we sometimes get a general description of how he looks (on the order of "tall, fair" or "large, gray-haired, very ugly");

[68] Sheehan, "Losing Face," 145.

iii.   Cet asks who it is, and everyone says the challenger's name;

iv.   Cet points out a shameful flaw in his opponent;

v.   the man sits down, and Cet demands that the contest continue.

Cet rebuffs seven challengers in all. The eighth, Conall Cernach, arrives late, and after he recites his exploits, Cet yields to him. But Cet jeers that if his brother Ánlúan were there, Conall would face a tougher contest. Conall delivers the immortal line "He is, though," and hits Cet in the chest with Ánlúan's freshly severed head.

Cet dismisses his challengers by declaring them disabled, and the rhetoric of these dismissals deserves to be studied in detail.[69]

---

[69] This has been done before to reach different conclusions: besides Sheehan, "Losing Face," see the thorough discussion by Ailís Ní Mhaoldomhnaigh, "Satirical Narrative in Early Irish Literature" (Ph.D. dissertation, National University of Ireland Maynooth, 2007), online at http://eprints.nuim.ie/1333/1/Satirical_Narrative_in_Early_Irish_Literature. pdf, 63-79; the comparative study by William Sayers, "Serial Defamation in Two Medieval Tales: The Icelandic *Ölkofra Þáttr* and The Irish *Scéla Mucce Meic Dathó*," *Oral Tradition* 6.1 (1991): 35-57, online at http:// journal.oraltradition.org/files/articles/6i/6_sayers.pdf; and the further discussion by Sayers, "The Laconic Scar," 488-492. Bruce Lincoln, in *Death, War, and Sacrifice: Studies in Ideology and Practice* (University of Chicago Press, 1991), has suggested that in this text, "wounds of the head (eye and voice) correspond to sovereign figures, of the arm or hand to warriors, and of the lower torso (foot and genitals) to the lower social strata" (255-256), which seems to work for the sovereign figures Éogan and Cúscraid, but the distinction between "warriors" and "lower social strata" is not clear, when all these characters are competing as warriors. But Sayers makes a similar claim: "These seven confrontations between Cet and the Ulstermen move on ideological spectra from active warrior initiation to impotent old age, from base social condition to the kingship, from foot to head, from wound to stump and scar. Here, too, the tripartite cosmos is imminent, in the discrete eye (head), arm (upper body), and leg (lower

Cet's first challenger is Lóegaire Búadach. In other texts such as *Mesca Ulad*, "The Intoxication of the Ulstermen," or *Fled Bricrenn*, "Bricriu's Feast," Lóegaire is presented as the third-ranked Ulster hero after Cú Chulainn and Conall Cernach; since neither of these others is present, it makes sense for Conchobor to encourage Lóegaire to step forward. Cet declares that Lóegaire once met him at the border and retreated shamefully: "you abandoned your horses and chariot and charioteer and escaped with my spear through you. Is that how you propose to take the pig?"[70]

The next challenger is Óengus, son of Lám Gábaid (*Lámgubha* in Oxford, Bodleian Library ms. Rawlinson B 502).[71] Cet asks if anyone knows why Óengus's father was called Lám Gábaid, 'Hand of Peril' (or Lámgubha, 'Hand-Wail'). The Ulstermen ask why, and Cet tells them that when he raided Ulster, Lám Gábaid was one of those who tried to stop him; he cast a spear at Cet and Cet flung it back, cutting off his *lám* (hand) so that it lay on the ground. "What could bring his son to challenge me?" Óengus sits down.

The next challenger is Éogan mac Durthacht, king of Fernmag.[72] He is described as tall and fair. Cet reminds Éogan that once, when Cet was driving off his cattle, Éogan came and threw a spear at him. It stuck in Cet's shield and Cet threw it back, taking out one of Éogan's eyes. "That is why you are one-eyed before the men of [Ireland]." Éogan sits down.[73]

The next challenger[74] is Muinremor mac Gerginn, 'Fat-Neck, son of Short-Head.' Cet dismisses him quickly: "It is not six days since I took three warriors' heads about the head of your first-born son from your land"–meaning that he killed four warriors, including

---

body) references. Their sum is the complete human body, in the form of both the warrior and his progeny–or lack thereof" ("The Laconic Scar," 490-491).

[70] §9; trans. Gantz, *Early Irish Myths*, 183.

[71] §10; trans. Gantz, *Early Irish Myths*, 184.

[72] §11; trans. Gantz, *Early Irish Myths*, 184.

[73] Éogan appears in other texts, notably *Loinges mac nUislenn*, "The Exile of the Sons of Uisliu," and the Boyhood Deeds of Cú Chulainn in the *Táin*. In these there is no mention of his being blind in one eye.

[74] §12; trans. Gantz, *Early Irish Myths*, 184.

Muinremor's son, and took their heads, while they were notionally under Muinremor's protection. Muinremor sits down.

The next challenger[75] is Mend mac Sálchada, 'Noteworthy,[76] son of Heel of Battle.' Cet laughs at "sons of [churls] with nicknames" who dare to challenge him, and says: "I am the priest who baptized your father with that name, for I struck his heel [*sál*] with my sword so that he took but one foot away. What could bring the son of a one-footed man to challenge me?" Mend sits down.

The next challenger[77] is Celtchar mac Uthechair. He is described as large, grey-haired, and ugly. Cet says that he once came to Celtchar's house, and that Celtchar cast his spear at him, "but I cast another one at you so that it pierced your thighs and your testicles. Since then you have fathered no sons or daughters. What could bring you to challenge me?" Celtchar sits down.

The next challenger[78] is Cúscraid, son of Conchobor. Everyone says that he has the look of a royal heir (more literally, "he is the makings of a king with respect to his appearance"). Cet reminds him that when Cúscraid came to the border to attempt his first feat of arms, "[y]ou abandoned one third of your retinue and left with a spear through your neck, so that today you have not a proper word in your head–the spear injured the cords in your throat. Since then you have been called Cúscraid Mend [Cúscraid the Stammerer]." Cúscraid sits down.

In this way, the text says, Cet has put *tár* (disgrace) upon the whole province.

This text has a number of interesting features. Most striking from the disability perspective–and overlooked in the scholarship–is the fact that there is no objective account of each man's impairment. We are not told, for example, that Éogan is missing an eye when he first

---

[75] §12; trans. Gantz, *Early Irish Myths*, 184.

[76] Both Mend mac Sálchada and Cúscraid Mend Machae appear to have the same element (*Mend*) in their names. In fact these are homonyms. See *DIL* svv. 1 menn (mend*)* (meaning "clear, evident, visible; conspicuous, remarkable, notable") and 2 menn (mend), "stammering, inarticulate."

[77] §13; Irish text cited from the edition by Rudolf Thurneysen, *Scéla mucce Meic Dathó* (Dublin: Dublin Institute for Advanced Studies, 1935); trans. Gantz, *Early Irish Myths*, 184-185.

[78] §14; trans. Gantz, *Early Irish Myths*, 185.

stands up, or that Cúscraid is heard to stammer. Impairment *per se* is not actually relevant to the contest. This looks like what Lois Bragg has called "a general disinterest in impairments as they might affect a character's competence [with] almost no hint of marginalizing pity or consequent charity anywhere to be found."[79] Actually what matters to Cet is whether an injury testifies to an opponent's shameful defeat at his hands. As readers of this text, we only 'see' impairment when Cet introduces it to us as disability by telling a disparaging story about it.

Also, physical impairment is only one of the ways in which Cet associates his opponents with shameful defeat at his hands. It makes no difference whether an embarrassing injury was inflicted on a warrior or his father, if it is memorialized in a nickname assigned to the father, which the son continues to bear. Everyone actually says that Óengus is a better warrior than Cet (§10), and Cet never denies it; but whether it is true or not is irrelevant, since Óengus "cannot deny the shame he carries through his father[;] the father's shame is visited upon him as if it were his own."[80] As regards his claim to the champion's portion, Óengus is disabled *without* being impaired.

Óengus's father's nickname is actually ambiguous. To quote Ailís Ní Mhaoldomhnaigh, it is:

> a name which could normally be expected to signify aggression and hostility–Hand of Peril. If one did not know the manner in which Óengus' father acquired this epithet, one would presume this to mean that Óengus was a warrior of repute having inherited his skill from him. However, by informing us of the aforementioned details, the author succeeds in completely undercutting this epithet, changing its meaning rather to 'endangered hand'.[81]

I would prefer to say "Cet succeeds" rather than "the author succeeds"; it is Cet who informs the assembled warriors what the situation is. He is telling them about more than a biological fact: what matters is not the father's missing hand *per se*, but how he lost it. Not all injuries are shameful. In law, for example, a king who is wounded in the back

[79] Bragg, "From the Mute God," 175.
[80] Ní Mhaoldomhnaigh, "Satirical Narrative," 65.
[81] Ní Mhaoldomhnaigh, "Satirical Narrative," 66.

effectively loses his kingly rank if he was fleeing from the enemy, but not if he broke through the enemy lines.[82] It is essential to be able to read wounds.

The wound-reading expert in early Irish literature is the physician Fíngin, who, in *Táin bó Cúailnge*, examines the injured Ulster warrior Cethern.[83] There is no doubt, in this instance, that all of Cethern's wounds were honorably received in battle against invading forces, but on examining them Fíngin is able to give a detailed description of the people who inflicted them.[84]

Cet does not have Fíngin's diagnostic skill, but he has the privileged knowledge to make up for it: he knows about the wounds because he inflicted them himself. Both Cet and Fíngin read bodies– and, by telling the story of how they were received, they add the *surplus* of meaning that Marie de France, in the famous Prologue to her *Lais*, considered essential to the process of glossing.

Cet is a glossator of both words and bodies. 'Hand of Danger' and 'Heel of Battle' sound as though they might connote prowess; Cet glosses them by supplying the correct interpretation, backed up by an evidential story. Interestingly, he approaches nicknames and physical conditions in opposite ways. We might imagine the following sequence: "A tall, fair warrior of the Ulstermen stood up. He was missing one eye. 'Who is this?' asked Cet. 'Éogan mac Durthacht,' said everyone. 'Do you know why he is missing an eye?' asked Cet. 'Let me tell you…'" But that is not how Cet proceeds. An impaired body may corroborate dishonor, but Cet's approach explicitly disallows the bad logic of concluding dishonor from an impaired body.

---

[82] Kelly, *Guide*, 19.

[83] O'Rahilly, *TBC I*, 209-213.

[84] Based on Cethern's subsequent choice to be healed only so that he can keep attacking the invaders, instead of with the hope of permanent recovery, Sayers argues that

"[s]ince scars are ambiguous and a sickbed may be dishonoring, a hero may accept wounds but prefer not to live with their consequences" ("The Laconic Scar," 484). How one feels about Cethern's choice must surely reflect how one feels about the *Táin* as a whole: is it a celebration or a critique of the "Heroic Age" warrior ethos? This is of course a much-debated topic.

Indeed–and this, I believe, is a conclusive reply to Sheehan–in another context it is an *unimpaired* body that would indicate dishonor.

A fourth paradigm: impairment as a sign of intact values; the "intact" body as a sign of shame

We have seen Cethern in the *Táin*, whose wounds are evidence of valiant fighting. At the end of "The Destruction of Da Derga's Hostel," in an example also adduced by Sayers,[85] the king's defender Conall Cernach escapes the titular hostel and goes to his father Amairgen, who greets him with the question "Is your lord alive?" Conall answers, "He is not alive." His father says, "I swear by the gods by whom the great tribes of Ulster swear, it is cowardly for a man to have gone out of there alive, having left his lord with his foes in death."[86]

The reader knows that King Conaire died because he failed as a ruler. While his defenders fought, he was overcome by a supernatural thirst that the rivers and lakes of Ireland refused to quench, in a reversal of a well-known motif, the female personification of Sovereignty conferring sovereignty upon a king by giving him a drink.[87] Conall does not try to explain this to his father. What he does is to offer his body as evidence that he is no coward:

> "My wounds are not white, you old hero," Conall said. He showed him his shield-arm, on which there were three times fifty wounds, which had been inflicted on it. The shield that guarded it is what saved it. But the right arm had been worked over, as far as two thirds of it, since the shield had not been guarding it. That arm was mangled and maimed and wounded and pierced, except that the sinews kept it to the body without separation.[88]

---

[85] Sayers, "The Laconic Scar," 473-474.
[86] §166; trans. in Koch and Carey, *The Celtic Heroic Age*, 183.
[87] The two classic instances of this are in *Echtra mac nEchdach* (the story about the hag at the well) and *Baile in Scáil*, "The Phantom's [Prophetic] Frenzy," ed. and trans. Kevin Murray, *Baile in Scáil* (Dublin: Irish Texts Society, 2004).
[88] §§166-167; trans. in Koch and Carey, *The Celtic Heroic Age*, 183.

Amairgen contemplates the butchered arm dangling by its tendons and says, "That arm fought tonight, my son," indicating satisfaction with Conall's effort. Probably any lesser impairment would have made him suspicious that Conall could have done more to defend the king.

Ralph O'Connor sees Conall as a mirror-image for Conaire's physical perfection, and proposes that "his body now becomes the site of a dreadful transformation from order to chaos: his broken appearance at the end of the saga echoes the king's dismemberment and, by implication, the shattered state of Conaire's realm."[89] That may be so, but it doesn't speak to the dynamics of the interaction between Conall and his father. When the king is dead, impairment is the *correct* condition for Conall. "Mulligan contends that the saga ends on an image of 'bodily integrity'," says O'Connor, "but I would add 'only just' and suggest that the narrative framing (contrasting with earlier images of wholeness) emphasizes the fragility of what remains."[90] Disagreeing in part with both these scholars, and aligning myself more with Sayers, I am now saying that the saga ends on an image of bodily impairment, not bodily integrity, but that this impairment confirms the integrity of the underlying value system that expects justice from kings and loyalty from warriors. It indicates that although there has been a failure at the top, the foundations of society remain intact, and the moral order of the universe is affirmed rather than compromised by Conaire's downfall.

"Bricriu's Feast" goes even farther in its celebration of a mutilated body. Competing for precedence with the women of Ulster, Cú Chulainn's wife Emer not only praises her husband for his skill in combat, and his ability to wound others and bloody his weapons, she mentions in an almost erotic way the damage that has been inflicted on his body: he has *créchta ina cháin cnis*, (gashes in his fair skin, and *álta ina thóeb liss*, (wounds in his smooth side),[91] and these are also to be praised. We might imagine from examples in the *Táin* itself[92] that a greater achievement would be to wound others without being

---

[89] O'Connor, *The Destruction of Da Derga's Hostel*, 224-225.
[90] O'Connor, *The Destruction of Da Derga's Hostel*, 225n131, referring to Eichhorn-Mulligan, "*Togail Bruidne Da Derga*," 18.
[91] Text from George Henderson, *Fled Bricrend: The Feast of Bricriu* (London: David Nutt for the Irish Texts Society, 1899), 26; my translations.
[92] E.g. O'Rahilly, *TBC I*, 140.

wounded in return, but apparently the proper sort of wounds are even more compelling evidence of honor, masculinity, and power.[93] In fact, Cú Chulainn's heroism becomes most apparent in the *Táin* as he fights on in spite of increasingly grievous wounds. The ultimate expression of this is the daunting iconic spectacle of his dead body strapped to a standing stone,[94] which retains the ability to chop off an enemy's hand or arm (*lám*) when carelessly approached. The Christian version of this would be how the faith of the saints is most fully realized through martyrdom and debilitating contempt for the body, which Irish tradition broadly celebrates but not without ambivalence.[95]

An extreme case of physical impairment is decapitation that does not immediately result in death. Speaking severed heads are not uniquely Irish,[96] but they do seem distinctively so, especially considering the linguistic and cultural focus on the head as the seat of identity. Examples include Conaire's head lauding his champion's loyalty in "The Destruction of Da Derga's Hostel";[97] Súaltaim's head crying out a warning to the court of Ulster in the *Táin*;[98] and Donn Bó's making good on his pledge to entertain his king on the night after

---

[93] Sayers makes a similar case for the proper sort of scars: "Deconstructive in real life, wounds are the very making of epic literature, and scars are their close-mouthed, echoic voices" ("The Laconic Scar," 494).

[94] Kimpton, *The Death of Cú Chulainn*, 43.

[95] See Carey, *King of Mysteries*, 246-258, for stories of the Céili Dé starving themselves and the surreptitious efforts of their community to feed them

[96] On medieval severed heads in general, including some that speak, see *Heads Will Roll: Decapitation in the Medieval and Early Modern Imagination*, ed. Larissa Tracy and Jeff Massey (Leiden and Boston: Brill, 2012). There are said to be more than 120 cephalophore (head-carrying) saints, perhaps most famously Saint Denis, some of whose heads get reattached, as with Winifred in Wales. Bendigeidfran in the Second Branch of the Mabinogi is the outstanding Welsh example of a severed head that still has a social life. It provides companionship–"you will find the head to be as good company as it ever was when it was on me" (trans. Sioned Davies, *The Mabinogion* [Oxford University Press 2007], 32), Bendigeidfran says before being beheaded–and also protects Britain from invasion once it's buried in London, but the text never says that it actually speaks, or quotes it as saying anything.

[97] Koch and Carey, *The Celtic Heroic Age*, 182.

[98] O'Rahilly, *TBC I*, 217.

the battle in *Cath Almaine*, "The Battle of Allen."[99] These are radical cases of impairment that defies becoming disability, at least for a little while (as per the critical realist model of disability, biology does assert itself as well). Like Conall Cernach with his arm dangling by the sinews, the characters whose heads have been severed express their values in a way that is only enhanced by their physical state.

Donn Bó deserves special attention, because his decapitation is miraculously reversed, and there is more than one paradigm in play. The heir of Colum Cille (Saint Columba) promised his mother that he would come home safe and sound, and so he does. His head is found singing sweetly to the corpses of the defeated Uí Néill; then, when he is claimed as a trophy by the victorious Leinstermen, he sings them a heartbreaking dirge. (To the extent that it is any *more* heartbreaking for being performed by a severed head, this is again "impairment as the price of power and art.") The warrior who took his head returns it to his body, and, thanks to Colum Cille, it reattaches, and Donn Bó seems fully restored to life. Hence the religious miracle, which returns us to Metzler's mainstream Christian paradigm (2)–the reason Donn Bó loses his head is so that the power of the saint can put it back– comes only *after* the severed head has spent the night singing: it doesn't seem as though the saint had anything to do with that part. It seems to be Donn Bó's sworn word that makes it so his head can speak and sing. Donn Bó's integrity of character is most fully realized when the integrity of his body is most lacking.

Conaire's head is complicated, too: his bodily impairment–his thirst and beheading–expresses the failure of his kingship, stemming from his Dumézilian "single sin of the sovereign," and the breakdown of the body politic, hence our Irish paradigm (1); but the fact that his head continues to function, to give Mac Cécht his due before he dies, confirms this as an isolated failure (one that does not compromise the institution of harmonious kingship or the ideology of *fír flathemon*, but rather supports it), and offers Conaire some measure of redemption as Mac Cécht gives him his drink of sovereignty at last. Likewise Cú Chulainn's non-decapitation at the end of "Bricriu's Feast" is a paradoxical mix of two paradigms: when he is challenged to a beheading game by the disguised Cú Roí, the correct condition of Cú

---

[99] See Ó Cathasaigh, *Coire Sois*, 442-446.

Chulainn's head is *off*, since it is dishonorable for him to shun the ax (paradigm 4); but since he welcomes the ax, his body is allowed to stay intact, which expresses the intact state of his honor (paradigm 1). Súaltaim is condemned to die for the crime of "inciting the king," so his headlessness might be said to reflect that offense (paradigm 1); but the manifest injustice of punishing him for being, as Conchobor immediately confirms, *correct* in his warning, makes him rather seem to be a martyr for the good of Ulster (paradigm 4).

As of this writing, I am not aware of any speaking severed heads of women in early Irish literature, but there seems to be no reason why the larger paradigm would not be available to them. The shattered head of Deirdriu at the end of "The Exile of the Sons of Uisliu" shows her honor intact.

Further complications: On the socially-ratified royal "blemish"

The examples I have talked about so far suggest that the law and the sagas agree about the socially-constructed nature of disability, and the need to gloss impairment as disabling or not, according to its etiology. But the *ainim* (blemish) that makes a king unfit to rule seems to contradict this. Such a blemish (basically any serious physical impairment) might be inflicted on the king for unjust rule or bad behavior, but it could also be caused by an accident, including an honorable accident like a wound in battle. Honorable impairment might be all right for warriors, but it is problematic for kings,[100] since the consequences of a royal blemish are the same regardless. The paradigmatic example is King Núadu of the godlike Túatha Dé Danann in "The (Second) Battle of Mag Tuired" who has to relinquish the kingship when he loses an arm in battle (§11, §14). He becomes king again once he gets a prosthesis (§53), a silver arm that functions like a natural one. This makes it clear that his moral fitness for the throne was never at issue. In the same text, the young king Bres proves to be so unjust and ungenerous that he is deposed; he is physically perfect (so beautiful, in fact, that people used to call every beautiful thing in the kingdom "a Bres"), and never suffers any injury, although he does become the target of satire. Although presumably the principle of physical perfection had some religious underpinning–i.e. the

---

[100] Sayers, "Kingship and the Hero's Flaw," makes it clear that the disfigurement he is dealing with is particular to warriors.

perfection expected of the king was related to his sacral function and his quasi-contractual relationship with the supernatural Otherworld[101]–the royal "blemish" is still, I argue, socially constructed, and the texts understand it as such.

In general, a king's fitness to serve had to be socially ratified. So did his expulsion from the kingship. This is clear from the way the texts describe unjust judgments. It was believed that the validity of a king's judgments–known as *fír flathemon* 'ruler's truth'–was a violation of his relationship with the Otherworld, and was directly responsible for the prosperity of his reign and the fertility of the land.[102] If the king was unjust the crops would wither. However, in the ninth-century tale *Cath Maige Mucrama*, "The battle of Mag Mucrama," the king of Tara, Lugaid Mac Con, pronounces a false judgment, and nothing happens. Only when the judgment is rectified by Cormac mac Airt, the son of the previous king, *and everyone responds with acclaim*, does the side of the house in which the false judgment was pronounced collapse; this is followed by crop failure, until Mac Con abdicates in favor of Cormac.[103] In "The Destruction of Da Derga's Hostel" Conaire's false judgment on his foster-brothers

---

[101] Stacey, *Dark Speech*, 42, doubts that the prohibition on blemished kings was ever "fully realized in the everyday politics of eighth-century Ireland," but explores a metaphor for the king as head of the *túath* (polity or "tribe") that suggests the importance of keeping the king intact; the strange requirement to compensate a king for a head-wound by giving him a man-at-arms with a breastplate, she argues, mixes the metaphors of king as head of his people and king as breastplate of his people. Meanwhile, Sheehan's ecclesiastical examples ("Losing Face," 135) may use the same vocabulary but should be treated separately from kings, since there is a Biblical background for a distinction between blemished and unblemished priests that seems more immediately relevant (see, e.g., Hector Avalos, Sarah J. Melcher, and Jeremy Schipper, eds., *This Abled Body: Rethinking Disability in Biblical Studies* [Atlanta: Society of Biblical Literature, 2007], 82-84, discussing Leviticus 21:17-23).

[102] The clearest expression of this ideology is the wisdom-text *Audacht Morainn*, "The Testament of Morann," ed. and trans. Fergus Kelly, *Audacht Morainn* (Dublin: Dublin Institute for Advanced Studies, 1976). It emphasizes the mutual obligations of king and people and the benefits that are produced by *fír flathemon*.

[103] O Daly, *Cath Maige Mucrama*, §§63-68.

arguably becomes non-retractable and binding when everyone acclaims it, even though it is not actually carried out (Cormac immediately orders something different, and for purposes of his justice this seems not to count).

Within the need for social ratification there seems to be some wiggle room. According to *Bechbretha*, the law-tract on bees, Congal Cáech was both king of Tara (the pre-eminent kingship of Ireland) and king of Ulster when he was stung in the eye by a bee, leaving him blind in that eye. This was enough of a "blemish" for him to lose the kingship of Tara, but not enough for him to lose the kingship of Ulster as well.[104] Here there is no doubt about the impairment; the uncertainty is to what extent that impairment translates to disability with respect to kingship.[105]

In Conchobor's death-tale,[106] the legendary king of Ulster, while raiding Connacht, is injured in the head by Cet mac Mágach using the calcified brain of a king named Mes Gegra, which remains embedded in Conchobor's skull. The physician Fíngin offers to treat the wound,

---

[104] Kelly, *Guide*, 19, 239.

[105] Sheehan's summary that "a king who is blinded in one eye loses his kingship" ("Losing Face," 136) disregards this aspect of the matter. Congal's subsequent death in the battle of Mag Rath is attributed squarely to his unrighteousness in the same part of *Bretha Éitgid* that discusses Cenn Fáelad's injury (and this is enlarged upon in the full saga; see Marstrander, "Battle of Mag Rath," and Jacqueline Borsje, "Demonising the Enemy: a Study of Congal Cáech," in *Proceedings of the Eighth Symposium of Societas Celtologica Nordica,* ed. Jan Erik Rekdal and Ailbhe Ó Corráin [University of Uppsala, 2007], 21-38); but there seems to be no claim that he was at all responsible for the bee-sting he suffered. Kelly, *Guide*, 239, discusses how Congal tried and failed to claim the beekeeper's eye in compensation, but was denied because the beekeeper was himself a king. Another king who loses an eye is Cormac mac Airt in "The Expulsion of the Déisi." This arguably reflects his failure to take notice of a rape committed by his son (we might say he 'turned a blind eye' to it), because the avenger who kills the son takes out Cormac's eye in the process. In that case the versions of the story differ as to whether Cormac had to abdicate as a result (see Ó Cathasaigh, *Coire Sois*, 309-310).

[106] Ed. and trans. Kuno Meyer, *Death-Tales of the Ulster Heroes* (Royal Irish Academy Todd Lecture Series 14. Dublin: Hodges, Figgis, 1906), 2-21.

but says "it will be an *athis* 'blemish' for the king.[107] The Ulstermen reply: "It is easier for us [. . .] to bear the blemish than his death."[108] There is no question that Conchobor is impaired: even after he sews up and disguises the wound, Fíngin tells Conchobor to abstain from horseback riding, sex, feasting, and running. However, the Ulstermen would prefer not to consider their king unfit to rule, so they don't. He continues on the throne for another seven years, even though he is not an *engnamaid* (active warrior),[109]until he hears about Christ's Crucifixion. This sends him into an apoplectic rage, which causes the brain-ball to burst out, killing him and baptizing him in his own blood even before the advent of Christianity in Ireland.

Lest we consider Conchobor a special case,[110] *Echtra Fergusa meic Léti*, "The Adventure of Fergus mac Léti"[111]–a saga which is preserved in a legal manuscript, and owes its survival to its value as precedent on a point of land law[112]–observes the distinction between

---

[107] Meyer, *Death-Tales*, 8-9: *bid athis duit.*
[108] Meyer, *Death-Tales*, 8-9: *'Is asso dún ... ind athis oldás a éc-som'*
[109] This is the only example *DIL* gives for engnamaid, glossed "one proficient in arms, an active warrior"; cf. *engnam*: "skill, dexterity; skill at arms, valor, prowess; an exploit, valorous deed, warlike action." The examples for engnam as "associated with *enech* [face, honor], with contamination of meaning" are late, and generally consist of pairs, e.g., "*a einech ⁊ a eangnum*"; [I do not dispute that there is a general association] between martial skill and honor.
[110] Knowing that a bad judgment, i.e. a violation of fír flathemon, was liable to blight the land, the Ulstermen were supposedly reluctant to allow Conchobor to pass any judgments at all (this is, however, belied by the judgments Conchobor renders in the *Táin* and his legal authority in the texts discussed by Stacey 2007, 154-55). There might have been a general willingness to exempt him from the full scope of royal duties rather than confront the flaws he might display in exercising them.
[111] Ed. and trans. Daniel A. Binchy, "The Saga of Fergus mac Léti," *Ériu* 16 (1952): 33-48. As this is a third example of an Ulster king, I wonder if Ulster might have been, or seemed to be, unusually tolerant of 'blemished' kings.
[112] Most recently, Stacey, *Dark Speech*, 69, 158, 214, and Neil McLeod, "Fergus mac Léti and the Law," *Ériu* 61 (2011): 1-28, mention various aspects of this tale's function in the legal context; see also Ruairí Ó hUiginn, "Fergus, Russ and Rudraige: a Brief Biography of Fergus mac Róich," *Emania* 11 (1993): 31-40.

impairment and disability even more explicitly. These two conditions are separated by the fact that the upper echelons of society decline to treat a particular impairment as a disability, for as long as they can get away with it.

Fergus, king of Ulster, is out one day with his charioteer, Muena, when he is captured by leprechauns[113] who take away his sword and carry him down to the seashore. He reacts by seizing three of them, and demands three wishes in exchange for sparing their lives. The only wish that he actually makes is for a charm that allows him to breathe underwater, so that he can travel "under seas and pools and lakes."[114] The leprechauns grant him this, by giving him herbs to put in his ears or a cloak to wrap around his head, but they tell him that he must never enter Loch Rudraige (now Dundrum Bay in County Down). In the end, Fergus cannot resist violating the prohibition. This leads to a traumatic encounter:

> When he dived under the lake he saw there a *muirdris*, a fearful water-monster which kept alternately inflating and contracting itself like a smith's bellows.[115] At the sight of it his mouth was wrenched back as far as his occiput, and he came out on land in terror.[116]

Fergus senses a change in himself–he is terrified–but seems unsure of how his emotional state has affected him physically. He asks his charioteer for confirmation. Muena replies that he looks *olc* (bad, wrong), but encourages him to sleep it off:

> He said to his charioteer: 'How do I appear to thee?'
> 'Ill is thy aspect', said the charioteer, 'but it will be

---

[113] On the etymology of this word (*lúchorpáin*), see Jacopo Bisagni, "*Leprechaun*: a New Etymology," *CMCS* 64 (2012): 47-84, and Patrick Sims-Williams, "Leprechauns and Luperci, Aldhelm and Augustine," in *Sacred Histories: a Festschrift for Máire Herbert*, ed. John Carey, Kevin Murray, and Caitríona Ó Dochartaigh (Dublin: Four Courts Press, 2015), 409-418.

[114] Binchy, "Fergus mac Léti," 42. The occiput is the back of the skull or head.

[115] On this monster, see Borsje, *From Chaos to Enemy.*

[116] Binchy, "Fergus mac Léti," 42.

nothing more (?); sleep will take it from thee.'
Thereupon the charioteer laid him down and he fell
asleep.[117]

How sincere is Muena in giving Fergus this advice? It reads at
least partly as a ruse to help him get away from Fergus, because as
soon as the king is asleep, the charioteer races to the court at Emain
Macha to report what has happened and ask who will take Fergus's
place as king. His understanding is that Fergus has a permanent
impairment, and that it qualifies as a blemish that makes him unfit to
rule. But the text does not say how the charioteer knows that Fergus's
condition will be permanent. He may have hoped that sleep would do
the king some good, and decided to tell the court only after noticing
that it was having no effect. Alternatively, he understands that the
king's face reflects the condition of his honor after fleeing in terror
from the monster, and that under the circumstances the damage is
irreparable.[118] In any case, Muena assumes that he knows how the wise
men of Ulster will react to his news, so rather than ask them what
should be done about Fergus, he immediately asks who will replace
him:

> While [Fergus] slept the charioteer went in the
> meantime to the wise men of Ulster who were
> [assembled] in Emain Macha and told them of the
> king's adventures and his present condition. He
> inquired of them what king they would take in his
> stead, since it would not be proper to have a
> blemished king in E[main] M[acha].[119]

Surprisingly, though, the wise men of Ulster want to keep Fergus as
king. This is viable as long as Fergus himself is not made aware of his
impairment:

---

[117] Binchy, "Fergus mac Léti," 42-43.
[118] This aspect is discussed by Jan Erik Rekdal, "The Value of the Face:
Face, Fear, Flaw and Shame in an Irish King's Saga," in *Literature and
Honour*, ed. Aasta Marie Bjorvand Bjørkøy and Thorstein Norheim (Oslo:
Universitetsforlaget, 2017), 95-102, online at https://www.idunn.no/doi/
book/10.18261/978-82-15-02955-9-2017.
[119] Binchy, "Fergus mac Léti," 43.

> The decision of the wise men of Ulster was that the king should come to his house, and that beforehand a clearance should be made of all the base folk so that there should be neither fool nor half-wit therein lest these should cast his blemish in the king's face; and further that he should always have his head washed while lying on his back so that he might not see his shadow in the water.[120]

Sheehan describes this as "keep[ing] out of public view,"[121] but it is not at all clear that he is ever prevented from leaving his house after coming home to it, which would unquestionably have tipped him off to suspect special treatment. The point, in any case, is not to convey that there is something wrong with him; it is, precisely, to *avoid* conveying that there is something wrong with him.

The wise men do not say why they want to go to all this trouble, whether it is because they love Fergus or they do not want the hassle of replacing him. (The text gives us no indication one way or the other, but the late medieval *Aided Fergus meic Léide*, "The Violent Death of Fergus mac Léide," which survives in a sixteenth-century manuscript, begins with the comment that Fergus was a righteous king who judged fairly.) In any case, the plan works: "For seven years he was diligently guarded [in this manner]."[122]

The text does not say whether Fergus is aware of this diligent guarding, but his quality of life seems unaffected by it.[123] He is impaired but not disabled. Binchy is surely right in saying that the impairment must be hidden from Fergus because, if he were aware of it, his honor would demand that he abdicate—that is, he would construe the impairment as a disability, and impose this interpretation of it on his people.

---

[120] Binchy, "Fergus mac Léti," 43.

[121] Sheehan, "Losing Face," 136.

[122] Binchy, "Fergus mac Léti," 43.

[123] The words translated by Binchy as "fool nor half-wit" are *drúth* and *óinmit* (see *DIL*, s.vv., and Boyd, "Competing Assumptions about the *drúth*"), both of which can refer to professional jesters or entertainers. So it is possible, though by no means certain, that the elimination of "base folk" from the court has deprived Fergus of his customary entertainment.

Appropriately, the sequence of events that ends the seven-year idyll starts with Fergus demanding to have his head washed, presumably while lying on his back:

> One day he told his bondmaid to wash his head. Thinking that the woman was too slow in carrying out this [*sic*], he gave her a blow with his whip. Resentment overcame her and she taunted him to his face with his blemish. He gave her a blow with his sword and cut her in two. Thereupon he turned away and went under Loch Rudraige; for a whole day and night the loch seethed from [the contest between] him and the *muirdris* [. . .] Eventually he emerged on the surface of the loch, holding the head of the monster, so that the [Ulstermen] saw him, and he said to them: 'I am the survivor.' Thereupon he sank down dead, and for a whole month the loch remained red from [the battle between] them.[124]

The tale concludes with a verse commemorating Fergus's impairment: "King Fergus, son of Léte / Went on the sandbank of Rudraige; / A horror which appeared to him–fierce was the conflict–/ Was the cause of his disfigurement."[125]

The way Fergus goes to fight the monster when he sees his own face at last shows that he himself is reading his appearance as a reflection of his cowardice–paradigm (1) all over again. As far as we know, given how the condition arose, he is absolutely right to read himself this way. (His redemption is accompanied by further impairment–death–which suggests that the only way out is through; and this in turn affirms paradigm 4.)

What this story indicates, and what I am arguing in general, is not that the social construction of impairment as disability is *optional* (again, to draw on the critical realist model, biology may assert itself in ways that make it unavoidable), but that early Irish literature was acutely aware of when it happened, and was sometimes willing to devote significant attention to it.

---

[124] Binchy, "Fergus mac Léti," 43-44.
[125] Binchy, "Fergus mac Léti," 44.

In light of the surveys by Metzler and others, this degree of awareness seems to be remarkable for the European Middle Ages. *Unique* may not be too strong. It deserves further study in itself and as part of a historically-oriented Disability Studies and a Medieval Studies that can learn from relevant advances in contemporary theory. And choosing to suspend society's judgment on physical impairment for long enough to take some "thinking space" is not at all a poor precedent for approaching disability issues in our own time.

Conclusion

To sum up, while I made no attempt here to catalog every instance of physical impairment in the early Irish sagas, I tried to cover enough of a range to establish that the major paradigms proposed for medieval Christian Europe–"impairment as the result of sin" and "impairment as something that required healing"–would not cover all the situations that arise. The further patterns that emerge (the first two an adjustment of these broader European paradigms from Metzler), with many of the supporting examples, are as follows. However, these paradigms can overlap; that is, they can apply to different aspects or different ways of reading the same situation.

> (1) Impairment as the result of shame, injustice, or violation of the supernatural:
> - dishonorable wounds, which might not even register as wounds until glossed as dishonorable (the competitors in "Mac Da Thó's Pig")
> - Fergus mac Léti's face contorted after fleeing from the monster
> - targets of satire and curses (the *ces noínden* debility as Macha's curse)
> - violation of *geissi* 'supernatural taboos' (Cú Chulainn's arm and thigh wither when he takes dog meat)
> - violation of *fír flathemon* 'the truth and justice of the ruler' and the king's relationship with the Otherworld (Ailill Ólomm's ear destroyed; bodily breakdown in "The Destruction of Da Derga's Hostel," including Conaire decapitated)
> - Brigit's brother's eye destroyed for disrespecting her
> - can be reverse-engineered to make impairment a *cause* of shame (Derbforgaill) or disqualification (the socially

ratified royal "blemish," sometimes open to negotiation or consciously delayed effect as with Congal Cáech, Conchobor, Fergus mac Léti)

(2) Impairment as the "before" condition of a positive transformation:
- poets whose "eloquence is born of dumbness, vision of blindness, and radiance of loathsomeness," including the Ash-Lad scenario (Amairgen)
- the Sovereignty ("wolfish," old, and horrible, then young and gorgeous)
- Brigit's eye, insofar as it is restored on her becoming a nun
- Donn Bó's head, insofar as it sets up a miracle of Colum Cille

(3) Impairment as the price of power, status, knowledge, art, or God's favor:
- Balor's baleful eye, the children of Calatín's gouged eyes, the Ulster heroes' self-mutilated groupies, Finn's thumb of knowledge, Brigit's blind boy, Cenn Fáelad's scholarship, Suibne's poems
- Brigit's eye, insofar as she uses it to deny herself to the world and consecrate herself to God without expectation of healing, and the Cailleach Bhéara's
- Donn Bó's music, insofar as being sung by a severed head amplifies its pathos

(4) Impairment can express honor, and non-impairment can be the result of shame:
- severe wounds are the honorable condition of the martial hero defending his lord (Conall Cernach in "Da Derga's Hostel") or his land and people (Cú Chulainn in the *Táin*); even being alive in such a scenario invites a challenge that only the wounds can refute
- the Ulstermen who do not make themselves available for beheading in "Bricriu's Feast" embarrass their province

- speaking severed heads (Súaltaim, Conaire, Donn Bó) demonstrate a commitment to their values that is only enhanced by their impairment

These paradigms seem to apply across genders, with due allowances for the different social roles available to men and women. But I have not exhausted this topic.

I hope that, moving forward, my framework will be useful for Celtic Studies scholars to think with as they explore more examples of non-normative bodies in early Irish literature and the issues that they raise, and productive in communicating to other medievalists and Disability Studies scholars some of the complexities of this material. No doubt the framework will invite further expansion and adjustment, especially as Disability Studies continues to evolve. Our fields ought to stay in touch.

Acknowledgements

I appreciate the suggestions of the anonymous reviewer for *PHCC*.

APPENDIX: SOME EARLY IRISH TERMS FOR PHYSICAL IMPAIRMENT

Definitions from eDIL (https://dil.ie/).

ail, "disgrace, reproach; act of reproaching; in physical sense, blemish, defect; name of a type of satire; misfortune (esp. of death or wounding in battle)"
ainim, "blemish," etc.
aisc, "act of reproaching; reproach, blame; disgrace (as a result of a deed); in concrete sense, blemish, disfigurement";
aithis, "insult, reproach, reviling; disgrace, ignominy; blemish, disfigurement"
anáeb, "that which is unpleasant; discomfort, distress; discourtesy; blemish, disfigurement"
béim, "act of striking; cutting, hewing, taking (off, away), removing, stripping (clothes, etc.) [...] blow, stroke of feeling; emotion; reproach, offence; blemish, fault, disgrace"
brell, "blur, spot, stain, etc.; slur, blemish, etc."
ceó, "mist; fault, stain, blemish" (with cen ceó, "without ceó," meaning "unharmed" or "faultless");
dainim, "a fault, blemish"
locht, "fault, shortcoming, vice; offence; (physical) blemish"
nescóit, "an imposthume or abscess; a blemish, disgrace (a boil on the face being a traditional symbol of dishonour"
1 on, "a blemish or disfigurement; in early sagas used of a blister(?) raised by a poet's satire on the face of his victim, and hence fig. a blot or stain on one's reputation, a social disgrace or disqualification"
smál, "ember, glowing coal, fire; ashes, dross; in moral sense, blemish, taint (of sin)"; cf. teimel, "darkness, gloom [...] stain, fault, sin"

See also Sayers, "The Laconic Scar," 476, on the terminology for wounds and scars: he lists álad, cned, cnía, crécht, gáel, guin, mairc, mersce, oenach, and tregmad.

Saints, Druids and Sea-Gods: Imagining the Past in Iona's Namescape

Thomas Owen Clancy

This article emerges from the research of the project 'Iona's Namescape: place-names and their dynamics in Iona and its environs', funded by the UK's Arts and Humanities Research Council.[1] Among the objectives of this project, the key aim of which is to provide a full survey of the place-names of the island of Iona, is the posing of questions about the dynamics of place-names: How are they understood and re-imagined? On what authority are names created, transmitted, and enshrined? What gives a name, or the interpretation of a name, authenticity? This article dwells on some of these questions, in considering how the past of the island was imagined through its place-names, and through the interpretation of those place-names. The linguistic context of the island is important. Iona was a majority Gaelic-speaking island into the twentieth century, but no longer has a Gaelic-speaking population native to the island, and has not done for some time. The dynamics of place-names and their interpretations, and the balance between authority and authenticity, are thus also to be found in the interaction between Gaelic and English.

The purpose of this article is to investigate the way in which figures one might think of as holy, sacred, numinous or the like (to borrow Joseph F. Nagy's description, "angels and ancients") have been read into and out of the landscape via place-names. Iona, the site of the monastery founded by St. Columba around A.D. 563, and where his successor, Adomnán, wrote his Life, the *Vita Sancti Columbae*, a

---

[1] The project (AHRC number AH/T007044/1)runs from 2020 to 2024 at the University of Glasgow; I am the Principal Investigator, joined by Prof. Katherine Forsyth and Dr. Alasdair Whyte as Co-Investigators; and Dr. Sofia Evemalm-Graham, Dr. Mairi MacArthur and Gilbert Márkus as Researchers, with Brian Aitken as Systems Developer. For more detail on the project, see https://iona-placenames.glasgow.ac.uk/. Note that by the end of 2023 it is hoped that all the names discussed here will be able to be explored in more depth through a place-name resource accessible through this website. I am grateful to all my fellow project team members for various forms of input into the research behind this paper.

hundred years later, has constantly over its history been seen as a numinous place, a 'thin place', a 'special place' and its namescape displays various responses to that notion.[2] The iconic quote from Samuel Johnson in 1775, in the heady first decades of the early modern Hebridean tour, sets the scene for this elevation of the island to romantic sublimity:

> Whatever withdraws us from the power of our senses; whatever makes the past, the distant, or the future predominate over the present, advances us in the dignity of thinking beings. Far from me and from my friends, be such frigid philosophy as may conduct us indifferent and unmoved over any ground which has been dignified by wisdom, bravery, or virtue. That man is little to be envied, whose patriotism would not gain force upon the plain of Marathon, or whose piety would not grow warmer among the ruins of Iona![3]

This viewpoint continued throughout the late eighteenth and nineteenth centuries, and was amplified in the period of the Celtic revival, as witness the comments of the problematic William Sharp, who wrote under the name 'Fiona MacLeod':

> A few places in the world are to be held holy, because of the love which consecrates them and the faith which enshrines them. Their names are themselves talismans of spiritual beauty. Of these is Iona. [. . .] In spiritual geography Iona is the Mecca of the Gael.[4] This aspect of the 'specialness' of Iona has also been

---

[2] For the Life of Columba and general discussion of early medieval Iona, see Richard Sharpe, *Adomnán of Iona: Life of Saint Columba* (Harmondsworth: Penguin, 1995); Alan Orr and Marjorie Ogilvie Anderson, *Adomnán's Life of Columba* (Oxford: OUP, 1961; revised edition, 1991). On the long-term history and reception of the island, see E. Mairi MacArthur, *Columba's Island: Iona from Past to Present* (Edinburgh: EUP, 1995).

[3] Samuel Johnson, *A Journey to the Western Islands of Scotland* (London: W. Strahan and T. Caddell in the Strand, 1775), 346-7.

[4] Fiona MacLeod, *The Divine Adventure: Iona: By Sundown Shores. Studies in Spiritual History* (London: Chapman and Hall, 1900), 91.

investigated in the present day in the excellent
ethnographical study of Dr. Krittika Bhattacharjee.[5]

The notion that the island *ought* to be special, even at its most
mundane, can be found affecting place-names and their interpretations
in various ways, and it is worth beginning this exploration with a
cautionary tale. A modest man-made feature, a ring of stones of
uncertain but probably modern date, had by the late eighteenth century
at the latest acquired a name probably similar to *Cobhan Cùilteach,
usually now rendered Cobhain Cuildich.[6] This name almost certainly
meant something like 'secluded hollow', but by the time of the Old
Statistical Account in 1795 had already begun to be reinterpreted as
meaning 'Culdee's cell or couch'–culdee (from Early Gaelic *Céle Dé*
'client or servant of God') having become shorthand for early
medieval monks or hermits during the early modern period in
Scotland.[7] Despite some scholarly pushback against it, this (false)
etymology then got reified into the English version of the name: The
Hermit's Cell, by which it is still known.[8] A little coda to this, to

---

[5] Krittika Bhattacharjee, "Once upon a place: the construction of specialness
by visitors to Iona" (PhD thesis, University of Edinburgh, 2018) available
at: https://era.ed.ac.uk/handle/1842/31532
[6] For the site itself, see CANMORE, s.n. "Iona, Cobhain Cuildich": https://
canmore.org.uk/site/21632/iona-cobhain-cuildich ; a detailed discussion of
the name can be found on a blog on the Iona's Namescape project site: T.
O. Clancy, "The Trouble with Cobhain Cuildich" (blog, December 2020):
https://iona-placenames.glasgow.ac.uk/the-trouble-with-cobhain-cuildich/
[7] Rev. Dugald Campbell, "Kilfinichen and Kilvickeon", *Statistical Account
of Scotland* [a.k.a. 'Old Statsitical Account'], vol. XIV (Edinburgh: William
Creech, 1795), 200: "One place in I [Iona] is still called the Culdee's
Cell†", "†Cathan, or Cothan Cuildich, signifies the Culdee's cell or couch".
On the (inappropriate) proliferation of the term 'Culdee', see William
Reeves, *The Culdees of the British Islands as they appear in history, with
an appendix of evidences* (Dublin: Gill, 1864).
[8] For some pushback, see e.g. William F. Skene, "Notes on the history and
probable situation of the earlier establishments at Iona, prior to the
foundation of the Benedictine monastery in the end of the twelfth century",
Proceedings of the Society of Antiquaries of Scotland 11 (1874-1876): 330-
49, at 337. It is not at present clear when 'Hermit's Cell' rather than
'Culdee Cell' or similar, gained currency in English.

illustrate a further problem with tackling names on Iona (the unreliability of Ordnance Survey forms of names), is the horrific transformation of gothic C to gothic T to plain letter T in the spelling of the name across recent maps, creating on current OS maps the nonce-name Tobhain Tuildich.[9] Leaving that problem to one side, however, the elevation of this humble location to a site of slightly mysterious religious activity indicates some of the tendencies this article explores.

One of the clearest places on Iona to see these processes at work is also a place with one of the oldest recorded names, confirming that this is not simply a modern phenomenon. In Adomnán's *Vita Sancti Columbae*, "The Life of St. Columba", written c.700, we are given the tale of Columba's encounters with angels on a certain hill. Witnessed by one of his monks, the hill, we are then told, is called, in Gaelic, Cnoc Angel.

> *Vnde hodieque et locus illius angelici condicti rem in eo gestam suo proprio protestatur uocabulo, qui latine potest dici colliculus angelorum, scotice uero cnoc angel.*

> And hence even today the place also of that angelic conference bears witness to the event that occurred in it, in its proper name, which may be rendered in Latin 'knoll of the angels', and in [Gaelic] *cnoc angel.*[10]

The name, in more or less this form, resurfaces in the eighteenth century as Angel Hill and Cnoc nan Aingeal.[11] This poses a question– had the name survived in this form all this time, or is this an antiquarian revival based on knowledge of the anecdote from Adomnán? Meanwhile, also beginning in the eighteenth century, we

---

[9] See images on Clancy, "The Trouble".

[10] Anderson and Anderson, *Adomnán's Life of Columba*, ii.16. Anderson and Anderson render *Scottice* as 'In Irish' which, while not incorrect, is a less capacious linguistic term than 'Gaelic'.

[11] 'Angel Hill': Richard Pococke, *Tours in Scotland, 1747, 1750, 1760*, ed. D. W. Kemp (Edinburgh: Scottish History Society, 1887), 78; 'Cnoc nan Aingeal', 1771 account, in Richard Sharpe, "Iona in 1771: Gaelic tradition and visitors' experience", *The Innes Review* 63 (2012): 161-259, at 193, and discussion, 240.

begin to hear of a separate name for the same site, Sìthean (a term usually translated as 'fairy hill'), and we begin to see traditions of this site being a fairy mound, with all the usual legends that accompany such sites.[12] What is the direction of travel here? Had this always been a site associated with the otherworld, repurposed as angelic in the new world of Columba's monastery in the seventh century? Or were the angels a new response to a new landscape, only later assimilated to prevalent popular views of fairy-hills? My colleagues Dr. Sofia Evemalm-Graham and Gilbert Márkus have explored this constellation of names in some detail,[13] and so I will not delve further into the issue here, but it does foreground some of the potential complexities involved: what were the motivations of namers and renamers?

It also highlights a feature of the namescape that I turn to now: the presence and absence of saints in it. The place-names of Iona have no shortage of examples of 'hagiotoponyms', place-names which contain the names of saints: wells, hills, crosses, inlets, all with Gaelic

---

[12] The name appears as Sion in an anonymous account from 1776: "Near the midst of the island are two beautiful hills called the high and low Sion hills. Here was a grand place of worship to which they went on white horses mounted". The account appears in the miscellaneous manuscript of Allan MacDonald of Knock, "Some hints regarding the dress, customs and manners of the Gaelti [sic], thrown together, loosely, by an officer, on board a transport in Chebucto Harbour, before Hallifax, Nova Scotia, 1776", National Library of Scotland, MS 14876, p. 87 (the manuscript has been digitised and is accessible via the NLS website: https://digital.nls.uk/gaelic-manuscripts-of-scotland/archive/117623672#?c=0&m=0&s=0&cv=0&xywh=-3517%2C-490%2C12432%2C9785).

[13] Sofia Evemalm-Graham, "A hill of angels and fairies: Sìthean Mòr, Iona and the dynamics of Scottish onomastics", *Namn og nemne. Tidsskrift for norsk namneransking* 39 (2022): 51-68; also, eadem, "Angels, Fairies and St Michael: some thoughts on Sìthean Mòr" (blog, September 2021): https://iona-placenames.glasgow.ac.uk/angels-fairies-and-st-michael-some-thoughts-on-sithean-mor/); see also Gilbert Márkus, "Cnoc Angel–articulating a ritual landscape" (blog, October 2021): https://iona-placenames.glasgow.ac.uk/cnoc-angel-articulating-a-ritual-landsdcape/

names, indicate their presence.[14] Numerous saints are represented, some with obvious associations with Columba and Iona. Perhaps the most prominent is St. Odhran or Oran, about whom Gilbert Márkus has written extensively recently, and around whom there grew up a considerable body of folklore, probably prompted by the prominence of the site of Reilig Odhrain as Iona's main cemetery in the medieval and early modern period.[15] Adomnán is present too, in a cross and a harbour which bear his name; as is St. Cainnech, who features in Adomnán's "Life of Columba," and whose name was contained in a lost chapel-name, 'Cill Chainnich.'[16] But there are also universal saints contained in the names of crosses and chapels: Martin, Matthew, John, Mary; and some of very uncertain identity, such as the saints commemorated in the sites called Cill MoNeachdain and Cill MoGhobhannain.[17] Our work on the project has uncovered uncertainty about some of these, for instance, the saint in Teampull Rònain, 'St. Ronan's Church,' appears in earliest forms as *Ronad* or *Ronag*, prompting a question about whether in fact this is dedicated to St. Adomnán's mother Rònnat.[18] How old some of these associations are is problematic, and although we have a rich collection of early modern traveller and antiquarian accounts of the island, we are more challenged for the period before 1700. There are some interesting and contrasting signals we can see among these names–e.g. the antiquarian, effectively Old Irish, spelling of Adomnán's name found in William Reeves' 1857 collection of names and the maps in his

---

[14] I engaged in a detailed discussion of hagiotoponyms in Scotland more generally in T. O. Clancy, "Saints in the Scottish landscape", *Proceedings of the Harvard Celtic Colloquium* 33 (2013): 1-34.

[15] Gilbert Márkus, "Replicating a sacred landscape: the cult of St. Odrán in Scottish place-names", The Journal of Scottish Name Studies 15 (2021): 10-31; idem, "Inventing Odrán: saints, pilgrims and politics in medieval Iona", The Innes Review 73 (2022): 1-30; see also idem, "Four blessings and a funeral: Adomnán's theological map of Iona", The Innes Review 72 (2021): 1-26.

[16] William Reeves, *The Life of St Columba, Founder of Hy* (Dublin: Irish Archaeological and Celtic Society, 1857), 417.

[17] Reeves, *Life*, 417, 420-1; 418.

[18] I explore this possibility in T. O. Clancy, "The church of Teampull Rònain: his or hers?" (blog, October 2022): https://iona-placenames. glasgow.ac.uk/the-church-of-teampull-ronain-his-or-hers/

edition of the Life of Columba, in 'Crois Adomnain', compared to representations of attested local pronunciations of the saint's name from the nineteenth century–including from Reeves himself–of the saint's name as 'Aodhanan' or similar. That mid-nineteenth-century 'restoration' of a good Old Irish spelling of a well-known name is something that will become relevant later on in this article.[19]

Interesting as these hagiotoponyms are to pursue, I am more interested here in an absence, or perhaps an absent presence. Aside from the admittedly non-trivial example of the name of the island itself, there are no Gaelic place names on Iona containing Columba's name. The island, as Í Choluim Chille or Ì Chaluim Chille or variants thereof, has been identified with Columba since at least c.800, when it first begins to be attested in this form in the Irish annals.[20] That identification is so close that occasionally we find the island simply being called 'Columbkill' or the like, as on Blaeu's Atlas in 1654.[21] But beyond this, there are no hagiotoponyms invoking Columba's name in Gaelic, including the names of churches and chapels, although we know from Scandinavian sources that one building, almost certainly that now referred to as Columba's Shrine, was called in Old

[19] William Reeves, *The Life of St Columba, Founder of Hy* (Dublin: Irish Archaeological and Celtic Society, 1857), map, opposite p. 424 (Crois Adomnain); list, p. 427 (Crois Aodhanan); the saint's name is similarly represented in the nearby Port Adhamhnain, which Alexander Carmichael renders as Port Aona'ain, attributing this to his "kindly old informant, now dead", John MacInnes: see Alexander Carmichael, "Place-names of Iona III", *Scottish Geographical Magazine* 3.5 (1887): 242-7, at 242.
[20] Seán Mac Airt and Gearóid Mac Niocaill, *The Annals of Ulster to A.D. 1131* (Dublin: Dublin Institute for Advanced Studies, 1983), at AU802.9 *I Columbae Cille a gentibus combusta est*, "Ì Coluim Chille was burned by the heathens [i.e., by Vikings]". This collocation is periodically attested in the Irish annals thereafter, e.g. AU986.3; Seán Mac Airt, *The Annals of Innisfallen* (Dublin: Dublin Institute for Advanced Studies, 1944, rep. 1976), at AI1026.4; and in other sources also. For some discussion and further forms, see Gilbert Márkus, "Í > Ioua > Iona", (blog, July 2022): https://iona-placenames.glasgow.ac.uk/i-ioua-iona/
[21] Johannes Blaeu, *Atlas Novus* vol. 5: Atlas of Scotland (Amsterdam: Blaeu, 1654), "Mula insula", viewable online at https://maps.nls.uk/atlas/blaeu/browse/111

Norse *Kolumkilla kirkju inni lítlu* 'little St. Columba's church.'[22] Interestingly, where we do find him is in English-language place-names, many of fairly modern vintage (St. Columba's Table, St. Columba's Pillow, and especially St. Columba's Bay.) Why is this?[23]

My sense is that Columba is in the Gaelic landscape of Iona, but as an implied presence in various names which triggered, or were designed to trigger, associations with the saint. We have seen the example of Cnoc nan Aingeal already. But there are others. One prominent example is Port a' Churaich on the south of the island. First attested (though in the wrong place) by Mánus Ó Dónaill, and now regularly called (in English), St. Columba's Bay, this is where Columba's *curach,* a traditional small boat, is reputed to have come to shore when he first came to Iona.[24] A natural mound of stones has, over the centuries, been pointed to as a memorial of the curach, and is sometimes referred to as An Curachan.[25] The place thus evokes Columba in Gaelic, not through his name, but through association with an aspect of his life and miracles. This is despite the name being, on the face of it, potentially a very common one, simply meaning 'port of the coracle'.

---

[22] Finnur Jónsson, *Snorri Sturluson, Heimskringla: Nóregs Konunga Sögur* (Copenhagen, 1893), 245. This reference, from the thirteenth-century saga of Mágnus Barelegs, refers to events in the 1090s. The veracity of the events described cannot be certain, but since Iona was in the early thirteenth century technically within the Norwegian diocese of the Suðreyjar, subject to Niðarós (Trondheim), it is likely that the Old Norse name for the church is accurate.

[23] We might also note the slightly complicated case of the farm called Columba, which is only very indirectly named from the saint. It takes its name from the Columba Hotel, whose farm it was, initially, at any rate. According to Mairi MacArthur (pers. comm.) "The Columba Hotel was named in 1868 after the former Free Church Manse was adapted to that purpose. Adjoining fields, previously worked by crofters, were included in the lease to become the Columba farm holding."

[24] A. O'Kelleher and G. Schoepperle (ed. and trans.), *Betha Coluim Chille. Life of Columcille, compiled by Manus O'Donnell in 1532* (Urbana: University of Illinois, 1918), §355. In this account, he has located *Port an Curaigh* where the current main harbour is. For other early mentions of the place and its names, see Sharpe, "Iona in 1771", 226-8.

[25] Reeves, *Life*, 423, 427.

Another example of this phenomenon of the implied presence of Columba is Càrn Cùl ri Èirinn. This is the place where, reputedly, Columba climbed to confirm that he could no longer see Ireland. (It should be noted that this is a legend told of several places in the Hebrides.) Again, and perhaps even more so, the name only really makes sense as an evocation of a tradition regarding Columba; but equally in Gaelic this evocation seems not to need his name attached to it. The tradition dates back at least as far as the eighteenth century, but there may well be traces of it present in a Middle Gaelic poem perhaps of the twelfth century.[26] In verse 6 of the poem, the speaker wishes to be on the breast of an island: *Conaicind a traigh sa tuile / ina reimim, /Comad h-e m'ainm run no-t-raigim / "Cul re h-Eirinn"*. ("That I might see [the sea's] ebb and flow / in their sequence, / that this might be my name, a secret I tell you: / 'Back towards Ireland.'")[27] These are the names of this sort which have remained, but many more may be lurking in common-seeming names where we can no longer discern an earlier association.

---

[26] First mentioned as such in Thomas Pennant's account: "He repeated here the experiment on several hills, erecting on each a heap of stones; and that which he last ascended is to this day called *Carnan-chul-reh*-EIRINN, or the eminence of the back turned to *Ireland.*" *A Tour in Scotland, and Voyage to the Hebrides MDCCLXXII* (Chester: John Monk, 1774), 278-9. The poem is that which begins "Mellach lem bith i n-ucht ailiuin", edited from a Brussels manuscript by Kuno Meyer, *Zeitschrift für celtische Philologie* 5 (1905): 496-7; and from a manuscript in the National Library of Scotland [NLS] by Donald Mackinnon, *Descriptive Catalogue of Gaelic Manuscripts* (Edinburgh: Constable, 1912), 82. I translated the poem in T. O. Clancy, *The Triumph Tree: Scotland's Earliest Poetry, AD 550–1350* (Edinburgh: Canongate, 1998), 188. See also Sharpe, "Iona in 1771", 245-47, though he seems to have been (rather uncharacteristically) unaware of the NLS version of the poem or Mackinnon's edition of it.
[27] Mackinnon, *Descriptive Catalogue*, 82; translation from Clancy, *Triumph Tree*, 188. I discuss this poem and its context in more depth in a forthcoming article, "*Tír, tráig, tuile* / land, strand and tide: Colum Cille and the Poetics of Place". For some discussion of similar poems in the voice of Columba, see Máire Herbert, "Becoming an exile: Colum Cille in Middle Irish poetry'" in *Heroic Poets and Poetic Heroes in Celtic Tradition: studies in honor of Patrick K. Ford*, ed. Joseph Falaky Nagy and Leslie Ellen Jones (Dublin: Four Courts, 2005), 131-40.

As noted already, Sìthean / Cnoc nan Aingeal is a potential example of this. In turning to my next category, druids, it is interesting that antiquarians wanted to see druids here, as well. In a letter from John Stuart to Thomas Pennant in 1773, he notes: "There are hardly any monuments of Druids now remaining in this island, excepting a Druidical circle, 15 feet in diameter, which is to be seen on the top of Cnoc-nan-aingeal. "[28] Pennant himself then notes in his tour: "On my return [from Port a' Churaich] saw, on the right hand, on a small hill, a small circle of stones, and a little cairn in the middle, evidently druidical, but called the hill of the angels, *Cnoc nar-aimgeal* [sic]; from a tradition that the holy man had there a conference with those celestial beings soon after his arrival."[29]

Columba's medieval hagiography is not notably druid-heavy. Aside potentially from encounters in Pictland (with characters called *magi* in Adomnán's Life), they really do not feature in the early hagiography of Columba (contrast this with Patrick or Brigit, for instance), and not at all in connection with Iona. They only really appear on Iona for the first time, to my knowledge, in Mánus Ó Domhnaill's compendious Life in 1532. There, he tells the story of Columba's arrival on Iona:

> *Oidhc[h]e cingcísi do cuatar a tír 'san oilen sin, ₇ do batar draithe 'san oilen sin ₇ tancutar a rectaibh espog d'indsoighe C[oluim] C[ille]. Acus adubratar ris nar coír do tect do'n oilen sin ₇ go rabutar fen and remhe ag siladh creidmhe ₇ crabaidh ₇ nach rainic se a les daíne naemtha eli da bennughadh. 'Ni fir daib-si sin,' ar C[oluim] C[ille], 'oir ni hespoig iar fir sib act draithe diablaide ata a n-agaidh creidimh, ₇ fagbuidh an t-oilen-sa, ₇ ní daeib do deonaigh Dia é.' Agus do fagbhatar na draithe an t-oilen le breithir C[oluim] C[ille].*

> On the eve of Pentecost they cast anchor on that island; and there were druids there, and they came in the guise of bishops toward Columcille. And they said

to him that it was not right for him to come on that island and that themselves had been there afore him sowing the Faith and piety, and it had no need of other holy men to bless it. 'It is not true what ye say,' saith Columcille, 'for ye be not bishops in truth, but druids of Hell that are against the Faith (*oir ni hespoig iar fir sib act draithe diablaide ata a n-agaidh creidimh*). Leave this island. Not to you hath God granted it.' And at the word of Columcille the druids left the island.[30]

This is an intriguing episode, since it is patently an elaboration of an episode in the Middle Irish Life of Columba, which Máire Herbert has dated to mid-twelfth century and assigned to Derry. Iona is a bit of an afterthought in this Life, but when Columba does eventually get there, there are bishops there–but it is revealed to him that these are not proper bishops and he expels them.

> *Luid iarum fo shomenmain co roacht in inud dianad ainm Híí Coluim Cille indiu. Adaig chengcisi tra ro siacht. Tancutar dí epscop bátar isin tír do gabail a láma ass. Ro fhollsig tra Dia do Colum Cille naptar epscuip iar fir, conid air sin forfacsat an innsi lais o ro indis forru a tuirtechta 7 a tindrium ndíles.*

Then he set out in good spirits and reached the place called today Iona of Colum Cille. It was the night of Whitsun [= Pentecost] when he arrived. Two bishops who were in the land came to expel him. God then revealed to Colum Cille that they were not genuine bishops (*naptar epscuip iar fír*), whereupon they abandoned the island to him when he made known their identity and description.[31]

---

[30] O'Kelleher and Schoepperle, *Betha Coluim Chille*, §204.

[31] Máire Herbert, *Iona, Kells and Derry: The History and Hagiography of the Monastic* Familia *of Columba* (Oxford: OUP, 1988; Dublin: Four Courts, 1991), 237, 261. It should be noted this episode has not been much considered in terms of its significance for twelfth-century Iona and the wider Columban context. It would repay some attention.

In Mánus's Life, as we have seen, these are clearly identified as druids disguised as bishops. In the absence of any other evidence, the 'druidificiation' would appear to me to be Mánus's doing, though we cannot rule out an intermediary. This is an intriguing episode, and prompts some interesting questions about the meaning behind assigning druidic identities to false bishops during the Reformation century. Be that as it may, this anecdote may underlie much of what follows it relating to druids having been on Iona.

The idea of the residents of Iona immediately previous to Columba being druids resurfaces again in the late seventeenth century.[32] In a passage from 1693 potentially echoing the account in Mánus Ó Domhnaill, John Fraser, the dean of the Isles, noted: "In this Ile was a societie of the Druids when Columbus came there, but it seems they were none of the best for he banished them all."[33] The druidic trope persists through the eighteenth century and beyond, now reinforced by a growing general obsession with druids among antiquarians, especially following on from the publication of John Toland's work in the early eighteenth century.[34] Some of these early modern accounts are rather extraordinary. The anonymous 1771 account of a visit to Iona tells us:

> Some maintain that the druids were massacred by St. Columba, whence the adjacent harbour is called The Martyrs Port. It is improbable, however, that the rancour of their Christian enemies would have dignified the Pagan priests with the name of martyrs. It is not fair to accuse the saint of such shocking

---

[32] I should note my debt in this next section of the paper to the work of the late Richard Sharpe, in his "Iona in 1771", where he identifies key texts and passages and discusses, inter alia, the druidic tendency.

[33] John Fraser, "A short description of I or Iona 1693", in *Geographical Collections relating to Scotland, compiled by Walter MacFarlane*, ed. A. Mitchell and J. T. Clark, 3 vols (Edinburgh: Scottish History Society, 1906–8), ii, 216-17. This rather begs the question of what "the best" druids would be like.

[34] John Toland, "A Specimen of the Critical History of the Celtic Religion and Learning, containing and account of the Druid", in *The Miscellaneous Works of Mr. John Toland* (London: Whiston / Baker / Robinson, 1747), 1-228; first published in 1726.

barbarity without good authority; and indeed the most specious opinion is, that the druids were extirpated before his time.[35]

Perhaps the most extreme version of this aspect of Columba as vengeful exterminator of the druids comes from another anonymous account, from 1776:

> The Druids possessed the Island on Columba's landing; they were slain by his order, and the last of their slain Corpses thrown into a Pit called *Slochd na m Biast*, or the Hole of the beasts, meaning the Pagans or Druids.[36]

The idea of druids on Iona found its toponymic home in two place-names, one real but misunderstood, the other probably conjured out of thin air. The first is Cladh nan Druineach, a small non-natural feature on the east side of the island. Gaelic *cladh* means graveyard, and indeed bones have been found at the spot. From the eighteenth century, antiquarians and visitors interpreted the word *druineach* as meaning 'druids'. Witness, for instance, the description of Dugald Campbell, author of the Iona entry for the Statistical Account of Scotland in 1792:

> A green eminence, close to the Sound of I, is to this day called the Druid's burial place. A cottager some years ago, planting potatoes in this spot and digging earth to cover them, brought up some bones which the

---

[35] Sharpe, "Iona in 1771", 195. The reference here is to the place generally called *Port nam Mairtir*; the author is correct to doubt that this has anything to do with druids.

[36] For the 1776 account, see fn. 12 above. The location of Slochd nam Biast is unknown, though Gaelic *sloc* "gully", is well attested as a place-name generic element on the island, appearing in some sixteen names, several of them containing animals as their specific elements, e.g., Sloc nam Muc "gully of the pigs / dolphins".

people of the island immediately concluded to be the bones of the Druids.[37]

This association of the site with druids persisted despite the fact that, as later writers clarified, the name meant nothing of the sort (and Gaelic speakers should probably have known this). As Hector MacLean pointed out in 1887:

> Cladh-nan-Druineach, more correctly Cladh nan Druinneach, does not mean 'burial-ground of the Druids' but 'burial-ground of the artists' [. . .] There are good grounds, therefore, for inferring that Cladh nan Druinneach in Iona is the burying ground of gravestone sculptors residing there.[38]

In fact its probable original meaning is 'embroideress', and this has given rise to an important forthcoming exploratory paper by my colleague Prof. Katherine Forsyth.[39]

I suspect that it is from the extraordinary morass of ideas about druids and this place, Cladh nan Druineach, that the name 'Innis nan Druineach', ostensibly meaning 'island of the druids' was invented–in this particular case I suspect the name had no currency at all before it was conjured into being in the mid-eighteenth century. It is first recorded by Bishop Richard Pococke in 1760, but I doubt he was the originator.

> A quarter of a mile to the north east of the great church, on a piece of ground which is at present

---

[37] Campbell, "Kilfinichen and Kilvickeon", 199. See Sharpe, "Iona in 1771", 241-43, for a full run-down of references to this place, first noted by Pococke in 1760 as "the Druids' Burial-place" (Pococke, *Tours*, 86).

[38] Hector MacLean, "Notes on place-names of Iona", *Scottish Geographical Magazine* 3 (1887): 37. The matter may be a bit more complex than the rather black and white picture I am painting here. It does seem possible that the word *druinneach*, whatever its original meaning, came to be understood in the eighteenth or nineteenth century in a toponymic context as having the meaning 'druid', despite this being incorrect.

[39] Katherine Forsyth "Iona's embroideresses", forthcoming. For the early meaning, see Dictionary of the Irish Language s.v. "druinech" at http://dil.ie/18873.

morassy, are two stones about seven feet high with a stone laid across at top, and some other stones near it set up on end, which they say were the first buildings St. Columb erected here; but I take them to be the remains of a Druid Temple, and the rather, as this isle was anciently called Inish Drunish, or the Isle of the Druids.[40]

Whatever the origin of the idea, Thomas Pennant then made the idea well-known, elaborating Pococke's earlier account:

[F]or Bishop Pocock mentions, that he had seen two stones seven feet high, with a third laid across on their tops, an evident Cromlech; he also adds, that the Irish name of the island was Inish Drunish, which agrees with the account I have somewhere read, that Jona had been the seat of Druids expelled by Columba, who found them there.[41]

It is interesting to see how the name gains a kind of spurious currency in writings on the island. For instance, Donald Campbell in the *New Statistical Account* in 1845 positions it first in his list, although he goes on to give the two genuinely most common names for the island: Ì Chaluim Chille, or simply Ì.

To the Highlanders of the present day, Iona is known as 'Innis-nan-Druidhneach,' or *the Island of the Druids*—as 'Ii-cholum-chille,' or *the Island of Colum, of the Cell, or Cemetery*, from whence the English word Icolymkill is derived; and *par excellence*, by I,

---

[40] Pococke, *Tours*, 85. The monument he refers to is likely to be that at Cladh an Dìseirt, pictured early on with a door-lintel remaining, somewhat resembling a cromlech. See Royal Commission on the Ancient and Historical Monuments of Scotland, *Argyll IV: Iona* (Edinburgh: HMSO, 1982), 243 for illustration.
[41] Pennant, *Tour*, 295.

or the island pronounced by the sound of *ee* in English, and which is the most general name it goes by, in the parish and surrounding neighbourhood.[42]

Nonetheless, we might note the inverted priorities of this list. It is this gradual replacement of the quotidian by the fabulous which is so symptomatic of nineteenth-century writing about Iona.

Informed by these wider contexts, we turn finally to a problematic yet intriguing name. Dùn Mhanannain is a small rocky hill on Iona's west coast. On the face of it, it appears to carry the name of the famous Gaelic "god of the sea", Manannán mac Lir.[43] And yet this form of the name first appears in the record of place-names in Bishop Reeves' edition of the Life of Columba in 1857 (as 'Dun Mhanannain').[44] That we have no earlier record of it is not surprising: the features of the west and north of the island are generally recorded later than many others, because it was not on travellers' itineraries. Nonetheless, the form of the name and the lateness of its recording gives me pause. The form of Manannán's name is, to my eye, suspiciously the way someone well-versed in early Irish literature would spell it; someone like Reeves himself, for instance.[45]

One reason for circumspection is the form of the name found on the two Ordnance Survey 6" to the mile maps (in 1881 and 1900): 'Dùn Manamin'. As we have already seen, the authority of the Ordnance Survey can be somewhat suspect on Iona names, and mere minim confusion (i.e., '*-min*' for '*-nain*') might lie behind this

---

[42] Donald Campbell, "Kilfinichen and Kilvickeon", *New Statistical Account of Scotland* (Edinburgh and London: Blackwood, 1845), 313.

[43] I will use the Early Gaelic (i.e., Old Irish) spelling to denote the character's name in what follows; variants will represent spellings in later texts and place-names. For a detailed account of the character of Manannán in Gaelic literature, see Charles W. MacQuarrie, "The Waves of Manannán: a study of the literary representations of Manannán mac Lir from Immram Brain (c. 700) to Finnegans Wake (1939)" (PhD thesis, University of Washington, 1997); revised and published as *The Biography of the Irish God of the Sea from The Voyage of Bran (700 A.D.) to Finnegan's* Wake *(1939): The Waves of Manannán* (Lampeter: Edwin Mellen, 2004).

[44] Reeves, *Life*, 428.

[45] See my comments above on his spelling of the name "Adomnán," in the monument name of Crois Adomnain.

spelling. Nonetheless, the evidence of the Ordnance Survey Name Books shows local people attesting to this form of the name, so we cannot completely dismiss it.[46] It gives us pause about Manannán being in the name, although the name otherwise is difficult to parse.[47]

One approach to this problem is to ask if people in the early modern Gàidhealtachd knew about Manannán, and if so, how did they spell his name? Thanks to the work of an eighteenth-century Mull poet, preserved in the important Hector MacLean Manuscripts in Nova Scotia, we can say that at least some local people were familiar with the name of Manannán. Iain mac Ailein (d.1760) composed both a prose text and a poem describing the migration of a number of the Tuatha Dé Danann to Scotland; in the course of these two texts he has cause to mention Manannán.[48] These texts were edited by A. MacLean Sinclair, and while he tidied up Iain mac Ailein's spelling, the Hector MacLean Manuscript itself allows us to see less standardised forms: "Cleun ni Mananain" (rendered by MacLean Sinclair as "Cliodhna nighean Manannain") and "Maninan" (rendered as "Manannain"). I think this gives us grounds for some confidence in the current form of

---

[46] The Ordnance Survey Object Name Books record the various authorities for the spellings of names, as well as other details, such as interpretations. In this case, they are two local farmers and the postmaster. For the record, see Argyll Name Book vol. 77: OS1/2/77/51, online at: https://scotlandsplaces.gov.uk/digital-volumes/ordnance-survey-name-books/argyll-os-name-books-1868-1878/argyll-volume-77/51 The idea of a simple spelling mistake is also made problematic by a derived name, Slochd Dùn Manamin.

[47] Failing better suggestions, one might suggest it is a rendition of Gaelic *meanmna* (g.s. *meanmain* 'spirit, intellect'), i.e., a version of *Dùn Meanmain (pronounced /mɛnɛmɪNʲ/), but that seems an implausible name for a dùn. It should be noted that "Manamin" here fails to comply by the basic Gaelic spelling rule regarding broad and slender vowels, which are almost universally observed otherwise in the spelling of Gaelic topographical names on the island on the Ordnance Survey 6" maps (the other exception being Eilean Musimul, a name which incorporates a Scandinavian existing name). All this perhaps supports the notion that this is a scribal error of some sort.

[48] A. Maclean Sinclair, *Na Baird Leathanach: The MacLean Bards. Vol. 1, The Old Maclean Bards* (1898)pp. 138 and 140. I hope to edit and discuss these intriguing texts in the near future.

the place-name (Dùn Mhanannain), and in it containing the name of Manannán mac Lir. This is bolstered by further traces of traditions of Manannán in the area, such as a charm recorded by John Gregorson Campbell, ostensibly received from an individual who flourished in the mid-eighteenth century, which invokes "Manannan" or "Manaman mac Leth." Gregorson Campbell initially published only an English translation of the charm:

> I will close my fist,
> Faithful to me is the wood;
> It is to protect my abusive words
> I enter in.
> The three sons of Clooney will save me
> And Manaman MacLeth
> And St Columba, gentle cleric,
> And Alexander in heaven.[49]

Alexander Carmichael, however, subsequently supplied a Gaelic original for the charm, giving the name as "Manannan mac Leth."[50] In light of the Ordinance Survey spellings of the name as "Dùn Manamin," the form in the English version with the spelling "Manaman" is interesting, and perhaps suggestive of a genuine name-variant.

It is also worth noting Alexander Carmichael's account of libations given to the sea which, Mairi MacArthur tells us, were latterly associated with Dùn Mhanannain, though the exact trajectory of this is hard to pin down. MacArthur notes:

---

[49] John Gregorson Campbell, "Charm for a Law Suit", in *Witchcraft & Second Sight in the Highlands and Islands of Scotland* (Glasgow: James Maclehose, 1902), 83. Note the spelling of the name as "Manaman" and compare with the early OS map forms discussed earlier.

[50] A full account of this original and Carmichael's subsequent alteration of it can be found in Ronald Black, *The Gaelic Otherworld* (Edinburgh: Birlinn, 2005), 219 and 482-3. See further, Ronald Black, "I thought he made it all up: Context and Controversy", in D. U. Stiùbhart (ed.), *The Life and Legacy of Alexander Carmichael* (Port of Ness: Islands Book Trust, 2008), 57-81 at page 61. I am very grateful to Dr Sìm Innes for supplying information and copies on this matter.

In two places, Iona and Lewis, [Alexander] Carmichael also recorded the custom of casting oatmeal or ale into the sea in order to assure a plentiful supply of seaweed to enrich the soil for the year's planting. He claimed that in Iona in 1860 he had talked with a middle-aged man whose father, when young, had taken part in the ceremony. It happened on Thursday before Easter, 'Diardaoin [a' Bh]rochain Mhòir' (Thursday of the great porridge): "As the day merged from Wednesday to Thursday a man walked to the waist into the sea and poured out whatever offering had been prepared, chanting:

A Dhè na mara
Cuir todhar 's an tarruinn
Chon tachair an talaimh
Chon bailcidh dhuinn biaidh

O God of the Sea,
Put weed in the drawing wave
To enrich the ground,
To shower us with food.

Those behind the offerer took up the chant and wafted it along the seashore . . . " Local tradition connects this event with Dùn Mhanannain on the west coast, the hill of 'Manann[an]' who was a god of the sea.[51]

There is room for uncertainty about the validity of this latter connection. For one thing, the topography is not propitious, and one might wonder if in fact such rituals took place elsewhere instead, for instance, somewhere where seaweed was more regularly harvested. Equally, if the good Christian residents of Iona were casting porridge into the sea hoping for bountiful seaweed in the nineteenth century, it is highly unlikely that the "Dè na Mara" they were invoking was anyone but the one God almighty. It is entirely possible that the connection between this prayer and Dùn Mhanannain was only made

---

[51] E. Mairi MacArthur, *Iona: The Living Memory of a Crofting Community*, *1750–1914* (Edinburgh: EUP, 1991), 179, citing Alexander Carmichael, *Carmina Gadelica* vol. I (Edinburgh: Oliver & Boyd, 1900), 163.

subsequent to Carmichael's publication. Having said that, it seems to have been well entrenched among Iona's Gaelic speakers by the early twentieth century, to judge by the account of the Rev. Colla Domhnullach (Coll A. MacDonald), in a radio broadcast published in 1938:

> "Cha bu mhath leam di-meas a dheanamh air Mac an Leigh," arsa an tàilleir, "ach tha mi cinnteach gu'm bi saobh chreidimh ann an *Africa* mar a bha saobh-chreidimh ann an I mìle bliadhna an dèidh searmonachadh Chaluim Chille. Nach aithne dhuit Dun-mhananain? B'ann do Mhananan a bha iad ag aoradh, oir nach b'esan a bha riaghladh na mara ann am beachd nan treubhan Ceilteach, agus chuala mise gu'm biodh muinntir I a' dortadh measan bhrochain, anns a' mhuir mar iobairt do Mhananan aig toiseach na naodhamh linn deug. Bha iad ag cur ubh na h-eireige dh'iarraidh ubh a' gheoidh. Bha fiughar aca gu'n cuireadh Mananan feamainn a' Cheitein 'na mill air na cladaichean."[52]

It is, I think, important to note that there must be a mild fictionalising in the conversations he constructs among the locals; and I find it hard to separate the tailor's description of the ritual which he precedes with "chuala mise" (I have heard), from Carmichael's account, with which the author, Domhnullach, was undoubtedly familiar.

---

[52] Colla Domhnullach, 'Eilean I', in *Am measg nam bodach: co-chruinneachadh de sgeulachdan is beul-aithris a chaidh a chraobh-sgaoileadh air an fhritheud eadar Samhuinn, 1936, agus An Gearran, 1937* (Glasgow: An Comunn Gaidhealach, 1938), 28. ["'I don't like to cast aspersions on Livingston," said the tailor, "but I am sure there is superstition in Africa like there was superstition in Iona a thousand years after the preaching of Columba. You're acquainted with Dùn Mhanannain? Manannan was worshipped by them, because it was he who regulated the sea in the opinion of the Celtic tribes, and I myself heard that the folk of Iona would place a portion of porridge in the sea as an offering to Mannanan at the beginning of the nineteenth century. They gave a chicken egg in exchange for a goose egg. They expected that Manannan would put the May seaweed in heaps on the shores.'" Translation mine.] I am grateful to Dr. Mairi MacArthur for calling my attention to this source.

Certainly by the twentieth century, Manannán had become a feature of the fertile imagination of spiritual tourists to the island, such as the already-mentioned William Sharp, who wrote under the name 'Fiona MacLeod'. It is instructive to see from what slender roots such overblown imaginings originated:

> It is a place to this day called Dûn Mananain. Here, a friend who told me many things, a Gaelic farmer named MacArthur, had related once a fantastic legend about a god of the sea. Manaun was his name, and he lived in times when Iona was part of the kingdom of the Suderöer. Whenever he willed he was like the sea, and that is not wonderful, for he was born of the sea.
>
> . . .
>
> Probably some thought was in my mind that there, by Dûn Mananain, I might find a hidden way. That summer I had been thrilled to the inmost life by coming suddenly, by moonlight, on a seal moving across the last sand-dune between this place and the bay called Port Ban. A strange voice, too, I heard upon the sea. True, I saw no white arms upthrown, as the seal plunged into the long wave that swept the shore; and it was a grey skua that wailed above me, winging inland; yet had I not had a vision of the miracle?
>
> But alas! that evening there was not even a barking seal. Some sheep fed upon the green slope of Manaun's mound.[53]

Even more extraordinary is the account by Ella Horsey from the 1960s. She describes:

> a grassy mound bearing the name of one of these– Manaanan, God of the Mist. Suddenly I became conscious of the pressure on my head and sensation of spider-webs covering my face which make me aware of unseen presences. I looked up and a patch of

---

[53] MacLeod, *Divine Adventure*, 112-13.

white mist floating slowly along the slopes of Dun I
attracted my attention. There was no sign of cloud or
mist elsewhere. Manaanan, whose symbol of old was
the mist! Could there possibly be a connection? . . .
the Unseen Presences were all about me–anything
might happen . . . [54]

Horsey had strong ideas about reincarnation, and about herself she
said, "I had been told through several channels that I had lived in Iona
in former lives and my friend, Lucy Bruce, had seen me clairvoyantly
as the child of a Druid priest on the island."[55] Here, the various
speculations on Iona's deep past, and their relevance to visitors in the
more recent past (and perhaps present) seem to collide and coalesce.

Leaving these modern speculations aside, if we can accept the
name Dùn Mhanannain at face-value, as containing the name of the
medieval Gaelic character Manannán, what is it doing here? Is it an
echo of the period of time when Iona was a key site within the
Kingdom of Man and the Isles (thinking here of Manannán's
legendary connection with the Isle of Man)? Does it perhaps have an
echo of a story in which Columba conversed with Manannán, much as
he did with (perhaps) Mongán in the Early Gaelic story of "The
Dialogue of Colum Cille and the Youth at Carn Eolairg"?[56] Is there
any enlightenment to be had from the reference to "Dún Manannáin"
in a bawdy seventeenth-century Irish poem?[57] Or was there a legend

---

[54] Ella Horsey, *Erraid. Seven Years on a Scottish Islet* (London & New
York: Regency Press, 1967), 40-1. I am grateful to Dr Mairi MacArthur for
supplying me with this quote and information about Ms Horsey.
[55] Ibid.
[56] For which see John Carey, "The Lough Foyle colloquy texts:
Immacaldam Choluim Chille 7 ind óclaig oc Carraic Eolairg and
Immacaldam in druad Brain 7 inna banfátho Febuil ós Loch Febuil", *Ériu*
52 (2002): 53-87.
[57] See Máirín Ní Dhonnchadha, "The poem beginning 'A Shláine inghan
Fhlannagáin", *Ériu* 46 (1995): 65-70, at p. 69 for the reference. In this
bawdy poem, full of double entendres, the addressee is called "a bhean ó
Dhún Manannáin", "O woman from Dún Manannáin" (poem, line 6c).
Regarding the name, Ní Dhonnchadha suggests that it is perhaps an allusion
to a brothel or similar: "Conversely, however, the placename 'Dún

in which Manannán was resident in the island, and if so, how old was that?

The place-names of Iona, with their record spanning 1300 years, have a great deal to offer both toponymists and those interested in Gaelic history and culture more widely, and many of the names permit decent and detailed explanation. Sometimes, however, as with trying to understand what a name like Dùn Mhanannain is doing on Iona, how old it might be, and what its original meaning might have been, it is hard to resist engaging in the same sort of speculation that gave rise to the stories and antiquarian fabulations of the past. In the Iona's Namescape project, we are well aware of the authority that will likely accrue to our survey once complete, and aware that any explanations we might put forward have the potential to create the basis for future imaginings about Iona past. The balance between authority and authenticity is a matter for the future, as well as the past.

Manannáin' (§6c) may well have been used to invoke a place of the imagination. Manannán's Otherworld abode is often located in 'Tír Tairngire', the land of eternal youth and uncircumscribed sex, and the poet may have intended to portray the addressee's abode as a place of similar promise." (p. 66) However, given the poem addresses a probably real woman as an abbess (line 6b), and that one of the only places known to me with a Dùn Mhanannain on it is Iona, which had a late medieval nunnery, perhaps there is more to think about here.

The Mysterious Book of Patrick O'Keeffe

Brian Frykenberg

On May 12, 2021, The Éire Society of Boston received a request from Mary Porter for assistance deciphering a curious little book held by The Scituate Historical Society, of which she is Archivist.[1] Mary had been contacted by Eilís Lyons of Mary Immaculate College, Limerick, about a reference to the volume in Pádraig de Brún's *Treoirliosta* of 1988.[2] In March of 1987, George E. Ryan, resident of Scituate, Éire Society Gold Medal recipient, and Senior Editor of *The Boston Pilot*, had published an article in "The Hiberno-File" column of *The Boston Irish News* entitled "The Mysterious Notebook of Patrick O'Keeffe."[3] The piece was intended to call forth further detailed study of the book, but beyond the inquiries of the late Breandán Ó Buachalla in 2005 that plea awaited attention.[4] When examined by Ryan the book held a clipping, a letter "To the Editor of

---

[1]Form submitted on "Eiresociety.org" (info@eiresociety.org) to then Éire Society President Mimi McNealy Langenderfer, circulated among board-members of the society, with response by me on that day. Scituate is a small town on the coast to the south of Boston.

[2]E-mail correspondence ("Irish Language Manuscript") between Eilís Lyons and Mary Porter from February 24 to March 23, 2021. Mary Porter subsequently sent a description of the book, accompanied by images, to Eilís Lyons. For the guide, see Pádraig de Brún, *Lámhscríbhinní Gaeilge: Treoirliosta* (Dublin: Dublin Institute for Advanced Studies, 1988), 34: "SCITUATE, Massachusetts: Scituate Historical Society 1 Ms."

[3]Pages 30-32. Ryan was awarded the medal in 1981: "Gold Medal," "Eire Society of Boston" (sic), https://www.eiresociety.org/events/gold-medal, last accesssed December 10, 2022. Ryan died on September 19, 2000.

[4]Prof. Ó Buachalla had telephoned the previous Scituate Historical Society Archivist, Carol Miles, regarding the volume on the morning of March 18, 2005, and requested photocopy images, which were arranged for the following day and eventually sent to him, along with a copy of Ryan's article: Email correspondence ("Irish' book") between Ó Buachalla and Miles, March 18-19, 2005. Ó Buachalla's letter of thanks for receipt of the materials is handwritten on University of Notre Dame Department of Irish Language and Literature stationery, dated "6/5/05," and indicates his likely

The [Boston] Sunday Globe" for December 22, 1878 by a pseudonymous "Aodh Beag" of the Boston Philo-Celtic Society, pleading for study of the Irish language in the context of Ireland's antiquity and contribution to European education set against its calumniators and detractors.[5]

The volume itself, entirely handwritten, is a personal book or 'commonplace' self-identifying as "Patrick O'Keeffe's" or "Pat Keeffe's" "Book." At 216 by 140 by 12 millimeters it fits the hand well, a single gathering of forty-six centrally stitched, unfoliated, unpaginated leaves, seven of which have been torn away leaving mere stubs. The booklet is bound by its single saddle-stitch to a weathered leather cover, faintly blind-stamped with swirls, which shows thread-fragments at the turn-ins that may have been used to tie the front and back covers together for protection. The binding includes reinforcement at the spine in quarter-leather. The slightly soiled laid paper produced by Curteis & Sons, Carshalton, Surrey sometime after 1791,[6] horizontally-ruled somewhat sporadically, is occasionally torn

---

location at the Keogh Institute (Newman House) in Dublin "for the Summer." Miles indicates that Ó Buachalla visited the Society in person at some point to view the book (personal conversations with Mary Porter, communicated to me in e-mails dated September 12, and October 12, 2022). To the best recollection of the Society, no further scholars came to examine the manuscript first-hand.

[5]"The Irish Language. Its Antiquity and Richness–A Strong Appeal By A Celt for its Revival." "All interested in the revival of the Irish language are invited to attend" Tuesday evening and Sunday afternoon meetings of the Society at "756 Washington street." The Boston Philo-Celtic Society was founded in April, 1873. See Matthew Knight, "An Army of Vindication: The *Irish Echo*, 1886-1894," in ed. Natasha Sumner and Aidan Doyle, *North American Gaels: Speech, Story, and Song in the Diaspora.* McGill-Queen's Studies in Ethnic History. Series Two 49 (Montreal; Kingston; London; Chicago: McGill-Queen's University Press, 2020), 163-200, at 165.

[6]The characteristic ornamental fleur-de-lis on a shield above scepter and initials, crown with trefoils on plinth or column, surmounted by fleur-de-lis is visible e.g. at fols. 23v-24r (transverse left-to-right across the gutter at the central stitch); and "Curteis & Sons" e.g. at fol. 28v (reading foot-to-head at the gutter). The company was recognized by this name by 1787, and

or worn at the edges, the first and final leaves showing signs of earlier mold and pest damage.[7] Every leaf has, or had, a conjugate; but despite various dates given internally, it is difficult to ascertain in what order the contents were included or copied. The texts, inscriptions, marginalia and other matter are in English cursive or in Irish of a traditional script, in various manuscript inks, with notes in pencil. The dimensions of the written space are well executed for larger texts (e.g. fol. 24r), including ornamental, zoomorphic, or swash capitals, dividers, and tables (e.g. fol. 40r).[8] Elsewhere the content has been accommodated to any possible area, that is: written upside-down (where indication of similar use on conjugates is lacking, such as at fol. 45 [fol. 2 excised]) even on pages which contain text running the opposite direction (e.g. fol. 4r);[9] transverse, whether foot-to-head starting at the gutter (such as the scribal attribution and macaronic disclaimer at fol. 27r mentioned below at note 38) or head-to-foot beginning at the fore-edge; or otherwise occupying the same area as alternative matter.

---

produced "white paper" by 1791: wandle.org/mills/ papermillcarshalton.pdf (especially pages 2-3 and notes), last accessed December 10, 2022.

[7]The full Conservation Treatment Report (including digitization) is by Bexx Caswell-Olsen, Director of Conservation, Northeast Document

[8]See **figures 1a and 1b (p. 109 below)**. "A note on editorial method" utilized throughout is included at the end of this bibliographic study, together with appendices comprising short lists of first lines and marginalia for literary works.

[9]See page at fol. 45(r) at **figure 2a (p. 110 below)** (oriented foot-to-head, i.e. 'upside-down'); also at fol. 4r at **figure 2b (p. 110 below)** (head-to-foot) "[Pá]dr*aig* ui Chaoimh," "Daniel Lane of Johnstown"; (foot-to-head) aphorism " … from numbers and art / never will fairly depart …." Fol. 4r includes a series of '1s' and '0s', perhaps encoding a binary number. I am grateful to Prof. David Stifter and Dr. Deborah Hayden for answering my queries on this matter.

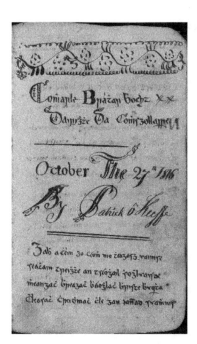

Fig. 1a - fol. 24r: well laid-out literary text at central stitching of volume

D L	A	2	3	D	E	F	8
Jan. Oct	Sun	satur	Frid	Thu	Wen	Tue	mun
May	mund	Sund	Satu	Frid	Thu	Wen	Tue
August	Tues	mund	Sund	Satu	Frid	Thu	Wen
Feb. Mar Novem	Wene	Tue	mund	Sun	Satu	Frid	Thu
June	Thur	Wene	Tues	mund	Sund	Satu	frid
Sep. Decem	Frid	Thur	Wen	Tues	mund	Sun	Satu
April July	Satur	Frid	Thur	Wene	Tues	mun	Sun

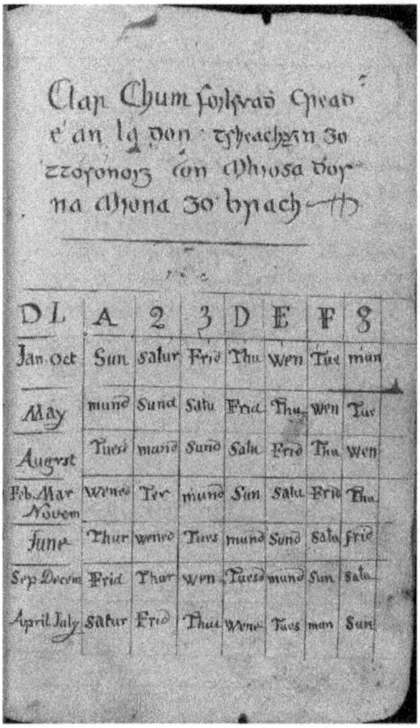

Fig. 1b - fol. 40r: clearly arranged calendrical table

Fig. 2a – fol. 45r: oriented foot-to-head ('upside-down')

Fig. 2b - fol. 4r: oriented head-to-foot (texts running in opposite directions)

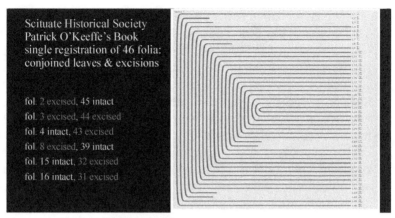

Scituate Historical Society
Patrick O'Keeffe's Book
single registration of 46 folia:
conjoined leaves & excisions

fol. 2 excised, 45 intact
fol. 3 excised, 44 excised
fol. 4 intact, 43 excised
fol. 8 excised, 39 intact
fol. 15 intact, 32 excised
fol. 16 intact, 31 excised

Fig. 3 - Collation per VCEditor (UPenn VisColl Project)

Fig. 4a - fol. 1v (text primarily reading from fore-edge)

We do not know at what point the missing leaves were removed. Their absence, however, tallies with some aspects of how the existing texts are arranged.[10] The initial removal, of two leaves following the first leaf at the front of the book, is partly mirrored by loss of a conjugate for the first of these excisions. Another removal of a single leaf precedes the longest poetic item of the collected writings. The next two, consecutive, removals precede an autograph and a transition to computistic subject-matter. The final removal, again of two consecutive leaves after a page and a half of personal computations, comes before a brief recurrence of literature on the final two leaves, and indeed also of authorial metadata and of certain early dates that appear to correspond to the beginning of the book.

The verso of leaf one, following a fragment on the recto of "Eachtra an Amadain m*h*or," contains faint notes of passage to and from Glanmire, Co. Cork, along with a "Capt. Leahy," and otherwise introduces the manuscript: "Patt Keeffe his Book / Dated June the 21st 1815 / wrote by Michael Keeffe ... / County of Cork . Borrowing of / Domhnall o Mahnuma" (sic).[11] Although the next surviving leaf, after the double excision (fol. 4, the recto seen at figure 2b), consists mostly of computations, Patrick O'Keeffe's name is given (in Irish) along with that of a "Daniel Lane of Johnstown," a designation which occurs once more on the verso of this leaf together with those of "M J [J J] Keefe," "Patrick O'Keeffe" again (now in English), and "Fermoy miles." It is not completely clear whether the Johnstown mentioned is one of two such townships which are close to Glanworth and Fermoy (see note 40 below), or perhaps less likely, Johnstown near to Glanmire and Cork Harbor.

---

[10]See **figure 3 (p. 111 above)** for the collation, utilizing VCEditor, available from the VisColl Project at UPenn.

[11]See **figure 4a (p. 111 above)** (reading from the fore-edge). Parts of certain inscriptions are as yet opaque to me. Wherever this is the case, such as with some of the text here, or in further references, I employ brackets or ellipses. Thus for the fourth line of the dedication: agus *ar* [abbreviation, then six-character word] *ch*uige *et* [words of two, two, and five characters (plus suspension-stroke and punctum)]. Furthermore, certain pages (e.g. fol. 7v: see figure 6b) appear to reveal palimpsest which will benefit from further analysis.

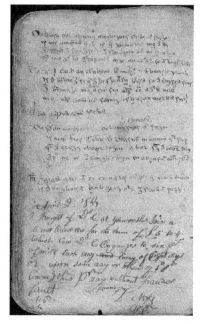

Fig. 4b - fol. 45v: (at head) five aisling verses (incomplete); (at foot): initialed deed for sale of cow, dated "April 2, 1855," "Bought of Dl L" (?) at "Glanworths Fair"

The final two leaves, at the end of the manuscript, offer, first, part of an account of expenses for 1817 and 1818 on the recto (seen upside-down at Figure 2a); and on the reverse, some stanzas of an *aisling* song followed, intriguingly, by an initialed record of the purchase of a cow at "Glanworths Fair," "April 2 1855," which will call for further mention.[12] Lastly, there are seven quatrains of a Fenian lay capped by an English aphorism,[13] then back-matter (including a scribal disclaimer) signed by "Patrick O'Keeffe, June the 22nd 1815," with

---

[12]See **figure 4b** (fol. 45v). There are five aisling verses, the third merely part of a first line, and the fifth just half of a verse. The series commences "Do bhíosa am aonar an uaigneas séal am shúighe . . . "

[13]The page (fol. 46r) is oriented upside-down, and the ornately written aphorism reads "Learning and manners / are charming companions." For the identical Fenian verses, compare ed. An Seabhac (Pádraig Ó Siocfhradha), *Laoithe na Féinne .i. Ceithre Laoithe agus Trí fichid den bhFiannaigheacht* (Dublin: Clólucht an Talbóidigh, 1941), 16-17 (ll. 905-48), from 'Agallamh Oisín agus Phádraig' (MS dated 1772). For several versions of the lay, see now the Fionn Folklore Database by Natasha

mention (reading from the head) of "Desmond," "Smith" and (from the foot) "Patrick Leddy" (twice).[14]

I will now briefly describe the remainder of the contents of "Patrick O'Keeffe's Book" in two unequal parts beginning at the second double excision, that is, the last third of the manuscript. On the recto of the leaf immediately after this double excision, at fol. 33r, is written "Boston February 20th 1847 … Boston, Och; But Old Érin na / [mech?] linn nó nár bpairt / June 30th 1847 Pat Keefe a Aois an tan so L.iv bliadhan / June 27th 1847 / Air na sgriobha a midhe meain an tsamhraidh / xxvii …":[15]

Fig. 5a - fol. 33r: dated indication of Patrick O'Keeffe's age with concurrent mention of Boston

Sumner, at https://fionnfolklore.org/#/lays/aop, last accessed December 20, 2022.

[14]This final page (fol. 46v) largely reads from the fore-edge, such as the autograph, which is headed by the disclaimer including "… you see this English / plain I am scarce …."

[15]Part of this inscription (see **figure 5a**) is as yet unclear to me (see the comment for fol. 1v, **figure 4a (p. 111 abov)** at note 11,), as is the case with parts of fol. 46v, mentioned in note 14 just above.

If this mention of Boston amounts to more than a quizzical comment, we appear to have a record here by Patrick O'Keeffe of his possible presence, or at least interest, in Boston for the times mentioned, at age 54, and thus evidence that O'Keeffe was born in 1792 or 1793.

Four leaves later comes a marginal inscription apparently indicating an earlier date: "Boston" and "Fermoy" with subtraction of the year "1816" from that of "1846" for a remainder of "30"; this calculation comes up yet again on the succeeding leaf.[16] There are occasional notes relating to shoemaking expenses and materials; to various as yet unidentified associates, and to occasions (such as a "fairday," a "wedding," and "Patricks day"); or to food, drink, business transactions, recreation ("Bowling Sunday"), and "Pennance / a Rosary ... for the / course of 2 weeks" dated "June the 9th 1819."[17]

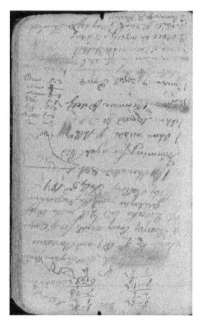

Fig. 5b - fol. 41v (reversing MS orientation to the reader)

---

[16]Thus fol. 37r (in pencil): "Boston / Fermoy" (l.h.); "1846 [-] 1816 / 30" (r.h.), while fol. 38r includes a table of golden numbers, epacts, and dominical letters from 1816 to 1846.

[17]See fols. 41v and 42r (each reversing MS orientation to the reader) at **figures 5b and 6a (p. 116 below)**; at fol. 45r (reversing MS orientation) is a note mentioning "... a horse for a load of Turf."

Fig. 6a - fol. 42r (reversing MS orientation to the reader)

Aside from this, the bulk of the last third of the book is taken up with computistical tables and explanations for determining epacts and positions of the moon, golden numbers, dominical letters, days of the weeks and months, leap-years, and of course Easter, according to the nineteen-year Dionysian lunar cycle.[18] After all of this, yet preceding the final two-leaf excision that separates the final leaves and their folkloric matter from the foregoing, comes a one-page Irish synopsis of the *Leabhar Gabhála Éireann* (Book of the Taking of Ireland).[19] This appears again to reflect the computistical, as well as the

---

[18]E.g. fols. 33b-37r, 38r-41r, and cf. **figure 1b (p. 109 above)** (fol. 40r). See fol. 35r: "The Julian Calender." However, problematic marginal readings for fols. 7v and 37r (Appendix 2 below, and cf. **figure 6b (p. 117 below)**, apparently mention Gregorian reckonings.

[19]"*Partholanus* mac Seara an [t-]*ochtmhadh* / glúin ó Noah *agus* do t*hir*ibh Magog … do g*h*louis o t*hír* . *Mhigdonia* … do / g*h*aibh tala*mh* . an Inb*h*er Sceine san / dtaob*h* t*hí*ar de M*h*um*h*ain . san mbl*iadhain* an / Dom*h*ain … 1978 …." The chronology of 'the Taking of Ireland' ends with the "Fir Bolgs . A.M . 2503" and "Slainge," briefly adding reigns of "Rúraidhe" and "Geanan*n*" (fol. 42v with foreign terms in cursive script).

historical, interests of O'Keeffe, or of the O'Keeffes. (Michael signs his name to one item in the series of computistic pages.)[20]

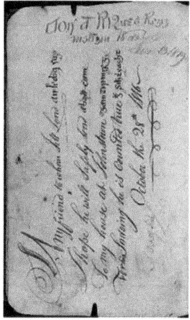

Fig. 6b - fol. 7v (text primarily reading from fore-edge): macaronic verse on loan of Patrick O'Keeffe's book

Along with other material included in the computistic section are alphanumerological estimations. The first of these allows one to tell which of a married couple will be first to die: write the woman's and the man's proper names in Latin, add the numerical values of all the letters in their names using a superscribed table, and divide by seven; if the resulting number is even, the woman will die first, if odd, the man.[21] The second is for ascertaining the fidelity or otherwise of a woman:

---

[20]Directions for such a table on a facing page (fol. 41r) signed at the foot of fol. 40v "By Micheal O Keeffe." The page which carries the inscription, as so many others, displays ornamental, perhaps serendipitous, pencil-scribbling.
[21]My synopsis of the Irish at fol. 37v, beneath which is (as follows) a somewhat different section in English: "To find whether it is a male or female / that is in its mothers womb, write the Father and mothers name and

A way to know whether a woman / bee geanmuid*he*
no Druiseamhuil [chaste or lascivious] ɔ / Firs[t] write
her own name and her Mothers name and give their
own / No to every letter and add to *the* total / No 15
and divide by 7, and if the and [end] No bee Even she
is geanmach / if odd Druiseamhuil ~ / Dated
December 14 1829 [22]

Several of the computistic entries are in English only. Nowhere
in the manuscript does Michael O'Keeffe's autograph or other
mention of him occur in Irish. However, some of the calendrical
explanations include Irish along with the English, as does the
estimation of a woman's fidelity, which is followed by a promissory
note initialled by "M K" and by two others. As mentioned, Patrick
O'Keeffe signs and dates the manuscript's very last page: his
autograph here follows a kind of deprecatory English-verse
colophon.[23] The signed and dated sale of the cow at "Glanworths Fair"
possibly by one "D¹ L" (Daniel Lane perhaps?) in "1855" on the leaf
preceding this, again, is difficult to explain if the manuscript indeed
came to Boston by 1847 or 1846. It is unlikely that such a record would
be of more than local use.[24]

---

the month / She Conceived add *the* whole together and / Divide by 7 if Even
it is a Daughter / if odd a son - / to know whether the Infant will live long or
not the Father and moth*ers* / name and the name of *the* day it will / be born
add 25 to the No and D by 7 / if even quickly and odd long life."
[22]At the head of fol. 34v. At the foot is an agreement made out to "Patrick O
Keeffe" (erasure of "Mich-" preceding) for a payment on "November next,"
which is dated the "16th" day of February 18230" (sic). The small
(punctuating?) character in the section quoted here is not intelligible to me.
See my comment at note 58 below and cf. the mark at fol. 46v (Appendix
2). Various markings (many of which appear to be isolated) occur
throughout the manuscript, awaiting expert palaeographical analysis,
including assessment of hands and inks.
[23]See fol. 46v (from the fore-edge) comparing note 14 above: "In Writing
fair you Plainly see / I am D(*ene*)generateing free / And no wonder indeed /
for my fingers are cramped I feel ...."
[24]See **figure 4b (p. 113 above)**: initialed deed for sale of cow, dated "April
2, 1855," "Bought of D¹ L" (?) at "Glanworths Fair" (fol. 45v at foot).
Written upside-down at the foot is "I demand."

The first two thirds of the O'Keeffe Book differ markedly from the final third, again discounting the surviving leaves that commence the volume. These leaves appear to mimic those at the end in the apparent miscellaneous nature of their popular literary items, or by their table-of-contents-like mention not just of person and time of writing, but also of place, if not of cause. The chronology ranges from "June the 21st 1815," recorded on the effective title-page, as seen, to "November the 12th … 1816" within the bodies of these largely-writ texts, except that marginal notes also mark "March 13 1819," as well as "April 7th, 1818."[25]

Immediately after the front matter is a collection of proverbs entitled "Com*har*le na ba*i*rr [bard-] scológe *dá* m*h*ac" ('Advice of the rustic-poet to his pupil') many of which are familiar to Irish-speakers from recent decades.[26] This popular text is included, for example, in commonplaces such as Royal Irish Academy Manuscript 23 K 9, written during 1821 in Co. Kerry,[27] which also contains devotional and

---

[25]Thus for the large poem concluding at fol. 30v: "Finished November the 12th Anno Domini 1816 &c" (at the foot of the page is a separate inscription, largely erased and all but illegible). "March 13 1819" (fol. 7v reading from head of page). "Matrimon April 7th, 1818" (fol. 12r marginal inscription at foot). A date "1814-9" appears at fol. 46v (see Appendix 2).
[26]They were sufficiently well known during the middle of the twentieth century to be included in school-certifications or school textbooks. See, for example, ed. Aindrias Ó Muimhneacháin, *Dánta Meán-Teastais, 1963-64*. Téacsa Gaedhilge le haghaidh na Meadhon-Scol (Dublin: Comhlucht Oideachais na h-Éireann, 1963-64), at 52-53: "Ná bí crua is ná bí bog …"; cf. the O'Keeffe book at fol. 5v: "Na bí bóg *et* na bi c*rú*aig …." A "Comhairle na Bardscolóige dhon bhFear Óg a bhí ag Lorg Mná," related to our text by its use of proverbial advice, occurs in the *dúchas.ie* Main Manuscript Collection, Volume 0328, Page 0029 (November 1, 1935; Cloghane, Co. Kerry; Seán Óg Ó Dubhda, collector; Séamus Ó Muircheartaigh, informant): https://www.duchas.ie/en/cbe/9000321/ 7158787/9071684, last accessed December 10, 2022. I am grateful to Andreas Vogel of Muintearas, Tír an Fhia (e-mail, September 6, 2022), for pointing to this source as well as to further traditions of the *bardscológ*.
[27]Fol. 5r (head) to 6v. The upper margin contains the inscription "Patrick Leddy" (cf. fol. 46v, reading foot-to-head). For the collection of proverbs and other materials, compare ed. Kathleen Mulchrone, *Catalogue of Irish*

grammatical materials, *barántas* or 'warrant' poetry, and a poem by "Seaghan Rúadh Ó Seitheachain," of which more shortly. A two-and-a-half-quatrain fragment of "Téallach flait*h*is fine c*h*aoim*h*" (sic) a poem written to Art mac Airt Uí Chaoimh (Keeffe) by Tadhg mac Dáire Mac Bruaideadha, Clare poet and bard to the Fourth Earl of Thomond, Donnchadh Ó Briain, follows this.[28] Mac Bruaideadha is known as instigator, in 1616, of 'The Contention of the Bards' (*Iomarbhágh na bhFileadh*), representing Ireland's Southern Half in challenging the Northern disciples of a legendary early Irish poet, Torna Éigeas.[29] After this, and preceding the excision of a single leaf comes a dated macaronic (Irish and English) quatrain asking borrowers of the book to return it to O'Keeffe in Johnstown.[30]

Following the excision, and continuing for twelve leaves, is the manuscript's longest item, a translation of a celebrated poem by the Iveragh poet and spuriously reputed bishop John O'Connell. Entitled "Tuireamh na hÉireann," also termed "Aiste Sheáin Uí Chonaill," the poem was composed between 1655 and 1659; it is here called "John O'Connell's Poem," in ninety-two simplified English verses capped with a concluding prayer. This account of Ireland's national myth or fate, interweaving biblical, classical, local, and confessional history from the Flood up to post-Cromwellian depredations and exile, was

---

Manuscripts in the Royal Irish Academy, Fasciculus IV (Dublin: Hodges, Figgis & Co.; London: Williams & Norgate, 1929), no. 192, 511-13, especially at 513 (MS pp. 57-58).

[28]"Tag*h*dg m*a*c Daire c*e*cin*i*t / Téallach flait*h*is fine c*h*aoim*h* ... " (fol. 7r), cf. the Bardic Poetry Database at https://bardic.celt.dias.ie/ displayPoem. php?firstLineID=1810, last accessed December 10, 2022. O'Keeffe has written initial letters for the last two lines of the incomplete quatrain, affording the viewer a glimpse of the copying process. The same page (foot-to-head) includes an itemized account for cash, wine, candles, and sugar.

[29]Ed. Lambert McKenna, *Iomarbhágh na bhFileadh: The Contention of the Bards*. Irish Texts Society Vols. 20-21. (London: Irish Texts Society, 1918-19 [1920]). See Joep Leerssen, *The Contention of the Bards (Iomarbhágh na bhFileadh) and Its Place in Irish Political and Literary History*. Irish Texts Society Subsidiary Series 2 (London: Irish Texts Society, 1994).

[30]See fol. 7v at **figure 6b, (p. 117 above)** (reading foot-to-head from the fore-edge). This brings to mind the inscription "Borrowing of / Domhnall O Mahnumna" at fol. 1v, **figure 4a (p. 111 above)**.

enormously popular, and portable, and often occurs more than once within several of the over one-hundred manuscripts that include it.

O'Keeffe's English version, which he dates at its finale to "October the 15th 1816," begins, "Irish heroes when I remind," a translation attributed variously to Diarmuid Ó Conchubhair in National Library of Ireland Manuscript G210, written in 1811 and of Limerick provenance; or, in a Cork manuscript of 1823 (Royal Irish Academy 23 G 10), to Daniel Cantlon of Drumcolliher. In a third manuscript of 1839 (24 C 26), the scribe merely credits the English to "a hedge-school-master."[31] Beyond its affinity to the south of Ireland, along with other materials compiled in the book, what is most remarkable about this poem's inclusion in our manuscript is its witness to O'Keeffe's integrative traditional view of history. As indicated, O'Connell's poem concludes with a prayer for pardon from sin. This is repeated at the head of the following leaf, and large swash letters with animal forms emphasize its ornate *finis*. That conclusion, if not also the piece on the following leaf, is signed "Wrote by Patt O'Keeffe" at the foot of that opposite leaf.[32]

---

[31]The poem, thus dated with a flourish on its last page, commences at fol. 9r and continues to fol. 20v, the introduction reading "... written by Patrick Ó Keeffe ... October *the* 13th / anno domini 1816 &c"; cf. "October an xvi m*h*adh lá deg 1816" (fol. 15v). See ed. Cecile O'Rahilly, *Five Seventeenth-Century Political Poems* (Dublin: Dublin Institute for Advanced Studies, 1952), Chap. 4, 50-82 (at 57), notes, 132-63. Cf. ed. Nessa Ní Shéaghdha, *Catalogue of Irish Manuscripts in the National Library of Ireland.* Fasciculus VI . Mss. G 208 - 257 (Dublin: Dublin Institute for Advanced Studies, 1980), at 2 (G 210 Tuireamh na hÉireann): "'Honeypound County Limk.' 1811 (p. 1) ... [Page 2] 'Eachtra tSeaghain Ui Connuill sonn arna haistriughadh ... go Bearla le Diarmaid O Concubhar' ...["The Adventure (?) of Seán Ó Conaill here ... translated to English by Diarmaid Ó Conchubhair"] 368 lines in numbered quatrains (92) with English translation beg. *Irish heroes when I remind ....*" For O'Keeffe's own apparent attribution of English renditions of some of the verses drawn upon for his text to one "David Mahoney" see the marginal entry for fol. 21v at Appendix 2 below.

[32]At fol. 20v the finale of the poem, preceding the ornate *finis*, reads "That pardon for our sins we may obtain / may Irish their rights regain / that our Religeon may turn the scale / So let all Christians say **Amen**." The pencil

O'Keeffe remains true to his patriotic theme, moving forward and taking to task, it would seem, the notorious Cork satirist Aonghus Ruadh na nAor Ó Dálaigh (c. 1550-1617), who amidst varying loyalties was eventually compelled by Sir George Carew to lampoon the Irish poets. There ensues a formal introductory mock 'warrant', again in macaronic Irish and English, summonsing Aonghus to the court of poetry to receive a verbal lashing for his crimes.[33] The fluid

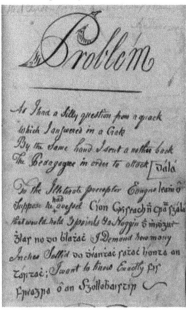

Figure 7a - fol. 21r: versified English and Irish prologue directed to "Eangus leamh Ó \Dála/"

inscription at fol 21r (head) reads: "I Do Implore the father son & Holy gost / that pardon for our sins we may obtain / A me-" [? =Ame[n]]. Verses 3, 64, 74 and 89 are hypermetric (brackets for insertions used for the last three of these).

[33]See **figure 7a** (fol. 21r): a versified English and Irish ad hominem prologue directed to "*Eangus* leam*h* Ó \Dála/," with the ensuing formal poetic warrant (fol. 21v at **figure 7b (p. 123 below)** likewise presented to "*Eangus* leam*h* Ó Dala" (italicization of the forename here indicating anglicization). Each text concludes with an *explicit* (*forcheann*). For the career of the satirist, see e.g. Darren McGettigan, "Ó Dálaigh, Aonghus (Aengus O'Daly)," *Dictionary of Irish Biography*, https://www.dib.ie/biography/o-dalaigh-aonghus-aengus-odaly-a6327, last revised October, 2009 (DOI: https://doi.org/10.3318/dib.006327.v1).

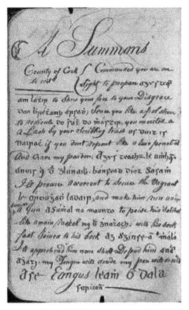

Fig. 7b - fol. 21v: formal poetic warrant presented to "Eangus leamh Ó Dala"

association of confessional, patriotic, and poetic concerns continues through the next item, a sixteen-quatrain poetic spiritual remonstrance by "Seaghan Rúadh / Ó Seitheachain" (so far unidentified) to his former pupil, "Dá[i]th[í] Ó Mhathghamhna" (sic) which censures the recipient for abandoning the Catholic faith in favor of the Protestant "teampcoill" [= church], marrying an English or Protestant woman, and using English law to bring about oppression.[34]

This plea for national and credal unity equates Ó Mathghamhna's decisions with the deadly sin of gluttony, and levels at him the

---

[34]Fol. 22r: "Seaghan Rúadh / Ó Seitheachain cecinit ///// [ornamental divider] Cé gur bhfada mé am mhaighea[s]tair air feraibh desmhúneach ...." ['Although I was long a master of the men of Desmond ...'] The poem continues to fol. 23v. Its four-line prologue (elided before the divider above) reads: "Do Dháth: Ó Mhathghamhna [sic] .i. sgolare bócht do thoig se air / a sgoil, diompuig chum teampcoill, ₇ do phós / bean galldha, et do bhí acúr an dlighe dforsa air / [MS: Csean?] go ndubairt Seaghan &c&c&c ₇-c" (to Dáithí Ó Mathghamhna, that is, a poor scholar whom he raised in / his school, who converted to the [protestant or English] church and who married / a [Protestant or English] woman, and he was putting the law of force upon [him?] / [?] so that Seán said ...). I am grateful to Aidan Doyle for pointing out the semantics of 'gallda'.

threatening prospects of mortality and a grim afterlife, contrasted with the reward for those, such as the author, who heed historical examples and obey the Pope. Like the "Comhairle na bard-scolóige dá mhac", this work which, like its introductory texts, finishes with an *explicit* ("*finis or* fórc*hean*n"), also appears in Royal Irish Academy Manuscript 23 K 9 in sixteen quatrains. An eighteen-quatrain version of the poem may be found in Harvard Irish Manuscript 9, a commonplace compiled circa 1833 in Co. Tipperary.[35]

The next contribution, begun right after the central stitching, is another teagasg poem, the "Counsel of Encouragement by a Poor Brother to his Fellow-Scholar." This consists of fifteen eschatalogically-tinged quatrains of exhortation drawing upon classical exempla, described at their conclusion as a "Piouswork" and with a Latin flourish) as a "Petision."[36] Following this, on the verso-leaf, is a metrical aphorism in two verses, the second of whichis translated into Irish,[37] and the next leaf bears a macaronic proverbial

[35]Citation at note 27 above, text at MS pages 37-40. The Harvard version occurs at pages 69-71 of that MS. See Cornelius G. Buttimer, *A Catalogue of Irish Manuscripts in Houghton Library, Harvard University* (Notre Dame, Indiana: University of Notre Dame Press, 2022), 44. For an "Ó Seitheacháin, Pilip (Philip Hyde)," mentioned in RIA MS 23 N 23, fl. 1778-79 likely in Co. Cork ("agus, b'fhéidir, sa Chóbh" ['and, perhaps, in Cove']), see Breandán Ó Conchúir, *Scríobhaithe Chorcaí 1700-1850*. Leabhair Thaighde. An 41ú hImleabhar (Dublin: An Clóchomhar, 1982), 176.

[36]At fol. 24 recto, **figure 1a, (p. 109 above)**: "Com*h*arle Brát*h*ar bocht . x x / Daiing*hth*e [sic] da C*h*om*h*sgolla*i*rre ..." (with ornate header); the poem concludes ornately (fol. 26r): "Finis With that" "Piouswork" / "Petisionque." A version of An t-Athair Uilleam Ua hÍcidhe's admonishments (1684) to Cian Ó Mathghamhna to take religious orders rather than marry a woman of high rank. Compare ed. Cuthbert Mhág Craith, *Dán na mBráthar Mionúr, Vol. 1.* Scríbhinní Gaeilge na mBráthar Mionúr. Imleabhar 8. (Dublin: Dublin Institute for Advanced Studies, 1967), 331-35. I am thankful to Andreas Vogel for these references (e-mail, September 6, 2022).

[37]Fol. 26v: "Kinsmen ... // If you be poor be sure no freedom make / for you are a fool tho sure and wise you spoke / But if you be rich and Spring from the race of Clowns / Your actions are good and words of high renown

disclaimer by the scribe followed by "Patrick O'Keeffe's Book" with calculations continuing on the verso.[38]

These precede a sixteen-stanza version of Eoghan Ruadh Ua Súilleabháin's "A Éigse is Suadha" or "Barántas an Hata," which is headed by a prologue in praise of the poet, and which, as we have seen, concludes with the statement "Finished November the 12th Anno Domini 1816": The poet's stolen hat, with powers that would coax heroines from Irish and classical mythology, functions as a metaphor for his amorous and poetic achievements, which have been illegitimately credited to another, and as a device to introduce significant places of poetic assembly in Ireland's Southern Half. "Barántas an Hata", again in sixteen stanzas, makes up part of the same Harvard Irish Manuscript 9 that contains a copy of Seán Ruadh Ó Seitheacháin's poem.[39]

In O'Keeffe's manuscript the second major loss of two leaves comes immediately after Ua Súilleabháin's "Barántas an Hata," the next surviving page, leaf 33 recto, being that which seems to mark O'Keeffe's presence in, or cognizance of, Boston during 1847. Upside-down on this is a note in English, "Osia[n] to Oisin son of Finn," which is curious given the snippet of *fiannaíocht* on the

---

// Spare not nor spend too much be this your care / Spare but to Spend and only spend to spare / For he that spends too much may want & so Complain / But he spends best that spares to spend a gain // Translation of [the second half of] the above // na caith is na taisg ar feadh do sholáthair / taisg chum chaite is caith chuim cimeata / an té chathionn go leamh biadh aneasbaidh et gearánfadh / san té taisgios chuim caite is fearra baranta ...." The selection concludes with an *explicit* ("forcheann leis an méid sin").

[38]Fol. 27r (head-to-foot) includes calculations and calendrical reckonings together with the name "Armstrong"; and (reading towards the fore-edge from the gutter) a scribal disclaimer in English and Irish: "All ye Courtious Readers do chioinn gach locht / That I with Speed do sgriobh ann so / Excuse me mar na bionn púinn gan lócht / And the Vices unseen by me deisíg gán doic."

[39]Fol. 28r and 28v present the encomiastic introduction of the poet and the formal prologue; the poem commences on fol. 28 v and continues to fol. 30v. Compare ed. Pádraig Ó Fiannachta, *An Barántas I: Réamhrá-Téacs-Malairtí* (Maynooth: An Sagart, 1978), 34-36 (the identical prologue and sixteen stanzas) with the version in Harvard Irish MS 9, p. 19 ff., consisting of eighteen stanzas with a short preamble (personal inspection).

reversed recto of the final leaf, folio 46. Whether or when Patrick O'Keeffe came to Boston, his book spent an unspecified time near Cork Harbor. However, as seen, it seems to have had at least one foot well planted in northern Co. Cork near Fermoy.[40] The jottings in the booklet contain several names, including "Mick." (Is this Michael O'Keeffe, perhaps Patrick's brother? The term "father" comes up separately in these accounts, although whether the scribe is Michael or Patrick is uncertain.)[41] Little is known to date about the other names; they partly overlap and mirror one another according to the

---

[40]Johnstown East, Civil Parish of Dunmahon, Barony of Fermoy: https://www.logainm.ie/10286.aspx, lat., long. 52.1686, -8.35229. Another Johnstown, farther north, Civil Parish of Kilgullane, Barony of Condons and Clangibbon, near Mitchelstown seems less likely: https://www.logainm.ie/12811.aspx, lat., long. 52.2518, -8.33321.

[41]Thus fol. 45r at figure 2a (reversed, foot-to-head) "To 2 removes *payed* [?] Mich*eal*," "1 remove *payed* [?] Mich*eal* ..."; but fol. 41v (reversed, foot-to-head) "4 Nails *payed* [?] Mick *the* day before ...," and fol. 45r "... Mick 1 Gall of a Sunday ...." Cf. fol. 45r "To [For] ... 2 removes *pay* [?] father ...." Fols. 41v and 42r (see **figures 5b (p. 115 above)** and **6a, (p. 116 above))** contain several further such examples.

[42]

Names, fols. 1-5r		Names, fols. 46-41v	
(2, 3 excised):		(44, 43 excised):	
Capt. Leahy	1v	Lowry, **D-1**	46v
Domhhnall o Mahnumna		**Patrick Leddy**	
Woo(d?), S(a?)m Penrose(?)		Desmond?	
Elizabeth, Dau(id?)		Smith [Coss?]	
Catherine o Niul	4r	Conn [Ciam(h)sa?]	
E(CS?) [reverse]		Initials (ML? M? M+I? T+S?)	45v
Daniel Lane	4r, 4v	Mich*eal*, father, Mick,	45r
John Everton	4v	Jerry, Madden	
Patrick Leddy	5r	Madden, Mrs Leddy, Tim, Fintin	42r
		Eoghan Roach, Curtin, Delor,	
		Lanes, Th*om*as, J*oh*n,	
		Daniel Lane , J-n S*iur*tin	
		Larry Sulevan, J. Curtin	
Additional names or initials:		Mrs Ryan, father, Mick,	41v
Armstrong	27r	Patsy Slattery, Th*om*as [Wh- ?]	
MK, E+Tly[?],	34r		
M+Tly{?}			
('+' = "marks")			

126

layout of the O'Keeffe volume.[42] No person putatively on the North American continent other than Patrick O'Keeffe himself is mentioned.

We have here a portable, personal volume that may have arrived in Boston in the midst of the Great Famine, but this is altogether uncertain. At any rate, O'Keeffe's fortunes during both this calamity and the decades between it and the period of the great majority of earlier entries in the volume (c. 1815 x 1818) are opaque. It would seem that he made his living reasonably well early on, as a shoemaker (mentioning iron, steel, nails, trimming, mending, soles, removes, washers, and pens); he keeps accounts of his trade and of foodstuffs (dairy and eggs); and notes the volumes and quantities of these, as well as of barley and sugar (possibly for poteen), whiskey, spirits (*biotaile*), medicaments (*leasa*), cash, and turf.[43]

Nothing is altogether peculiar about O'Keeffe's, or the O'Keeffes', cursive English scripts, occasional orthographic oddities, catch-words and insertions, bits of scribal Latin, marks of local English plausibly originating in Irish (for which several apologies are made), or Irish dialect. The compilers, Patrick foremost, it appears, switch fluently between well-learned, though not polished, English, less straitened English, and colloquial or formal Irish which is always written in traditional script, albeit with a mildly irregular range of pre-standardized Modern Irish spellings and abbreviations.[44] Hands in the

---

[43] As indicated (see notes 17 and 41), most of these accounts are listed on fols. 41v, 42r, and 45r, each with inverse orientation ('upside-down') to the reader. See further figures 5b, 6a, and 2a. Briefer lists (strictly of consumable items) occur at fols. 33r (see figure 5a) and 7r (reading foot-to-head).

[44] Irish orthography: -*n* for -*nn*, -*u*- for -*a*-, -*io*- for -*ea*-, -*cc*- for -*g*-, lack of glide vowels (consonant quality), irregular markings of length and lenition, double spellings to mark length, e.g. at fol. 23v úgh*dar* (vs. *údar* or *ughdar*). English orthography: e.g. myselve 4v, deseid 21v, courtious 27r, Calender 35r, centuary 36r, colums 40v, derection 40v, peid 41v. Scribal features: e.g. prepositions *do* and *go*, conjunction *nó*, as consonant plus double suspension-stroke with or without punctum delens. English morphology, syntax, pronunciation: e.g. countay 1v, points (pints) 21r, goeth 36r, As I ... believes 37r, Excuse any ... Defects that is here 37r, As you .... sees 38v, Fir Bolgs 42v. Local Irish dialect (arguably O'Keeffe(s)

manuscript vary in formality, emphasis, and style. As mentioned, the punctuation and capitalization amount to a pause and effect augmented by spacing, dividers, ornaments, and variation in the size of scripts in brown or black inks, or in pencil.

This highly selective, sometimes quirky, bilingual collection of devotional, monitory, patriotic, poetic, and personal history might have come to Scituate at almost any time in any number of ways. That having been said, O'Keeffe's book would *appear* to have arrived there previous to the advent of Irish mossing during the American Civil War and the extensive development of the mossing business in Scituate by Daniel Ward of Coleraine thereafter. (Ward came to Scituate from Boston in 1847.)[45] But it is difficult to tell. Sources possibly shedding light on the career of a Patrick O'Keeffe in North America, or of Michael, if either one of them came here at all, from 1846 onwards, have turned up nothing conclusive in local archives–governmental, ecclesiastical, or amalgamated personal sources–whether online or otherwise.[46] Records of ship arrivals in New York City and in New England during this time have been similarly unproductive.[47] The

---

vs. possible transcriptions): e.g. c*hum* (chugam) 7v, bánfead (vs. bainfidh mé) 21v, do *chioinn* (fheiceann) 27r, na bion*n* (nach mbíonn) 27r, ma t*h*igid*h* (má thagann) 37v, do c*hidhfear* (feicfear) 39v, so (seo) 39v, ttosónóig 40r. Latinate admixtures: Petisionque 26r, Finis with that Piouswork (ibidem), but som is nothingum 37r. For in-depth treatment of some of these features of language, see Aidan Doyle, *A History of the Irish Language* (Oxford: Oxford University Press, 2015), Chap. 6 "A New Language for a New Nation (1800-70)," 107-160, especially at 141-57: "The Shape of the Language (1800-70)."

[45]Barbara Murphy, *Irish Mossers and Scituate Harbour Village* (Scituate: Scituate Historical Society, 1980), 1 (Daniel Ward moves to Scituate), 21-22 (1862-63 earliest mention of mossing activities in Scituate). I am grateful to Mary Porter for directing me to this excellent book.

[46]Among sources in the search for a Patrick or Michael O'Keeffe coming to Greater Boston Area, those consulted but otherwise not listed below include FamilySearch, the Boston Archdiocesan Archives, the Massachusetts State Archives, the Massachusetts Historical Society, and the New England Historic Genealogical Society, and Irish Genealogy.

[47]E.g. New York, New York, *Index to Passenger Lists, 1820-1846*, NARA microfilm publication M261, rolls 50 [m] and 74 [o] (Washington, D.C.:

remainder of this study therefore merely offers a few examples or directions for further enquiry, some of which may be disappointing (if instructive), while others may prove promising if additional evidence comes to light.

A request concerning "PATRICK O'KEEFE native of Glanmire, county Cork, who sailed from Liverpool in ship Virginia for New York about 12th March 1846 . . . by his brother, JOHN, care of Mr. PATRICK MCCARTHY, Northampton Street Boston Ms." is entered as an advertisement in *The Boston Pilot* for November 22nd, 1851.[48] Intriguingly, a "P. O'Keeffe" is listed for *The Boston Pilot* as a subscriber in 1849, and a "Patk O'Keeffe" in November of 1847 as a possible member of the non-sectarian Boston Confederation for Repeal of the Union of Ireland with Britain.[49] However, there are no provable connections here.

National Archives and Records Administration, n.d.), archives.gov/research /immigration/customs.records-1820-1891.html#nyk. Ed. Ira A. Glazier and Michael Tepper, *The Famine Immigrants: Lists of Irish Immigrants Arriving at the port of New York, 1846-1851* (Baltimore: Genealogical Publication Company, 1983), with thanks to Prof. Emerita Catherine B. Shannon for this reference. I am likewise grateful to John McColgan, Archivist, City of Boston Archives, and to Assistant Archivist, Meghan Pipp, for guidance in consulting the *Superintendent of Alien Passengers Lists, 1837-1847* (3 vols); the *Record of the Proceedings of the Alien Passenger Committee* (Deer Island Hospital listings) (June, 1847-); and the *Boston Directory*, 1846-58 (see note 50 below).
[48]*The Boston Pilot* (1838-1857), Volume 14, Number 47, November 22, 1851, Page 4, Advertisements, Column 3 ("INFORMATION WANTED"), https://newspapers.bc.edu/?a=d&d=bpilott18511122-01.2.8.3&e=-en-20--1-txt-txIN-. Many ships came to North America from Cork via Liverpool during the Famine. I am thankful to Meghan Pipp (e-mail, October 22, 2021) for sharing a copy of the June 5th 1855 Boston City Census record for Ward 11 which lists "Patrick McCarty" as one of three male occupants of a home on Northhampton Street, and the contemporary Ward 11 tax assessment, which lists the same "Pat McCarty" as a "Shoemaker."
[49]*The Boston Pilot* (1838-1857), Volume 12, Number 47, November 24, 1849, Page 7, Advertisements, Column 2 (receipt from "P. O'Keeffe" of "Newton Corner" for $1 subscription), https://newspapers.bc.edu/ ?a=d&d=bpilott18491124-01.2.29.2&e=-en-20--1--txt-txIN--. *The Boston*

An "O'Keefe, John, bootmaker" appears in The Boston Directory between 1854 and 1856; a "McCarty, Patrick, shoemaker" of "83 Northampton" is listed at that address from 1851 to 1858; and an "O'Keefe" or "Keefe," "Patrick, shoemaker," is noted at various addresses on "Ann" [Street] between 1846 and 1852. There are further listings, of an "O'Kee[f]fe, Patrick, shoemaker" for 1853 at "467 Commercial," and of a "Keefe, John, laborer," "476 Commercial" for the same year.[50] Despite the interesting correspondence between "Patrick McCart[h]y" of "Northampton" noted here and in The Boston Pilot advertisement and 1855 Boston Ward 11 census and tax records, any pertinence to an O'Keeffe having to do with our manuscript remains conjectural.

There is a very problematic record of the arrival of a "Patrick Keeff" in New York on the *Virginian* on April 28th, 1847; this is over two months beyond the "Boston February 20th 1847" inscription by Patrick O'Keeffe in his book (which admittedly may be a desideratum or other utterance rather than a statement of arrival), not to mention

---

Pilot (1838-1857), Volume 10, Number 47, November 20, 1847, Page 7, Advertisements, Column 2 ("Patk O'Keeffe" listed at $1 among "NAMES OF CONTRIBUTORS" to the "BOSTON CONFEDERATION"), https://newspapers.bc.edu/?a=d&d=bpilott18471120-01.2.28.2&e=-en-20-1-txt-txIN-.

[50]*The Boston Directory* (Boston: Adams, Sampson, 1846-1858) (no results for 1847, 1857; 1850 lacking):

1846: (p. 93, col 2): Keefe Patrick, shoe maker [sic], house 275 Ann.
1848-9: (168, 1) [the same]
1851: (139, 2) Keefe, Patrick, shoemaker, house 259 Ann
       (166, 1) McCarty Patrick, shoemaker, h. Northampton
             (shoemakers Patrick McCarty [166] and David O'Keefe
             [188] listed respectively at h. 5 and 12 Sullivan place)
1852: (194, 1) O'Keefe Patrick, boarding, 109 Ann
       (171,1) McCarty Patrick, shoemaker, h. Northampton
1853: (188, 2) McCarty Patrick, shoemaker, h. 38 [83] Northampton
             (shoemaker Patrick O'Keefe [214, 3] h. 467 Commercial;
             laborer John Keefe [160, 1] h. 476 Commercial)
1854: (234, 1) O'Keefe John, bootmaker, house rear 809 Wash.
1855: (201, 2) McCarty Patrick, shoemaker, h. 83 Northampton
1856: (257, 1) O'Keefe John, bootmaker, house 11 Channing
       (224, 2) McCarty Patrick, shoemaker, h. 83 Northampton

the possibly earlier "Boston" jottings therein, unless O'Keeffe, whatever age he was, disembarked and reboarded at different ports of call.[51]

The most promising, if inconclusive, lead not inconsistent with O'Keeffe's having resided temporarily in Boston is a certification of United States citizenship dated "October 26th 1855" for a Patrick Keeffe, of East Bridgewater, some twenty miles southwest of Scituate, who claims to have arrived in Boston on May 30th, 1847 (fourteen-and-a half months after the sailing of the Virginia noted in The Boston Pilot), but who also happens to be fifty-five years old in 1855 and born on March 17th, 1800.[52] His place of origin is said to be the townland and parish of Kilworth, Cork, a short distance east of Glanworth and north of Fermoy, in the Barony of Condons and Clangibbon. In the Federal Census for 1850 this Keeffe, designated as a "laborer," is already in East Bridgewater, with his wife Catherine, who is forty-three, and his seven children, who are spaced by two years each,

---

[51]"The New York, U.S., Immigration Arrival Records, 1846-1851" list a "Patrick Keeff: *Age 800*" [sic! for *80*?] without any date of birth: "Embarkation: Liverpool . Ship: Virginian . Occupation: *Grower* . Compartment: Cabin . Native Country: *Great Britain*. Arrival Place: New York, New York . Arrival Date: *28 Apr 1847*." I have italicized the several troublesome aspects of this record. Search on *Ancestry.com* communicated to me October 29, 2021, photocopy via e-mail, August 17, 2022, by Scituate Historical Society volunteer Charlie Cook.

[52] "Massachusetts, U.S., State and Federal Naturalization Records, 1798-1850. District Court, Massachusetts . Primary Declarations of Intention, Vol. 10A (Cont, P 264-End) - V 11 (P 1-623, Cont), 1855-1857." A certificate of naturalization, dated at its foot "October 26th 1855" reads in part: "... *Patrick Keeffe* of *East Bridgewater* in the District–an alien and a free white person born at *Kilworth Ireland* in the *County of Cork* on or about the *Seventeenth* day of *March*, in the year of our Lord eighteen hundred and ~~ and is now about *Fifty five* years of age: that he arrived at *Boston* in the District of *Massachusetts* the United States of America, on or about the *Thirtieth* of *May* [?] in the year of our Lord eighteen hundred and *forty seven* . . . " [Patrick Keeffe's name inscribed and notarized with "this mark" 'X']. I am thankful to Charlie Cook for making note of this record (e-mail, October 19, 2021), and to Robin Sarah Penick, Archive Technician, National Archives, for making an image of this record available to me (e-mail, October 22, 2021).

ranging from eighteen to six, the two eldest (John and Michael) listed as shoemakers.[53] By the 1865 Massachusetts Census, however, he adjusts his age to seventy-three while making no such augmentation for his wife (she is fifty-six).[54] Seventy-three is just the age our own Patrick O'Keeffe would be in 1865, having been born in 1792. Whoever this person in East Bridgewater was, he was creative with numbers: in the 1870 Federal Census he is back to age seventy and his wife has only aged to fifty-seven.[55] His signature of choice is uniformly an 'X', which appears odd for a literate person. In 1865 and in 1870 (for the second of which he is termed a "farmhand") it is noted that he is able neither to read nor to write (his wife indicated in 1870 as merely unable to write).

Lists of Kilworth famine deaths in 1847 were compiled for the local landlord, Lord Mount Cashell, when he presented his case to Captain Forbes of the U.S.S. Jamestown in an effort to secure a portion of that ship's provisions to be sent to feed the starving community of his area. Included here are a David Keefe of Graig townland, a Peter Keeffe of Ballinooher, with his three children, and an Arthur Keeffe of Kilclogh with one child.[56] Further information may result from pursuing personal names that occur in the O'Keeffe manuscript, particularly those with a plausible origin in northern Co. Cork, or

---

[53] "Schedule I: Free Inhabitants in *East Bridgewater* in the County of *Plimoth* State of *Mass* enumerated by me, on the 25th day of July, 1850 ..." (etc.). I am grateful to Charlie Cook for this record (copy e-mailed October 25, 2021).

[54] "INHABITANTS in the Town of *East Bridgewater*, in the COUNTY of *Plymouth*, in the STATE OF MASSACHUSETTS, enumerated by me, the 21st & 22nd day of June 1865 . . ." (etc.). I am again grateful to Charlie Cook for copies of this and of the following record (e-mail, August 17, 2022) .

[55] "[Page No. 64} ... Schedule 1.–Inhabitants in *East Bridgewater*, in the County of *Plymouth*, State of *Massachusetts*, enumerated by me on the *17* day of *June*, 1870 . . . " (etc.).

[56] "Deaths by Starvation in the District of Kilworth from the 1st January last," dated 17 April 1847, submitted by the Earl of Mount Cashell to Captain R. B. Forbes of the U.S.S. Jamestown. Laurence M. Geary, "A Famine Document," *The Dublin Review of Books*, April 8, 2013, https://drb.ie/articles/a-famine-document. I am very thankful to Catherine Shannon (e-mail, October 24, 2021) for this reference. Use of this and of records listed in the preceding notes is my own responsibility.

similarly from searching for local records especially on the East Coast of North America.

A question also remains, given interests manifested in the *Boston Globe* newspaper column written by "Aodh Beag" of the Boston Philo-Celtic Society in 1878, and likewise by the contents of our manuscript, as to whether Patrick O'Keeffe, if he indeed came to New England and lived long enough, may have been acquainted with "Aodh Beag" or with the Society, provided inclusion of this clipping within "Patrick O'Keeffe's Book" goes farther than its ephemerality may allow us to see.[57] There is certainly much left to be discovered in the O'Keeffe book, including the origin and purpose of certain symbols and of what appears to be an owner's, or a seller's, stamp.[58] Whether or not the book ever came to Boston, might it have simply made its way to New England, even particularly to Scituate, via an antiquarian, book-dealer, or other person not necessarily related to the O'Keeffes who possessed some interest in the language, traditional history, and political fortunes of Ireland?

Thanks to the efforts of Mary Porter and the Scituate Historical Society the O'Keeffe manuscript has been analyzed and conserved by the Northeast Document Conservation Center (NEDCC) in Andover, Massachusetts. It will be made available for online access as a digital flip-book accompanied by a simplified online guide based upon the present study.[59] Several of the poetic and prose pieces within it deserve

---

[57] See note 5 above.

[58] An example of the former (fol. 39v, very small, foot-of-page) so far escapes me. The latter (at fol. 27r) appears to read "Harvey H. Small" (?). To date I have been unable to ascertain the identity of this person.

[59] Following the initial correspondence with Mary Porter (see note 1 above) my first viewing of the manuscript was on May 19, 2021. I worked from photocopy images up until October 13th of that year, when our team, Mary, myself, Charlie Cook, and Catherine Shannon, met to consult and correspond about the volume. By March 16, 2022, NEDCC was ready to supply the Scituate Historical Society with preliminaries of their report, which was completed during May. High-resolution images were made available to me on August 1, 2022 on my visit to Scituate: these and renewed personal inspection of the book revised several of my original opinions, as did a subsequent visit (August 17, 2022) to view watermarks and small or difficult images under strong light.

consideration, or even edition, in their own right.[60] Meanwhile, with the support of The Éire Society of Boston, plans are underway to celebrate the upcoming publication in Scituate of this mysterious little book, and to point to its value and accessibility as a witness to early nineteenth-century bibliographic, literary, and personal history.

Acknowledgements

I wish to thank The Éire Society of Boston for encouraging this project. I also wish to note that this study was partly inspired by a presentation on October 6, 2017, at the 37th Annual Harvard Celtic Colloquium, by Katie Hill (Old Sturbridge Village), Elizabeth Kading (Mystic Seaport), and Brendan Kane (University of Connecticut), regarding another Irish 'commonplace' volume found in the United States, "William Helys Book: Introducing a Previously Unknown Irish Manuscript, c, 1825." I am likewise grateful to Brendan Kane, Christina Cleary, Deirdre Nic Cárthaigh, and Emmet de Barra for the guidance offered to several of us who participated in the Celtic Studies Association of North America's Early Modern Irish palaeography mini-course which met during June, 2022, offered conjointly by the Learn Early Modern Irish project (léamh.org).

---

[60]I am grateful to Prof. Breandán Ó Conchúir for corresponding with me concerning the O'Keeffe manuscript and its inclusion in his catalogue of Irish manuscripts in North America.

BRIAN FRYKENBERG

Appendix One

*A note on editorial method

Patrick O'Keeffe's book is a commonplace volume belonging to the Irish manuscript tradition rather than to the world of printed books. I have chosen a middle path of transcription adapted to Irish script, italicizing expansions, compendia, and marks of lenition indiscriminately. I endeavor to convey indications of emphasis (capitalization, superscripts, heavy script) wherever these are apparent in quoted selections of Irish or English text. Word division has been introduced silently. Since many excerpts in English quote sections of the manuscript, italics are not used for English translations, but rather are employed in a manner similar to the treatment of Irish, for emphasis and expanding contractions, and are otherwise limited to titles.

Short list of incipits and first lines for literary works

fol. 1r: Eachtra an Amadain m*h*or a*n* so … [incomplete]

fols. 5r-6v: Com*h*arle na ba*i*rr sgológe *dá* m*h*ac / Mo c*h*oma*r*le d*h*uit a m*h*ic df*h*uil Eog*h*uin d*o* s*h*il airt …

fol. 7r: Tag*h*dg m*a*c Daire c*ecini*t / Téallac*h* flait*h*is fine Chaoim*h* … [two-and-a-half quatrains]

fols. 9r-20v: John Connells / Poem Translated by Some / Unknown Composer … // … Written by Patrick O'Keeffe / for his own use … // Irish heroes when I remind [ninety-two quatrains plus benedictory envoi (93), nos. 3, 64, 74, and 89 hypermetric]

fol. 21r: A Problem / As I had a silly question from a quack … [macaronic English and Irish] (addressed to "*Eangus* leam*h* ó \Dála/")

fol. 21v: A Summons / County of Cork / to wit / Commanded you are on / sight to prepare agus tea*cht* / am láthir … [macaronic English and Irish] (addressed to "*Eangus* leam*h* Ó Dala")

fols. 22r-23v: Seag*h*an Rúad*h* / Ó Seit*h*eac*h*ain c*ecini*t / do Dhát*h*: Ó Mhathghamhna … ///// [ornamental divider] Cé g*u*r b*h*fada mé am m*h*aig*h*ea[s]tair a*i*r f*e*raibh desm*h*úne*ach* … [sixteen quatrains]

fols. 24r-26r: Com*h*arle Brát*h*ar bocht . x x // Daiing*h*t*h*e [sic] Da Chom*h*sgolla*i*rre / October the 27ᵗʰ 1816 / By Patrick O'Keeffe / Gab*h* a c*h*éin go caom*h* mo t*h*eagasg uaimse … [fifteen quatrains]

135

fols. 28r-30v: Con*n*tæ C*h*orchoe mar aon . / le mor C*h*uaird Éirion*n* / uile x x x x x x / le heog*h*an ua Suilliob*h*ain ... //// AG so órdúag*h*a fuin*n*eam*h*uil feid*h*mlaid*ir* ... //////// [fol. 28v] ///// EIGSE su*air*ce [sic] s*h*léib*h*e luac*h*ra éistig lin*n*e red / a laoid*hth*ib*h* éifiacht dib*h* go leig*h*ead*s*a fé m*ar* sg*r*iosad*h* mé ... [sixteen stanzas]

fol. 42v: *Partholanus* m*a*c Seara an [*t*-]*och*tmhadh / glúin ó Noah *agus* do t*h*ir*ī*bh Magog m*a*c / *Japheth*, do g*h*louis o t*h*ír . *M*h*igdonia* ... [*Leabhar Gabhála Éireann*, fragmentary synopsis]

fol. 45v: Do b*h*íosa séal am aon*ar* an uaigneas sleib*h*e a*m* s*h*úig*h*e ... [five *aisling* verses, fragmentary first line only for verse three, half-verse only for verse five]

fol. 46r (reverse orientation, reading foot-to-head): m*o* c*h*ú sa no*ch*t go br*a*th F*ionn* f*a*o*i* mar ata ab*h*fad on rint / dfag me g*a*n deoc*h* g*a*n b*h*ia fa s*h*uil na ccli*ar agus* Chri*os*t . . . [seven quatrains]

Appendix Two

Short list of occasional inscriptions and marginalia:

**As indicated in the discussion above (e.g. at notes 22 and 58), cursory marks, inscriptions, and calculations are characteristic of this volume, particularly in the computistic sections. Unless they appear to point to further significant information on the present viewing of the manuscript, they are not included in this brief account.

fol. 1v: [head-to-foot] (JO?) [four-to-six-letter word erasure] / is cra / all (h?)ou(rs?) / (d?)ay of on(l?) [symbol?] / (of or?) / tom- (t)ha(t) / (b?)y that place ... [at foot] Da(u?)(-d?) [six letters illeg.]

[from fore-edge] To 1 to Cork – From ... (s?) / To 1 F(r)o*m* [or initial?] – Woo(d?) – (6?) [or marking end of line?] / To 1 From Glanmire – S(a?)m Pen(rose?) – (6?) / To 1 to passage – Capt Leahy – (6?) / Glanmire / (mcm?) (inch?) [illeg.] 1 ... / Countay ... / Elizabeth

[from gutter] Patrick

fol. 4r: [head-to-foot] (Pá)dr*aig* ui c*h*aoim*h* / [initial] ag*us air* n*a* sg*r*iobha / and he are (?)(?) / County of Cork / to wit fi(nis?) / John o Connell / John o Conn / [series of '1s' and '0s' possibly encoding binary number] / John o Connell / perpetual / John o C / Catherine / o Niul / Daniel Lane of Johnstown ... / Su(m?) / Sum / fir / si(?)

[foot-to-head] [scribbling] Come to me [two initials (g?g?)] / County of Cork / July *the* 14th 1815 / Dan*iel* / My Dear E(CS?) I do (I do?) lend / Joh(s?) si D / December the 30th / (e/l?cs?) / Dear L(?)(?) [six-letter word] / C / Pay / [five or six-letter word] / Pay / perpetuel / from numbers and art / never will [I] fairly depart

[from fore-edge] Paying [ten-letter word]

[from gutter] ~ / (a)men

fol. 4v: [head-to-foot] (initials) … John Everton / M J J J Keeffe / from myselve … M(O)K / M / Fermoy miles / By Patrick / O Keeffe / Daniel Lane / of Johnstown

fol. 7v: [head] Aois *an* K(a)l(en)*da*(s?) *an* t(*an*) do K(alend)(*is?*) g(?)ig / m(?)n*n* (s?/g?)in 18 day / March 13 1819 [foot-to-head from fore-edge] [initials (numbers?): (S?) d d d *us* . his / (?) / (?)]

fol. 11r: [foot] Otherwise Gaol Glas [ornament, or initials]

fol. 12r: [foot] Matrimon April 7th, 1818 [foot r.h.] 1846 / 1818 / 28 [followed by characters with erasure: MJ-K?]

fol. 12v: [foot] agus b*adh* truagh am*h* sín

fol. 13r: [interlinear] viz. eire fodla and banaba their names [proper names in traditional Irish script]

fol. 15v: [interlinear (in pencil)] Hymn [foot] October an xvi m*hadh* lá deg 1816

fol. 18r: [foot (in pencil)] This M-(?) [illeg.]

fol. 20r: [head] I Do Implore the father son & Holy gost / that pardon for our sins we may obtain / A me- (?)

fol. 21v: [foot (bracketed)] Turn Over for the Remainder / of those Verses which was / Composed by David Mahoney

fol. 23r: [foot] i .. e or .i. Promoter or Institutor of the / Protestant religeon ~ [of Luther]

fol. 25r: [foot] October the 27th 1816 By P. Keeffe [erasure underneath (possibly initials)] fol. 25v: [foot] (be*artha*) [b*arra* [=b*ach*ta?] tu*ar*(ga?)st (an) [ornament, or initials]

fol. 26r: [interlinear after explicit] Piouswork [foot] Petisionque [paragraphus]

fol. 29r: [foot] [ornament, or initials, with centered cross]

fol. 29v: [foot] Reader Turn over to the other side [ornament underneath]

fol. 30r: [foot] A Good deed for he merited more the / Suffering rogue (of punisment meted out to perpetrator) [paragraphus]

fol. 30v: [foot] And do[o]es [fairly?] Co[?]mm[ent? p?]nge another / [twelve-or-thirteen- letter word] very [three five-letter words erased, mostly illeg. ("likely living"?)] [word of four letters] spa(?)(oi?)l / [one five-letter word erased] Daily Labour & [one five-letter word (illeg.)] ~

fol. 33r: [head] Johns Johns and J?(//?)s [interlinear following date (pencil)] (*The* s- [=Ye s-?]) ~

fol. 34r: [foot] Finished December 3rd 1816

fol. 35r: [foot] Anseo v. 12 is the G. N.-

fol. 36r: [foot] [sums with binary, initials or symbols]

fol. 36v: [foot] [sums, initials or symbols]

fol. 37r: [head] Aois [o, i, s with diagonal descenders right-to-left] *an* K(a)l(en)(das?) an t(*an*) d*o* K(a)l(en)(das?) g*ar* d(o?) g('x'?) m*i*l(-?) 18-

fol. 37r: [bracketed at r.h.] Written or Wrote by me / i.e. Patrick O'Keeffe of / Johnstown – November the 22nd / Anno domini .. 1816 & sixteen / I so hereby request and pray / the Readers to Excuse me for any / vices or Defects that is here / unseen by lapse or / oblivion ~ &c [foot (in pencil)] Boston 1846 – 1816 / 30 / Fermoy

fol. 39v: [foot] [special symbol (see figure 10a)]

fol. 40v: [foot] By Michael O Keeffe

fol. 42v: [foot-to-head] [top] special symbols [bottom] 9 pence packing

fol. 46r: ['head' of page in reverse orientation (foot)] Learning and manners / ~ [abbreviation or symbol: (To-l-s?) illeg.] / are Charming companions [from fore-edge (reverse orientation)] Erin

fol. 46v: [head] September – 6 / D D-l D-l / June the 22nd [initials] / Desmond / July [initials] Desmond / c [symbol] Smith Coss / [bird on branch (illustration)] 1814-9

[from fore-edge] Conn Ciamhsa(eh)   7tember 8tober / 7tember 8tober / Conn Ciamsa ////

June *the* 22nd 1815 / Lowry

[reverse orientation (from foot)] Eiríg suas at s*h*uighe / [several words at present illeg.] / (sé?) feuch ar(us?)(airm?) ab a*n* baill [two symbols illeg.] . . .

"Nid wy'n adnabod neb o'r rhyw fenywaidd": An examination of the feminist and postcolonial elements in *Y Storm*, Gwyneth Lewis's Welsh translation of William Shakespeare's *The Tempest*.

Manon Gwynant

The focus of this paper will be the Welsh translation of William Shakespeare's play, *The Tempest*, *Y Storm*, by Gwyneth Lewis, a former student and fellow at Harvard University.[1]

Gwyneth Lewis is one of Wales's leading contemporary poets and was Wales's First National Poet from 2005–2006, and her work includes poetry, non-fiction, original plays, and translations. Lewis's translation of Shakespeare's *The Tempest* was commissioned in 2012 by the National Theatre of Wales as part of the World Shakespeare Festival and the artistic programme for the Olympic Games.[2] A production of the translation was performed at the National Eisteddfod of Wales in The Vale of Glamorgan by the National Theatre of Wales in the same year, and there were further performances in Carmarthen and Bangor.[3] This particular play by Shakespeare was also translated by another of Wales's most notable modern poets, Gwyn Thomas, in 1996, under the title *Y Dymestl*.[4] Although the focus of this paper is Gwyneth Lewis's translation, there will be some examples where examining this earlier work will also be beneficial. This paper will examine the feminist and postcolonial elements in *Y Storm*, taking into consideration Lewis's own work and outlook as a prolific bilingual female poet and translator.[5] *The Tempest* is a drama full of ambiguity

---

[1] William Shakespeare, *Y Storm*, trans. Gwyneth Lewis (Cyhoeddiadau Barddas, 2012).
[2] "Bywgraffiad Gwyneth Lewis", accessed 1 October 2022, http://www.gwynethlewis.com/bywgraffiad.shtml.
[3] "Plays–Y Storm", accessed 1 October 2022, http://www.gwynethlewis.com/plays_ystorm.shtml.
[4] William Shakespeare, *Y Dymestl*, trans. Gwyn Thomas (Dinbych: Gwasg Gee, 1996).
[5] It is important to note that in the context of this paper, Wales will be looked at as a 'postcolonial' country (note the lack of hyphen). For further

and potential for reinterpretation and experimentation, and Lewis takes full advantage of this in her Welsh adaptation. The paper will focus specifically on Miranda and on her relationship with her father.

To contextualize Gwyneth Lewis's translation, it is important to look at the history of translating Shakespeare into the Welsh language. The first known translation of Shakespeare into Welsh was *King Henry IV, Part 11*, translated by David Griffiths in response to a competition at the National Eisteddfod of Wales in Aberffraw, 1849.[6] The first full translation into Welsh was of *Hamlet* by David Griffiths in 1864, also in response to a National Eisteddfod competition, and this was published in *Yr Eisteddfod*, a Welsh periodical, in 1866.[7] Others in the nineteenth century include a translation of *King Lear* and *Macbeth* by Jonathan Reynolds,[8] a partial translation of *Julius Caesar* by Llywarch Reynolds in 1872,[9] and a translation of *King Lear* by O. N. Jones in 1884.[10] The twentieth century saw further complete translations, including *Macbeth* by T. Gwynn Jones, published fully in 1942, *Breuddwyd Nos Ŵyl Ifan* (A Midsummer Night's Dream) translated in 1999 by Gwyn Thomas,[11] as well as five complete plays translated by J. T. Jones, *Hamlet* (Hamlet, 1960),[12] *Marsiandwr Fenis*

explanation, see Chris Williams, "Problematizing Wales" in *Postcolonial Wales*, ed. Jane Aaron and Chris Williams (Cardiff: University of Wales Press, 2005), at 3-17.
[6] Emyr Edwards, *Shakespeare yn y Theatr Gymraeg* (Caerdydd: Emyr Edwards, 2016), 10.
[7] William Shakespeare, "Hamlet, Tywysog Denmarc", trans. David Griffiths, *Yr Eisteddfod*, 6/2 (1866): at 97-192.
[8] Edwards, *Shakespeare yn y Theatr Gymraeg*, 14.
[9] William Shakespeare, "Cyfieithiad o Julius Caesar, 1872", trans. Llywarch Reynolds, NLW MS 997B.
[10] A full history of the Welsh translations of Shakespeare can be found in Emyr Edwards' volume, *Shakespeare yn y Theatr Gymraeg.*
[11] William Shakespeare, *Breuddwyd Nos Ŵyl Ifan*, trans. Gwyn Thomas (Caerdydd: CBAC, 1999).
[12] William Shakespeare, *Hamlet*, trans. J. T. Jones (Aberystwyth: Cymdeithas Lyfrau Ceredigion, 1960).

(The Merchant of Venice, 1969),[13] *Nos Ystwyll* (Twelfth Night, 1970),[14] *Romeo a Juliet* and *Bid Wrth Eich Bodd* (Romeo and Juliet and As You Like It, 1983).[15] At the turn of the century, further translations emerged, including a new translation of *Hamlet* by Gareth Miles in 2004,[16] the translation concerning this paper by Gwyneth Lewis, and a new translation of *Macbeth* by Gwyn Thomas in 2017.[17]

Translating Shakespeare's plays into Welsh, as with any translation from a major language into a minor one, leads to many interesting considerations. Angharad Price refers to the Italian saying "traduttore traditor" (the translator is a traitor, described by Price as a "doethair cynganeddol", meaning an apothegm in cynghanedd), but argues that we should concentrate on the things gained, "y cyfoethogi", that derives from translation, leading to a process of "*cysylltu, magu cydraddoldeb a chadarnhau perthynas ieithoedd â'i gilydd*" (connecting, nurturing equality and confirming the relationship between languages).[18] This important cultural process also demonstrates the robustness of the Welsh language, adequately adopting Shakespeare's words and worlds, whilst also placing the Welsh language in a wider context of a global Shakespeare. Sonia Massai notes that "translation, as much as adaptation, has proved crucial to the dissemination of Shakespeare worldwide,"[19] a reminder that Shakespeare's prominence across the globe would not be as far-reaching or influential without translation. As Andrew Dickson notes, "run your fingers over many world cultures and, sooner or later, you

---

[13] William Shakespeare, *Marsiandwr Fenis*, trans. J. T. Jones (Caernarfon: Gwasg Tŷ ar y Graig, 1969).

[14] William Shakespeare, *Nos Ystwyll*, trans. J. T. Jones (Aberystwyth: Cymdeithas Lyfrau Ceredigion, 1970).

[15] William Shakespeare, *Romeo a Juliet / Bid Wrth Eich Bodd*, trans. J. T. Jones (Caernarfon: Gwasg Gwynedd, 1983).

[16] William Shakespeare, *Hamlet*, trans. Gareth Miles (Caerdydd: Gwasg APCC, 2004).

[17] William Shakespeare, *Macbeth*, trans. Gwyn Thomas (Cyhoeddiadau Barddas, 2017).

[18] Angharad Price, "Cyfoeth Cyfieithu", *Taliesin*, 100 (Haf 1997): 11-39, at 26.

[19] Sonia Massai, "The Wide World" in *Shakespeare in Ten Acts*, ed. Gordon McMullan and Zoë Wilcox (London: British Library, 2016), 74.

will touch something that feels Shakespearean."[20] Countries and communities across the globe have adapted and adopted Shakespeare, moulding his works to reflect their own beliefs and worldviews, and Wales and the Welsh language are no exception.

Helena Buffery states: "When a Catalan translator produces a version of a Shakespeare play, he creates an intertext which has at least as many links with texts in Catalan as it does with a possible English source text."[21] This quotation can be applied to a translation of Shakespeare in any language, and it is especially applicable to the Welsh translation of Williams Shakespeare's play in question here. *The Tempest* is an extremely important play in the context of a global Shakespeare because as Brinda Charry notes this particular play is "among the best-known and widely acclaimed works of literature" in the world,[22] and "[it] has been re-read and re-enacted and has spoken very differently to different generations and cultures."[23] Gwyneth Lewis's translation, *Y Storm*, introduces a Welsh context to this well-known play and allows us to re-visit it with fresh eyes. It is also important to note that by staging a production of this Welsh translation alongside productions of Shakespeare in a variety of languages from across the globe, a Welsh Shakespeare is placed in the heart of a global Shakespeare, confidently leaving a Welsh stamp on the Shakespearean canon, one that continues to grow and develop over 400 years since the death of its original creator.

Chantal Zabus also draws attention to this play's wider role, noting that "in its nearly four centuries of existence, *The Tempest* [....], through its rewritings has helped shape three contemporaneous movements–postcoloniality, postfeminism or postpatriarchy, and postmodernism."[24] The first two movements noted in the above quotation leads back to the subject of this paper, and before turning to

---

[20] Andrew Dickson, "Global Shakespeare", accessed 11 December 2018, www.bl.uk/shakespeare/articles/global-shakespeare.
[21] Buffery, Helena, *Shakespeare in Catalan* (Cardiff: University of Wales Press, 2007), 145.
[22] Brinda Charry, The Tempest: Language and Writing, (London: Bloomsbury, 2013), x.
[23] Charry, *The Tempest: Language and Writing*, 117.
[24] Chantal Zabus, Tempests After Shakespeare (Basingstoke: Palgrave, 2002), t. 1.

the translation itself, it is important to define feminism and postcolonialism in the context of this paper because as John McLeod says, "it is as challenging to define 'feminism' as it is to define 'postcolonialism'."[25] A recent definition of postcolonialism runs thus:

> it [. . .] covers a very wide range of writings from countries that were once colonies or dependencies of the European powers. There has been much debate about the scope of the term: should predominantly white ex-colonies like Ireland, Canada, and Australia be included? [. . .] In practice, the term is applied most often to writings from Africa, the Indian sub-continent, the Caribbean, and other regions whose histories during the 20th century are marked by colonialism, anti-colonial movements, and subsequent transitions to post-Independence society. [. . .] Postcolonial theory considers vexed cultural-political questions of national and ethnic identity, 'otherness', race, imperialism, and language, during and after the colonial periods.[26]

Postcolonialism is a heavily loaded term that must be used cautiously. Wales has a complex relationship with colonialism; it is a country that has been both subjected to internal colonialism and a participant in overseas imperialism. Although it is not possible to label Wales as a postcolonial country in the same way as it is to do so when referring to countries in Africa, the Indian sub-continent and the Caribbean, it is still possible usefully and revealingly to apply postcolonial theory and thinking to Welsh works, and works by Welsh authors, in both Welsh and English. As Chris Williams notes, it is not "reasonable to view contemporary Wales as post-colonial", but it is "useful to think of a 'postcolonial Wales'".[27]

---

[25] John McLeod, *Beginning Postcolonialism* (Manchester: Manchester University Press, 2000), 173.

[26] *Oxford Reference*, s.v. "Postcolonialism," accessed 1 October 2022, https://www.oxfordreference.com/view/10.1093/acref/9780199208272.001.0001/acref-9780199208272-e-904.

[27] Williams, "Problematizing Wales", t. 3.

It is also important to recognise the relationship between postcolonial criticism and translation. Helena Buffery believes that "a common postcolonial view of translation [is] as a process that has aided cultures to reinforce their own dominance by assimilation, as a form of cultural and linguistic control."[28] Gwyneth Lewis's translation is an example of this at work, as she re-introduces this well-known play through the medium of Welsh. The act of translating a great playwright such as Shakespeare into Welsh can be seen as a postcolonial one, an act that shows the strength of a language in the face of adversity. As Macdonald P. Jackson notes in regard to the Maori language, "by showing that Te Reo Māori [the Māori language] can be a suitable medium for such a great English verbal icon as a Shakespeare sonnet, you demonstrate how robust the Māori language is."[29]

The key to a feminist and postcolonial reading can be found in the very fabric of the language of the play, and this is one of the elements of colonialism that resonates loudest within a Welsh context. In his collection of essays, *Decolonising the Mind*, discussing The Politics of Language in African Literature, Ngũgĩ wa Thiong'o argues that "language was the most important vehicle through which that power fascinated and held the soul prisoner. The bullet was the means of the physical subjugation. Language was the means of the spiritual subjugation."[30] He expands on this by noting that "the most important area of domination was the mental universe of the colonised, the control, through culture, of how people perceived themselves and their relationship to the world", and in his view, all the above can be traced back to, and are mainly carried through language.[31]

Lewis's use of language in her translation of *The Tempest* cleverly challenges the political and cultural tensions that remain between Wales and England, as well as the role of the woman within those tensions. Lewis does not change the plot of the play in any way,

---

[28] Buffery, *Shakespeare in Catalan*, 3.

[29] MacDonald P. Jackson, "Translating Shakespeare's Sonnets into Māori: An Interview with Merimeri Penfold", *Shakespeare Quarterly*, 52/4 (Winter, 2001), 492.

[30] Thiong'o, Ngũgĩ wa, *Decolonising the Mind* (London: James Currey, 1986), 492-8, at 9.

[31] Thiong'o, *Decolonising the Mind*, 9.

but she does take advantage of one of the main themes of the work. Language is at the heart of *The Tempest*, and as Brinda Charry notes, the language of the play invites, "even forces, the reader to notice it for its own sake."[32] As a poet who writes in both English and Welsh, it is no surprise that Gwyneth Lewis has a particular interest in language. As Angharad Price notes, in Lewis's work there is a clear delight "yn nheithi corfforol iaith", in the physical characteristics of language, and it is a clear theme in all her work.[33] One of Lewis's most interesting works in this context is her volume of poetry, *Y Llofrudd Iaith* (The Language Murderer),[34] that won the Arts Council of Wales Book of the Year Award when published in the year 2000,[35] adapted and reinvented in an English volume under the title *Keeping Mum*.[36] Both volumes explore language and emphasise the poet's belief that language is a convention ("confensiwn yw iaith"),[37] not to be taken too seriously, but also a powerful tool when used carefully and cleverly.

> Feminism, the second element at hand in this paper, in the words of Kim Solga, is "the best and most accurate term to use when thinking about gendered experience from a human rights perspective. Any human being worried about discrimination on the basis of gender or sexual orientation will have some affinity with this term, whether or not they realize it."[38] Solga also notes that "many of us who are politically aware [. . .] are also reticent about using

[32] Brinda Charry, *The Tempest: Language and Writing* (London: Bloomsbury, 2013), t. 73.
[33] Angharad Price, "Gwyneth Lewis", in *Y Patrwm Amryliw – Cyfrol 2*, ed. Robert Rhys (Cyhoeddiadau Barddas, 2006): 277-86, at 277.
[34] Gwyneth Lewis, *Y Llofrudd Iaith* (Llandybïe: Cyhoeddiadau Barddas, 2000).
[35] "Biography", accessed 19 September 2022, https://literature.britishcouncil.org/writer/gwyneth-lewis.
[36] Gwyneth Lewis, *Keeping Mum* (Bala: Bloodaxe Books, 2003).
[37] Angharad Price, "*Tu Chwith* yn Holi Gwyneth Lewis", 8 (Gaeaf 1997): 53-6, at 54.
[38] Kim Solga, *Theatre & Feminism*, (London: Palgrave, 2016), 1-2.

a term [feminism] that remains clouded by persistent stereotypes."[39]

The poem below, an English translation of Gwyneth Lewis's original Welsh-language poem "Bro Ceridwen", Ceridwen's Country, is from the perspective of the shape-shifting keeper of the cauldron of wisdom from the story of the mythical Taliesin, Ceridwen. Lewis's poem is written from the perspective of a woman who has grown to be defined in mythology as an outsider, an 'other'.

"Bro Ceridwen"

I was born, ignorant of the meaning of boundaries,
to a tribe defeated centuries ago
and left forgotten to farm the fields
on a margin of empire. From my mother's eyes
I learnt there's more to earth's imagination
than the hedges and acres of man's ownership.
A bailiff of shadows my father was,
a shepherd of light on the slopes of the moon.[40]

As an aside, it is also interesting to notice the parallels between Ceridwen in the above poem, and Miranda in *The Tempest*. Ceridwen was born "heb wybod beth oedd ystyr ffin",[41] ignorant of the meaning of boundaries, according to Lewis, as was Miranda, and both are defined by their relationship to men—Ceridwen the mother of Taliesin, and Miranda, the daughter of Prospero. Through Gwyneth Lewis's eyes, both women are given a chance to stand on their own two feet, a voice anew and a recognition as two human beings in their own right.

When discussing this poem, "Bro Ceridwen" in an interview with Richard Poole, the translator of this poem and of many of Lewis's works, Gwyneth Lewis claims that "It wasn't so much feminist as practical." Although Lewis is, as Solga notes above, reticent about

---

[39] Solga, *Theatr & Feminism*, 12.
[40] The original poem, "Bro Ceridwen", appeared in Gwyneth Lewis's collection *Sonedau Redsa a Cherddi Eraill* (Llandysul: Gomer Press, 1990), 47-56. This translation is taken from *PN Review 113*, 23/2, (January–February 1997), https://www.pnreview.co.uk/cgi-bin/scribe?item_id=899, accessed 1 October 2022.
[41] Gwyneth Lewis, *Tri Mewn Un* (Cyhoeddiadau Barddas, 2005), 47.

using the term feminist to describe this work, it is clearly a feminist poem as she reworks the mythical tale of Taliesin and places the women at the forefront. This demonstrates the importance of taking Lewis's full body of work into consideration when analysing this translation, as well as her views and opinions more broadly. It is not possible to fully appreciate the feminist and post-colonial elements in *Y Storm* without doing so.

Lewis utilises her various translations to compile and introduce some of her principles and beliefs, and this is reflected in her view on translation and the role of the translator, as will be shown shortly. Her other stage plays, *Clytemnestra* (2012),[42] and *Medeia* (2016),[43] both based on ancient Greek plays, the first in English and the second in Welsh, are further evidence that although Lewis does not see herself as a feminist writer, her experience as a woman living in a patriarchal society has shaped her worldview and interests. As she examines the role of women in both languages, Lewis utilises the original plays to introduce her own modern message regarding the status of women in a modern, bilingual society. More recently, Lewis published an English poem on the Wales Arts Review website under the title "Misogyny" that is nearly impossible not to describe as a feminist one. Dedicated to Amy Hungerford, it opens:

> I see you, great literary men, holding a party
> Just beyond me.
> You are loving and greeting
> Each other while I'm caught in the junk room
> Of your misogynies: mahogany furniture
> Shipped from crises on older continents,
> Is blocking my way.[44]

Another significant fact about Gwyneth Lewis, along with her prominent bilingualism as a poet, is that she has a strong connection and relationship with America. She notes that she learned a lot from American poetry, "ynglŷn ag uchelgais artistig", about artistic

---

[42] Gwyneth Lewis, *Clytemnestra* (Cardiff: Sherman Cymru, 2012).
[43] Gwyneth Lewis (cyf.), *Medeia* (Cyhoeddiadau Barddas, 2016).
[44] Gwyneth Lewis, "Misogyny", accesed 12 December 2018, https://www.walesartsreview.org/poem-misogyny-by-gwyneth-lewis/.

ambition,[45] and it is worth noticing the similarities between Lewis and one of America's most notable feminist poets in the twentieth century, H. D. Although H. D. never translated Shakespeare's works, an element of cultural translation can be found in her volume *By Avon River*, where Claribel, the King's daughter in *The Tempest* described by Marianne Novy as "a figure for female invisibility and silence,"[46] is re-christened. Susan Friedman notes that Claribel "becomes her [H.D.'s] persona",[47] "as [a] woman writer seeking her place in a dominant male literary tradition."[48] The same can be applied to Gwyneth Lewis and her depiction of Miranda in her Welsh translation. Although Miranda has a voice, unlike Claribel who is silenced completely, she is still confined to the patriarchal order of society and its expectations of her as a female. As will be shown shortly, in her translation of *The Tempest*, Lewis uses language to overturn some of the patriarchal elements in the play and subvert the original authorial intention, something Gwyneth Lewis may not describe as feminist, but as practical, and parallels can be drawn between Lewis and Miranda. After examining her body of work, it is possible to argue that Lewis's keenness to refute the term feminism does not mean that her works are not feminist, but rather that she refuses the stereotypes that have become so entwined with the term. There is no doubt that her work examines gendered experiences from a human rights perspective, and so it is apt to describe *Y Storm*, and her portrayal of Miranda in this translation, as a feminist one.

It is also important when studying this translation of *The Tempest* to take into consideration Gwyneth Lewis's own views on translation. Whilst discussing translations of her own works in another revealing interview with Richard Poole, she notes: "What I'm not interested in is reproducing a direct equivalent of a poem in one language in the other!" She adds: "I don't see the relationship between translator and

---

[45] Angharad Price, "*Tu Chwith* yn Holi Gwyneth Lewis", 8 (Gaeaf 1997): 53-6, at 55.
[46] Marianne Novy, *Women's Re-Visions*, (Chicago: University of Illinois, 1990), 8.
[47] Susan Stanford Friedman, "Remembering Shakespeare Differently: H.D.'s By Avon River", in *Women's Re-Visions of Shakespseare*, ed. Marianne Novy (Chicago: University of Illinois, 1990), 151.
[48] Friedman, "Remembering Shakespeare Differently", 144.

poet as one in which the translator is a kind of transparent being through whose work the original poem shines out. It's a collaboration, one in which the translator adds his own colours and flavours to the original work. [. . .] the secret is to achieve this 'added value' without ruining the starting point."[49] This added value is exactly what we see in relation to Miranda's character in Lewis's *Y Storm*.

In general, Lewis's salient strategy regarding translation involves domestication, a term first coined by Laurence Venuti, and described by Rhianedd Jewell as a decision on behalf of the translator "*yn ei ddawns*", in his dance, to adapt the translation and set it in the cultural context of the target language, ensuring that the audience understand the piece, as well as identify with its content. If a translator decides to adopt the strategy of domestication, according to Jewell, they are invisible.[50] Gwyneth Lewis's adaptation is a clear example of a text that employs the domestication strategy, whilst Gwyn Thomas's Welsh translation of the same text on the other hand, *Y Dymestl*, employs the foreignization strategy; a translation where the translator is visible and the text foreign to the target audience. Further differences between the two translations will be examined in due course, but it is worth noting here an obvious, but important difference between the translator's, namely their genders. As Richard Poole notes, a difference in the gender of a translator "adds another element to the otherness of the negotiation–a language, a culture, a gender."[51]

Miranda, the only female character given a voice in Shakespeare's *The Tempest*, is thus key to a feminist reading of Gwyneth Lewis's *Y Storm*, and her status on the Island is an interesting one. The daughter of sorcerer Prospero, the play's protagonist, Miranda has been raised an only child on a remote island, and although she is not a slave, she *is* under Prospero's control, objectified and looked at through the lens of the male gaze. Traditionally, Miranda is seen as a female living under the patriarchal order of things, a character that seems like an "unlikely model for the development of a

---

[49] Richard Poole, "Gwyneth Lewis in conversation with Richard Poole", *PN Review*, 24/3 (Jan–Feb 1998): 50-5, at 52.
[50] Rhianedd Jewell, *Her a Hawl Cyfieithu Dramâu* (Caerdydd: Gwasg Prifysgol Cymru, 2017), 66.
[51] Poole, "Gwyneth Lewis in Conversation", 53.

strong female protagonist" according to Gayle Greene.[52] However, Gwyneth Lewis takes full advantage of the ambiguous language of the play and gives Miranda a new lease of life, challenging the patriarchal structures of the play by quietly and subtly altering the language of the original. As noted in the introduction to Luise von Flotow and Hala Kamal's volume *The Routledge Handbook of Translation, Feminism and Gender*, "translation can subvert, rewrite, or question hegemonic definitions of authorship, as well as [. . . .] disrupt or dismantle intersecting regimes of power."[53]

Shakespeare's Miranda is often referred to as "something", an object on an island that belongs to Prospero, and nothing more. This terminology is set from the very first scene where we meet Miranda, scene two of act 1. Prospero says to his daughter:

> I have done nothing but in care of thee,
> Of thee, my dear one, thee my daughter, who
> Art ignorant of **what** thou art'[54]

Miranda echoes her fathers 'what', saying:

> You have often Begun to tell me **what** I am,
> But stopped
> And left me to a bootless inquisition,
> Concluding "Stay. Not yet."[55]

Gwyn Thomas translates both "what"s as "beth"–that is, reproducing in Welsh the original term–but Gwyneth Lewis's are as follows. The first:

> *Fe wnes i bopeth dim ond er dy fwyn,*
> *Ti, fy nghariad, fy merch sy'n gwybod dim*
> *Mwy am **bwy** wyt ti na phwy wyf fi.*[56]

---

[52] Gayle Greene, "Margaret Laurence's *Diviners* and Shakespeare's *Tempest*: The Uses of the Past', *Women's Re-Visions*, ed. Marianne Novy (Chicago: University of Illinois, 1990), 165-82, at 165.
[53] "Women (re)writing authority: A roundtable discussion on feminist translation"
[54] William Shakespeare, *The Tempest* (London: Bloomsbury, 2011), 172.
[55] Shakespeare, *The Tempest*, 173.
[56] Shakespeare, *Y Storm*, 15.

My daughter who knows no more about **who** you are
than **who** I am. ("fy *merch sy'n gwybod dim/Mwy am
bwy wyt ti na phwy wyf fi*").

Notice the quiet but crucial change from what to who. And the second:

> *Fe ddechreuaist ti ddweud*
> ***Pwy** ydw i'n aml, ond gan orffen adrodd*
> *Yr hanes gyda, "Na! Ddim eto!"*[57]

Not what I am, but *who* I am (***Pwy** ydw i*").

This small but significant change in language cannot be ignored as it
gives Miranda a new level of status, transforming her from something
to someone, no longer being objectified and instead, affording her a
human, and individual, identity. Sima Sharifi notes, as she presents
two excerpts of Margaret Atwood's *The Handmaid's Tale* (1985) "as
a case study that illustrates what can happen to a text that is 'translated'
across cultural boundaries into a theocratic receiving society such as
the Islamic republic of Iran" that "the purpose of the following
contrastive analysis is not to 'establish what has been 'lost' or
'betrayed' in the translation process;[58] merely for the sake of adhering
to the source text. The micro-level text analysis here is meant to
expose the way patriarchy is perpetuated through language use."[59] The
micro-level text analysis in this paper is also used to expose the
patriarchy perpetuated through language use, and demonstrate how
Gwyneth Lewis overturns it.

Although she refutes the term feminist as we have seen, it would
nevertheless manifestly go completely against the grain for Gwyneth
Lewis to translate Shakespeare's play and keep Miranda's character
as one who is totally subordinate to her father in a society controlled
by men. I would like to suggest that Miranda's character can be seen
as a symbol of Wales here, or more specifically, women's rights in
Wales, post-devolution. Following a degree of devolution in 1997
with the establishment of the Welsh Assembly, renewed attention was
given to women's rights in Wales, leading to changes such as women

---

[57] Shakespeare, *Y Storm*, 16.
[58] Bassnett, Susan, *Translation*. London: Routledge, 2014, 8.
[59] Sima Sharifi, 'Translation of women-centered literature in Iran', in *The
Routledge Handbook of Translation, Feminism and Gender*, t. 41

accounting for 41.7% of elected members, which, according to Paul Chaney, "led to the Assembly having the second highest proportion of women elected to a national government body in Europe", for example.[60] Lewis's role as the first Poet Laureate of Wales is a further symbol of this. Quietly and subtly, post-devolution Wales is characterized and symbolized by Lewis's Welsh Miranda, transformed from something to someone and given an identity anew.

This is also done to some degree in relation to other women in the play, namely mothers. As Kim Ballard observes, "interestingly, mothers are often absent" in Shakespeares plays and *The Tempest* is no exception.[61] The only reference to Miranda's mother in this play is when Prospero tells Miranda: "Thy mother was a piece of virtue, and / She said thou wast my daughter".[62] Interestingly, Lewis's translation runs thus: *Yr oedd dy fam yn wraig rinweddol, taerai / Mai ti oedd fy merch.*[63] "Your mother was a virtuous woman, and she insisted you were my daughter." Notice once again the change in language here, transforming Miranda's mother from an object to a human, not a piece of virtue, but a virtuous woman. As subtle as this change may be, it is an extremely important one in relation to this paper. Other women in *The Tempest* include Sycorax, the witch, and Claribel, previously mentioned in this paper, and just like Miranda, the readers rely on Prospero's descriptions of these women as they are not afforded their own voices. Therefore, in any translation of this play, attention must be paid to Prospero's language as not only does "the language used by individual characters to describe the world around them structure[s]

---

[60] Paul Chaney, "Women and the Post-Devolution Equality Agenda in Wales", A Paper Presented to the Gender Research Forum, Women and Equality Unit, Cabinet Office 11 February 2002, https://www.researchgate.net/publication/228783477_Women_and_the_post-devolution_equality_agenda_in_Wales#:~:text=Abstract%20Members%20of%20the%20women%E2%80%20%99s%20movement%2Cin%20Wales%20played,Act%20that%20founded%20the%20National%20Assembly%20for%20Wales, 5

[61] Kim Ballard, "Daughters in Shakespeare: Dreams, duty and defiance", accessed 4 February 2019, https://www.bl.uk/shakespeare/articles/daughters-in-shakespeare-dreams-duty-and-defiance.

[62] Shakespeare, *The Tempest*, 175.

[63] Shakespeare, *Y Storm*, 16-17.

their experience of the world",[64] as Brinda Charry notes, it also structures the experiences of the reader and viewer.

This is further proved by looking at Miranda's relationship with her father, Prospero. Symbolic parallels have already been drawn between Gwyneth Lewis and Miranda in this paper, and a further similarity is their relationship with their fathers. As Kim Ballard notes, "parent-child relationships feature heavily" in Shakespeare's plays,[65] and *The Tempest* features what Peter Rickson describes as a "motif of an idealized father-daughter relationship."[66] This is a theme that can be found in Lewis's other works, namely in her volume of poetry, *Treiglo*, that was on the Wales Book of the Year Short List in 2018.[67] This volume explores the poet's relationship with her father, and it is hard not to draw parallels between these poems and the translation in question here. Unlike *The Tempest*, it is the daughter who writes the father's story in *Treiglo*:

> *mae yma gorff, sef Gwilym Lewis,*
> *Fy nhad, wedi ei dreulio'n gerddi*
> *Ac ynddynt mae'n henwr ac yn ifanc,*
> *Yn annwyl ac eto'n dywyll.[68]*

> Here is a body, Gwilym Lewis,
> My father, digested into poems
> Where he is both an old man and young
> Dear but also dark.

A common element in both relationships is tension: the tensions between the child and father, as well as the tensions that arise between the kinder and darker sides of the fathers. It is important to take this volume into consideration when analysing Lewis's translation of *The Tempest* as the relationship between father and daughter is such an integral motif.

---

[64] Charry, *Language and Writing*, t. 34.
[65] Ballard, "Daughters in Shakespeare: Dreams, duty and defiance".
[66] Peter Rickson, "Adrienne Rich's Re-vision of Shakespeare", in *Women's Re-Visions of Shakespeare*, ed. Marianne Novy (Chicago: University of Illinois, 1990), 183-95, at 184.
[67] "News", accessed 29 September 2022, http://www.gwynethlewis.com/news.shtml.
[68] Gwyneth Lewis, *Treiglo* (Cyhoeddiadau Barddas, 2017), 10.

As noted, Gwyneth Lewis adapts and adjusts the language in *Y Storm*, resulting in a work that places the major emphasis on a domesticating strategy of translation. Prospero and Miranda's relationship is the key to this process of domestication. One of the main changes is that Lewis's Miranda does not greet her father, Prospero, as sir for the greater part of their conversation in the second scene of the opening act. Shakespeare's Miranda answers Prospero thus: "Certainly, sir, I can."[69] However, Miranda in Gwyneth Lewis's adaptation answers: "Rwy'n cofio."[70] I remember. For comparison, Gwyn Thomas's Miranda answers: "Yn sicir, syr, fe alla'-i.",[71] a direct translation of Shakespeare's original. Another example is the following question: "Sir, are you not my father?"[72], translated by Lewis: *Onid ti yw nhad?*[73] "are you not my father?", with the sir having been dropped by Gwyneth Lewis. By omitting the sir, alongside the use of the informal pronoun "ti", you, the relationship between Prospero and Miranda changes, and although it doesn't eradicate what Brinda Charry refers to as Prospero's "patriarchal authority" completely,[74] it transforms the conversation from one between a master and slave, to one between father and daughter, establishing a closer relationship between them.

Another decision that changes the nature of the play is not to include several of the royal terms or references. Prospero is not a "A prince of power" in *Y Storm*,[75] but a man *a chanddo rym*,[76] a man with power; ("yn d'wysog grymus" is Gwyn Thomas' choice, which is a much more literal translation).[77] Prospero in Shakespeare's original refers to his daughter as "his only heir / And princess, no worse issued",[78] but, crucially, she is *fy merch*, "my daughter," in Lewis's

[69] Shakespeare, *The Tempest*, t. 174.
[70] Shakespeare, *Y Storm*, t. 16.
[71] Shakespeare, *Y Dymestl*, t. 11.
[72] Shakespeare, *The Tempest*, t. 174.
[73] Shakespeare, *Y Storm*, t. 16.
[74] Charry, *Language and Writing*, 90.
[75] Shakespeare, *The Tempest*, t. 175.
[76] Shakespeare, *Y Storm*, 16.
[77] Shakespeare, *Y Dymestl*, 11.
[78] Shakespeare, *The Tempest*, 175.

translation.[79] Prospero's "princely trunk" isn't referred to at all by Lewis.[80] Additionally, towards the end of this particular conversation between father and daughter, Shakespeare's Prospero refers to "other princes";[81] in Gwyneth Lewis's translation, on the other hand, it is *tywysogesau*–that is princesses, not princes, to begin with, and princesses, not other princesses.[82] Changing princes to princesses makes the decision to dispense of the word "other" here even more notable, with the translator going out of her way to suggest that the Welsh Miranda is not a princess. This demonstrates the importance of a detailed and attentive reading of Lewis's version, as her use of language enables us to read Miranda in a different light.

Is it thus possible to discern here a commentary on the relationship between Wales and England in a contemporary setting? Omitting many of the references to royalty in this translation not only frees Miranda of her royal duties, but it also raises many questions in relation to the role of the monarchy in Wales. This is one example of how Lewis domesticises her translation, enabling Welsh speakers to use the work of one of the greatest icons of English literature as a vehicle to understand their own culture anew. Discussing her translation, *Y Storm*, Gwyneth Lewis notes:

> *Nid gweithred lefn, hawdd mo'r cyfieithu yma, ond rhywbeth sy'n agor drws rhwng dau fyd gwahanol–y tu fewn a'r tu allan [. . .]–ac, ymhellach, yn rhwygo, hollti, dinistrio'r gwreiddiol er mwyn porthi'r gwrandawr.[83]*

> Translating is not an easy, smooth act, but something that opens a door between two different worlds–the inside and the outside [. . .]–and

---

[79] Shakespeare, *Y Storm*, 17.
[80] Shakespeare, *The Tempest*, 175.
[81] Shakespeare, *The Tempest*, 183.
[82] Shakespeare, *Y Storm*, 19.
[83] Gwyneth Lewis, "I Mewn i'r Tempest ac Allan o'r Storm", accessed 2 October 2018, https://www.cyfieithwyr.cymru/files/I_Mewn_ir_ Tempest_ ac_Allan_or_Storm_Gwyneth_Lewis.pdf, 9.

furthermore, tears, splits and destroys the original to
feed the listener.

This could also be identified as a postcolonial strategy as it identifies and addresses the problems and consequences of the decolonization of a country, especially relating to the political and cultural independence of Wales. Gwyneth Lewis uses the work of one of the greatest writers in English literature as a gateway for the Welsh to access their culture anew, utilising language to introduce a version of *The Tempest* that will resonate with the people of Wales in a different way to the original play.

Through her subtle adaptions of terminology, Gwyneth Lewis uses her translation of *The Tempest* to emphasise the way in which society and its structures constrain the voices of women, demonstrating her clear awareness and understanding of the power-plays of language. It is also part of a larger canon, of a global Shakespeare, and therefore shares an intertextuality with all other translations, adaptations and works inspired by *The Tempest* by William Shakespeare. As we have seen, her translation also bespeaks the cultural and political tensions in contemporary Wales. This adaptation of Shakespeare is thus a vehicle that allows the target audience to examine that relationship by focusing on the crucial significance of what Lewis refers to as an "added value" that a skillful translator can bring to the text of a canonical work.

Porcine Ploughmen and Etruscan Diviners:
The Classical Myth of Tages in *Betha Adamnáin*

Jesse Patrick Harrington

Betha Adamnáin, the Middle Irish vernacular "Life of Adamnán" (d. 704), sainted ninth abbot of Iona, is a homiletic hagiography of the late tenth century, preserved in a single manuscript copy of the seventeenth century. It is a short text, comprising a mere 279 lines, or nine pages, in its modern edition.[1] These feature sixteen miraculous narrative episodes set during the life of the saint, ranging in length from one line to one page, structured as a homily on the biblical chapter Job 38. The sixteen episodes include nine aggressive confrontations between the saint and his secular royal opponents, invariably ending with Adamnán's pronouncement of a curse upon the offending royal dynasty. The remainder features a range of otherworldly encounters by the saint, many of which concern confrontations with demons in public assemblies and with individuals of strange and miraculous births.

In the nineteenth century, these episodes earned *Betha Adamnáin* an unfortunate and unwarranted reputation, as "a miserable production, full of absurdities and anachronisms."[2] In the last four decades, the text has undergone a welcome renaissance of critical reappraisal. In 1988, Máire Herbert and Pádraig Ó Riain edited the text and assigned it to a precise historical context, situating it in the concerns of the Columban community of Kells and its often-difficult relations with external churches and royal dynasties, c. 960–75.[3] The

---

[1] Máire Herbert and Pádraig Ó Riain, eds. and trans., *Betha Adamnáin: The Irish Life of Adamnán*, Irish Texts Society 54 (London: Irish Texts Society, 1988).

[2] William Reeves, ed. and trans., *The Life of Saint Columba, Founder of Hy, Written by Adamnan*, Historians of Scotland 6 (Edinburgh: Edmonston & Douglas, 1874), xl.

[3] Herbert and Ó Riain, eds., *Betha Adamnáin*, 4-8, 41-44; Máire Herbert, *Iona, Kells, and Derry: The History and Hagiography of the Monastic familia of Columba* (Oxford: Clarendon, 1988), 153-8, 168-9; with refinements regarding the date of composition, responding to the edition's

editors argued that it offered "a unique mid-tenth-century essay on Irish Church-State relations", with the various cursed dynasties standing in for opponents of Kells.[4] In an important essay on the saint's otherworldly encounters, John Carey restored a lost narrative episode to the text, while demonstrating the text's high degree of literary sophistication and careful attention to thematic coherence and internal narrative symmetry.[5] Thomas Owen Clancy elaborated the text's important place within the wider Columban literary tradition and showed that it responded to Adamnán's own writings.[6] Patrick Wadden explored a single episode of the text which he argued displayed an artful reworking of biblical motifs.[7] Most recently, I have argued that the seemingly disconnected sequence of narrative episodes can be understood as a sophisticated and coherent homily on Job 38, which addressed the fears and anxieties of the author's community in the third quarter of the tenth century. Each episode was designed to be

---

reviewers, which subsequently appeared in Pádraig Ó Riain, *Dictionary of Irish Saints* (Dublin: Four Courts Press, 2011), 53-55. For a full survey of the literature on *Betha Adamnáin* since this edition, see Jesse Patrick Harrington, "Adamnán, Kells, and Job: Reappraising *Betha Adamnáin* (the Middle Irish Life of St Adamnán of Iona) as a Tenth-Century Homily," *Eolas* 13 (2021): 51-88 at 51-55. The sole addition to that survey is the recent chapter on the text in Brian Lacey, *Adomnán, Adhamhnán, Eunan: Life and Afterlife of a Donegal Saint* (Dublin: Four Courts Press, 2021), 168-77. Nonetheless, Lacey's discussion is largely derivative of the arguments in Herbert and Ó Riain's edition, and although it briefly acknowledges the subsequent important contributions of their reviewers and of Thomas Owen Clancy, the chapter otherwise overlooks the contributions and refinements offered by the other scholars cited below.

[4] Herbert and Ó Riain, eds., *Betha Adamnáin*, quoted at 43.
[5] John Carey, "Varieties of Supernatural Contact in the Life of Adamnán," in idem, Máire Herbert, and Pádraig Ó Riain, eds., *Studies in Irish Hagiography: Saints and Scholars* (Dublin: Four Courts Press, 2001), 49-62.
[6] Thomas Owen Clancy, "Adomnán in Medieval Gaelic Literary Tradition," in Jonathan M. Wooding, Rodney Aist, Thomas Owen Clancy, and Thomas O'Loughlin, eds., *Adomnán of Iona: Theologian, Lawmaker, Peacemaker* (Dublin: Four Courts Press, 2010), 112-22.
[7] Patrick Wadden, "*Trácht Romra* and the Northumbrian Episode in *Betha Adamnáin*," *Ériu* 62 (2012): 101-11.

heard in careful dialogue with the narrative episodes which immediately precede and follow it, as well as in intertextual dialogue with the corresponding verses of Job 38, as interpreted in the exegetical commentary tradition of Gregory the Great (d. 604) and Laidcenn of Clonfert (d. 661). The overarching theme of the homily is the pride of the flesh and of the spirit, while an important secondary theme, drawing on Job, concerns intellectual pride, the proper exercise of knowledge, and the temptations of idle speculation in areas which are the strict preserve of the Christian prophet.[8]

In this paper, I will focus on the single narrative episode (henceforth, referred to as "the *Breviary* episode") which Carey identified and restored to *Betha Adamnáin*. I will argue that this episode reveals the anonymous homilist-hagiographer's hitherto unnoticed awareness of two other intertextual sources, which he carefully reworks to serve the broader argument of his homily. One is contemporary Patrician hagiography, while the other is the classical Latin tradition. This will be the first time that an extended influence from pagan classical literature has been proposed for *Betha Adamnáin*. This proposed influence involves not only that which was filtered through familiar late antique Christian writers, such as Isidore of Seville, but potentially also direct access to Ciceronian philosophical writing which has not previously been identified at such an early stage of the Irish literary tradition. To argue this will be an important addition to the critical knowledge and scholarly understanding of *Betha Adamnáin*, offering further evidence of its literary sophistication, of its fitting memorialisation of its learned protagonist, and of the continuing importance of the liberal arts within the Columban community in Ireland.

***

The *Breviary* episode does not appear in the lone surviving manuscript of *Betha Adamnáin*, but as the third lection in an abbreviated Latin version of the Life of Adamnán, contained in William Elphinstone's sixteenth-century *Breviary of Aberdeen*. This lectionary version of the Life contains other episodes that are clearly abbreviated or reworked from *Betha Adamnáin*, and this episode is no

---

[8] Harrington, "Adamnán, Kells, and Job."

different.[9] Carey has argued convincingly that the episode would originally have appeared between §§14–15 of *Betha Adamnáin*, but that it was lost at some point between the original composition and later copying of the Middle Irish Life.[10] Given its abbreviated Latin form in the *Breviary*, it is not clear that the tale survives with all its narrative particulars intact. Nonetheless, what does survive is enough to show that it was clearly integral to the Middle Irish homily.[11] The *Breviary* narrative runs as follows:

> *Cumque porci suo more terram verterent sub cespite quoquo euulso infans viuus repertus est. Quem cum Sanctus Adampnanus inuenit velut filium educauit et liberalibus artibus instrui laborauit. Tandem ante Dei virum ductus multa ei probleumata proposuit. Tunc sanctus facto signaculo crucis inimicum effugavit, qui in specie infantis beatum virum temptare voluit.*

> While pigs, according to their wont, were rooting up the earth, a living infant was found beneath a turned-up sod. When the holy Adamnán found him, he brought him up like a son, and exerted himself to have him trained in the liberal arts. When at length brought before the man of God he set him many questions. Then with the sign of the cross the saint banished the Enemy, who had sought to tempt the blessed man in the form of an infant.[12]

This short abstract provides the story of a strange child who is brought to Adamnán, revealed to be a demonic tempter, and banished

[9] For the text and discussion of the *Breviary* Life, see Herbert and Ó Riain, eds., *Betha Adamnáin*, 36-41; with text, translation, and commentary in Alan Macquarrie and Rachel Butter, eds., *Legends of Scottish Saints: Readings, Hymns and Prayers for the Commemorations of Scottish Saints in the Aberdeen Breviary* (Dublin: Four Courts Press, 2012), 232-3, 318-20.
[10] Carey, "Supernatural Contact," 55, 59-61.
[11] Harrington, "Adamnán, Kells, and Job," 72-5.
[12] The text of the episode is edited in Herbert and Ó Riain, eds., *Betha Adamnáin*, 37; with text and translation in Macquarrie and Rachel, eds., *Legends of Scottish Saints*, 232-3; and translation only in Carey, "Supernatural Contact," 55.

according to the saint's miraculous power and wisdom. It fits a broader narrative pattern in *Betha Adamnáin*: of demons who challenge the authority of the saint, and who tempt his intellectual pride with difficult, theologically speculative questions, but whom he shrewdly recognises and exorcises rather than attempting to answer.[13] In purely formal, literary terms, the restoration of the episode enhances the internal symmetry of the text. It provides an evil demon-child who tempts Adamnán, to mirror the good Christ Child who illuminates Adamnán in his cell in the chapter which immediately follows.[14] It offers a demonic questioner in human guise to complete a trio of such questioners—fulfilling the homiletic theme of Job thrice resisting Satan—with the opening and final chapters of the text.[15] It provides a seemingly unnatural birth from the ground to complete a trio of strange pregnancies with two earlier chapters.[16] In exegetical terms, the *Breviary* episode not only furnishes *Betha Adamnáin* with another illustration of guarding against intellectual pride, but it further provides the necessary image and moral commentary for the scrutinising of the earth in Job 38:18, without which the homiletic sequence on Job 38 is incomplete.[17] Altogether, Carey's proposed reconstruction and placing of the *Breviary* episode is both consistent and necessary for the themes, motifs, and narrative order of the episodes in *Betha Adamnáin*. Without it, these same episodes discussed lack their clear narrative trajectory and denouement. The episode is therefore essential to any understanding of the text as a coherent homily and narrative.

---

[13] Herbert and Ó Riain, eds., *Betha Adamnáin*, 34-5, 37-9, 48-51, 58-61, §§2–3, 16. The coincidence between the manner of the three demonic assaults in *Betha Adamnáin* and the *Breviary* was first observed by Reeves, ed., *The Life of St Columba*, lvii-lviii, though it was not until Carey that the three assaults were shown to belong originally to the same tenth-century text.

[14] Herbert and Ó Riain, eds., *Betha Adamnáin*, 58-9, §15; Carey, "Supernatural Contact," 55, 59-61.

[15] Herbert and Ó Riain, eds., *Betha Adamnáin*, 48-9, 58-61, §§2, 16; Harrington, "Adamnán, Kells, and Job," 72.

[16] Herbert and Ó Riain, eds., *Betha Adamnáin*, 48-51, 54-5, §§3, 11; Harrington, "Adamnán, Kells, and Job," 72-3.

[17] Harrington, "Adamnán, Kells, and Job," 71-2, 74.

Despite this work on the *Breviary* episode and its important place in *Betha Adamnáin*, two significant intertextual analogues have gone unnoticed. The first appears in another tenth-century hagiography, *Bethu Phátraic* (A Life of Patrick), also known as *Vita Tripartita S. Patricii* (The Tripartite Life of St. Patrick). *Bethu Phátraic* has a complex recension history. It appears to have achieved a stable narrative core by the tenth century, but it continued to be worked on until it was given a homiletic framework, perhaps as late as the twelfth century. During this time, the language of the text shifted progressively from Latin into Middle Irish.[18] In its extant form, *Bethu Phátraic* contains a story which resembles the *Breviary* episode, namely the story of Bishop Olcán.[19] It reports that while Patrick was passing through Dál Riata, a local king heard an infant crying in the earth and ordered that the nearby cairn be opened. It was discovered that the woman buried there had given birth after her death and burial, and the *mac béu* (live son) was found with the *máthair mairb* (dead mother). As an added marvel, the tomb smelled as wine when it was opened. The king's druid gave the child the name Olcán, because of the *olc* (evil) that he had lived seven days in the tomb. Patrick baptised the child and accepted him as his disciple, eventually appointing him bishop of Airthir Maige (Armoy). Nonetheless, the narrative continues that Patrick and Olcán were not always on good terms. The chief wedge between the two churchmen came when Olcán was compelled, under threat of further bloodshed, to baptise and bless a tyrant to whom Patrick had denied his baptism and blessing. Patrick maintained that Olcán had taken upon himself the tyrant's guilt and gave orders to run down his former disciple with his chariot, a summary judgement which was averted only by the charioteer's reluctance to run down a bishop. In lieu of his initial sentence, Patrick prophesied the death,

---

[18] Kenneth Jackson, "The Date of the Tripartite Life," *Zeitschrift für celtische Philologie* 41 (1986): 5-45 at 15-6.

[19] Kathleen Mulchrone, ed., *Bethu Phátraic: The Tripartite Life of Patrick* (Dublin: Hodges Figgis & Co., 1939), 96-9, lines 1869–1936; with translation in Whitley Stokes, ed. and trans., *The Tripartite Life of Patrick: With Other Documents Relating to that Saint*, vol. 1 (London: Eyre & Spottiswoode, 1887), 160-7. For Bishop Olcán, see also John O'Hanlon, *Lives of the Irish Saints*, vol. 2 (Dublin: James Duffy & Sons, 1875), 643-8; Ó Riain, *Dictionary of Irish Saints*, 521-2.

destruction, and hardship that would come upon the monastery of
Airthir Maige, and that jurisdiction over its lands would transfer to the
saints Mac Nisse of Connor and Senán of Inis Cathaig. Nonetheless,
he admitted that Olcán would be a saint and his merit would be great
in heaven.

The *mac béu* in *Bethu Phátraic* offers an important vernacular
analogue for the *infans viuus* of the *Breviary* episode, with its
marvellous discovery of a child in the earth who is raised by the saint
but later proves a difficult disciple. The *Breviary* episode might thus
be considered a borrowed trope from what was the most influential
vernacular Irish hagiography of the tenth century. Both stories deal
with the common theme of foundlings, whether they had been
orphaned (as Olcán) or more strictly abandoned, a social category to
which references can be found elsewhere in Irish literature.[20] An
interest in such children would have been appropriate to the historical
Adamnán, whose efforts to extend legal and political recognition of
the Church as ultimate "lordly guardian" and protector of *innocentes*
(children under the age of seven) formed an important principle of his
celebrated *Lex Innocentium* (The Law of the Innocents).[21] By the tenth
century, however, the Church had assumed an increasingly formalised
legal and social responsibility for foundlings, as evident, for example,
in the canons of Regino of Prüm (c. 906).[22] Child oblation was not
without its difficulties, and some early medieval ecclesiastical

---

[20] John Boswell, *The Kindness of Strangers: The Abandonment of Children
in Western Europe from Late Antiquity to the Renaissance* (New York:
Pantheon, 1988), 212-4.
[21] Daniel A. Binchy, "Betha Crólige", *Ériu* 12 (1938): 1-77 at 8–9, §7; Neil
McLeod, "Cáin Adomnán and the Lombards", in Anders Ahlqvist and
Pamela O'Neill, eds., *Language and Power in the Celtic World: Papers
from the Seventh Australian Conference of Celtic Studies, University of
Sydney, September 2010*, Sydney Series in Celtic Studies 10 (Sydney:
Celtic Studies Foundation, University of Sydney, 2011), 241-65 at 256.
[22] Regino of Prüm, *Libri duo de synodalibus causis et disciplinis
ecclesiasticis*, ed. F. G. A. Wasserschleben (Leipzig: Sumtibus Guil.
Engelmann, 1840), 2.68-71 (pp. 237-8); Boswell, *The Kindness of
Strangers*, 220-3.

authorities showed a marked ambivalence toward the practice.[23] Accordingly, the two stories might be considered as common reflexes of a tenth-century monastic anxiety regarding that responsibility, noting the difficulties and the dangers that younger members of the community of uncertain origins could pose to clerical and monastic discipline.[24]

There was additionally the tradition that Patrick had been enslaved as a swineherd, and *Bethu Phátraic* notably features several miracle stories involving pigs.[25] In one narrative section, Patrick cursed the thirteen chief idols of Mag Slécht, covered in the precious metals of gold, silver, and brass, to be swallowed by the earth.[26] Soon after, Patrick providentially discovered gold on a spot where pigs had been rooting, allowing him to pay a druid, more concerned with his golden idols than with the saint's offer of eternal salvation, for a plot of land on which to build his church.[27] The story arguably echoes Augustine of Hippo's favoured image of Moses' Israelites plundering "the gold out of Egypt" (Exodus 3:21–2, 11:2–3, 12:35–6), which the Egyptians had dug from the mines of providence and misused in their idols. Augustine had used this image to justify the incorporation of pagan knowledge in the liberal arts used by Christians, provided they could be removed from their former wicked and harmful service to demons and put toward the proper use of preaching the Gospel.[28] The

---

[23] Boswell, *The Kindness of Strangers*, 243-51; Mayke de Jong, *In Samuel's Image: Child Oblation in the Early Medieval West*, Brill's Studies in Intellectual History 12 (Leiden: Brill, 1996).

[24] I am grateful to the colloquium's participants for suggesting this possibility during discussion of the paper.

[25] Much of the section that deals with Patrick's role as swineherd is missing from the extant manuscripts of *Bethu Phátraic* and has been reconstructed from the Latin of John Colgan's seventeenth-century *Trias Thaumaturga*. See Stokes, ed. and trans., *Tripartite Life*, vol. I, 18.

[26] Mulchrone, ed., *Bethu Phátraic*, 55, lines 1004–18; with translation in Stokes, ed. and trans., *Tripartite Life*, vol. I, 90-3.

[27] Mulchrone, ed., *Bethu Phátraic*, 58, lines 1052–9; with translation in Stokes, ed. and trans., *Tripartite Life*, vol. I, 94-5.

[28] Augustine, *De doctrina Christiana*, ed. and trans. Roger P. H. Green (Oxford: Clarendon Press, 1995), 2.108, 2.144-51 (pp. 106-7, 124-31); ibid., *Confessiones*, II.ix.15. For the theme in Augustine, see John

reconciliation of Christian and pre-Christian knowledge was a key interest of medieval Ireland's learned elites, and the theme was especially prominent in the hagiographical traditions concerning Patrick.[29] The *Breviary* episode likewise concerns itself with the limits of what knowledge may be acceptably Christianised, while presenting its own swine-driven encounter between its saint (a teacher of the same liberal arts as Augustine) and a body of knowledge that cannot.[30]

Though the story of Patrick's swine in *Bethu Phátraic* is not linked with any miraculous discovery of children in the earth, the saint is said to have taken a tender youth (*maeth óclach*) herding swine as

---

Marenbon, *Pagans and Philosophers: The Problem of Paganism from Augustine to Leibniz* (Princeton: Princeton University Press, 2015), 27. For the theme in early medieval England, as preserved in the tenth-century Junius manuscript compiled around the time that *Betha Adamnáin* was composed, see Audrey Walton, "'Gehyre se ðe Wille': The Old English *Exodus* and the Reader as Exegete," *English Studies* 94.1 (2013), 1-10 at 2-3.

[29] Kim McCone, *Pagan Past and Christian Present in Early Irish Literature* (Maynooth: An Sagart, 1990). The Augustinian theme appears even more strongly in the later hagiographical tradition of Patrick. In Jocelin of Furness' twelfth-century *Vita S. Patricii*, Patrick's servitude is compared with the biblical Joseph's slavery in Egypt, figuratively tried as gold in a furnace, and is ended by an angel directing the saint to gold dug up by his herd of swine to pay for his manumission (§§13, 15-6). Thus, the gold necessary for Christian freedom is explicitly taken from the figurative land of Egypt. The foundation of his church (§106) is presented as a repeat of this miracle, with the pagan owner of the land returning the gold which he had received from Patrick, thereby emphasising that the riches possessed by the pagans have their ultimate source in the Christian God and are thus apt for Christian reclamation. See *Triadis Thaumaturgae, seu divorum Patricci Columbae et Brigidae, trium veteris et majoris Scotiae, seu Hiberniae, sanctorum insulae, communium patronorum acta, tomus secundus sacrarum ejusdem insulae antiquitatum*, ed. John Colgan (Louvain: Cornelium Coenestenium, 1647), cols. 67A-68A, 89B; with translation in James O'Leary, *The Most Ancient Lives of Saint Patrick: Including the Life by Jocelin, Hitherto Unpublished in America, and his Extant Writings*, Irish Fireside Library (New York: P. J. Kenedy, 1883), 147, 150-2, 256.

[30] Both Augustine and the *Breviary* episode refer explicitly to the *liberales disciplinae* (Augustine) or *liberales artes* (the *Breviary*). See Augustine, *De doctrina Christiana*, ed. and trans. Green, 2.145 (pp. 124-5).

another disciple; to have resurrected, baptised, and learned from another swineherd, who had thitherto spent a hundred years in his grave; and to have restored to life a child who had been torn apart and eaten by pigs, so that his parents and people could accept and believe the Christian message.[31] Thus, both sets of stories show the moral ambivalence and ambiguity of swine. They could serve the saint and his mission, but they could also be a force for danger and destruction.[32]

***

Nonetheless, the hagiographical analogue in *Bethu Phátraic* does not fully explain the various features of the *Breviary* episode. The tale of Bishop Olcán notably does not provide an analogue for the strange knowledge and specifically otherworldly character of the foundling in the *Breviary*, nor does it offer an obvious explanation for Adamnán's hostility to his questions. For this, one may additionally note the close resemblance with the ancient Etruscan myth of the Tyrrhenian Tages.[33] Classical Latin tradition claimed Tages as a founding prophet of the Etruscan religion, who taught the method of divination by slaughtering animals that was later undertaken by the Roman

---

[31] Mulchrone, ed., *Bethu Phátraic*, 25-6, 76-7, 119-20, lines 421–7, 1404–13, 2319–39; with translation in Stokes, ed. and trans., *Tripartite Life*, vol. I, 40-1, 122-3, 198-201.

[32] The destructiveness of swine is a central image of Patrick's negative prophecies in Mulchrone, ed., *Bethu Phátraic*, 107-8, 122-3, lines 2028-33, 2054–67, 2398–400; with translation in Stokes, ed. and trans., *Tripartite Life*, vol. I, 174-7, 204-5.

[33] Carey, "Supernatural Contact," 56, has already suggested the figure of Tages, with specific reference to Cicero's telling, as a non-Indo-European pagan analogue for the *Breviary* episode. Carey, however, did not consider the Etruscan myth to be a conscious analogue or potential source for the hagiographer, preferring to situate the story within an indigenous Irish and Welsh literary tradition. His passing reference has not been explored in subsequent scholarship. I am grateful to Brigid Ehrmantraut for independently suggesting to me the parallel between Tages and the *Breviary* episode, and to both scholars for graciously reading and commenting on this paper.

haruspices, or soothsayers.[34] He is an example of the *puer senex* (aged child), childlike in appearance but possessed of otherworldly wisdom.[35] About a dozen authoritative works in the classical and late antique Latin tradition (from the first century B.C. to the eighth century A.D.) refer to Tages. He appears in the poems of Ovid and Lucan, in the history of Ammianus Marcellinus, and in the discourses of Cicero, Columella, Sextus Pompeius Festus (later abbreviated by Paul the Deacon), Censorinus, Lactantius Placidus, Servius, Macrobius, Martianus Capella, and Isidore of Seville.[36] No single

---

[34] Marcus Tullius Cicero, *M. Tulli Ciceronis De Divinatione*, ed. Arthur Stanley Pease. University of Illinois Studies in Language and Literature 6–8 (Urbana: The University of Illinois, 1920), 2.50–51 (pp. 435-9); J. R. Wood, "The Myth of Tages," *Latomus* 39.2 (April-June 1980): 325-44; Jean-René Jannot, *Religion in Ancient Etruria*, trans. Jane Whitehead, Wisconsin Studies in Classics (Madison: University of Wisconsin Press, 2005), 3-4, 178; Nancy Thomson de Grummond, "Prophets and Priests," in eadem and Erika Simon, eds., *The Religion of the Etruscans* (Austin, Texas: University of Texas Press, 2006), 27-44 at 27-30.

[35] The terms *puer senex* and *puer senilis* were coined by Ernst Robert Curtius, *European Literature and the Latin Middle Ages* (London: Routledge & Kegan Paul, 1953), 98-101, who traced the topos to pagan antiquity. See also Teresa C. Carp, "*Puer senex* in Roman and Medieval Thought," *Latomus* 39.3 (1980): 736-9; Jerzy Linderski, "Review: The Bronze Liver of Piacenza: Analysis of a Polytheistic Structure by L. B. van der Meer," *Classical Philology* 85.1 (January, 1990), 67-71 at 68; Marie-Laurence Haack, "Puer senex," in Béatrice Bakhouche, ed., *L'ancienneté chez les anciens*, vol. 2 (Montpellier: Université Paul-Valéry Montpellier III, 2003), 371-83.

[36] The key classical and late antique Latin works which mention Tages, in the approximate chronological sequence of their authors' floruits, are as follows: Marcus Tullius Cicero, *De Divinatione*, in William Armistead Falconer, ed. and trans., *Philosophical Treatises*, Loeb Classical Library 154 (Cambridge, Mass.: Harvard University Press, 1979), 2.50-51; Ovid, *Metamorphoses*, ed. and trans. Frank Justus Miller, revised G. P. Goold, vol. 2. Loeb Classical Library 43 (Cambridge, Mass: Harvard University Press, 2014), 15.553-59; Lucius Junius Moderatus Columella, *On Agriculture*, ed. and trans. Harrison Boyd Ash, E. S. Forster, and Edward H. Heffner, vol. 3, Loeb Classical Library 408 (Cambridge, Mass.: Harvard University Press, 2014), 10.344-5; Lucan, *The Civil War: Pharsalia*, ed.

source among these, however, provides the details of the Tages legend complete.[37] Lucan, Columella, Festus, Lactantius, Servius, and Macrobius give only passing reference, in each case acknowledging Tages' status as a famous seer or founder of Etruscan haruspicy. Cicero, Ovid, Martianus, Ammianus, and Isidore provide at least a narrative abstract of the aetiological legend, in which Tages taught the Etruscans the secrets of haruspicy after they discovered him in a ploughed field. Of this list, some, such as Ovid, Lucan, and Isidore, were part of a general curriculum in the early medieval West; others, such as Cicero, Macrobius, and Martianus, were less common but not

---

and trans. J. D. Duff, Loeb Classical Library 220 (Cambridge, Mass.: Harvard University Press, 1928), 1.635-37; *Sexti Pompei Festi De verborum significatu quae supersunt cum Pauli epitome*, ed. Wallace M. Lindsay, Bibliotheca scriptorum Graecorum et Romanorum Teubneriana (Leipzig: B. G. Teubner, 1913), p. 492.6-8; Censorinus, *Censorini De die natali liber ad codicum denuo collatorum fidem*, ed. Ivan Cholodniak (St. Petersburg: Russian Imperial Academy of Sciences, 1889), 4.13; Ammianus Marcellinus, *History*, ed. and trans. John C. Rolfe, vol. I. Loeb Classical Library 300 (Cambridge, Mass.: Harvard University Press, 2014), 17.10, 21.10; Lactantius Placidus, *Lactantii Placidi in Statii Thebaida commentum*, ed. Robert Dale Sweeney. Bibliotheca Scriptorum Graecorum et Romanorum Teubneriana. vol. I (Stuttgart: Teubner, 1997), 4.516; Maurus Servius Honoratus, *Servii Grammatici qui feruntur in Vergilii carmina commentarii*, ed. Georg Thilo and Hermann Hagen, vol. I (Leipzig: B. G. Teubner. 1881), 2.781; Ambrosius Aurelius Theodosius Macrobius, *Saturnalia*, ed. and trans. Robert A. Kaster, Loeb Classical Library (Cambridge, Mass.: Harvard University Press, 2014), 5.13; Martianus Capella, *De Nuptiis Philologiae et Mercurii*, in James Willis, ed., *Martianus Capella*, Bibliotheca scriptorum Graecorum et Romanorum Teubneriana (Leipzig: B.G. Teubner Verlagsgesellschaft, 1983), 2.157, 6.637; Isidore of Seville, *Isidori Hispalensis episcopi Etymologiarum sive Originum libri XX*, ed. Wallace Martin Lindsay, vol. I (Oxford: Clarendon Press, 1911), 8.9.34.
[37] Wood, "The Myth of Tages," 325-8. Wood has argued that the most complete version of the myth is provided by the sixth-century Byzantine administrator Iohannes Lydus (John the Lydian) in his *De ostentis*, but this work was written in Greek rather than Latin, so its availability in the medieval Latin West may be doubted.

unknown.[38] Through these writers, and the later scholia and excerpts of their works, the story of Tages was transmitted to medieval readers in Ireland and elsewhere.

For example, the author of *In Cath Catharda* (The Civic Battle), the late Middle Irish translation-adaptation of Lucan's *De Bello Civile* dated to the twelfth or thirteenth century, adds an explanation of the Roman poet's brief allusion for his reader: *In Tages isin dano, da m-beith neach no iarfaighead, is e ro aircestar in ealadhain draidochta. Ni bui athair nó mathair occa, acht a focbail beo fo fotaibh in arathair chena.* (That Tages, then, if anyone should ask, was he who invented the science of augury. He had neither father nor mother but was found alive under the sods of the plough.)[39] These added details are consistent with those of Cicero, Ovid, Martianus, Ammianus, and Isidore, but not with that of Festus, who identifies Tages as a son of Genius and grandson of Jove. Cillian O'Hogan has argued that the "Irish Lucan" takes his details of the Tages myth from the DR scholia tradition on Lucan, which itself drew on Isidore: *iste Tages dicitur primus aruspicinam artem Etruscis tradidisse et postea non apparuisse. Dicitur hic, arante quodam rustico, subito exiluisse ex glaebis terrae et aruspicinam dictasse, quo die <et> mortuus est.* (This Tages is said to have been the first to hand down the art of haruspicy to the Etruscans, and afterwards he did not appear. When some rustic was ploughing, he is said to have leapt up suddenly from the sods of the earth and to have pronounced haruspicy, and on the same day he died.)[40] O'Hogan noted that the *fotaib* (sod) of *In Cath*

---

[38] Jesse Keskiaho, *Dreams and Visions in the Early Middle Ages: The Reception and Use of Patristic Ideas, 400–900*, Cambridge Studies in Medieval Life and Thought, Fourth Series 99 (Cambridge: Cambridge University Press, 2015), 21.

[39] Whitley Stokes, ed. and trans., *In Cath Catharda: The Civil War of the Romans: An Irish Version of Lucan's Pharsalia* (Leipzig: Hirzel, 1909), 76-7, lines 992–4.

[40] The sigla "D" and "R" refer respectively to two eleventh-century manuscripts which preserve in common the quoted scholium: Berlin, Staatsbibliothek, Ms. lat. fol. 35, saec. XI, and Munich, Bayerische Staatsbibliothek, Ms. lat. 14505, saec. XI. For discussion of these manuscripts and the text of the scholium on Lucan, *The Civil War*, 1.635,

Catharda could easily have been derived from the *glaeba* (sod) of the scholia. To this, O'Hogan added the *Commenta Bernensia* preserved in the tenth century: *hic Tages dicitur, cum terra araretur, subito natus*. (This Tages is said to have been born suddenly when the earth was being ploughed.)[41]

These commentaries could as easily gloss the *Breviary* episode, so well do they fit the circumstances of the unnamed and parentless child brought to Adamnán. The *cespes* (sod) in the *Breviary* episode could easily be a re-Latinisation of a vernacular term such as *fotaib* used to translate *glaeba*, a term which is notably found in the account of the myth in Ovid and Isidore.[42] Nonetheless, the *Breviary* episode displays certain motifs and moral messaging that cannot be accounted for solely by reference to scholia abstracts. The presence of swine, the child-like appearance of the strange figure on his discovery, the figure's demonic associations, and the hostility of the discoverer toward him are not found in the scholia on Tages. If the scholia served as inspiration, they have clearly been expanded upon by the homilist-hagiographer, quite possibly with reference to one or more of the fuller accounts of the Tages myth. This invites comparison with the more developed classical Latin authorities, two of which would especially account for the *Breviary*'s motifs. One is Isidore, whose work was certainly available in Ireland. The other, less obviously available though perhaps not inaccessible, is Cicero. Taken together alongside *Bethu Phátraic*, these two authorities might account for the *Breviary* episode in its entirety. This is not to exclude the possibility that the strange children in *Bethu Phátraic* and the *Breviary* may derive ultimately from an indigenous tradition or chthonic mythology; that they may have sprung from Irish, rather than Tyrrhenian, soil.[43] To

---

see *Supplementum adnotationum super Lucanum*, ed. Giuseppe A. Cavajoni (Milano: Cisalpino-Goliardica, 1979–90), vol. 1, xxxiii–v, 86; Cillian O'Hogan, "Reading Lucan with Scholia in Medieval Ireland: In Cath Catharda and its Sources," *Cambrian Medieval Celtic Studies* 68 (Winter, 2014): 21–49 at 33–4.

[41] *Scholia in Lucani bellum civile*, ed. Hermann Usener (Leipzig, 1869), 41; O'Hogan, "Reading Lucan," 34.

[42] Ovid, *Metamorphoses*, ed. Miller, 15.554; Isidore, *Etymologiarum*, ed. Lindsay, 8.9.34; *The Etymologies*, trans. Barney et al., 183.

[43] See footnote 33 above.

attempt to exclude this would be to prove a negative that cannot be proved. However, even if the stories did derive ultimately from an indigenous tradition (a question which could well be the subject of another paper in its own right), a medieval Irish author or audience could not have avoided those stories' obvious resonances with the familiar motifs and messages of the Latin Tages myth to which they had access. Therefore, it is those stories' probable relationship with the traditions surrounding Tages which form the remainder of my discussion today.[44]

It is worth starting with Isidore's *Etymologiae* as a source to which an Irish homilist-hagiographer could certainly have had easy access. Isidore discusses the myth of Tages in his chapter *De magis* (Concerning Magicians). He calls the myth a *fabula* (fable), a category of narration which he had previously defined as *non sunt res factae, sed tantum loquendo fictae* (not actual events that took place, but that were only invented in words).[45] Nonetheless, he accepted that fables

---

[44] For those wishing to situate the *Breviary* episode in a specifically "indigenous" context, a good starting point might be to explore the abundance of uncanny swine in the medieval insular literary tradition. See, e.g., William Hackett, "Folk-Lore. No. I. Porcine Legends," *Transactions of the Kilkenny Archaeological Society* 2.2 (1853): 303-10; John Rhys, *Celtic Folklore: Welsh and Manx*, vol. 2 (Oxford: Clarendon Press, 1901), 501-5; John Arnott MacCulloch, *The Religion of the Ancient Celts* (Edinburgh: T. & T. Clark, 1911), 209-11; Tom Peete Cross, "The Psalter of the Pig, an Irish Legend," *Modern Philology* 18.8 (December, 1920): 443-55 at 447; Sister Mary Donatus, "Beasts and Birds in the Lives of the Early Irish Saints" (Philadelphia: Unpublished Doctoral Thesis, University of Philadelphia, 1934), 73-80, 147-50; Anne Ross, *Pagan Celtic Britain: Studies in Iconography and Tradition* (London: Routledge & Kegan Paul, 1967), 308-21;Próinséas Ní Chatháin, "Swineherds, Seers, and Druids," in *Studia Celtica* 14--5 (1979–80), pp. 200-11; Patrick K. Ford, "A Highly Important Pig," in Ann Therese E. Matonis and Daniel F. Melia, eds., *Celtic Language, Celtic Culture: A Festschrift for Eric P..* Hamp (Van Nuys, CA: Ford & Bailie, 1990), 293-304; Miranda J. Green, *Animals in Celtic Life and Myth* (London: Routledge, 1992), 17-20, 164-6, 169-71.

[45] Isidore, *Etymologiarum*, ed. Lindsay, 1.40.1; translation in *The Etymologies of Isidore of Seville*, trans. Stephen A. Barney, W. J. Lewis, J.

might be used to make a moral point. Importantly, Isidore is the first source to associate Tages with the demonic. This is a crucial element of the *Breviary* episode, which assimilates the child to the other demonic questioners in *Betha Adamnáin* and provides the story with its Christian message:

> *Itaque haec vanitas magicarum artium ex traditione angelorum malorum in toto terrarum orbe plurimis saeculis valuit. Per quandam scientiam futurorum et infernorum et vocationes eorum inventa sunt aruspicia, augurationes, et ipsa quae dicuntur oracula et necromantia. [. . .] Aruspicinae artem primus Etruscis tradidisse dicitur quidam Tages. Hic ex oris aruspicinam dictavit, et postea non apparuit. Nam dicitur fabulose, arante quodam rustico, subito hunc ex glebis exiluisse et aruspicinam dictasse, qua die et mortuus est. Quos libros Romani ex Tusca lingua in propriam mutaverunt.*

Consequently, this foolery of the magic arts held sway over the entire world for many centuries through the instruction of the evil angels. By a certain knowledge of things to come and of things below, and by invoking them, *aruspicia* (divinations), auguries, and those things that are called oracles and necromancy were invented. [. . .] A certain Tages is said to have first given the art of *aruspicina* to the Etruscans. He pronounced divinations orally, and after that did not show himself. It is said in fable that when a certain rustic was ploughing, he suddenly leapt up from the clods and pronounced a divination, and on that day he died. The Romans translated these books from the Etruscan language into their own.[46]

A. Beach, Oliver Berghof, and Muriel Hall (Cambridge: Cambridge University Press, 2006), 66.
[46] Isidore, *Etymologiarum*, ed. Lindsay, 8.9.3, 8.9.34-35; *The Etymologies*, trans. Barney et al., 181, 183.

Isidore can thus account for the demonic aspect of the foundling and for Adamnán's consequent hostility to his conjectures, both of which are essential features of the *Breviary* episode. Nonetheless, Isidore makes no mention of the child-like appearance of Tages or of the presence of livestock at the discovery, which are equally important as literary motifs in the *Breviary* episode, if not as moral message. For these, the fullest classical narrative and commentary in Latin on the myth of Tages, and the closest version to the *Breviary* episode, appears to be that provided by the pagan philosopher Marcus Tullius Cicero in his treatise *De Divinatione* (On Divination). Cicero commanded a special interest during the Carolingian renaissance of the ninth century, when several important manuscript copies of his works were made within the Frankish Empire. Notably, his writings were known to the Irish scholars who were numerous in the Carolingian schools. The Irishman Sedulis Scottus, who compiled his *Collectaneum* at Liège in the middle of the ninth century, excerpted an impressive number of Ciceronian works.[47] By the third quarter of the ninth century, and continuing through the tenth century, several manuscripts of Cicero's philosophical works, including *De Divinatione*, were in active use at the abbey of Corbie.[48] Corbie has been described as "an important stopping point for travellers to and from" the insular world (a relationship attested in eleventh-century Irish saints' *vitae*), and as a major centre of book production whose manuscripts displayed significant artistic parallels with those of the Columban monastic federation (as respectively exemplified by the Corbie Psalter and the Book of Kells).[49] This would suggest an obvious conduit for

---

[47] Leighton Durham Reynolds, ed., *Texts and Transmission: A Survey of the Latin Classics* (New York: Doubleday, 1983), 73-4, 133, 141; idem, *Scribes and Scholars: A Guide to the Transmission of Greek and Latin Literature* (Oxford: Clarendon Press, 1991), 102-3.

[48] Reynolds, ed., *Texts and Transmission*, 124-5.

[49] David Ganz, *Corbie in the Carolingian Renaissance*, Beihefte zu Francia 20 (Sigmaringen: Jan Thorbecke Verlag, 1990), quoted at 41; Bernard Meehan, "The Book of Kells and the Corbie Psalter (with a Note on Harley 2788)," in Toby Barnard, Dáibhí Ó Cróinín, and Katharine Simms, eds., *'A Miracle of Learning': Studies in Manuscripts and Irish Learning: Essays in Honour of William O'Sullivan* (Aldershot: Ashgate, 1998), 29-39. The

transmission to Ireland, though it must be admitted that no direct evidence has been identified to date for access to Cicero's works in Ireland before the composition of *Betha Adamnáin*. Nonetheless, the Middle Irish poem *A Rí richid, réidig dam* (O King of Heaven, Clarify to Me), by the eleventh-century poet Gilla in Chomded úa Cormaic, refers to *Cicir* (Cicero) and his scribe Marcus Tullius Tiro, demonstrating that at least indirect knowledge of, and interest in, the Roman philosopher existed in Ireland by the eleventh century.[50] Given this accumulation of circumstantial evidence, there is little reason to suppose that the more important Irish monastic federations could not have gained access to *De Divinatione* through any one of these channels in the tenth century, when the later stages of the Carolingian renaissance made their impact felt in Ireland. Even if the homilist-hagiographer of *Betha Adamnáin* did not have ready access to *De Divinatione* in a Columban library, his interests in the limits of licit knowledge and prophecy would have made it worthwhile to have sought out a copy to lend further weight to his homiletic theme. This possibility will be considered in more detail later in the piece.

Cicero's version of the Tages myth is notably unique among the dozen or so authorities mentioned to digress at length on the childlike appearance of the sage at his discovery: an essential element of the myth nearly always noted in modern scholarship on Tages, and a crucial analogue with the *Breviary* episode. Cicero reports:

---

debate over whether the Book of Kells was produced in whole or in part at Kells, or at Iona or another monastic house within the Columban federation, need not distract from Corbie's connexions with the Insular world.

[50] Gilla in Chomded Úa Cormaic, *A Rí richid, réidig dam*, §16, in Richard Irvine Best and M. A. O'Brien, eds. *The Book of Leinster, Formerly Lebar na Núachongbála*, vol. 3 (Dublin: Dublin Institute for Advanced Studies, 1957), 574-87 at 576, lines 17787–90. Brent Miles, *Heroic Saga and Classical Epic in Medieval Ireland* (New York: D. S. Brewer, 2011), 48-9, has observed that the poet appears to have derived his knowledge of antiquity indirectly, through the synchronic world history in Eusebius/Jerome's *Chronica*. John Carey has suggested to me that, in this case, the poet may be drawing his information from Isidore, *Etymologiarum*, ed. Lindsay, 1.12.1; *The Etymologies*, trans. Barney et al., 51, a text he used in other instances too. I am grateful to Brigid Ehrmantraut for bringing this stanza to my attention and to Prof. Carey for his helpful comment.

Tages quidam dicitur in agro Tarquiniensi, cum terra araretur et sulcus altius esset impressus, exstitisse repente et eum adfatus esse qui arabat. Is autem Tages, ut in libris est Etruscorum, puerili specie dicitur visus, sed senili fuisse prudentia. Eius adspectu cum obstipuisset bubulcus clamoremque maiorem cum admiratione edidisset, concursum esse factum, totamque brevi tempore in eum locum Etruriam convenisse. Tum illum plura locutum multis audientibus, qui omnia verba eius exceperint litterisque mandarint. Omnem autem orationem fuisse eam qua haruspicinae disciplina contineretur; eam postea crevisse rebus novis cognoscendis et ad eadem illa principia referendis. Haec accepimus ab ipsis, haec scripta conservant, hunc fontem habent disciplinae.

A certain Tages is said to have sprung up in the territory of Tarquinii, when the earth was being ploughed and a deeper furrow than usual was pressed into it, and to have addressed the one who was ploughing. This Tages, moreover, as reported in the books of the Etrurians, is said to have appeared in *puerili specie* (a boyish form) but with the prudence of old age. When the *bubulcus* (herdsman) was surprised at the sight of him and uttered a great shout in astonishment, some people assembled, and before long, the whole of Etruria had come together at that spot. Then he [Tages] spoke many things to the crowd of hearers, who received all his words and committed them to writing. Moreover, all the discourse was that which was continued in *haruspicinae disciplina* (the science of the soothsayers), which was improved afterwards by the recognition of *rebus novis* (new events) and by referring them back to those same principles. From them, we received these things:

these writings that they preserve, this source of the
science that they hold.[51]

The narrative correspondences between the Ciceronian story and
the *Breviary* episode are close. Even in abbreviated abstract, the
childlike *species* (appearance) of the two otherworldly figures, their
unexpected discovery in the newly ploughed earth, and their
precocious posing of numerous arcane matters to their astonished
hearers make the association between the two stories clear. A close
reading of Cicero might also explain the introduction of swine to the
hagiographical narrative. In no classical source do swine appear at the
discovery of Tages. Ovid claimed that Tages was unearthed without
the help of human hands, which would not be inconsistent with the
image of swine rooting up the earth.[52] There was also the association
of livestock with haruspicy, which a medieval audience would have
known was based on the examination of animal entrails, though there
is evidence that some ancient diviners preferred not to use pigs.[53]
Cicero's *bubulcus*, however, can be interpreted a rustic or herdsman,
which might additionally imply the presence of livestock necessary to
speed the plough. In his *Etymologiae*, Isidore compared the meaning
of the word *bubulcus*, which he defined as 'cow-herd' (derived
etymologically from *bos*, cattle), with *subulcus*, 'swine-herd' (from
sus, swine).[54] There is nothing in the early medieval manuscript
tradition of *De Divinatione* to suggest that *subulcus*, an admittedly
rarer term in classical Latin, ever replaced *bubulcus* as a variant
reading of the text.[55] On the other hand, arguably, it did not have to. In

---

[51] Cicero, *De Divinatione*, 2.50.
[52] Ovid, *Metamorphoses*, ed. Miller, 15.554.
[53] For the well-attested use of pigs in Roman sacrifice, see Celia E. Schultz,
"Roman Sacrifice, Inside and Out," *The Journal of Roman Studies* 106
(2016): 58-76 at 63. For the ancient Greek view of the unsuitability of pigs
for divination, however, see Derek Collins, "Mapping the Entrails: The
Practice of Greek Hepatoscopy," *The American Journal of Philology* 129.3
(Fall, 2008): 319-45 at 334.
[54] Isidore, *Etymologiarum*, ed. Lindsay, X.S.263; *The Etymologies*, trans.
Barney et al., 229.
[55] For the variant readings of the principal manuscripts, see the critical
apparatus in Marcus Tullius Cicero, *De divinatione; De fato; Timaeus*, ed.

medieval Latin, *bubulcus* in addition to its etymologically primary meaning of 'cow-herd', acquired the further additional meaning of 'swine-herd'.[56] To a medieval Irish reader, this might suggest that it was not a cattle-driven plough but swine rooting up the earth that had been responsible for Tages' discovery. Such a sense may indeed have come most naturally to an Irish audience, when one considers that the Irish word for ploughshare, *socc*, originally meant 'pig' (cognate with Latin *sus*), and that early Irish legal terminology displayed a conscious affinity between *srúb tuirc* (the snout of a boar) and *srúb n-arathair* (the snout of a plough).[57] Alternatively, the Latin term *sulcus* (furrow), which is found in both Cicero's and Martianus' respective accounts of Tages, might evoke by more distant association images of the similar words, *sus* or *subulcus*, and hence swine inclined to digging furrows. To cap off these porcine associations, it is worth noting that the Latin synonym, *porca*, can itself refer equally to 'the ridge of a furrow' or 'a sow'.

Other narrative episodes and motifs within *Betha Adamnáin* offer further indirect evidence of association. For instance, Cicero is unique among the classical authors in having the whole of Etruria gather in an assembly (*concursus*) to hear the strange child. In that respect, the *Breviary* differs in having the child seemingly pose his message to a lone hearer. However, the *Breviary* is unusual in this instance. In *Betha Adamnáin*, most of the saint's activity takes place amidst an *airecht* (public gathering), *rígdáil* (royal assembly), or *slúag* (crowd

---

Otto Plasberg and Wilhelm Heinrich Ax (Stuttgart: B. G. Teubner, 1969), 85[b].

[56] *Dictionary of Medieval Latin from British Sources*, ed. Ronald Edward Latham, David R. Howlett, and Richard Ashdowne, vol. 1 (London: Oxford University Press, 1975), *s.v.* bubulcus.

[57] Fergus Kelly, *Early Irish Farming: A Study Based Mainly on the Law-texts of the 7th and 8th centuries AD*, Early Irish Law Series 4 (Dublin: Dublin Institute for Advanced Studies, 1997), 469-70. Compare the observation of Peter J. Reynolds, *Iron Age Farm: The Butser Experiment* (London: British Museum, 1979), 53: "It is possible [. . .] to use a herd of pigs in such a way as to prepare and manure a seed bed, clean up after harvest, and never actually employ a plough at all. The only human input is concerned with planting, hoeing, and reaping." Reynold's assessment has been endorsed by Green, *Animals in Celtic Life and Myth*, 19.

of people), or atop a *tulach* (hill of assembly).[58] Such assemblies are the public location of Adamnán's disputations and challenging questioners in human guise up to this point in the narrative. The setting of the action within royal assemblies is consistent both with the public career of the historical Adamnán and with the biblical narrative of Job, on which the hagiographical narrative and homily are based, in which the Devil challenges Job's case both in the royal assembly of Heaven (1:6–2:12) and later in the presence of Job's royal comforters.[59] In the *Breviary*, on the other hand, almost all reference to the public gatherings known from *Betha Adamnáin* is omitted. The sole instance which is retained is the demonic confrontation of Adamnán amidst the airecht and slúag of Munstermen in *Betha Adamnáin*, §2, revised as the second lection of the *Breviary* Life. Here, however, the *Breviary* states only that the people arrived (*advenit populus*)to hear the saint after his abbatial election, omitting any mention of the assembly's location or participants as specified in *Betha Adamnáin*.[60] Thus, it seems probable that the third lection–the *Breviary* episode–abbreviates a somewhat longer narrative which would have originally set the confrontation between Adamnán and the demonic child in a public assembly. Indeed, such a concursus may have been deliberately omitted from the third lection of the *Breviary* Life, as it was already implied by the *adventus populi* of the second lection. In *Betha Adamnáin*, such a setting would have drawn out the thematic parallels necessary to underscore the internal association of the demonic questioner with the earlier demonic questioners in the assemblies of §§2–3. If we accept the likelihood that the discovery and confrontation of the strange/demonic child was a public occasion in *Betha Adamnáin*, it offers another intertextual parallel with Cicero's account of Tages. While the author of the *Breviary* episode could have taken several of his key details from Ovid, Martianus, or Isidore, and indeed would probably have had one or more of those texts in mind when

---

[58] Herbert and Ó Riain, eds., *Betha Adamnáin*, 48-9, 52-3, §§2–3, 10, lines 46, 49, 100. See also the discussion of these terms in ibid., 67-8, 73. Such settings are not explicitly labelled, but are heavily implied to be the same, for the other secular episodes in ibid., 50-5, §§4–9.

[59] Harrington, "Adamnán, Kells, and Job," 61-4.

[60] Herbert and Ó Riain, eds., *Betha Adamnáin*, 37, 48-9; Macquarrie and Butter, eds., *Legends of Scottish Saints*, 232-3.

writing his account, Cicero offers the closest parallels with the stories in both the *Breviary* and *Betha Adamnáin* as they survive.

***

Cicero is an apt comparison for reasons other than narrative length and detail. Notably, he is unique among the Latin authors in his degree of outright hostility to the myth of Tages, in which he arguably surpasses even Isidore. Here it is worth considering the place of the myth within Cicero's work. *De Divinatione* is structured as a philosophical dialogue on divination. In the first book, the character Quintus (Cicero's brother) presents the case in favour of both the viability and efficacy of divination, while in the second book, a character bearing Cicero's own name presents the case against it. The myth of Tages as it appears in *De Divinatione* belongs to this second book. It should be noted that Cicero was not opposed to all forms of prediction per se. He did not object to the reality of the gods' attempts to communicate with humans, or to human attempts to establish relationships between the past, present, and future. Rather, what he opposed were the so-called "arts" of divination.[61] The dialogue concludes that while any answer to the question must be provisional, the case seems to weigh against divination.[62]

Such a philosophical and moral conclusion, offering a rejection of the divinatory arts coupled with an acknowledgement of the utter unknowability of the answers to certain speculative questions, is consistent with the homiletic theme of *Betha Adamnáin*. Cicero's argument is consistent with the moral message of the theophany in Job 38, which challenges the ability of humans to know those things which are veiled regarding the past, present, and future.[63] The pagan author's argument is also consistent with the message of the questioning

---

[61] Federico Santangelo, *Divination, Prediction, and the End of the Roman Republic* (Cambridge: Cambridge University Press, 2013), 13.

[62] It has been debated how closely the character of Cicero in the dialogue resembles the Roman orator's actual views, but this would not have detained a medieval audience. See Mary Beard, "Cicero and Divination: The Formation of a Latin Discourse," *The Journal of Roman Studies* 76 (1986): 33-46; Malcolm Schofield, "Cicero for and against Divination," *The Journal of Roman Studies* 76 (1986): 47-65; Santangelo, *Divination*, 11, 15-23.

[63] Harrington, "Adamnán, Kells, and Job," 59-62.

episodes in *Betha Adamnáin*. In these, Adamnán rejects the problems posed by his speculative questioners as *esamain* (audacious).[64] These would have made Cicero's text attractive to the Irish homilist. Moreover, the saint is perfectly willing to accept and admit that he does not know the answers and should not desire to. Far from making the wonder-working saint's response to such questions "uncharacteristically weak," as the text's editors have suggested, this depiction is remarkably consistent with the epistemic humility commanded by Job 38 and Gregory the Great.[65] It should come as no surprise that the homilist might also look to Cicero, a highly respected authority on divination, and add a moral exemplum inspired by that work to support his broader homiletic argument. For those who might question the use of a pagan philosopher and a reworked pagan myth to support this message, the homilist includes a self-referential justification within his narrative, by noting that Adamnán laboured in the study and teaching of the liberal arts. Since this curriculum rested, of course, on the writings of pagan authors such as Cicero, the invocation of Adamnán's authority clears the way for a moral exemplum adapted from the Roman orator.

With these points in mind, it is worth directly considering Cicero's comments on Tages. Immediately after providing the details of the myth, Cicero condemns it as nonsensical:

> *Num ergo opus est ad haec refellenda Carneade? Num Epicuro? Estne quisquam ita desipiens, qui credat exaratum esse–deum dicam an hominem? Si deus, cur se contra naturam in terram abdiderat, ut patefactus aratro lucem aspiceret? Quid? Idem nonne poterat deus hominibus disciplinam superiore e loco tradere? Si autem homo ille Tages fuit, quonam modo potuit terra oppressus vivere? Unde porro illa potuit, quae docebat alios, ipse didicisse? Sed ego insipientior quam illi ipsi, qui ista credunt, qui quidem contra eos tam diu disputem.*

---

[64] Herbert and Ó Riain, eds., *Betha Adamnáin*, 48-9, §2, line 41.
[65] Herbert and Ó Riain, eds., *Betha Adamnáin*, 69; Harrington, "Adamnán, Kells, and Job," 65.

Now do we need a Carneades or an Epicurus to refute
such nonsense? Who in the world is stupid enough to
believe that anybody ever ploughed up–which shall I
say–a god or a man? If a god, why did he, contrary to
his nature, hide himself in the ground to be uncovered
and brought to the light of day by a plough? Could not
this so-called "god" have delivered this art to
mankind from a more exalted station? But if this
fellow Tages was a man, pray, how could he have
lived covered with earth? Finally, where had he
himself learned the things he taught others? But
really, in spending so much time in refuting such
stuff, I am more absurd than the very people who
believe it.[66]

If the myth is so obviously nonsensical, one might ask why either
the hagiographical character Adamnán or his Irish audience should
have been any less critical of a similar situation. *Bethu Phátraic*
arguably sidestepped Cicero's first two objections by claiming that
Olcán was an ordinary child who had unusually been born within a
cairn, providing him the necessary air-pocket to live and breathe for
the seven days he spent underground. It also claims no special
knowledge on the part of Olcán, circumventing Cicero's third
objection to the myth.

At least initially, the homilist of *Betha Adamnáin* hints at the
same 'rationalising' explanation for his own story of the child dug up
from the earth. The preceding episodes establish that sometimes
infants can be born after their mother's death, and that sometimes
pregnant women can be interred in graveyards, without the
undertakers' knowledge of those pregnancies.[67] Given that the
historical Adamnán had noted the propensity of swine to uproot
graveyards, it seems probable that *Betha Adamnáin*'s audience was
being invited to imagine a 'coffin birth' that resembled that of Olcán
in *Bethu Phátraic*.[68] Indeed, this point may have originally been made
more explicit in the *Breviary* episode before it was abbreviated later.

---

[66] Cicero, *De Divinatione*, 2.50-1.
[67] Herbert and Ó Riain, eds., *Betha Adamnáin*, 48-51, 54-5, §§3, 11.
[68] Harrington, "Adamnán, Kells, and Job," 72-3.

According to the homilist's logic, this might then explain Adamnán's initial acceptance of the strange, but perhaps still human, child. In that respect, Adamnán's initial, sceptical acceptance of the strange child, before giving way to outright hostility once new information had presented itself, is notably consistent with the approach of the pagan author. Cicero's *De Divinatione* shows the philosopher's humble willingness to give the question of divination a hearing, before ultimately rejecting it.

A similarly negative attitude to the truth of the story is offered by Isidore, who, as already mentioned, calls the story a fabula. On the moral level, Isidore accepted that fables might be used to make a moral point.[69] Nonetheless, Cicero's dismissal of the story inevitably raised another possibility for the Christian reader that would not have been so obvious for the pagan philosopher. If this Tages could not be a god, but also could not be a man who lived under the earth, the reasonable Christian inference was that he must have been a demon from the underworld. This was precisely the view taken by Isidore when he attributed Tages *scientia futurorum et infernorum* (knowledge of things to come and of things below).[70] The Christian view was that demons posed as pagan gods and were ubiquitous and universal in all times and places.[71] If such a demon could infest and haunt the Etruscan past, it was just as plausible that such a demon could similarly infest and haunt Ireland in Adamnán's day. Here, for the Christian reader, Cicero's explicit recognition of the provisional nature of knowledge opens his conclusions regarding the myth of Tages to further explication and updating in the new light of Christian revelation.

These attitudes give a broader significance to the cluster of episodes in *Betha Adamnáin* which would originally have surrounded the *Breviary* episode. Notably, the episode of the demon in childlike guise would have been sandwiched between Adamnán's resurrection miracles and a story in which the saint is miraculously permitted in his cell to hold the Christ Child, a figure which had become an increased

---

[69] Isidore, *Etymologiarum*, ed. Lindsay, 1.40.1; *The Etymologies*, trans. Barney et al., 66.
[70] Isidore, *Etymologiarum*, ed. Lindsay, 8.9.3; *The Etymologies*, trans. Barney et al., 181.
[71] Isidore, *Etymologiarum*, ed. Lindsay, 8.11.4–5; *The Etymologies*, trans. Barney et al., 184.

object of devotion and affective piety in tenth-century Ireland.[72] Thus, in two immediately sequential episodes, the saint encounters an otherworldly visitor who appears in the form of a human child, bringing with him the promise of illumination regarding the meaning of Creation. As Jean-René Jannot has observed, "the child expert in things divine is a very widespread theme, extending into Christianity;"[73] indeed, the theme is most pronounced in the Gospel account of the twelve-year old Jesus teaching the elders in the Temple.[74] The modern mythographer's association between the *puer senex* and Christ may additionally have been natural for late antique and medieval commentators. Charles Murgia and Danuta Shanzer have suggested that Martianus' fifth-century account of Tages includes descriptions of Christ that were transferred to the Etruscan sage in conscious imitation.

> Martianus appears to have thought of the words of Prudentius which describe Christ's coming into the world and his takeover of Rome and to have used them to describe yet another child-god . . . the mysterious Tages, born from a furrow, and connected with the foundation of Etruria, and hence of Rome. Both gods first appeared to humble folk: Christ to the shepherds and Tages to a plowman.[75]

---

[72] Herbert and Ó Riain, eds., *Betha Adamnáin*, 56-9, §§13–5. See also Thomas C. O'Donnell, "'It is No Ordinary Child I Foster in My Little Cell': Fostering the Christ Child in Medieval Ireland," *Eolas* 10 (2017): 89-108; idem, *Fosterage in Medieval Ireland: An Emotional History*, The Early Medieval North Atlantic 9 (Amsterdam: Amsterdam University Press, 2020), Ch. 4.

[73] Jannot, *Religion in Ancient Etruria*, 3. See also Carp, "Puer senex", passim.

[74] Luke 2:41–52; Carp, "Puer senex," 737; Joseph Ratzinger (Pope Benedict XVI), *Jesus of Nazareth: The Infancy Narratives*, trans. Philip J. Whitmore (New York: Bloomsbury, 2012), 123-7.

[75] Danuta Shanzer, "De Tagetis exaratione," *Hermes* 115.1 (1987): 127-8 (quoted at 127) offered a reading of Martianus by analogy with Prudentius, following a suggestion of Charles Murgia. Jerzy Linderski, "A Non-Misunderstood Text Concerning Tages," in idem, *Roman Questions:*

In addition, both figures were associated with divine light.[76] Strikingly, the Irish homilist seems to have made a similar connexion, albeit one which reimagines Tages as a demonic mockery of Christ's Incarnation and Resurrection. Christ's Nativity underground in a cave in Bethlehem, which foreshadowed the three days spent in another cave before his Resurrection, was traditionally held to have occurred between an ox and an ass and to have been revealed to shepherds.[77] So too, the otherworldly visitor in the *Breviary* episode is held to have emerged from the ground in the company of swine, with his own, heavily implied, liminal, miraculous, and otherworldly associations of the 'coffin birth.' It is only once Adamnán has rejected the false promise of illumination by the demon in childlike (Tages-like) guise that he is able to receive the true promise of illumination by the Christ Child.

These associations may offer the most convincing explanation for the swine's role in the hagiographical narrative: that they were added to underscore the demonic dimension. On the one hand, Isidore had noted the symbolic association of swine with illegitimate children, and such an association would symbolically reinforce the implied 'rational' association of the child with unusual pregnancy.[78] On the other hand, demons, the dead, and swine could be closely linked in the Christian tradition. In biblical literature, the most memorable instance is the demonic legion which first possessed the demoniac who lived among the tombs of Gadara, and which thereafter, by Christ's permission, infested the Gadarene swine.[79] Patristic commentators suggested that the demons had targeted the swine because of how they lived, with a figurative emphasis on the pride of the flesh and spirit (or

---

Selected Papers, Heidelberger althistorische Beiträge und epigraphische Studien 20 (Stuttgart: F. Steiner, 1995), 590-1, 676-7, has questioned whether this is the original, authorial reading, but this does not preclude such an association being made by a medieval reader.

[76] Shanzer, "De Tagetis exaratione," 127.

[77] Pope Benedict XVI, *Jesus of Nazareth*, 67-9, 71-3.

[78] Jamie Kreiner, *Legions of Pigs in the Early Medieval West* (New Haven: Yale University Press, 2020), 32. Of course, Kreiner, ibid., 16-7, has also reminded that pigs are highly individual and their symbolic associations far from stable.

[79] Matthew 8:28–34; Mark 5:1–20; Luke 8:26–39; cf. Isaiah 65:4.

intellect), all of which were important to the homiletic theme of *Betha Adamnáin*.[80] Notably, the Gadarene swine rose to a new prominence in visual cycles of the life of Christ produced at around the time of *Betha Adamnáin*'s composition: in the Ottonian iconography of the latter part of the tenth century, which displayed a renewed emphasis on the demonic infestation.[81] In addition, Psalm 79 noted the dangers that swine posed to vineyards, which Irish exegetes interpreted figuratively as the destruction of graveyards (as the vineyards of the Lord), a destruction which might similarly be attributed to the demonic.[82] It has already been mentioned that the historical Adamnán wrote negatively of livestock grazing on cemeteries, a combination of naturalist observation with biblical exegesis which appears to be integral to the narrative logic of *Betha Adamnáin*.[83] Near the end of the hagiographical narrative, a revenant corpse arrives to question Adamnán, reinforcing the association of demons with graveyards.[84] Given that *Betha Adamnáin* is a text which foregrounds the demonic opposition to Adamnán in its opening chapter, it is reasonable to expect the *Breviary* episode's audience to have been attuned to potential markers of the demonic and to have detected the association. By adding pigs to the tale, this narrative framing of the episode furnishes a powerful narrative economy. This allows the hagiographer to dispense with Cicero's lengthy, explicit moralisation on the ungodly nature of Tages, a moralisation which Cicero had pronounced absurd to have to state explicitly.

***

The foregoing discussion has shown the ways in which the *Breviary* episode may be seen as consistent with tenth-century continental and insular currents in biblical exegesis, Christian iconography, classical literary revival, devotional piety, and hagiographical narrative. In moral terms, *Betha Adamnáin* clearly

---

[80] Kreiner, *Legions of Pigs*, 182-3. Also significant to patristic commentators on the swine was the theme of idolatry, which the Tages/Christ juxtaposition might further insinuate.
[81] Kreiner, *Legions of Pigs*, 187-95.
[82] Harrington, "Adamnán, Kells, and Job," 73. See also the literal examples in footnote 31 above.
[83] Harrington, "Adamnán, Kells, and Job," 72-3.
[84] Herbert and Ó Riain, eds., *Betha Adamnáin*, 58-61, §16.

warns its audience through moral exempla against difficult questions and speculations regarding the past, present, and future.[85] For the homilist, such speculation is a form of intellectual pride that does not spiritually edify or illuminate. Rather, it must be properly recognised as a kind of demonic temptation that only sows confusion, frustration, and disbelief. Of course, the author of *Betha Adamnáin* was not opposed to legitimate prophecy or to faith in divine and saintly promises regarding the future. The entire medieval exegetical enterprise was premised on an acceptance and an understanding of the intelligible relationships between past, present, and future, with a special focus on those relationships that were securely grounded in biblical scripture and hagiographical record. The Bible was filled with prophecy. The Columban federation honoured both Columba and Adamnán for their access to prophetic insight.[86] *Betha Adamnáin* is filled with negative prophecies uttered by Adamnán against his opponents, pronouncements of a dire future which is said to have been fulfilled.[87] The narrative concludes with the saint's prophecy of an affliction that would come upon the men of Britain and Ireland around the feast of St. John, which it identifies as a prophecy of Adamnán's own death.[88] The homiletic peroration offers conventional praise of Adamnán in terms of the biblical prophets, comparing him with St. Paul as a vessel for proclaiming truth.[89]

The homilist was keen, however, to emphasise that any such prophecy needed to come ultimately from Christ, to whom the exemplary figure of Job and the prophets pointed forward, and the figure of Adamnán pointed back.[90] At the same time, the sole direct appearance of Christ in *Betha Adamnáin* is juxtaposed with the deception of the diabolical Enemy in childlike guise. This offers an admonitory, parallel exegesis, in which the demonic deceptions and

---

[85] See episodes in Herbert and Ó Riain, eds., *Betha Adamnáin*, 34-5, 48-51, 58-61, §§2–3, 16.
[86] Carey, "Supernatural Contact," 59-62; Clancy, "Adomnán in Medieval Gaelic Literary Tradition," 115-22.
[87] Herbert and Ó Riain, eds., *Betha Adamnáin*, 49-57, §§2-10, 13.
[88] Herbert and Ó Riain, eds., *Betha Adamnáin*, 60-1, §17; Lacey, *Adomnán*, 174.
[89] Herbert and Ó Riain, eds., *Betha Adamnáin*, 62-3, §18.
[90] Harrington, "Adamnán, Kells, and Job," 79.

temptations of Job's comforters and of the Etruscans' Tages pointed forward mockingly to the Devil in the New Testament, and Adamnán's demonic questioners pointed back. The homilist of *Betha Adamnáin* is adamant that Adamnán's prophecies stand securely under divine inspiration, are valid in all times and places, and can be counted upon as worthy of confident belief. While doing so, he rejects any alternative speculations, predictions, or prophecies that may come from other, less secure sources of pride and intellect.

Having considered both the classical 'source' and moral message of the homiletic episode, it is worth asking why the homilist included them within his narrative. One possibility, given the analogue in *Bethu Phátraic*, is that the Tages-inspired story was intended as a rhetorical swipe at the tenth-century hagiography of Patrick. Such intertextual argument was not unknown in medieval Irish hagiography. It has been suggested, for instance, that the transformation of the British chieftain Coroticus into a fox in Muirchú's seventh-century hagiography of Patrick may have represented deliberate propaganda on the part of Armagh against its principal hagiographical competitor, Cogitosus' Kildare-sponsored hagiography of Brigit. The story might have been designed to discredit the story of Brigit's tame fox. The point, it has been argued, was that foxes are dangerous and not to be treated lightly.[91] One might detect a similar motive at work in the tenth century. The period saw increased competition following the Columban federation's relative diminution of status in favour of the Patrician federation, a development which drew complaint from the Kells homilist of *Betha Adamnáin*.[92] In drawing a figurative parallel between Tages and Olcán (whose name explicitly contains the onomastic element for 'evil'), while insinuating a demonic origin for a child found in similarly strange and otherworldly circumstances, the Kells homilist might have intended a similar rhetorical swipe at the expense of the Armagh federation. Likewise, the rooting of the swine in the earth–which had recovered pagan gold for Patrick, but a pagan god (or demon) for Adamnán–undercut the more positive patristic message which had arguably Christianised the formerly pagan learning in *Bethu Phátraic*. Some pagan learning was acceptable, as

---

[91] David R. Howlett, ed., *Muirchú Moccu Macthéni's Vita Sancti Patricii: Life of Saint Patrick* (Dublin: Four Courts Press, 2006), 182.
[92] Herbert and Ó Riain, eds., *Betha Adamnáin*, 13-6, 51, 70, §6.

endorsed by Augustine and by the Patrician hagiographers and exegetes of Armagh, but it was not without its real and lingering dangers.

Nonetheless, the *Breviary* episode suggests that the homilist's special concern was to shore up the status of Adamnán as prophet, while circumscribing prophecy within carefully defined limits. Neither need have been a direct response to *Bethu Phátraic*. Instead, the pressure may have come from within Kells and the Columban federation itself. The period of *Betha Adamnáin*'s composition was a difficult time for the federation and for the community of Kells. Around the turn of the century, Kells appears to have lost the subject church of Moone in Kildare and its wider influence in south Leinster to the expanding see of Glendalough. The federation suffered repeated Norse depredations on Iona and Kells, including the plundering of Kells in 951 and 970, when its relics of Columba and Adamnán may have been taken. It saw political pressure from its royal neighbours, a relegation in its privileged status, the emergence of a rivalry between Kells and Iona, and laxity among its tenants.[93]

In the face of such hardship and uncertainty, it would be understandable that members of the monastic community should begin to doubt their position in the world. They would have had questions regarding both the past–in the causative sin which presumably underlay their suffering–and the future. There may have been the special temptation either to doubt Adamnán's prophecies and continuing protection of his community as valid in all times and places, or to turn to speculation and divination for answers. The biblical promise and example that the homilist set before his audience to counter these two tendencies were those of Job, whose attributed virtues he mapped onto the life of their exemplary abbot and saintly patron Adamnán. The homilist urged his community to reject idle speculation and demonic temptation, to bear their suffering patiently and manfully, and to double down on monastic discipline. Provided they did so, they could be full in the confidence that God would bring about an eventual end to their sorrows, with a restoration of good fortune that would surpass even their greatest days.[94]

---

[93] Harrington, "Adamnán, Kells, and Job," 80-4.
[94] Harrington, "Adamnán, Kells, and Job," 84-5.

For those tempted to turn to idle speculation outside the biblical promise of Job, the writings of Cicero and Isidore criticising divination offered a damning critique. While determining such literary influences is always a difficult and slippery task, it bears repeating that tenth-century Irish exegetes had access to Isidore and could easily have had access to Cicero, the two classical sources whose motifs and moral message most satisfactorily account for the *Breviary* episode. It should also be recalled that the *Breviary* episode does not reject the liberal arts outright. Indeed, it accepts the importance of the liberal arts, noting that Adamnán himself taught them. Rather, the episode addresses those who trained in the liberal arts with a story with which they must surely have already been familiar. These are no pearls before swine; instead, the respected authority of Cicero, the virtuous pagan, and Isidore, the episcopal encyclopaedist, concerning the foolishness of divination is rendered more powerful in the ventriloquised mouth of Adamnán, the saintly voice of God, who warns that divination is inspired by demonic teachers.

Bibliographic Additions and Corrections to *PHCC* 41

Boyd, Matthieu, "Modeling Impairment and Disability in Early Irish Literature"
Page 73, line 2 for Cormac read Conaire

Harrington, Jesse Patrick, "Porcine Ploughmen and Etruscan Diviners: The Classical Myth of Tages in *Betha Adamnáin*"

Additional bibliography, page 190

Page 164, additions to footnote 21:
> Kuno Meyer, ed. and trans. *Cáin Adamnáin:An Old-Irish Treatise on the Law of Adamnán.* Anecdota Oxoniensia, Mediaeval and Modern Series 12 (Oxford: Clarendon Press, 1905); Gilbert Márkus, trans. *Adomnán's 'Law of the Innocents': A Seventh-Century Law for the Protection of Non-Combatants* (Glasgow: University of Glasgow, 1997); Pádraig P. Ó Néill and David N. Dumville, eds. and trans. *Cáin Adomnáin and Canones Adomnáni,* Basic Texts in Gaelic History 2 (Cambridge: University of Cambridge,2003), 20-51; Máirín Ní Dhonnchadha, "The Law of Adomnán: a translation" in Thomas O'Loughlin, ed. *Adomnán at Birr, AD 697 Essays in Commemoration of the Law of the Innocents* (Dublin: Four Courts Press, 2001), 53-68.

Page 172, additions to footnote 44:
> David Sproule, "Politics and Pure Narrative in the Stories about Corc of Cashel," *Ériu* 36 (1985):11-28 at 22-8; Karen Jankulak, "Alba Longa in the Celtic Regions? Swine, Saints and Celtic Hagiography," in Jane Cartwright, ed., *Celtic Hagiography and Saints' Cults* (Cardiff: University of Wales Press, 2003), 271-284; Will Parker, "'The Topographical Pig': A Cambro Gaelic Insular Ecotype?", *Cambrian Medieval Celtic Studies* 84 (Winter, 2022):51-82.

Sounding different in medieval Wales: unorthodox speech in the poetry of Beirdd yr Uchelwyr (*c. 1300–c.* 1600)

Llewelyn Hopwood

Little is known about Barbra, the wife of Siors Mathau, M.P. (d. 1557), apart from one detail: she had excellent Welsh. Lewys Morgannwg (*fl.* 1520–1565) spends most of his eulogy to her husband praising her instead, specifically her speech: *Dilediaith di-ŵyl ydyw,* / *ym mrig iaith Gymräeg yw* (Without patois, brave is she, / she is at the height of the Welsh language).[1] This is not an uncommon description. In the previous century, Mathau Goch is described as *Cymro da ei Gymräeg* (A Welshman with excellent Welsh), and Sir Huw Iolo is *Syr Huw, dda ei Gymräeg* (Sir Huw, good his Welsh).[2] Indeed, most eulogies praise some aspect of the individual's speech, language, or linguistic knowledge.

If having 'good Welsh' was the norm, this suggests that everything else could easily be deemed abnormal: unorthodox and unacceptable. In order to examine what was considered to be unorthodox speech in late medieval Wales, this article mines the poetry of *Beirdd yr Uchelwyr* (the Poets of the Nobility, *c.* 1300–*c.* 1600) for descriptions of the sounds of Wales's languages. It finds that faulty language was a key feature in the portrayal of outsiders and that

---

[1] Lewys Morgannwg, "Moliant Siors Mathau, Radur, a Barbra ei wraig," in *Gwaith Lewys Morgannwg*, ed. A. Cynfael Lake (Aberystwyth: University of Wales Centre for Advanced Welsh and Celtic Studies, 2004), 2: 43-45, lines 39–40. Unless otherwise noted, all translations are my own save for those with the works of Dafydd ap Gwilym (Dafydd Johnston et al., *Gwefan Dafydd ap Gwilym*, Swansea University and the Centre for Advanced Welsh and Celtic Studies, University of Wales, published 2007, (accessed 11 January 2023, www.dafyddapgwilym.net)); Guto'r Glyn (Ann Parry Owen et al., *Gwefan Guto'r Glyn*, Centre for Advanced Welsh and Celtic Studies, University of Wales, published 2013, (accessed 20 March 2023, http://www.gutorglyn.net/)), and Iolo Goch (*Iolo Goch: Poems*, ed. Dafydd Johnston (Llandysul: Gomer, 1993)).

[2] Guto'r Glyn, "Moliant i Fathau Goch o Faelor," in *Gwefan Guto'r Glyn*, line 71; Lewys Glyn Cothi, "I Ofyn Cyfrwy a Harnais March gan Syr Huw Iolo a Hywel ab Ieuan," in *Gwaith Lewys Glyn Cothi*, ed. Dafydd Johnston (Cardiff: University of Wales Press, 1995), 343-344, line 5.

attacking and mocking such languages (English and Irish) or language use (Welsh) was part of an attempt to uphold the social standards of the bardic institution, thus justifying its existence. Moreover, the myriad failings found in both faulty Welsh and non-Welsh languages are all shown to involve perceptions of control, or lack thereof.

To appreciate what is meant by language control in a medieval context, we must first listen, and listen with late medieval Welsh ears. We shall begin, then, by contextualising sound and auditory perception in the medieval world as well as the close relationship between sound and language. Next, the social circumstances of late medieval Welsh poets shall be outlined by examining a series of grammatical texts known as *Gramadegau'r Penceirddiaid*, or simply the bardic grammars. This will then allow us to listen firstly to the sound of unorthodox Welsh, before turning to examine the alien sounds of Irish, Latin, and English. For convenience, I use the term 'bad Welsh' for the former and 'foreign languages' for the latter.[3]

*

The founding philosophy of 'historical sound studies,' which is the general context for this avenue of enquiry, is that sound is period-, location-, and culture-sensitive.[4] A student's phone ringing in the middle of a lecture is a disruption, but the same ringtone from the same phone is the sound of rejoicing if it is finally heard from the back of the sofa after an hour spent searching for it. Sounds can also change over time–new sounds appear, old ones disappear or transform–but even with those that stay the same, people's perception

---

[3] While variations on the phrase '*Cymraeg da*' (good Welsh) do appear in the poetic record, '*Cymraeg gwael*' (bad Welsh) does not. Furthermore, although the other languages studied were not necessarily 'foreign' to Wales in the late medieval period–nor in the modern period in the case of English–since I am using this term to describe languages that listeners did not necessarily speak or understand and/or languages that listeners would have associated with regions outside of Wales, it remains a useful term.

[4] See, for example, Alain Corbin, *Village Bells: Sound and Meaning in the 19th-Century French Countryside*, trans. Martin Thom (London: Papermac, 1998), Bruce R. Smith, *The Acoustic World of Early Modern England: Attending to the O-Factor* (Chicago: University of Chicago Press, 1999), and Adin E. Lears, *World of Echo: Noise and Knowing in Late Medieval England* (Ithaca and London: Cornell University Press, 2020).

of those sounds are highly variable from place to place, period to period, and culture to culture. This is the starting point for all research in this field, which, including this study, seeks to reveal new meanings in historical texts by paying close attention to and contextualising the sounds of a particular place at a particular time. In this case, these are the sounds of unorthodox speech in late medieval Wales.

Speech is, of course, sound, and so too is language; the boundary between the two is often porous. A particularly inspiring demonstration of this fact is the experimental art piece by Alvin Lucier, *I am sitting in a room.*[5] In this performance, Lucier sits in a room and speaks a paragraph into a microphone that instantly plays the sound back into the same room on repeat, thereby creating a feedback loop. The effect on the listener's perception of Lucier's English is explained in the first half of the paragraph itself:

> I am sitting in a room different from the one you are in now. I am recording the sound of my speaking voice and I am going to play it back into the room again and again until the resonant frequencies of the room reinforce themselves so that any semblance of my speech, with perhaps the exception of rhythm, is destroyed.[6]

This breakdown of a semblance of speech is the backdrop to this article's exploration of the perception of unorthodox language in late medieval Wales. It is most applicable to the poets' presentation of foreign languages. However, it also applies when considering standards of diction in a known language, in this case, Welsh. Standardised written Welsh did not yet exist–not even at the later end of our period of study, as the great variety in spelling certain letters during the early printing period attests–and so what made Welsh 'good' or 'bad' is necessarily a sound-studies question, since language

---

[5] The piece was composed and first recorded in 1969 at Brandeis Electronic Music Studio, Brandeis University (Waltham, MA), but the earliest surviving recording is Alvin Lucier, *I am sitting in a room*, Source Records, 1970. The latest recording with Lucier's voice before he passed away in 2021 is Alvin Lucier, *Alvin Lucier: Two Circles*, Mode Records, 2016.
[6] Alvin Lucier and Douglas Simon, *Chambers* (Middletown, CT: Wesleyan University Press, 1980), 30-31.

usage was, for most vernacular speakers at this time, a spoken language. Thus, listening to language as "an extrasemantic experience and expression of sound," as Adin E. Lears puts it, remains relevant at all times.[7]

What made language and indeed any sound pleasant in the premodern period was a sense of order, regulation, and, ultimately, control. In the Middle Ages, it was believed that sound did not have any meaning in and of itself: it only carried the sense within the speaker's mind to the listener's ear, who then sought to grasp the initial sense encased within the sound.[8] Thus, the semantic aspect of language was far more important than the somatic experience of language. But, despite its potentially sinful hazards, language was necessary to communicate with other humans and with God, and Christ was the Word of God made flesh.[9] The only way to square this circle was to proceed with great caution and only engage very carefully and correctly with language so that it would not become meaningless noise. Hence, then, the need to speak properly and the high regard in which poets–the most proper of all speakers–were held.[10]

---

[7] Lears, *World of Echo*, 4. It is extremely difficult for people to imagine their own language(s) as sound without any linguistic meaning, though there have been some artistic efforts to imagine the sound of English, including a short play entitled *skwerl* (Brian Fairbairn and Karl Eccleston, "How English sounds to non-English speakers," YouTube, posted October 8, 2011, accessed January 11, 2023, https://www.youtube.com/watch?v=Vt4Dfa4fOEY, with the text at @briandkarl, "SKWERL," tumblr.com, posted February 9, 2015, accessed January 11, 2023, https://www.tumblr.com/brianandkarl/110560981278/we-get-a-lot-of-emails-asking-for-the-skwerl) and a pop single ("Prisencolinensinainciusol," track A2 on Adriano Celentano, *Nostalrock*, Clan Celentano, 1973).
[8] *Grammatici Latini ex Recensione Henrici Keilii*, ed. Heinrich Keil (Lipsiae: B. G. Teubneri, 1857), 2: 5; *Medieval Grammar and Rhetoric: Language Arts and Literary Theory, AD 300–1475*, ed. Rita Copeland and Ineke Sluiter (Oxford: Oxford University Press, 2012), 172-89.
[9] Augustine, *Confessions*, trans. William Watts (Cambridge, MA: Harvard University Press, 1997), 2: 168; see also Eric Jager, *The Tempter's Voice: Language and the Fall in Medieval Literature* (Ithaca: Cornell University Press, 1993).
[10] Lears, *World of Echo*, 137-145.

In this sense, Welsh poets are a fantastic example of how to use language carefully, since they composed in metres that used *cynghanedd* (harmony): a set of rules on consonance and internal rhyme that had euphony as their end goal.[11] These rules only got stricter over time: poets who deviated from them received increasingly short shrift from their peers and in order to increase compliance, the rules themselves were assembled, enhanced, and codified, thereby creating the bardic grammars.

Considering the history of the bardic grammars helps us consider the historical context too, namely the seemingly precarious social situation of Welsh poets from about 1300 onwards. During the Middle Ages, poets had always maintained a prestigious social position, patronised mostly by princes. However, in 1282, Llywelyn ap Gruffydd, the last native prince of Wales, was killed in a skirmish with King Edward I of England's soldiers, triggering the Edwardian Conquest of Wales and bringing an end to the royal patronage of poets. A new class of Welsh nobles, now serving the English rather than Welsh crown, did manage to continue patronising poetry–thus giving this period's poets their modern title, the Poets of the Nobility–and indeed this was an immensely fruitful period for Welsh poetry. Nonetheless, this short crisis at the end of the thirteenth century startled poets into realising that their privileged way of life may not last forever. This was then compounded by the growth in popularity of other forms of entertainment–the free metre poetry of minstrels and instrumental music, much of these being associated with England and Ireland–which undermined, sullied, and ultimately threatened the high standards of Welsh bardism.[12] This, then, was a period of growing anxiety for professional Welsh poets who felt threatened throughout the fourteenth, fifteenth, and sixteenth centuries, worrying that their profession could disappear.

One effect was that the higher standards of language use in poetry were increasingly expressed and enforced. This is most clearly displayed in the codification of the bardic grammars and the

---

[11] Mererid Hopwood, *Singing in Chains*, second edition (Llandysul: Gomer, 2016).

[12] *Urban Culture in Medieval Wales*, ed. Helen Fulton (Cardiff: University of Wales Press, 2012), *passim*.

proliferation of its copies as the Middle Ages came to a close.[13] While parts of at least one section–that on letters–were likely compiled in the early thirteenth century, i.e., before the Edwardian Conquest, surviving copies date from *c.* 1330 and many more date from the fifteenth and sixteenth centuries: it seems that two may have been compiled in the early fourteenth century; two later that century; four in the fifteenth century; and eighteen in the sixteenth century.[14]

Whether or not the grammars came into existence in some form– oral or written–before or after the great social changes brought about by the Conquest does not particularly matter for our purposes.[15] This is due to the fact that numerous copies are found from the fourteenth century onwards, confirming that they came to be–even if they were not at the beginning–a manifestation of the literary classes' concern with the preservation and codification of traditional material and of the re-definition of panegyric poetry after the loss of its traditional

---

[13] David N. Klausner, "The 'Statute of Gruffudd ap Cynan': a window on late-medieval Welsh bardic practice," in *Gablánach in scélaigecht: Celtic studies in honour of Ann Dooley*, ed. Sarah Sheehan, Joanne Findon, Westley Follett (Dublin: Four Courts Press, 2013), 265-275.

[14] For dating, see Michaela Jacques, "The Reception and Transmission of the Bardic Grammars in Late Medieval and Early Modern Wales," unpublished doctoral dissertation (Harvard University, 2020), esp. 28-29 and Table 0.2 (22-26), forthcoming as *Grammar and Poetry in Late Medieval and Early Modern Wales*, (Cardiff: 2024). See also Daniel Huws, *A Repertory of Welsh Manuscripts and Scribes* (Aberystwyth: National Library of Wales and University of Wales Centre for Advanced Welsh and Celtic Studies, 2022).

[15] On the early dating circulation of parts of the grammars, see the following articles by Thomas Charles-Edwards: "Bardic Grammars on Syllables," in *Celts, Gaels, and Britons: Studies in Language and Literature from Antiquity to the Middle Ages in honour of Patrick Sims-Williams*, ed. Erich Poppe, Simon Rodway, and Jenny Rowland (Turnhout: Brepols, 2022), 239-256; "The Welsh bardic grammars on *Litterae*," in *Grammatica Gramadach and Gramadeg: Vernacular grammar and grammarians in medieval Ireland and Wales*, ed. Deborah Hayden and Paul Russell (Amsterdam: John Benjamins Publishing Company, 2016), 149-160; and Thomas and Gifford Charles-Edwards, "The continuation of Brut y Tywysogion in Peniarth ms. 20," in *Ysgrifau a cherddi cyflwynedig i Daniel Huws*, ed. Tegwyn Jones and Edmund Boleslav Fryde (Aberystwyth: National Library of Wales, 1994), 293-305.

patrons.[16] (That the grammars manifest this concern remains true even when considering the fact that they appear to be closer to philosophical essays on the nature of Welsh bardism rather than practical handbooks.)[17]

This proliferation seems to coincide with a tightening of bardic discipline and standards; an argument complemented by the appearance of eisteddfodau at which rules were agreed upon, and prizes given to the best poets. The most significant eisteddfodau were held at Carmarthen in 1451 and Caerwys in 1523 and 1567, and the most significant document, other than the grammars, is one formulated at one of these eisteddfodau (the first Caerwys eisteddfod); a document known as *The Statute of Gruffudd ap Cynan*:

> There is no question that the profession of bard suffered a serious downturn in its reputation and social standing around the end of the fifteenth and the beginning of the sixteenth century, and that the Statute of Gruffudd ap Cynan was intended to remedy this situation.[18]

The very conception of these events and institutions suggests that there was a need at this time to outline the unique features of the professional poets, namely their education. Some form of bardic institution is likely to have existed in Wales in the central Middle Ages, but there is no clear evidence until the fifteenth century, where the eisteddfodau and the Statute can be viewed as the gradual formalization of the bardic guild in light of social change. One of their

---

[16] Ann Matonis, "Problems Relating to the Composition of the Early Bardic Grammars," in *Celtic Language, Celtic Culture: A Festschrift for Eric P. Hamp*, ed. Ann Matonis and Daniel Melia (Van Nuys, California: Ford and Bailie, 1990), 273-91 at 287-88; Ann Matonis, "Gutun Owain and His Orbit: The Welsh Bardic Grammar and Its Cultural Context in Northeast Wales," *Zeitschrift Für Celtische Philologie* 54 (2004), 154-69 at 155-56; R. Geraint Gruffydd, "Wales' Second Grammarian: Dafydd Ddu of Hiraddug [Sir Joh Rhŷs Memorial Lecture]," *Proceedings of the British Academy* 90 (1995), 1-28 at 20.
[17] Dafydd Johnston, *Llên yr Uchelwyr* (Cardiff: University of Wales Press, 2005), 23-24.
[18] Klausner, "The 'Statute of Gruffudd ap Cynan'," 272.

primary functions was to make it harder for uneducated, amateur poets to practice the profession. The Statute describes in detail the six- to nine-year education that was required of a trainee poet, including what steps they must take and what poetic skills they must obtain, e.g., which metres, before they could climb the profession's ladder to reach the highest position: *pencerdd* (chief poet). This poet was expected to be able to compose in every verse, every genre, and knew everything there was to know: *Penkerdd a ddyly gwybod y kwbl* (The pencerdd should know everything).[19]

The most useful–and uniquely Welsh–section of the grammars that demonstrates the texts' conception of language as sound and their emphasis on the importance of control is the final section, consisting of a set of *trioedd cerd* (poetical triads).[20] Particularly revealing are the "conceptual triads," as Paul Russell calls them–those that, in Morfydd Owen's words, are "chiefly concerned with what might be called the ethics of the poetic profession"–as opposed to the "factual triads," which "simply provide a classification of the rules of grammar and prosody," e.g., *Teir rann ymadrawd yssyd: henw, a rachenw, a beryf* (There are three parts of speech: noun, and pronoun, and verb).[21]

Crucially, this first type of triad, concerned with the rights and wrongs of poetry, becomes more common in later recensions, coinciding with the increased concern for the standards of professional

---

[19] *Records of Early Drama: Wales*, ed. David Klausner (London: British Library, 2005), 160.

[20] Most other sections are modelled on the Latin grammars of fourth-century Roman, Aelius Donatus, and sixth-century north-African grammarian, Priscianus Caesariensis (Priscian). The relationship between the Welsh bardic grammars and these earlier texts is explored in excellent detail in Jacques, "The Reception and Transmission of the Bardic Grammars."

[21] Paul Russell, "Poetry by numbers: The poetic triads in *Gramadegau Penceirddiaid*," *Grammatica, gramadach and gramadeg: vernacular grammar and grammarians in medieval Ireland and Wales*, ed. Deborah Hayden and Paul Russell (Amsterdam: John Benjamins Publishing Company, 2016), 161-80 at 163-64; Morfydd E. Owen, "Welsh Triads: an overview," *Celtica* 25 (2007), 225-250 at 238; *Gramadegau'r Penceirddiaid*, ed. G. J. Williams and E. J. Jones (Cardiff: University of Wales Press, 1934), 17 (Red Book of Hergest, i.e., Oxford, Jesus College MS 111, 1382 x *c*.1405).

Welsh poets. As Paul Russell puts it: "while the Peniarth 20 triads seem [. . .] to be concerned with how to compose verse, the triad collections appended to the other versions are more interested in how to be a poet."[22]

Most importantly, from a sound studies perspective, these "conceptual triads" include sets of triads on what type of performances and sounds can adorn or sully a poem. Here, it becomes instantly apparent that clear declamation was essential. The sound of good poetry is clearly described as an unhindered, fluent performance: *Tri pheth a anghyweiriant gerdd nev ymadrodd: pwl ddadkaniad, ac anghywraint ssynnwyr, ac annystyriol ddyall y parablwr* (Three things disturb a poem or speech: dull declamation, and crude sense, and the speaker's thoughtless understanding).[23] *[A]nghyweiriant* can also be translated as 'unyoke' or 'bring disharmony to,' thus emphasising both the controlled and auditory nature of *cynghanedd* (harmony) poetry.

Among the other things that "spoil" and "disgrace" poetry are "sluggish" and "untimely" declamations:

- *Tri pheth a anhoffa kerd: llesc datkanyat, a sathredic dychymic ac anurdas y prydyd*

- *Tri pheth a warthruda kerd ac a'e hanurda: y datkanu yn anamser, a'e chanu yn amperthynas, nyt amgen noc y'r neb nys dylyei, ac eisseu kerdwyr y barnu* (*Gramadegau'r Penceirddiaid*, 17 [Red Book of Hergest])

- Three things spoil a poem: sluggish declamation, vulgar imagination, and a poet's dishonour

---

[22] Russell, "Poetry by numbers," 177.
[23] *Gramadegau'r Penceirddiaid*, 135 (Oxford, Jesus College MS 15, mid-sixteenth century), 36 (Aberystwyth, National Library of Wales, Llanstephan MS 3, mid-fifteenth century).

- Three things disgrace and sully a poem: its
  untimely declamation, and its inappropriate
  performance, namely not to those who do not
  deserve it, and the poets' misjudgements.

These prohibitions all point to the importance of regulation and order in one's speech, none more so than those against *anwadalwch* (inconstancy)–one of the three things that are not admissible in or that do not harmonise in a poem (*Tri pheth ny chynghein mywn kerd*)–and those against poetry that is *anosparthus* (disorderly), like those of the lower grade minstrels known as *beirdd y glêr* (hereafter *Clêr* poets): *ny ellir dosparth ar glerwryaeth, kanys kerd anosparthus yw* (order cannot be imposed on *Clêr* minstrelsy, for it is a disorderly verse).[24] *Anwadalwch* and *anosparthus* are two words that clearly relate to the ideal that a performance should be controlled.

In terms of poetic performance and the importance of clear declamation, the most recently discovered fragment of the grammars is also, in many ways, the most revealing. The so-called *Gramadeg Gwysanau*, found in the Flintshire Record Office and published for the first time by Ann Parry Owen in 2016, reveals that, contrary to previous belief, it was in fact quite common for *Beirdd yr Uchelwyr* to write down their poetry and that this correct recording was key for correct declamation. *Gramadeg Gwysanau* seeks to stress that "poets must realise that they also have a responsibility to convey their poems as clearly and intelligibly as possible, and if they fail to do that, then they are partly responsible for the failure of the poem."[25] This relationship between composing and performing poetry and the importance of transmission–at one point demonstrated rather remarkably through the unreadability of an *englyn* (a four line poetic form) without spaces between words–is the take-home message of the fragment that has survived from this standalone and colourful

---

[24] *Gramadegau'r Penceirddiaid*, 17 (Red Book of Hergest), 135 (Jesus 15), 35-36 (Llanstephan 3).
[25] Ann Parry Owen, "*Gramadeg Gwysanau*: A fragment of a fourteenth-century Welsh bardic grammar," in *Grammatica Gramadach and Gramadeg: Vernacular grammar and grammarians in medieval Ireland and Wales*, ed. Deborah Hayden and Paul Russell (Amsterdam: John Benjamins Publishing Company, 2016), 181-200, at 190.

recension of the grammars. Nonetheless, its emphasis on declamation is key and astonishing in its clarity and seemingly original imagery.

Dyrchauel [y]r adeilat y vyny yw y datkanv yn vchel groyw [ ] eglur a gwniaw pob geir yn y le yn hirlaes, ac ar wahan, yspys, didra[m]gwyd, val y gallo dynyo[n] hydysc y gwy[b]ot a'e dysgv. Ac onys datkenir yn da yspys, tebic yw hynny y rodi kledeu yn llaw dyn a'r parlis arnaw—y kledeu yn da ac yn llym, yntev heb allel d[im] ac efo—am na ellir dyall peth a dywetto.

The raising up of the building is the loud and clear reciting of it [i.e. the poem] distinctly, binding each word in its place long and at full length, separately, clearly, without impediment, so that skilled men can understand and learn it. And if it is not recited well and clearly, it would be like placing a sword in the hands of a paralyzed man–the sword being good and sharp, but he being unable to do anything with it–because one cannot understand what he [i.e. the reciter] is saying.[26]

Therefore, according to all recensions, bad-sounding poetry had very little semblance of control. These descriptions of poor speech and poor poetic declamation match those found in the poetic corpus itself, which shall be considered next.

Stuttering Welsh

Once a person's language is heard as seemingly out of their control, it quickly ceases to be understood as 'sound' and soon becomes non-human 'noise.' A famous example of such noisy Welsh appears in an eight-poem debate between Gruffudd Gryg (*fl.* 1350–80) and Dafydd ap Gwilym (*fl.* 1340–70), in which Dafydd accuses Gruffudd of plagiarism and low standards of poetry.[27] As we have

---

[26] Owen, "*Gramadeg Gwysanau*," 197-99.
[27] Poems 23-30 in *Gwefan Dafydd ap Gwilym*. For a Middle English comparison, see Julie Orlemanski, "Margery Kempe's 'Noyse' and Distrusted Expressivity," in *Voice and Voicelessness in Medieval Europe*, ed. Irit Ruth Kleiman (New York: Palgrave Macmillan, 2015), 123-138.

seen, the second of these was a growing concern, and although this debate was light-hearted–or at least began in a light-hearted manner before Dafydd took insult–the underlying concerns regarding a poet who is bringing down the standards of the bardic guild were in fact very real.[28] One of the main ways Gruffudd is presented as an insubstantial poet is through his inability to perform his own poetry in a fluent and clear voice, perhaps due to his suffering from some sort of speech disability.[29]

Here, we remember that inconstant, sluggish, dull, and disorderly declamation went against the expected standards of 'good poetry.' A detailed examination of the accusations levelled in this debate reveals a correspondence between the bardic grammars and the poets' descriptions. Firstly, Gruffudd's name–Gruffudd Gryg–carries a meaning similar to 'Hoarse Gruffudd' or 'Stuttering Gruffudd,' which is exploited by Dafydd.[30] As with most disabilities, speech disabilities did not become objects of scientific investigation until the early modern period and so, when considering their portrayal in the Welsh poetic record, it must be borne in mind that, in the medieval period, speech was believed to be dependent on rational thought.[31] With the spectrum of deaf-muteness in mind, speaking with a stutter also applies to Mara Mills's statement that "prelingual deafness seemed

---

[28] On the seriousness of the debate, see *Gwaith Gruffudd Gryg*, ed. Barry Lewis (Aberystwyth: University of Wales Centre for Advanced Welsh and Celtic Studies, 2010), 10-19.

[29] This section uses 'disability' and related terms advisedly, since I am concerned with descriptions that associate physical conditions, such as deafness, muteness, or speech impediments, with social stigma rather than with the conditions themselves, recognising that physical conditions such as these only become disabilities through environmental factors. While some medieval authors treated these conditions with a remarkable degree of sympathy and nuance, very few feature among Beirdd yr Uchelwyr. See Jonathan Hsy, "Symptom and Surface: Disruptive Deafness and Medieval Medical Authority," *Journal of Bioethical Inquiry* 13, no. 4 (2016): 477-483, and *Disability in the Middle Ages: Reconsiderations and Reverberations*, ed. Joshua Eyler (Farnham: Ashgate, 2010).

[30] *Geiriadur Prifysgol Cymru* (*GPC*), s.v. cryg, accessed January 12, 2023, https://geiriadur.ac.uk/gpc/ gpc.html.

[31] Mara Mills, "Deaf," in *Keywords in Sound*, ed. David Novak and Matt Sakakeeny (Durham: Duke University Press, 2015), 45-54, at 46.

inextricably linked to muteness; in turn, deaf people seemed incapable of intelligence and moral reason."[32] As we shall see, then, comparing bad poetry to stuttering speech was a serious accusation.

Dafydd opens by addressing his opponent as *Gruffudd Gryg, wŷg wag awen, / grynedig, boenedig ben* (Gruffydd, empty and worthless muse, / with his painful trembling mouth), before later labelling him *y mab ataliaith* (the stuttering lad) and *cryglyfr bost, craig lefair beirdd* (the cowardly stuttering boaster, echo–stone of the poets).[33] It seems that the cruel auditory imagery in this last line plays on the sonic features of a stutter, namely repeating parts of a word over and over again. In the context of accusations of plagiarism, this is what Gruffudd does to other poets' works: he steals their work and repeats it, but in an inferior and incomplete form.

There seems to be a similar multi-layered joke in a comparison to a red grouse: *grugiar y gerdd* (poetry's red grouse).[34] A red grouse is a bird that makes a repetitive, gulping-like sound, which Dafydd ap Gwilym believes to be similar to a stuttering human.[35] Furthermore, this bird's name, *grugiar*, might sound as though it contains the same adjective as that which is applied to Gruffudd: *cryg*. It in fact derives from *grug*, meaning 'heather' or 'heath,' and *iâr*, meaning 'hen,' making this a 'heather hen' or a 'heath hen.' Nonetheless, in an aural setting, where spelling is irrelevant, and particularly in the hands of a poet such as Dafydd ap Gwilym who marvelled in wordplay, listeners may well have identified the first element of this word as near-homophonous with Gruffudd Gryg's sobriquet. It could thus be a 'cryg' hen: a 'hoarse hen' or a 'stuttering hen.'[36]

---

[32] Mills, "Deaf," 46.

[33] Dafydd ap Gwilym, "24. Cywydd Ymryson Cyntaf Dafydd ap Gwilym," *Gwefan Dafydd ap Gwilym*, lines 1–2, 61, 60.

[34] Dafydd ap Gwilym, "28. Trydydd Cywydd Ymryson Dafydd ap Gwilym," *Gwefan Dafydd ap Gwilym*, line 2. My translation.

[35] ESL and Popular Culture, "Grouse ~ Red Grouse Bird Call and Pictures for Teaching BIRDSONG," YouTube, posted 21 May 2014, accessed January 11, 2023, https://www.youtube.com/watch?v=zfgFY-hgiOk.

[36] For more on Dafydd ap Gwilym's wordplay see Dafydd Johnston, *"Iaith Oleulawn:" Geirfa Dafydd ap Gwilym* (Cardiff: University of Wales Press, 2020), especially 231-259; *GPC*, s.v. grugiar.

The return of this gulping sound confirms that Gruffudd's name is more likely to refer to a stammer rather than a hoarse voice. In a rare instance of Middle Welsh onomatopoeia, Dafydd's use of *cuc cuc* seeks to convey the guttural sound of 'glug glug,' followed then by the sound of a drunken dog eating a crow: *cuc cuc yn yfed sucan, / ci brwysg yn llyncu cyw brân* (a glug glug noise like someone drinking gruel, / or a drunken dog swallowing a crow chick).[37] Here, Dafydd enhances the dehumanising effects of comparing a human voice to animalistic noise by noting that this is a 'drunk' dog: a dog that has lost all control of its physical and mental capacities, and one that is gorging on a particularly noisy bird. This ensures that we hear Gruffudd's poetry as sub-standard at best.

It bears repeating that this is largely a comedic exchange, and accusations of Gruffudd's stammer are likely exaggerated, not least because it must have been impossible to make a living as a poet without being able to speak and perform poetry unhindered. Nonetheless, while Dafydd may be making a mountain out of a molehill, it is revealing that stuttering speakers were go-to reference points when satirising poets who had produced unacceptable poetry.

The ostracization of stuttering humans in medieval Wales is reflected in their apparently reduced legal rights. One passage in the Blegywryd recension of the Law of Hywel Dda reads: *Tri dyn yssyd ny digawn vn ohonunt bot yn vrawdwr teilwg o gyfreith* [. . .] *dyn ny allo dywedut, megys cryc anyanawl* (Three men who are not fit enough to be a judge of law [. . .] any man who cannot speak, such as a congenital stammerer).[38] Therefore, when Dafydd later asserts that Gruffudd has corrupted the world's poetry with his mouth (*Gwyrodd â'i ben gerdd y byd*), we hear that the corruption comes as much, if not more, from his stuttering voice as from the primary fault: his alleged plagiarism.[39]

---

[37] Dafydd ap Gwilym, "30. Pedwerydd Cywydd Ymryson Dafydd ap Gwilym," *Gwefan Dafydd ap Gwilym*, lines 41–42.
[38] *Cyfreithiau Hywel Dda yn ôl Llyfr Blegywryd (dull Dyfed): argraffiad beirniadol ac eglurhaol*, ed. Stephen J. Williams and J. Enoch Powell (Cardiff: University of Wales Press, 1942), 104.
[39] Dafydd ap Gwilym, "24. Cywydd Ymryson Cyntaf Dafydd ap Gwilym," *Gwefan Dafydd ap Gwilym*, line 34.

A poet whom we only known as Ieuan is also described as *cryg*, again as a reference to some speech disability. In an anonymous satire, Ieuan is mocked about how he trips over his words and is referred to as *cryg* on several occasions: *gwae ef, crog lef cryglafar* (curse him, with his loud, hoarse croak) and *cranc crynryw, croglyw cryglef* (a shivering crab, harsh-voiced hangdog).[40] We conjecture that this may be a reference to some speech impediment due to the fact that many physical defects to do with his feeble mouth (*finllyth*) are either mocked or wished upon him, e.g., *nef ni'th fydd, dwyll feddydd dall, / neb ni'th gâr, byddar bawddull* (there will be no heaven for you, deceitful, blind drunkard, / nobody loves you, filthy deaf man).[41] Onomatopoeia returns–*dwp-dap, a'i glap a'i naper* (dip-dap, and his clapper and his linen)–probably in reference to the clapper that would be used to warn others of a leper's presence, judging by accusations of leprosy elsewhere in the poem, e.g., *molog moel ddosog ddisech* (ulcer-eyed bald man dripping with sweat).[42] Again, animalistic auditory imagery floods the poem as well as scatological comparisons: *min tarandin toryndwll* (arse-farting mouth [rips a] hole in your mantle).[43] More importantly, this imagery filters into how the bad poet is once again linked to animals and the lowly *Clêr: clerwriaidd fab ab ebwch* (*Clerwr*-like son, with an ape's howl).[44] The apparent lack of control in Gruffudd's speech was enough to label him as different–a mere rhymester–and thus cast him out of the traditional guild of highly trained poets.

Unrestrained Welsh

Even if a speaker had no physical disabilities that affected the pitch and texture of their voice, problems of tempo and restraint could still mean that they spoke in an unorthodox way. Free-flowing speech, often expressed in terms such as *ffraeth* (witty), *berw* (bubble), and *rhugl* (fluent), could be a feature of the most impressive speakers,

---

[40] Anonymous, "Dychan i Ieuan," *Gwaith Prydydd Breuan a Cherddi Dychan Eraill o Lyfr Coch Hergest*, ed. Huw Meirion Edwards (Aberystwyth: University of Wales Centre for Advanced Welsh and Celtic Studies, 2000), 99-102, lines 30, 54.

[41] Anonymous, "Dychan i Ieuan," lines 1, 61-62.

[42] Anonymous, "Dychan i Ieuan," lines 36, 110.

[43] Anonymous, "Dychan i Ieuan," line 69.

[44] Anonymous, "Dychan i Ieuan," line 91.

since it showed they had great wit and a sharp mind as well as the crucial ability to control their speech. More commonly, however, it had connotations of unregulated language, which, as we have seen, was perceived to be a shortcoming.

Free-flowing speech that is out of instead of under control is the issue with Addaf Eurych (*fl.* first half of the fourteenth century). Hywel Ystorm (*fl.* first half of the fourteenth century) mocks Addaf on the grounds that he does not know when to be quiet. Addaf has no restraint and does not stop spouting sub-standard poetry. In a sharp satire that reverses typical eulogistic motifs–Addaf's home is cold, unwelcoming, and silent–the poet's own loud, blabbering, overly-prolific voice is one of the few sounds that feature:

> *Addaf gau ni thau, iaith ennig–frithgyrdd,*
> *Â'i freithgerdd ddrewiedig;*
> *Can ni thau garrau goriedig,*
> *Can ni phaid tarw diraid terrig,*
> *Can ni myn emennydd ysig*
> *Ymadaw â'i ffrost, ffeniglbost ffig*[45]

Addaf the liar does not shut up, little language of confused song
And his stinking disordered poem
Because of his puss-filled legs,
Because an evil, stiff bull does not stop,
Because a wounded brain cannot command,
Begone with his tumult, useless, fennel-branch idiot

While Gruffudd, Ieuan, and Llywelyn had speech disabilities relating to their tongues, mouths, and throats, Hywel Ystorm suggests that Addaf was mentally unwell–*Can ni myn emennydd ysig*–and that this was hindering his ability to speak in a measured way. Once again, this is a comedy poem and so exaggeration is to be expected, but comic hyperbole was a way of reminding everyone of the same underlying

---

[45] Hywel Ystorm, "Dychan i Addaf Eurych," in Prydydd Breuan et al., *Gwaith Prydydd Breuan a Cherddi Dychan Eraill o Lyfr Coch Hergest*, ed. Huw Meirion Edwards (Aberystwyth: University of Wales Centre for Advanced Welsh and Celtic Studies, 2000), 65-68, lines 119–124.

message: the aim of every speaker should be total control over how one spoke.

The importance of moderating one's speech and restraining any desire to let language flow unchecked helps to explain a small sub-genre within the poetry of Beirdd yr Uchelwyr where poets berate their own tongues for speaking out of turn as if they had a life of their own.[46] Llywelyn ab y Moel (*fl. c.* 1395–1440) is the author of the most well-known example and certainly the one with the greatest element of self-deprecation. Having lost control of his tongue, Llywelyn curses it and demands that it stays quiet.

> *Pa ddiawl a wnei pan ddêl nos,*
> *Na fedri, eithr ynfydrym,*
> *Yleni dewi er dym?*
> *Adde'r wyd, o ddireidi,*
> *Addail tir i ddiawl i ti,*
> *Awr daw hyd ar dalm o'r dydd*
> *aml ferw yn ymleferydd;*
> *mwy no rhegen mewn rhagnyth,*
> *am nith Fair, ni thewi fyth,*
> *aelod fochwal ddiwala,*
> *yn sôn am ferch dynion da.*[47]

What devil must you do when night comes,
You cannot, foolish alien,
Shut up for anything's sake this year?
You confess to be, by mischief,
worthless leaves, Devil take you,
When daytime comes
greatly do you bubble and babble
more than a quail in a nest,

---

[46] Eurig Salisbury, "Tair Cerdd Dafod," *Dwned* 13 (2007): 139-168.

[47] Llywelyn ab y Moel, "I'r Tafod," in Dafydd Bach ap Madog Wladaidd et al., *Gwaith Dafydd Bach ap Madog Wladaidd, 'Sypyn Cyfeiliog' a Llywelyn ab y Moel*, ed. R. Iestyn Daniel (Aberystwyth: Canolfan Uwchefrydiau Cymreig a Cheltaidd, 1998), 104-106, lines 10–14.

by Mary's son, you never shut up,
insatiable cheek-walled organ
making noise about the daughter of good men.

This is strikingly similar to Hywel Ystorm's attack on Addaf Eurych
and his inability to control his speech. Unlike Addaf, the precocious
tongue has a right to reply and refuses to be silent, though it does admit
that even it has little control over this, since its noise is the product of
some uncontrolled *berw*.

> *"Ni thawaf," heb y tafawd,*
> *"ni thau gwynt yn nithiaw gwawd.*
> *Berw a ddwg, fal mwg mawr,*
> *O'r cylla megis callawr"*[.]
> *(Llywelyn ab y Moel, "I'r Tafod," lines 15–18)*

"I won't shut up," said the tongue,
"the wind doesn't shut up when winnowing praise.
Bubbling comes, like a great smoke,
From the stomach like a cauldron" [.]

Counterintuitively perhaps, despite the great energy of these
scenes, speaking in an unrestrained fashion was seen as a sign of
laziness. Both stammering and unrestrained speech were the product
of a lazy tongue and a lazy mind that had made no effort to be selective
when it spoke. To combat such a failing, medieval homilies and moral
treatises would often cite 'Tutivillus,' a word-collecting demon who
punished careless speech and idle talk as symptoms of the sin of
sloth.[48] Though Tutivillus himself is absent in the Welsh poetic record,
there are occasional links between idle talk, tongues, and the Devil.

A particularly gruesome example of the tongue being targeted as
the source of devilish sound comes through Llywelyn ap Gwilym
Lygliw (*fl.* late fourteenth century). Hell was a raucous place in the
medieval auditory imagination, and Llywelyn uses this in his poem on
St. Paul's vision of Hell where, among the croaking crows and hissing
snakes, he hears the incessant wailing of sinners: *A mil o eneidiau*

---

[48] Margaret Jennings, "Tutivillus: The Literary Career of the Recording
Demon," *Studies in Philology* 74, no. 5 (1977): 1-95; Kathy Cawsey,
"Tutivillus and the 'Kyrchateras': Strategies of Control in the Middle
Ages," *Studies in Philology* 102, no. 4 (2005): 434-451.

mân, / *Ochi anferth a chwynfan* (a thousand little souls, / great groaning and lamentation). He then alludes to the common image of sinners being hung from their tongues–often a symbolic punishment that fits the crime, usually blasphemy or sloth–but by focussing particularly on the sound that would come from these now disabled sinners.

> *Ynghrog pob gradd onaddun*
> *A bach drwy dafod pob un:*
> *Rhai yn griddfan rhag annwyd*
> *A rhai dan blwm tawdd mewn rhwyd*
> *A chythraul ar ei chwethroed*
> *Â bêr cam mwy no bar coed*[49] [,]

> Each class of them hanging
> With a hook through each of their tongues:
> Some of them groaning from cold
> And some in a net under molten lead
> And a demon upon her six-feet
> With a skewer larger than a bar of wood [,]

Speaking in an unstoppable torrent was thus undesirable and could be deterred through both comedic mocking and stern warning. This is one extreme of having no control over one's language: speaking in tongues. On the other extreme is being tongue-tied: total silence.

Mute Welsh

Metaphorical muteness was not always unorthodox and often had neutral connotations as a stock auditory image in elegies. Mourners could become 'mute' in their grief and corpses themselves are 'mute' by their nature. Poets often mourn the fact that a patron or fellow poet who was once so eloquent is now totally silent: *nid hawdd ymadrawdd*

---

[49] Llywelyn ap Gwilym Lygliw, "Gweledigaeth Pawl yn Uffern," in Gruffudd Llwyd, et al., *Gwaith Gruffudd Llwyd a'r Llygliwiaid Eraill*, ed. Rhiannon Ifans (Aberystwyth: University of Wales Centre for Advanced Welsh and Celtic Studies, 2000), 39-41, lines 39–40, 55–60.

â mud (it is not easy to converse with a mute) is a phrase that echoes throughout the Beirdd yr Uchelwyr corpus.[50]

This imagery is understandable for a period in which most knowledge, including about health and existence itself, was gathered through sound, since proof by vision is largely a product of the Enlightenment.[51] A speaking human was a healthy human, and so a completely silent human was as good as dead. This is what is signalled by the muteness of the half-dead Irishmen in the Second Branch of the *Mabinogi*, and this is what Iolo Goch (*c*. 1320–*c*. 1398) plays with when he uses the aforementioned dead patron's phrase to describe a man lying in a drunken stupor: *ni wyddiad neb p'le'dd oeddud, / nid hawdd ymadrawdd â mud* (no one knew where you were, / it is not easy to converse with a mute).[52]

Nonetheless, while becoming 'mute' in death and mourning was in no way regarded to be a physical failing, nor was it linked to concepts of stupidity such as in the English words 'dumb' and even 'mute' today, it was still an involuntary act; something that was out of the speaker's control, unlike, for example, monastic silence.[53]

---

[50] E.g., *nid diboen na'm atebud, / nid hawdd ymadrawdd â mud* (it is not unpainful that you won't answer, / it is not easy to converse with a mute), Dafydd ap Gwilym, "Marwnad Llywelyn ap Gwilym," *Gwefan Dafydd ap Gwilym*, lines 27–28.

[51] "There is no doubt that the philosophical literature of the Enlightenment– as well as many people's everyday language–is littered with light and sight metaphors for truth and understanding," Jonathan Sterne, *The Audible Past: Cultural Origins of Sound Reproduction* (Durham: Duke University Press, 2003), 3; see also Trevor Pinch and Karin Bijsterveld, "New Keys to the World of Sound," in *The Oxford Handbook of Sound Studies*, ed. Trevor Pinch and Karin Bijsterveld (Oxford University Press, 2012), 1-15, and Veit Erlmann, "But What of the Ethnographic Ear?," in *Hearing Cultures: Essays on Sound, Listening, and Modernity*, ed. Veit Erlmann (Oxford and New York: Berg, 2004), 1-20.

[52] *Pedeir Keink y Mabinogi*, ed. Ifor Williams (Cardiff: Wales University Press, 1930), 44; Iolo Goch, "Ymddiddan yr Enaid â'r Corff," in *Iolo Goch*, 56-63, lines 25–26.

[53] There are no direct references to monastic silence in the Welsh poetic record, but see Paul F. Gehl, "*Comptens Silentium*: Varieties of Monastic Silence in the Medieval West," *Viator* 19 (1987), 125-160; George,

Unintentional silence was certainly another feature of unorthodox speech.

Rhys ap Dafydd Llwyd ap Llywelyn Lygliw (*fl.* fourteenth-fifteenth century) epitomises this feature as he recounts the humiliation of such silence during a failed adventure to meet a girl. After trudging through overgrown fields for hours, Rhys finally reaches her house, but despite his plans to charm her with wit and eloquence, when the time comes, he is dumbstruck and cannot muster a single word.

> *A phan ddeuthum y bûm bŵl*
> *Fegis dyn hurt ryfygwl;*
> *Ni ddôi o'm pen air gennyf,*
> *Ni chawn lun iawn gan liw nyf.*
> *Ffraeth yn ei habsen, wenferch,*
> *Fyddwn pan soniwn am serch,*
> *Ac yn ei gŵydd ni lwyddai*
> *Barabl ym, a'm berw, by lai?*[54]

And when I came, I became dim
Like a frightened fool;
Not a single word came from my mouth,
I could not get a full phrase, on account of the one
with the colour of heaven/Nyf,
In her absence, pure girl, I was loquacious
Speaking about love,
But in her presence, not a word
Came to me, and my [usual] fluency. Why not?

Along with the word *mud*, referring to anything from complete silence to a stutter, we also note the adjective *pwl*: a highly significant word, that also appears in the bardic grammars signifying many sensory disabilities. Its principal and etymological meaning is 'dim' or 'dull'

Devereux, "Ethnopsychological Aspects of the Terms 'Deaf' and 'Dumb'," *Anthropological Quarterly* 37, no. 2 (1964): 68-71.
[54] Rhys ap Dafydd Llwyd ap Llywelyn Lygliw, 'I Ferch,' in Gruffudd Llwyd, et al., *Gwaith Gruffudd Llwyd a'r Llygliwiaid Eraill*, ed. Rhiannon Ifans (Aberystwyth: University of Wales Centre for Advanced Welsh and Celtic Studies, 2000), 65-66, lines 13–20.

in terms of light, but this can broaden to cover 'dull (of senses),' 'dim(-sighted),' and 'hard of hearing.'[55] The entertainment here, then, is based on the audience's shared understanding that this poet's silencing was as unorthodox as suffering from a disability; not being able to control when one spoke was a failing, albeit a humorous and embarrassing one on this occasion.

Returning to the *Mabinogi*, in the First Branch, Pwyll Pendeuic Dyuet (Pwyll Prince of Dyfed) exhibits the deficiencies of both speaking too much and not enough. Pwyll's name ('Patience' or 'Deliberation') is highly ironic as he consistently speaks without thinking. Pwyll promises to grant the stranger, Gwawl ap Clud, his wish before even hearing what it is, leading him to give away his wife. Then, once he realises his mistake, he is dumbstruck and cannot muster a single word to fix the problem: *Kynhewi a oruc Pwyll, cany bu attep a rodassei* (Pwyll was silent, for there was no answer he could give).[56] The tale shows that being in a position of authority without control over one's speech was dangerous and there is undoubtedly a link between this lesson and a proverb common in *Beirdd yr Uchelwyr* poetry, which can also be found in the Legal Triads: *ni roddir gwlad i fud* (land is not given to a mute person).[57] A lack of control over one's faculty of speech was not only the key tenet of unorthodox Welsh, but also a matter of social concern.

---

[55] *GPC*, s.v. "pŵl(1)," accessed January 12, 2023, https://geiriadur.ac.uk/gpc/gpc.html.

[56] *Pedeir Keink*, 14; *The Mabinogion*, ed. and trans. Sioned Davies (Oxford: Oxford University Press, 2007), 12.

[57] E.g., Gruffudd ap Maredudd, "Serch gwrthodedig," Gruffudd ap Maredudd, *Gwaith Gruffudd ap Maredudd*, ed. Ann Parry Owen (Aberystwyth: University of Wales Centre for Advanced Welsh and Celtic Studies, 2007), 3:87-88, lines 35–36: *Na roddir, ferch lawir lwyd, / Gwlad i fud, gloywdwf ydwyd* (A country, grey, generous girl, / is not given to a mute, you are a bright growth); Proverb §801 in *Diarhebion Llyfr Coch Hergest*, ed. Richard Glyn Roberts (Aberystwyth: CMCS Publications, 2013), 89-90; Triads X37, Q74, and Y160 in *The Legal Triads of Wales*, ed. Sara Elin Roberts (Cardiff: University of Wales Press, 2007), 58-59, 128-131, 364-365.

Foreign Languages

Even more different than unorthodox Welsh, however, was a language that was already different in the first place. In general, most non-Welsh languages were perceived to be the same as 'bad Welsh': uncontrolled noise. The remainder of this article will examine the perceived sounds of two such languages: Irish and English. A further handful of languages were spoken in Wales during the later Middle Ages but very few feature in the poetic corpus: French and Flemish are each referred to once and given only the briefest of descriptions, while Cornish simply appears in a list.[58]

A notable exception is Latin: the transcending language of ecclesiastical, scientific, and courtly authority, which had a fantastic auditory reputation. Simply knowing this language was praiseworthy: Ffwg Salbri, dean of St. Asaph, is praised by Tudur Aled as *Gŵr llên llwyd, gorllanw Lladin* (Grey, man of letters, Latin's high tide), and William Herbert, Earl of Pembroke, was *Y iarll hydr a ŵyr Lladin* (The mighty earl who knows Latin).[59] In terms of sound, Latin was heard as the purest of all languages: the phrase *Ladin dilediaith* appears frequently and it is often described as *cyson* (harmonious), itself a

---

[58] The absence of French does not reflect the presence of French in medieval Wales, particularly during the central Middle Ages. See Matthew Siôn Lampitt, "The 'French of Wales'? Possibilities, Approaches, Implications," *French Studies* 76, no. 3 (2022), 333-349. For the most recent survey of early medieval Flemish settlement in Wales, see Gerben Verbrugghe, Timothy Saey, and Wim De Clercq, "Mapping 'Flemish' settlements in South Wales: electromagnetic induction (EMI) survey at the villages of Wiston (Pembrokeshire) and Whitson (Monmouthshire)," *Archaeologia Cambrensis* 170 (2021): 251-274; for Cornish, see Y Nant, "I ofyn gŵn gan yr Abad Wiliam," *Gwaith y Nant*, ed. Huw Meirion Edwards (Aberystwyth: Centre fore Advanced Welsh and Celtic Studies, 2013), 42-44, lines 25–32. Non-European languages are not mentioned in the poetic corpus, but see Natalia Petrovskaia, *Medieval Welsh Perceptions of the Orient* (Turnhout: Brepols, 2015).

[59] Tudur Aled, "Cywydd i Ffwg Salbri, Deon Llanelwy," in *Gwaith Tudur Aled*, ed. T. Gwynn Jones (Cardiff: University of Wales Press, 1926), 1:92-94, line 49; Hywel Dafi, "Moliant Wiliam Herbert, ail iarll Penfro," in *Gwaith Hywel Dafi*, ed. A. Cynfael Lake (Aberystwyth: University of Wales Centre for Advanced Welsh and Celtic Studies, 2015), 2:393-394, line 1.

borrowing from Latin *consonus* (agreeing, harmonious).[60] Its secondary meaning, 'constant,' may seem to be a perplexing way to describe a language, but it is related to its primary meaning, 'harmonious,' given the close relationship between mathematical proportions and music in medieval and Classical thought.[61] Constancy is also synonymous with regularity and, as we have seen, a regulated language is a controlled, good-sounding language.

That Latin was admired as a controlled language is one reason why it easily entered Welsh poetry in wholesale, linguistic units, and in mostly earnest poems. The other reason is that Latin pervaded Welsh society to the extent that it was the most common second language in Wales and that everyone in medieval Wales was either passively bilingual, with fluency in the vernacular and a smattering of mostly liturgical Latin, or more extensively so, with proficiency in both.[62] This Latin interference occurs either in short snippets, such as in this couplet by Gruffudd ap Maredudd–*Erglyw fi, fy Nêr uwch sêr ysydd, / Eurglo in caelo medd seilm Dafydd* (Hear me, my Lord who is above the stars, / golden lock in heaven, says David's psalms)–or

---

[60] E.g., *Sierôm wyd, oes ŵr am iaith / Ar Ladin mor ddilediaith*? (You are Jerome, is there another man [who knows] such a language / As [his] unpolluted Latin?), Huw ap Dafydd ap Llywelyn ap Madog, "Moliant Syr Siôn Aled, ficer Llansannan," *Gwaith Huw ap Dafydd ap Llywelyn ap Madog*, ed. A. Cynfael Lake (Aberystwyth: University of Wales Centre for Advanced Welsh and Celtic Studies, 1995), 45-46, lines 35–36; *GPC*, s.v. "cyson," accessed January 12, 2023, https://geiriadur.ac.uk/gpc/gpc.html.
[61] See, for example, Boethius, *Anicii Manlii Torquati Severini Boetii, De instituione arithmetica libri duo, De institutione musica libri quinque, accredit Geometria quae fertur Boetii*, ed. Gottfried Friedlein (Leipzig: B. G. Teubneri, 1867); *Boethius, Fundamentals of Music*, trans. Calvin Bower (New Haven: Yale University Press, 1989).
[62] Elizabeth M. Tyler, "Introduction. England and Multilingualism: Medieval and Modern," in *Conceptualizing Multilingualism in Medieval England, c. 800–c. 1250*, ed. Elizabeth M. Tyler (Turnhout: Brepols, 2011), 1-14, at 10; Ad Putter and Keith Busby, "Introduction: Medieval Francophonia," in Keith Busby and Christopher Kleinhenz (eds.), *Medieval Multilingualism: The Francophone World and its Neighbours* (Turnhout: Brepols, 2010), 1-14.

on a larger scale, such as Ieuan ap Rhydderch's ode to the Virgin Mary:[63]

> *Mam Grist Celi, seren heli,*
> *Luna celi, lain y suliau.*
> *Oportere nos habere,*
> *Miserere, moes ar eirau.*

(Ieuan ap Rhydderch, "I Fair," lines 65–68)

Oh mother of Christ of the Lord, star of the sea,
moon of Heaven, gem of Sundays,
it is proper for us to have–
show mercy–courtesy in our words.

Greek and Hebrew had similar reputations with *Ebryw* (Hebrew) often followed by the adjective *llwybraidd* (orderly); the significance of describing a language and its sound as 'orderly' need not be repeated.[64] Thus, despite sounding different from Welsh, difference was not perceived to be a problem with these languages. This is not true of Irish and English.

Irish

Very few Welsh-speakers spoke Irish. Furthermore, although Welsh and Irish are both Celtic languages, they are not mutually intelligible. In this way, hearing Irish as non-linguistic sound would have been the only way most people in late medieval Wales would have perceived this language.

---

[63] Gruffudd ap Maredudd, "Awdlau i Dduw," in *Gwaith Gruffudd ap Maredudd*, ed. Barry Lewis (Aberystwyth: University of Wales Centre for Advanced Welsh and Celtic Studies, 2003–7), 2:39-46, lines 259–260; Ieuan ap Rhydderch, "I Fair," in *Gwaith Ieuan ap Rhydderch*, ed. R. Iestyn Daniel (Aberystwyth: University of Wales Centre for Advanced Welsh and Celtic Studies, 2003), 103-105. For further examples and discussion see Llewelyn Hopwood, "Creative Bilingualism in Late Medieval Welsh Poetry," *Studia Celtica* 55 (2022): 97-120.
[64] E.g., *Ebryw mor llwybraidd* (such orderly Hebrew), Tudur Aled, "Cywydd i'r Esgob Dafydd ab Owain," in *Gwaith Tudur Aled*, 1:84-87, line 54.

When hearing a language that we do not understand, how we perceive that language is heavily affected by our prejudices and–if the language can be identified–the reputations of that language's speakers. There is nothing inherently romantic, charming, harsh, or ridiculous about any language's phonology, but each can be described as such, purely based on the relationship between speaker and listener.

As was shown in the discussion on speech impediments, 'noise' was, and still is, used to describe the sounds of outsiders in order to emphasise their otherness. Nowhere was this clearer in the Middle Ages than when describing foreign languages, as in Ranulf Higden's passage on the language of Ethiopians: *Some diggeþ caues and dennes, and woneth vnder erþe and makiþ hir noyse wiþ grisbaytynge and chirkynge of teeþ more than wiþ voys of þe þrote* (Some dig caves and dens and dwell underground and make their noise more by grunting and gnashing their teeth than by using their throat's voice).[65] Higden's racist remarks characterize Ethiopians as animals and magnifies their distance from literate, English standards of behaviour and speech.

This is close to how Irish appears in Welsh poetry. There was a strong derogatory sense to words like *Gwyddel* (Irishman) and *Gwyddelig* (Irish), often appearing, for example, in lists of spiteful labels for odious antagonists, such as the stock figure of the Jealous Husband called *Eiddig*, who sometimes appears as *Eiddig Wyddelig* (The Irish Jealous One), or in the description of Llywelyn ab y Moel's tongue as a sinful, Irish priest: *Offeiriad meddw gweddw, Gwyddel* (A widowed, drunken priest, [and] Irishman).[66] These xenophobic ethnic

---

[65] Ranulf Higden, *Polychronicon Ranulphi Higden monachi Cestrensis together with the English Translation of John Trevisa and of an unknown writer of the fifteenth century*, ed. J. Rawson Lumby (London: Longman, 1865), 1: 159.
[66] E.g., Anonymous, "Gŵr Esyllt," in *Selections from the Dafydd ap Gwilym Apocrypha*, ed. Helen Fulton (Llandysul: Gomer, 1996), 37, line 25; Llywelyn ab y Moel, "I'r Tafod," *Cywyddau Iolo Goch ac Eraill*, ed. Henry Lewis, Thomas Roberts, and Ifor Williams (Cardiff: University of Wales, 1937), reprint 1972, 208-210, l. 61; *GPC*, s.v. "Gwyddel(1)," "Gwyddelig," accessed January 12, 2023, https://geiriadur.ac.uk/gpc/ gpc.html.

labels have been studied in some detail, but what has not yet received its due attention is how these labels are often to do with sound.[67]

One of the primary connotations of Irishness in medieval Wales was music.[68] Instrumental music as its own art seems to have come to Wales from Ireland. As such, the presence of Ireland's talented harpists had given Irishness both positive connotations of music and negative connotations of noise. Since foreign languages are often perceived as non-linguistic sound, it is inevitable that the Irish language could become part of this 'music' or this 'noise.' In the poetic record, Irish is nearly always the latter, since these musicians were playing on foreign soil within earshot of a group of paranoid rival entertainers, Beirdd yr Uchelwyr.

As with Eiddig Wyddelig, the noisy connotations of Irishness often appear in labels pinned upon opponents during bardic flytings. Iolo Goch chose to make particularly extensive use of this auditory imagery in two connected satirical poems involving Irish stock characters. Dafydd Johnston has argued convincingly that these poems were composed as part of a humorous bardic competition, in which the participants were set tasks by the poet Ithel Ddu (*fl.* second half of the fourteenth century), probably at Christmas time.[69] Iolo was first given the task of composing an elegy to *Hersdin Hogl* (Arse-Arse of the Hovel), a fictional old woman who was a stock figure of fun; another poet presumably responded with a now-lost poem in the voice of Hersdin Hogl's son, another stock figure, *Y Gwyddelyn* (The Irishman), satirising Iolo for being disrespectful towards his dead mother. Iolo then responded with the second of his two poems,

---

[67] For more on the history of Irish people in medieval Wales, see Karen Jankulak, "How Irish was medieval Ceredigion? Pseudohistory, history, and historiography," in *Gablánach in scélaigecht: Celtic studies in honour of Ann Dooley*, ed. Sarah Sheehan, Joanne Findon, and Westley Follett (Dublin: Four Court Press 2013), 253-264, and Patrick Sims-Williams, *Irish influence on Medieval Welsh literature* (Oxford: Oxford University Press, 2011), 16-20.

[68] Sally Harper, *Music in Welsh Culture Before 1650: A Study of the Principal Sources* (Aldershot: Ashgate, 2007), especially 7-159; A. O. H. Jarman, "Telyn a Chrwth," *Llên Cymru* 6 (1960–61): 154-175.

[69] Dafydd Johnston, *Iolo Goch*, 186.

focussing entirely on mocking the Irish son and his noisy, faulty language.

While Iolo does pay attention to the noise of Hersdin in the first poem–she is compared to various farmyard animals and is a *gythwraig, ymddanheddwraig haidd* (a grumbling woman, one who squabbles over barley), with typical synaesthetic mixing of stench and sound–it is her old age and leathery skin that bears the brunt of his mockery.[70] However, when Iolo targets the son, he focusses much more on speech and the physical features that impede it. *Gwae'r mab gwedy gwyro'r min* (Woe to the lad with the twisted mouth), Iolo cries, before describing the Irishman and his brother as lepers begotten by the devil; lepers whose "clap"–a semantically empty onomatopoeic sound–is the only sound heard at their mother's funeral.[71]

> *Ei gwlan a'i chwpan a'i chap*
> *A'i deuglaf yn rhoi dwyglap.*
> *I ddiawl oedd ohoni ddyn,*
> *I ddiawl yntau Wyddelyn.*

(Iolo Goch, "Dychan i Hersdin Hogl," *Iolo Goch*, 144–149, lines 85–88).

> Her wool and her cup and her cap
> And her two lepers giving two claps.
> She bore a son to the devil,
> May the devil take him, Gwyddelyn.

Attacks on the Irishman's unclean language crystallise in the second poem, targeting his *barf rydlyd, berw afradlawn* (rusty beard, vain hubbub) and closing with the biting couplet *Yswain morchwain mawrchwaith, / Ŷs faw diawl, aswy fu d'iaith* (Lice-ridden knave of great sourness, / eat devil's dirt, clumsy was your language').[72]

Revealingly, this Irishman is portrayed as a minstrel trying to undermine the bardic profession, and while this poem was, once again, all in jest and performed in the context of parody, this jibe is surely a

---

[70] Iolo Goch, "Dychan i Hersdin Hogl," *Iolo Goch*, 144-149, line 10.
[71] Iolo Goch, "Dychan i Hersdin Hogl," *Iolo Goch*, 144-149, line 59.
[72] Iolo Goch, "Dychan i'r Gwyddelyn," *Iolo Goch*, 148-153, lines 32, 91–92.

revealing and honest expression of Iolo's anxieties towards what appeared to him to be a dwindling Welsh profession in light of increasingly popular forms of entertainment coming from outside of Wales. We must remember that Iolo's fabricated ire comes in the context of a poetic debate, and so Iolo is responding to the previous poem and mocking it in the only way a poet knows how: by calling it 'bad poetry.' Thus, *iaith* (language) here is not just the Irish language, but also the language that made up the poorly put-together poem that the 'Irishman'–some Welsh poet–had just performed: Welsh. The primary concern, then, is that Y Gwyddelyn is trying to confront an established, trained poet, even though his standard of poetry is no higher than a lowly minstrel's verse.

> *Gad atad, o'th gyd-wtir,*
> *Bob eilwers, fab yr hers hir,*
> *Twncl ar y tafod tancern,*
> *Tincer gwawd, wyneb tancr gwern.*

(Iolo Goch, "Dychan i'r Gwyddelyn," *Iolo Goch*, 148–153, lines 83–86)

Get yourself, if you are driven out together,
Every so often, son of the long arse,
A toncuer[73] on your sharp pointed tongue,
Peddler of poetry, face like an alderwood tankard.

Portraying "Y Gwyddelyn" as a minstrel, *tincer gwawd*, characterizes him as one of the troublesome Clêr poets, as Iolo did more explicitly earlier in the same poem: *Cipiwr crainc, iangwr copr crin, / Cyffeithdy clêr cyffeithdin* (Crab snatcher, wrinkled copper knave / minstrels' tannery with pickled arse).[74] He is a *[p]uror iawn*

---

[73] The poem's seaside scene leads Dafydd Johnston to parse the otherwise unattested word "twncl" as a borrowing from English "toncuer," a Norfolk dialect name for the fish commonly known as "sole." See *Iolo Goch*, 188, and *English Dialect Dictionary*, ed. Joseph Wright (Oxford: 1898–1905), s.v. "toncuer."

[74] Iolo Goch, "Dychan i'r Gwyddelyn," *Iolo Goch*, 148-153, lines ll. 11–12.

(a 'proper singer'), where *puror* is a common poet, unlike Iolo who is a *prydydd* (trained poet).[75]

> *Nid synnwyr ffôl wrth ddolef,*
> *Nid clêr lliw'r tryser llawr tref,*
> *Nid beirdd y blawd, braw heb rym,*
> *Profedig feirdd prif ydym.*

(Iolo Goch, "Dychan i'r Gwyddelyn," *Iolo Goch*, 148–153, lines 51–54)

No foolish sense at the top of our voices,
No minstrels of the marketplace coloured like the
three stars
No flour-begging poets, powerless judgement,
We are proven master poets.

"Tincer gwawd" also puts the Irishman in an urban context. As we shall soon hear, Welsh poets associated English speakers, whom they largely held in contempt, with the towns. Whenever the language is heard in a poem, its associations with the hubbub of town life is turned against its speakers. Despite occasionally marvelling in urban life, Welsh poets often saw urbanity as a foreign blight. Judging by the amount of urban and indeed seafaring terminology that litters the scene and its auditory landscape–dogs, metal heaps, tanneries, beggars, markets–Iolo's satire seems to suggest that the negative connotations of urbanism in Wales was not limited to English; it was also a negative association of Irish, and perhaps all foreign languages. To a Welsh poet's ears, then, Irish was a different and uncontrolled form of speech.

English

Like Irish, English mostly appears as a barbarous, animalistic sound. Despite the gradual integration of the English and Welsh nobilities after 1282, ethnic identities maintained a sharp distinction, and it seems that this distinction found its clearest expression in poetry: *Na ad, f'arglwydd, swydd i Sais, / Na'i bardwn i un bwrdais* (Do not, my lord, allow any office to an Englishman, / nor give any

---

[75] Iolo Goch, "Dychan i'r Gwyddelyn," *Iolo Goch*, 148-153, lines 31.

burgess his pardon), says Guto'r Glyn.[76] What has gone largely unnoticed is that such antagonism against English people often focusses on the English language and its barbarous sound. This final section addresses this oversight.

Although there is much Anglophobic sentiment in medieval Welsh poetry, the sociolinguistic landscape was not unambiguous. By the late Middle Ages, the Welsh-speaking nobility had begun to live hybrid, diglossic lives as they increasingly acquired English to obtain cultural and political power, meaning that English was becoming the high-status vernacular of Wales in commerce, bureaucracy, and law. Crucially, however, it was not becoming the high-status vernacular of literary expression: Welsh men and women could be English in terms of politics and class but Welsh in terms of poetic patronage, often leading to strong expressions of anti-English resentment in poetry. This allowed Welsh to maintain its prestige in the literary world at least.

We have seen that knowing Latin, Greek, Hebrew, and French was a praiseworthy trait in medieval Wales. There are no such descriptions for Irish and the closest instance for English is in Lewys Morgannwg's portrait of Sir Rhisiart Bwclai Hen: *Ni thyfai iaith ddoeth o fin / Well garbron Lloegr a'i brenin* (No better language sprang from any mouth / before the English and their king).[77] Furthermore, while English could be praised indirectly when praising a polyglot, e.g., Rhydderch ab Ieuan Llwyd who was a *Gyweithas ieithydd* (amiable linguist), it is never mentioned by name.[78]

Nonetheless, the reality was that the upper classes in Wales were often expected to be at least bilingual in Welsh and English. While having eloquent Welsh was a virtue towards which all noblemen and women should aspire, it seemed to have been unquestionably inferior

---

[76] Guto'r Glyn, "21. Moliant i Wiliam Herbert o Raglan, iarll cyntaf Penfro, ar ôl cipio castell Harlech, 1468," in *Gwefan Guto'r Glyn*, lines 61–62.
[77] Lewys Morgannwg, "Moliant Syr Rhisiart Bwclai Hen," *Gwaith Lewys Morgannwg*, 2:466-468, lines 35–36.
[78] Dafydd ap Gwilym, "10. Marwnad Rhydderch ab Ieuan Llwyd," *Gwefan Dafydd ap Gwilym*, line 39. See also: Dafydd ap Gwilym, "6. Marwnad Llywelyn ap Gwilym," *Gwefan Dafydd ap Gwilym*, line 12; and Guto'r Glyn, "6. Cwyn am absenoldeb yr Abad Rhys ap Dafydd o Ystrad-fflur," *Gwefan Guto'r Glyn*, line 24.

to being eloquent in more than one language, even if that language was English. This can be gleaned from Guto'r Glyn's praise of monoglot nobleman Dafydd Llwyd ap Gruffudd. His panegyric is predicated on the fact that it would usually be unacceptable for a nobleman to only know Welsh, at least if he wished to have a favourable reputation outside of the Welsh-speaking heartland. But Dafydd was respected by both Englishmen and Welshmen *despite* only knowing the latter's language.

> *Mil a ddywod wamaliaith,*
> *Maen' ar ôl, am na ŵyr iaith.*
> *Ni bydd Dafydd heb dyfiad,*
> *Ni ŵyr iaith ond iaith ei dad.*
> *Er eu sôn mwy yw'r synnwyr*
> *No dau o'r gorau a'i gŵyr.*
> [. . . .]
> *Arglwyddi Lloegr ogleddiaith*
> *A'i peirch er na wypo'u iaith.*

> (Guto'r Glyn, "86. Moliant i Ddafydd Llwyd ap Gruffudd o Abertanad," *Gwefan Guto'r Glyn*, lines 21–26, 31–32.)

> A thousand spoke a mocking speech
> because he doesn't know language, they're
>   behind.
> Dafydd won't be without progress,
> he knows no language except the language of his
>   father.
> Despite their talk the wisdom's greater
> than two of the best men who can speak it.
> [. . . .]
> England's northern-speaking lords
> respect him even though he doesn't speak their
>   language.

Dafydd was the exception that proved the rule. There is even a sense of admiration in the fact that he only spoke Welsh, especially in the context of everyone else's *sôn* (talk, noise), suggesting that some may have thought it better to speak one language purely than to speak several languages poorly.[79]

It seems that this sort of hybrid 'Wenglish' was how the speech of Elen, wife of Aberystwyth burgess Robert le Northern, sounded to Dafydd ap Gwilym; it was a *lediaith lud* (halting patois).[80] If this is the case, Guto'r Glyn and Dafydd would be predicting the complaints of sixteenth-century grammarian Gruffydd Robert, who begins his 1567 Grammar by lamenting the mongrelisation of both Welsh and English in the mouths of unintelligent Welshmen who are blinded by England's bright lights: *i cymraeg a fydd saesnigaidd, ai saesneg (duw a wyr) yn rhy gymreigaidd* (their Welsh will be English, and their English (God knows) too Welsh).[81] Thinking back to Barbra, wife of Siors Mathau, it should be noted that she was an Englishwoman from Somerset, and so it may be with a sense of surprise that Lewys Morgannwg remarked that she was "without patois."[82]

Another sign that the rise of English-Welsh bilingualism did not sit comfortably with most Welsh poets is that its praise is always subdued and with much more focus on Welsh than English. The aforementioned one-foot-in-one-foot-out situation of bilingual Welsh noblemen and women, for which Helen Fulton uses the post-colonial term 'doubling,' partially explains this phenomenon.[83]

---

[79] This is the opposite attitude to many language activists in Wales and Ireland today who believe that using what little grasp one has on the language in question is better than not using it at all: "gwell Cymraeg slac na Saesneg slic" (loose Welsh is better than slick English), modelled on the Irish "Is fearr Gaeilge bhriste ná Béarla cliste" (broken Irish is better than clever English). Dylan Foster Evans, "Dala'r slac yn dynn," *O'r Pedwar Gwynt* 12 (2020).

[80] Dafydd ap Gwilym, "120. Dewis Un o Bedair," *Gwefan Dafydd ap Gwilym*, line 18.

[81] Gruffydd Robert, "*Dosbarth Byrr Ar Y Rhan Gyntaf i Ramadeg Cymraeg 1567*," in *Rhagymadroddion 1547–1659*, ed. Garfield H. Hughes (Cardiff: University of Wales Press, 1976), 46-48.

[82] Lewys Morgannwg, "Moliant Siors Mathau," line 39.

[83] Helen Fulton, "Class and Nation: Defining the English in Late-Medieval Welsh Poetry," in *Authority and subjugation in writing of medieval Wales*, ed. Ruth Kennedy and Simon Meecham-Jones (Basingstoke: Palgrave Macmillan, 2008), 191-212, at 195; Homi Bhabha, *Locations of Culture* (London: Routledge, 1994), 57-93, 121-131.

This neutral and subdued praise of English suggests uneasiness with the realpolitik of Wales's diglossia wherein English was a necessity. After all, in the absence of statehood, what defined the Welsh nation as distinct from the English was the Welsh language: Middle Welsh *iaith* could mean both 'language' and 'nation.' So, for it to have to share the stage with English was an uncomfortable reality.[84] These poems seem to contain the now familiar sense of dread bubbling away under the surface; a sense that the Welsh language was less and less the language of the noble court, especially of Welsh homes close to or in England.

Eulogies containing such praise primarily concern marcher families such as the Herberts of Raglan and the Vaughans of Abergavenny. For example, the bilingualism of Thomas ap Roger Vaughan's home at Hergest was a cause for praise in the eyes and ears of Bedo Brwynllys (*fl. c.* 1460): *Dinas yw dy dŷ annedd, / Dwy iaith dan ei do a wedd* (The house in which you dwell is a refuge, / It is befitting that two languages are under its roof).[85] After Thomas was killed in the Battle of Banbury in 1469, his son Watcyn ap Tomas (Watkin Vaughan) took over his post as the constable of Huntington, modern-day Shropshire, as well as the praiseworthy ability to maintain two languages in the same home of Hergest. Lewys Glyn Cothi (*fl.* 1447–1486) praises the house as heaven on earth: *Ystad yw costio dwy iaith, / A rheoli rhai eilwaith* (It is of great dignity to maintain two languages, / And to manage more again).[86]

Even though these are all figures with close ties to the English Crown who lived close to or in England in a distinctly English auditory

---

[84] *GPC,* s.v. "iaith," accessed January 12, 2023, https://geiriadur.ac.uk/gpc/gpc.html; John Davies, *A History of Wales*, revised edition (London: Penguin, 2007), at 164, 198. This polysemy echoes Bede's definitions of the 'nations' of Britain as the speakers of the same language. See Bede, *Bede[:] The Ecclesiastical History of the English People*, ed. Judith McClure and Roger Collins (Oxford: Oxford University Press, 1999), 9-12.

[85] Quoted in Francis Payne, *Crwydro Sir Faesyfed* (Llandybïe: Llyfrau'r Dryw, 1966–68), 1: 33.

[86] Lewys Glyn Cothi, "Moliant Watcyn ap Tomas," *Gwaith Lewys Glyn Cothi*, 285-286, lines 7–8. An alternative reading would give "maintain two peoples" referring to Thomas's cross-border lordship over Welsh and English tenants.

environment, no mention is made of English itself. In both instances, bilingualism is only praised in general terms with a suggestion of specific admiration towards the individuals' ability to keep Welsh alive in their households despite the pressures of English.

The scarcity and even absence of English on these occasions are telling because, otherwise, it is clear that the English language occupied a negative and noisy place in the Welsh auditory imagination. Poets' references to English as a stand alone language–rather than in a Welshman's home or in a bi- or multilingual mind–are consistently unflattering if not hostile. It is regularly portrayed as an inhuman, barbarous noise.

For example, when Guto'r Glyn's praises William Herbert, Earl of Pembroke and one of Wales's most powerful noblemen at the time, animalistic imagery abounds: *Gwell arglwydd Cymro i'm bro o'm bryd / No Sais yn cyfarth Saesneg hefyd* (Better a Welsh lord to my land, in my opinion, / Than an Englishman barking in English).[87] English can also sound harsh, like in Lewys Glyn Cothi's prophetic poem to Jasper Tudor, in which the poet foresees him routing the English, including the English language itself: *a'r Saesneg wangreg i wâl–yr eigion* (and the weak, harsh English language, driven to the hidden depths).[88] Similarly, it can have a grating quality. Dafydd Llwyd of Fathafarn (*c.* 1420–*c.* 1500) also imagines the routing of the English, who are once again described in auditory terms: *dilyn y Saeson dilwydd, / garw eu sain, a gyr o'u swydd* (follow the failing Englishmen, / harsh their sound, [and] drive [them] from their office[s]).[89]

This negative auditory perception goes some way to explain a peculiar feature of bilingual poetry from medieval Wales, which is the fact that the handful of poems that blend English and Welsh are all

---

[87] Hywel Swrdwal, "Awdl Foliant Wiliam Herbert," in *Gwaith Hywel Swrdwal a'i Deulu*, ed. Dylan Foster Evans (Aberystwyth: University of Wales Centre for Advanced Welsh and Celtic Studies, 2000), 31-33, lines 49–50; for a particularly Anglophobic poem, see poem 7 in the collection.
[88] Lewys Glyn Cothi, "Awdl Frud i Siasbar Tudur," *Gwaith Lewys Glyn Cothi*, 37-39, line 71.
[89] Dafydd Llwyd o Fathafarn, "Cywydd Proffwydoliaeth," in *Gwaith Dafydd Llwyd o Fathafarn*, ed. William Richards (Cardiff: University of Wales Press, 1964), 37-40, lines 79–80.

comedy poems.[90] Macaronic poetry has been associated with comedy since at least the sixteenth century.[91] However, as was briefly mentioned, macaronic Welsh-Latin poems are anything but humorous. They are instead products of piety, of a concern for literary craft, and of a desire to infuse Welsh with the prestige of Latin. Why, then, are English-Welsh poems different?

Like with the Welsh-Latin poems, concerns of prestige remain at the heart of why Welsh-English poems are almost exclusively comedy poems, but it is Welsh that now has the upper hand. Welsh maintained a monopoly as the language of poetry in Wales even while English was steadily becoming the language of social authority. Therefore, the moment English trespasses into this poetic territory in which it is a second-grade language, it loses its authority, and the rug can be pulled from beneath its feet. Here, English is heard as different, uncontrolled, and, so, nonsensical. The humorously imbalanced situation benefits the Welsh-speaking audience who, unlike the English language, 'belong' in this arena, and their inflated sense of linguistic pride, especially the bilingual members.

One poem must suffice to outline the standard relationship between English and Welsh in this regard: a satire on the town of Flint by Tudur Penllyn (*c.* 1420–*c.* 1485–1490).[92] Flint is close to the

---

[90] Two possible exceptions are Dafydd Llwyd o Fathafarn, "Cywydd Moliant i Syr Rhys ap Thomas," in *Gwaith Dafydd Llwyd o Fathafarn*, 113-115, and two free-verse stanzas in Aberystwyth, National Library of Wales MS 16031, discussed in Simon Meecham-Jones, "Code-switching and contact influence in Middle English manuscripts from the Welsh Penumbra – Should we re-interpret the evidence from *Sir Gawain and the Green Knight*?," in *Multilingual Practices in Language History: New Perspectives*, ed. Päivi Pahta, Janne Skaffari, and Laura Wright (Berlin: De Gruyter, 2017), 97-119, at 109-110. A third poem that needs mentioning is Ieuan ap Hywel Swrdwal, "Awdl i Fair," in *Gwaith Hywel Swrdwal a'i Deulu*, 124-126: an earnest Marian lyric in strict-metre but written entirely in English. For a full discussion, see Hopwood, "Creative Bilingualism," 110-113.
[91] Teofilo Folengo, *Teofilo Folengo: Baldo*, ed. and trans. Ann E. Mullaney, 2 vols (Cambridge MA: Harvard University Press, 2007–2008).
[92] Tudur Penllyn, "Dychan i Dre'r Fflint ac i'r Pibydd," in *Gwaith Tudur Penllyn ac Ieuan ap Tudur Penllyn* (Cardiff: University of Wales, 1959), ed. Thomas Roberts, 51-53.

modern-day border with England and was indeed under the Earldom of Chester at the time of composition, and like all burgess towns in late medieval Wales–either planted by the English Crown or with a great deal of English speakers–its auditory environment had a distinctly English flavour.[93] This is what Tudur plays with in his satire, which sees him visiting a wedding feast, hoping to entertain the crowd with a beautiful strict-metre poem of his own making. His proposals, however, are scornfully and dynamically rejected in a bilingual couplet in favour of an English musician playing the bag pipes: *"Ywt,"* *ebr Sais, drais drysor,* / *"Y nelo mynsdrel na mor"* ("Out," said the violent, English doorman, / "I want no more of a minstrel").[94] Breathlessly, Tudur lashes out at everyone present and focusses in particular on their English language: not only does he describe the sound of the English bouncer who kicks him out as *aneglur* (unclear), but he also goes to great lengths to deride the excruciating racket of the piper who upstaged him, *rhygnu, syndremu, swn drwg,* / *rhwth gaul, a rhythu golwg* (a grating sound, an aghast stare, an awful noise, / a big, slack belly, and a swelling sight).[95] Tellingly, he regards Flint a captive town, seeing its hybrid Anglo-Welsh identity, and indeed its bilingualism, as a mongrel vice: *[t]ref ddwbl, gaergwbl, gyrgam* (a fully-fortified, crooked, double town). This is a more outspoken version of other poets' cautious attitudes towards bilingualism and their derision of *llediaith* (half-language, patois, barbarism).[96]

Most Welsh-English poems have a similar atmosphere, and each plays on how English sounded unorthodox in a Welsh poem; the unexpected being a crucial element of comedy.[97] Despite the humour, each betrays the same fear of what will become of the bardic profession. Tudur Penllyn's satire is a particularly poignant example.

---

[93] For more on burgess towns during the earlier period, see Matthew Frank Stevens, *Urban Assimilation in Post-Conquest Wales: Ethnicity, Gender and Economy in Ruthin, 1282–1348* (Cardiff: University of Wales Press, 2010); for the later period, see Harper, *Music in Welsh Culture*, 297-370.
[94] Tudur Penllyn, "Dychan i Dre'r Fflint ac i'r Pibydd," lines 15–16.
[95] Tudur Penllyn, "Dychan i Dre'r Fflint ac i'r Pibydd," lines 26–26.
[96] Tudur Penllyn, "Dychan i Dre'r Fflint ac i'r Pibydd," line 3.
[97] Matthew Bevis, *Comedy: A Very Short Introduction* (Oxford: Oxford University Press, 2013), 49-51. For more examples, see Hopwood, "Creative bilingualism."

Overall, Welsh comes out on top: the narrative of a Welsh poet scoffing at English-speaking drinkers who fail to recognise good poetry clearly demonstrates the notion that English was the prestigious vernacular of all social spheres bar the literary. This is shown even in minor details: English is associated with low-brow topics, like peas and dung–*Sôn am bys, Wiliam Beisir, / Sôn o'r ail am dail i'w dir* (William Beiser speaks of peas, / The other speaks of dung for his land)– while Welsh is associated with high-brow verse.[98] Within the poem, there is no doubt that the high literary status of Welsh is maintained, whereas the socio-economic status of English is undermined as it becomes an uncontrolled, lower-grade language now that it has set foot in the unfavourable realm of Welsh poetry.

Nonetheless, although we laugh at the English musician, like we did at the Irishman and the stuttering Welshmen, this is the exact sort of situation that Welsh poets dreaded: a form of entertainment that is not strict-metre poetry–and that is not even Welsh–becoming popular with Welsh audiences. The poet's hostile reaction to this popular sound stems from the same motive behind the hostile reaction to the speakers of bad Welsh we heard earlier. Bad Welsh poetry and the bad sounds of new, foreign forms of entertainment both threatened the Welsh poet's line of work: a line of work that was all about high standards of good sound.

*

Assessing the sounds of Wales's languages by looking exclusively at the poetry of Beirdd yr Uchelwyr yields biased results. These were poets who were composing at a perceived time of crisis intrinsic to every situation where a professional group attempts to assert a monopoly of authority. This, then, meant that they needed to justify their existence by emphasising their distinctly high and praiseworthy standards of language usage. The result is that their descriptions of all other forms and sounds of speech and language will almost by necessity be critical. Nevertheless, the very fact that they saw themselves as the gatekeepers of good diction means that their output provides a treasure trove of rich descriptions of the sounds of Wales's languages and their unorthodox speakers.

---

[98] Tudur Penllyn, "Dychan i Dre'r Fflint ac i'r Pibydd," lines 17–18.

Sound and Fury: the use of relics in ritual cursing and exorcism

Emer Kavanagh

Introduction

The use of bells and *bachall*s in Christian daily life and rituals was adopted early by the Church. *Bachall*s (Irish bachaill henceforth), also called 'croziers', were a type of staff that, visually, were reminiscent of a shepherd's crook. These staffs soon became a symbol of office for bishops and abbots of the early Church, although exactly when the tradition of them representing the Church's authority first developed is uncertain. Similarly, there is no real biblical basis for the use of bells by the clergy. This paper examines bells and bachaill both as relics and as objects used in the early Irish Church's rituals of exorcism and cursing, with particular interest paid to the sounds produced during the performance of such rites, and the effect these sounds would have had on bystanders.

***

The veneration of important community figures, whether they were warrior heroes, kings, ancestor figures or saints, is attested across many different cultures and religions. As such, it is not surprising that various cults dedicated to specific saints and martyrs appeared early in the Christian church. These cults are believed to have developed from the practice of worshipping at the tombs and burial places of the early martyrs, a practice that arose during Late Antiquity. Lucas has suggested that, as Roman cemeteries were typically placed outside of the city limits, there was ample space provided for adherents to build larger shrines and memorials to the dead.[1] By the end of the fourth century this practice had become so widespread that *martyria* could be found all over the Roman Empire. By 396, Bishop Victricius of Rouen had travelled to Britain, bringing with him relics that he had obtained in Rome, believing that they would not only protect him but

---

[1] A.T. Lucas, "The Social Role of Relics and Reliquaries in Ancient Ireland" in *The Journal for the Royal Society of Antiquaries of Ireland vol 116* (1986), p. 5.

that this blessing could be extended to the Christian community in Britain at that time.[2]

The interconnected nature of monastic settlements no doubt facilitated the spread of this tradition throughout Christian communities, but as Lucas has also noted, "the preservation and veneration of objects associated with persons who played an important part in the family, the tribe or the nation in the past seems to be a very ancient and very widespread human trait".[3] Thus, it appears that the cult of saints and the importance placed on the objects associated with them was simply an extension, or an overwriting, of practices that had previously existed, although now subsumed within a Christian context. Relics, then, are objects of particular religious significance, typically associated with a saint. There are many different types of relics, ranging from the most intimate, called corporal relics, which are the body parts taken from the deceased saint, to the associative, or the objects that were personally used by, or closely connected to, them.[4]

While there are some accounts of corporal relics in the Irish sources, the majority of textual evidence refers to associative relics. Many different types of objects could fulfil the role of a relic, for example the so-called *Cathach*, or 'Battler': a psalter that dates from the sixth century at the earliest, which was said to have been written by St. Colum Cille himself. The Cathach was believed to be a powerful protectorate in times of warfare and battle, and by the eleventh century a custom had evolved which saw it being carried three times around the battlefield, right-hand-wise, to ensure victory.[5] A note on the churches of Munster, which can be found on folio 44b of Rawlinson B 512, states that the five primary emblems of every church were a bachall, the service set, a cross, a bell, and the gospel, and in Ireland bachaill and bells are by far the most common objects depicted in the annals and literary texts as association relics. Visually, the imagery of flocks and shepherds conjured through the physical shape of the

---

[2] Ibid.
[3] Ibid.
[4] See Niamh Wycherley, *The Cult of Relics in Early Medieval Ireland* (Turnhout, 2015) for a full discussion of the use of relics in medieval Ireland.
[5] Wycherley, *The Cult of Relics,* p. 137.

bachall lends itself ideally to an object used by church men, not to mention as an emblem of their power and a marker of their status within medieval Irish society.[6]

There are a number of different words used to refer to relics in the Irish tradition. The Latin word *reliquiae*, meaning 'remains', was most commonly used in Latin-language texts, and was borrowed into Old Irish in the word *reilic*. However, reilic tends to refer to cemeteries rather than relics, as can be seen by the modern Irish word for cemetery, *roilig*.[7] Instead, the word *minn* is typically applied to relics in the early medieval period, although originally this word meant something like 'badge' or 'emblem'. A number of different texts depict abbots and high-ranking church members travelling with important relics that related to their founding saint, with these relics acting as an emblem of both their rank and affiliation. Further, during the medieval period it became common for such relics to be used in an official capacity, during oath-swearing and for binding agreements.[8] Thus, in modern Irish, the form *mionn* is the standard word for 'oath'.

Although the idea of a priestly caste carrying staves or rods as a mark of their status was present from before the time of the Roman augurs, who carried wands that were used to mark ritual spaces in the sky, the Biblical archetypes are, of course, Moses and his brother, Aaron, both of whom carried staves (or shared a single staff, depending on the interpretation), through which miracles were performed as proof of God's existence and supremacy. The first mention of Moses's staff comes in the Book of Exodus, 4:2 – 6, during the episode of the burning bush, when God imbues the staff with the power to turn into a snake, saying that it is to be used as the first sign of His power, to incite people's faith in Him.[9] Thereafter called the Staff of God, Moses (and possibly Aaron) used it to bring about a number of miracles, including the parting of the Red Sea during the

---

[6] See Fergus Kelly, *Guide to Early Irish Law* (Dublin, 1995), pp. 39-42 for a fuller discussion on the status of Clergy and the Church in medieval Ireland.

[7] eDIL s.v. *reilic* or dil.ie/34955.

[8] Wycherley, *The Cult of Relics,* pp. 130 - 140.

[9] *Exodus* 4:17.

Israelites flight out of Egypt[10], and the creation of a fresh source of drinking water during their time in the wilderness.[11] This episode would, have course, have been well-known in Ireland during the period, as evidenced, at the very least, by the fact that early Irish origin-legend in *Lebor Gabála Érenn* draws a parallel between the wanderings of the Irish settlers and those of the Israelites, as recounted in Exodus.[12]

In Ireland, the *Bachall Ísu* ('Staff of Jesus') was the most famous bachall. Its name invokes Moses's Staff of God and, like that staff, it was said to have been a gift from God, given to St. Patrick by way of a religious youth who lived on an island in the Tyrrhene Sea.[13] The bachall was considered one of the most important relics held by the Church of Armagh, along with a bell that was also said to have been owned by the saint. The Bachall Ísu first enters the public record in the Annals of Ulster under the year 789, when it and a number of other relics associated with St. Patrick were "dishonoured" by Donnchad son of Domnall, at an óenach in Ráth Áirthir.[14] As mentioned above, relics such as bachaill and bells became emblems, not only identifying the holder of such objects as high-ranking church members, but also serving to affiliate an individual church to its founding saint. Indeed, St. Bernard once wrote that the Bachall Ísu and the Book of Armagh were the two most important insignia of the Church of Armagh.[15] Thus, an attack on the Bachall Ísu was a strong political statement against either Armagh or the ruling family that were connected to that church, or even both. Although the Bachall Ísu remained a very public and venerated relic, it eventually became a symbol of the Catholicism

---

[10] *Exodus* 14:15-28.
[11] *Exodus* 17:5-7. Additionally, five of the plagues of Egypt were brought about through the use of the Staff.
[12] See Conor O'Brien, "The New Israel Motif in Early Medieval Origin Legends", in *Origin Legends in Early Medieval Western Europe*, (Brill, 2022), pp. 239-58 for a recent discussion of this.
[13] Ludwig Bieler, *Four Latin Lives of St Patrick: Colgan's Vita secunda, quarta, tertia, and quinta* (Dublin, 1971), p. 29; Wycherley, *The Cult of Relics*, p. 138.
[14] Wycherley, *The Cult of Relics,* p. 138.
[15] Myles V. Ronan, 'St Patrick's Staff and Christ Church' in *Dublin Historical Record vol 5* (Dublin, 1943), p. 122.

and idolatry of the Irish people. It was seized by the Anglican church in 1538, its reliquary was stripped of its gold and precious stones, and the staff itself was burned "as an object of superstition".[16]

While bells had no biblical basis, they were used for ritual acts in Antiquity, as was the case with staves and wands. For example, bells were used in exorcisms, which would in turn influence early Christians to adopt them into their own rite of exorcism. As Bitel notes, "Early Christians also began ringing bells at ceremonies of baptism, cursing, and blessing"[17], demonstrating how quickly and easily the Church was able to incorporate them into its various formalities. The most obvious feature of bells, especially church bells, is that they are loud and can be heard over long distances. Take, for instance, the idea that in London a true 'Cockney' is anyone who was born within the sound of Bow Bells, an area that stretches from Cheapside, where the Church of St. Mary-le-Bow is located, to Hackney, a distance of some six miles. In monastic communities of the early Middle Ages, bells played a fundamental role in marking time for the day's activities. They were used to announce the hour, call the community to prayer, to meals, and to their work. Thus, the sound of bells became an integral part, albeit through the background noise, of life in or near a monastic or clerical site.

As with the Bachall Ísu, it is St. Patrick who lays claim to the most famous bell relic in Ireland. Known today as 'St Patrick's Bell', this is a handbell made from two sheets of iron that were bent and riveted together, before a handle was added and the entire object dipped in bronze.[18] As with other early Irish handbells, St. Patrick's Bell was tongueless, and noise was created when it was struck against something, or if it was struck by a bachall. Due to the primitive nature of its design, the object is difficult to date, although the Annals of Ulster mention the "bell of the testament" as one of the relics taken from St. Patrick's grave by Colum Cille, to be given to new shrines in other churches.[19] In the 1100s an ornate shrine, or reliquary, was

---

[16] Ibid., p. 128.

[17] Bitel, "Tools and Scripts for Cursing", p. 7.

[18] Bitel, "Tools and Scripts for Cursing", p. 8.

[19] AU 553. Accessed November 23 2022, https://celt.ucc.ie/published/ T100001A/index.html. Although recorded under the year AD 553, the

created for the bell. Shaped as a trapezoid to match the shape of the bell, it was made from bronze plates topped by a decorative plaque that completely covers the handle of the bell. Indeed, the reliquary was riveted together, indicating that it was not meant to be opened, nor the bell to be used, after it was enshrined.[20] An inscription on the edge of the backplate of the shrine records the name of the craftsman who made the bell, along with the name of Domhnall Ua Lochlainn (d. 1121), who commissioned the making of the shrine. Both bell and shrine are currently on display in the National Museum of Ireland.[21]

Thus, while bells marked sacred spaces and times, dividing them between the personal and the religious, the bachall marked the holder as being sacred. Together, these symbols took on profound meaning for wider society. While technically not allowed to take part in the Mass, the local lay Christians and converts were certainly allowed to listen to it. As bells were adopted into some religious ceremonies early, it is very likely that people would have heard the sound of a handbell being struck during one of the occasions that they were permitted to attend the Mass.[22] They likewise would have heard Latin in the same way, as it was the language used in religious ceremonies during this period. Now, then, there is a convergence of three elements that are generally understood and observed as being integral parts of Christianity. Sound can trigger strong memories and elicit emotional responses in the listener. Along with a visual and auditory performance, it can combine to create an effect on the audiences' interpretation and response to a given situation. Thus, a man publicly

---

majority, if not all, of these extremely early dates were written at a much later time period. For the entry in question, the annalist reports that he himself found the information in 'the Book of Cuanu', a now-lost annal purported to be from the fifth and sixth century, indicating that he is recording it later, perhaps as part of an effort to fill out the early records of Ireland. The language of the entry itself can be dated to c.11th century.
[20] Bitel, "Tools and Scripts for Cursing", p. 9.
[21] Accessed November 23 2022, https://www.museum.ie/en-IE/Collections-Research/Collection/Resilience/Artefact/Test-5/8e122ba9-6464-4533-8f72-d036afde12a9. The artifacts can be found, in person, as part of the Treasury Gallery exhibition.
[22] See Bitel, "Tools and Scripts for Cursing", pp. 9-10 for the likelihood of bells being used at specific moments during the Mass from the sixth century onwards.

ringing a bell, particularly with a bachall, while chanting psalms in Latin, will certainly be viewed through the lens of human experience, and the crowd that he gathers around him will interpret his performance through that same lens. Through the performance, and the sounds generated by it, the space around him is transformed into a religious space, just as the audience are transformed into active participants as they witness whatever comes next.

Both exorcism and cursing begin in this way, with a public performance of chanted Latin, accompanied by the striking of bells. While no official rite of exorcism exists for medieval Ireland, there are many examples in the textual sources. We return, once again, to St. Patrick, specifically his *Vita* from the early fifteenth-century manuscript called the Leabhar Breac (Royal Irish Academy MS 23 P16) which contains an account of an exorcism performed by him. In this episode, Patrick had retreated to Cruachán Aigle (modern day Croagh Patrick) during the Easter festival, for a solitary period of fasting. During his fast,

> . . . the mountain was filled against him with devils in the shapes of black birds. Patrick sings psalms of cursing against them, and he weeps and strikes his bell, until a gap broke in it. [...] The devils flee at once upon the sea, as far as eye can reach, and drown themselves in that place, and no devil visited the land of Ireland from that time to the end of seven days and seven months and seven years.[23]

A second example can be seen from the Life of St. Berach:

> At this time there were many legions of demons in Glendalough fighting against Coemgen and his monks, and they caused trembling and terror to weak men, and hurt them, and caused plagues and many sicknesses in the glen; and they could not be cast out till Berach came. Then Berach went round the city,

---

[23] Whitley Stokes, *Three Middle Irish homilies on the Lives of saints Patrick, Brigid and Columba* (Calcutta, 1877), p. 38. Accessed November 25 2022, https://celt.ucc.ie/published/T201009/index.html.

and rang his bell, and sang maledictory psalms against the demons, and cast them out of the glen.[24]

As we can see from both accounts, a performative ritual is being described. Both require the performer to be in the area that is in need of an exorcism; both ring their bells against the supernatural agents; and psalms, described as 'cursing' and 'maledictory' in nature, are vocalised. Such a performance would generate a significant amount of noise, no doubt alerting people nearby that something was taking place, if not drawing them closer to witness it as bystanders. However, even as bystanders they now become active participants of the ritual. Just as a novel, or a text being read, can be interpreted through the lens of the reader's understanding and experience, so too can a visual performance.

In the case of Berach's exorcism, we are told that the ritual is taking place in Glendalough, a monastic site founded in the sixth century by St. Kevin. As a large, working religious settlement, the monastery was home to workshops, a scriptorium for the production of manuscripts, an infirmary and farms, as well as dwellings for the community that resided there, both lay and ecclesiastical. Thus, coming from a religious background, or at least such a Christian setting, the audience would probably already understand both the ritual they were witnessing, and the context for its performance. As Stacey has noted, in relation to public performances under the law, "a full understanding of what is taking place depends on the audience's recognizing that a performance is occurring, and an act of interpretation is required."[25] In this case, a clerical or lay religious audience would have known what an exorcism was, and what the desired outcome would be. Their knowledge and understanding then granted authority to the performer. Without the audience, the exorcist is simply a cleric ringing a bell and shouting loudly as he wanders around an area of land.

---

[24] Charles Plummer, *Betheda Náem nÉrenn: Lives of Irish Saints* (Oxford, 1922), p. 28. Accessed November 25 2022, https://celt.ucc.ie/published/T201000G/index.html.

[25] Robin Chapman Stacey, *Dark Speech: The Performance of Law in Early Ireland* (Philadelphia, 2007), p. 50.

What, then, does this mean for St. Patrick's exorcism? After all, his exorcism takes place atop Cruachán Aigle, during a forty-day period of solitary fasting. Is he simply a cleric wandering around, ringing his bell and being loud, without an audience to observe and grant legitimacy to his actions? Surely not: he achieves his goals, and the devils throw themselves into the sea and drown themselves. However, Patrick only achieves this once his emotions overcome him. In frustration, he begins to weep, before throwing his bell at the tormenting spirits so hard that he actually cracks it.[26] As Bitel notes, "God eventually granted Patrick's prayers, but at the expense of his dignity."[27] Reading this episode as a parody of other texts that rely on ritual performances to drive the action, may be a better way to interpret it. However, there are also clear parallels with Moses, who spent forty days fasting atop Mt Sinai. Additionally, Moses threw down the tablets containing the Commandments in anger, breaking them in a similar way to how Patrick broke his bell.

Regardless of whether or not the Saint Patrick episode is a parody or an allusion to Moses, the authors of such texts appear to be referencing some type of performance that existed. Other depictions of medieval Irish exorcisms are described in similar terms, including the ringing of the bell and the recitation of psalms which, in the examples highlighted, are referred to as 'maledictory' and 'cursing' respectively. While there are no texts from the period that detail exorcism step by step, there is another, more public ritual that is performed in a similar manner: that of cursing, specifically the type of cursing that is carried out by clerics and other ecclesiastics.

The Bible takes a clear stance on cursing: "But to you who are listening I say: love your enemies, do good to those who hate you, bless those who curse you, pray for those who mistreat you." (Luke 6:27); "If I have rejoiced at the ruin of him who hated me, or exulted when evil overtook him, I have not let my mouth sin by asking for his

---

[26] Cracked bells are a common trope in hagiographical literature, with the implication typically being that the saint is praying so hard, and so passionately, that he cracks his bell due to the enthusiasm with which he rings or strikes it. In Patrick's case, the bell is cracked when he loses his temper and throws it at the devils, rather than through exertion caused by the ritual.

[27] Bitel, "Tools and Scripts for Cursing", p. 6.

life with a curse." (Job 31:29-30); and even more succinct: "Bless those who persecute you: bless, and do not curse." (Romans 12:14). However, in a society that makes space and allowances for poetical satire, there appears to have been room for cursing within the religious sphere. This seems to have been achieved through the use of psalms, specifically those known as the imprecatory psalms.

There are around one hundred and fifty psalms, and it was standard practice for clerics to commit them to memory, typically in the first year or two of their religious training.[28] The word 'psalm' derives from the Greek word *'psalmoi'*, meaning 'instrumental music', or 'words accompanying music', which indicates that they may have begun their life as individual hymns collected to form a sort of anthology that was preserved in the Old Testament. As they vary in tone and content, with many being self-contained, particular psalms have been recited during certain times, or for specific purposes. For example, Psalm 23, beginning "The Lord is my shepherd" contains a message of comfort within the Christian faith, and has become associated with funerals. Conversely, the imprecatory psalms are those psalms that invoke judgement or call for God's wrath in a manner that curses the person the psalm is being used against. One of the most well-known of the imprecatory psalms is Psalm 69, which contains such lines as:

> May the table set before them become a snare; may it become retribution and a trap.
> May their eyes be darkened so they cannot see, and their backs be bent forever.
> Pour out your wrath on them; let your fierce anger overtake them.
> May their place be deserted; let there be no one to dwell in their tents.
> For they persecute those you wound and talk about the pain of those you hurt.
> Charge them with crime upon crime; do not let them share in your salvation.

---

[28] Dan Wiley, "The Maledictory Psalms" in *Peritia 15* (2015), p. 261. Translation from the Douay-Rheims bible online, http://drbo.org.

May they be blotted out of the book of life and not be
listed with the righteous.[29]

An imprecatory psalmodic ritual has been recorded in §32 of
Cáin Adamnáin.[30] The ritual, which is said to have been created by
Adamnan himself, follows the sanction clause laid out in §31-32, and
is created from a list of twenty psalms and the names of eighteen
saints, with one to be recited every day for twenty days, along with an
appeal to the saint that has been paired with it. A poem from Bodleian
Library, MS Rawlinson B 512 (f.51b1), which follows the copy of
Cáin Adamnáin recorded in that manuscript, gives a similar list with a
few changes. While the poem follows *Cáin Adamnáin,* and states that
Adamnan was the one who created the ritual and the arrangement of
its contents, the poem itself contains no mention of *Cáin Adamnáin,*
leading Wiley to argue that this "indicates that the ritual may be used
in other situations, a notion supported by references to the practice in
early Irish literature."[31]

The *Life of Saint Ruadan* describes in great detail an episode
where the saint and his clerics employ a ritualized ceremony of cursing
against Diarmait, who is named as "the king of Ireland in the time of
Ruadán".[32] In this text, the curse takes on a ritualized aspect. It is
described as follows: the gathered clerics "proceeded to ring their
bells, both large and small, against Diarmait so violently that they
damaged the bells in ringing them. They also sang psalms of cursing
and vengeance against him, but they could not obtain their will of the
king, but he treated them with great contempt."[33] The monks
congregate around Tara, within sight, or at least sound, of the royal
residence, and once begun they do not cease their chanting and bell-
ringing until they have achieved their goal. The public nature of this
action seems to invite onlookers to witness it: the ritual becomes a
spectacle for the consumption of the public.

---

[29] Psalm 69:22-28, New International Version.
[30] Kuno Meyer, *Cáin Adamnáin: an Old Irish treatise on the law of
Adamnan* (Oxford, 1905), p. 23.
[31] Wiley, "The Maledictory Psalms", p. 268.
[32] Plummer, *Betheda Naem nÉrenn,* p. 312.
[33] Ibid., pp. 314-315.

Making a legal claim against a king, especially one of Diarmait's high status, was difficult. The highest echelon of medieval Irish society was made up of those classed as *nemed,* or 'privileged'. They were made up of the elites: kings, lords; clerics; and poets, and these classes of people had special legal privileges. Take, for example, the process of distraint, known as *athgabál,* which is presented in a detailed manner in the legal text *Di Cetharślicht Athgabála.* This was the formal seizure of property, and a valid legal process of claiming restitution.[34] It also contains a number of features relating to time, space and public performances that are similar to the ritual of cursing. It began with the plaintiff giving formal notice (*apad*) to the defendant that the seizure of property would begin after a period of delay (*anad*). Notice had to be given early in the morning, and in front of witnesses. During the delay, the defendant is given the opportunity to respond and pay the fine, or perform the obligation, owed to the plaintiff. Should the defendant refuse to do so, the process of distraint proper is set in motion, and the plaintiff is now entitled to enter the defendant's land and begin removing cattle, or other valuable livestock, until the value of the fine is paid in full.

These types of elaborate, formal and performative rituals can be found elsewhere in the legal texts. For example, if a watchdog commits an offence, apad was given to its owner before a plank was placed across the dog's food vessel, and the dog is not fed until the owner has paid the compensation due. Should the owner ignore this, and continues to feed his dog, the crime then passes from the category of animal trespass to *duinechin* (human offence), and the fine is increased to reflect this.[35] *Bretha Comaithchesa* (Judgements of a Neighbourhood) outlines the process in place should livestock or a domestic pet trespass onto, or damage, a neighbour's property.[36] Should cattle graze on a neighbour's land, the injured party must "throw a stone over them three times in the presence of a witness".[37]

---

[34] Kelly, *Guide,* p. 177. See also Binchy, D.A., 'A Text on the Forms of Distraint', in *Celtica* 10 (Dublin, 1973), pp. 72-86; Binchy, D.A., 'Distraint in Irish Law', in *Celtica* 10 (Dublin, 1973) 22-71.

[35] Kelly, *Guide,* p. 180.

[36] See Thomas Charles-Edwards, *Bretha Comaithcheso* (Dublin, 2022) for the full edition of this legal text.

[37] Ibid.

After a period of twenty-four hours, if the cattle's owner refuses to pay the fine levied, the plaintiff can impound the herd where, after *díthim, lobad* is enacted and the herd is forfeit. In the case of offences caused by the very lowest level of society, unfree people who, of course, had no livestock, no part of the distraint procedure could be used. Instead, apad was given to the slave's master, after which a manacle and chain were placed on the slave.[38] They were then placed on lower food rations, similar to the treatment of a watchdog that commits an offence, until their master paid the compensation that was owed. This procedure was also used for other members of society that lacked the economic status of livestock owners, such as shepherds, cowherds, and *fuidir,* or 'tenants-at-will'.[39]

However, as the highest-ranking members of society, there was nobody the nemed could submit to or who could force them to honour their contractual obligations. Instead, different procedures, such as cursing, were needed to fill this gap in the legal code. An Old Irish triad states that it is unwise to act as surety against a king or another class of nemed because their *enech,* or honour, was too great for the surety to sue, or gain legal redress from, in the event that the nemed defaulted.[40] *Bretha Nemed Déidenach* goes as far as to say that "a contract with *nemeds* [nemthiu] is not a contract".[41] Additionally, *Tecosca Cormaic* says "do not buy from a high-ranking person".[42] Presumably, not all contracts with nemed were automatically void or invalid, but it would certainly be difficult to enforce one should the nemed renege. In the case of kings, they could substitute themselves for an *aithech fortha* (substitute churl).[43] Whenever the king broke the law or refused legal responsibility for wrong-doing, the plaintiff could instead begin the process of distraint against the substitute figure, and gain restitution from them.

There was, however, another special procedure which could be used, called *troscud,* or 'fasting', which was intended to pressure a

---

[38] Ibid., p. 182.
[39] Ibid.
[40] Kelly, *Guide,* p. 25.
[41] Ibid., p. 162.
[42] Kelly, *Guide,* p. 162; Kuno Meyer, *The Instructions of King Cormac mac Airt* (Dublin, 1909), section 19.
[43] Kelly, *Guide,* p. 25.

241

nemed or king into submitting to the law and accepting judgement.[44] This procedure was prescribed when a legal suit was brought against a defendant of elite status who refused to concede to judgement should the ruling go against him. When a plaintiff undertakes a fasting, it was performed outside the offending elite's home, with later commentators of *Di Cetherslicht Athgabála* noting that it usually took place between the hours of sunset and sunrise, no doubt to disrupt and halt the nemed's evening meal. The nemed was not allowed to eat during the fast, unless he made a guarantee that he would submit to the law. If he does eat, he must then pay twice the amount originally owed. If he still refuses the judgement, and the fast is considered justified and conducted correctly, the nemed loses his own right to legal compensation in the future, and effectively his rights within society.[45]

As with the above legal processes, the ritualized cursing carried out by Ruadan and his monks against Diarmait has a highly visible, public, and performative aspect to it. By bringing the performance to Tara–within earshot and perhaps eyeshot of the royal residence, considering how clearly the psalms and bell-ringing could be heard by those within the building–the monks are deliberately drawing public attention to the situation, and highlighting what they perceive to be an injustice against them and the legitimacy of Ruadan's authority. As with the performance of *troscud,* their presence–throughout the day and night, rather than just the hours of darkness, when the royal household would be enjoying their main meal and sleep–is designed to bring public pressure to bear on the king, shaming him into doing the right thing and submitting to Ruadan's will.

The second *Vita* of Máedóc of Ferns contains a number of instances of the saint threatening curses, and two instances of curses being used explicitly. In the first instance, no description of the ritual is given, and the curse is directed at a large rock that is broken into two halves.[46] In the second, the ritual is described in similar terms as the exorcism episodes above:

---

[44] Ibid., p. 182.

[45] Cf. Kelly, *Guide,* pp. 182-183, and Stacey, pp. 27-28, for discussions concerning *troscud.*

[46] Plummer, *Betheda Naem nÉrenn,* p. 219.

[H]e turned his bachalls and enduring relics round them three times widdershins. He rang his bells and handbells together against them, that is the *Mac Ratha* ('Son of Grace'), the bell of the brooch, the bell of the hours, which is called the white bell, and the bells of the clergy and congregation from that time forth; and he cursed them without delay.[47]

The 'turning' of the bachaill and relics around them three times is also reminiscent of the tradition of carrying the Cathach around the field of battle three times, as well as the traversing of the exorcism site while performing that ritual. Here, the direction is reversed as superstition placed a negative or unlucky aspect on a left-handed path, while the right-hand direction brought additional good luck and contributed to the performance of the Cathach ritual and the driving out of demons.

However, it is one of the implied threats that stands out, due to the purely aural nature of it. While *Cáin Adamnáin* lays out the steps for ritual cursing which, like the legal processes discussed, made allowances in timing for the subject to come to terms before the full curse is enacted, the period of apad or notice is conspicuously missing. However, as cursing is a process used against nemed in place of the legal procedures, we would expect the ritual to begin the same way, with formal notice given to the subject.

When Máedóc is returning from his sojourn in Wales, we are told that he could see a group of brigands near the coast, attacking pilgrims and other people using that road. As a saint and the head of a monastic community, Méadóc would, of course, have been familiar with pilgrims, and his monastery would have hosted them and performed all the rituals of hospitality one would expect during the time period, including offering protection. On seeing the brigands waylaying the pilgrims, Máedóc orders his ship to go ashore to help them. In the meantime, he begins to ring his bell, which is heard by the brigands and interpreted correctly by their leader, who reveals it to be "'the sound of the bell of a devout and godly man,' said he, 'and he rings his bell to bid us cease this work.' They let the pilgrims be after this."[48] In this instance, it is the sound of the bell, heard on the shore from the

---

[47] Ibid., p. 229.
[48] Plummer, *Betheda Naem nÉrenn*, p. 205.

boat, that gave notice to the brigands that a cleric was on his way and was displeased with the attacks they were carrying out. Here, the sound of the bell seems to act as a reminder that the Church had the power to deliver a powerful censure. The brigands may not be nemeds, but they are unlawful and, as such, acting outside of the legal codes. While the legal procedures may be difficult to enforce in such cases, the ecclesiastic processes could certainly be used against them in place of the law.

An episode from the fragmentary annals seems to hint that notice was indeed given prior to cursing, although verbally rather than through the use of bells.[49] The tale, which involves Adamnán, sees the cleric give verbal notice to king Fínnachta. However, the cursing ritual that follows is described in different terms than the others looked at so far, and vastly different from the ritual laid out in *Cáin Adamnáin*. In this instance, Adamnán sends a cleric from his retinue to Fínnachta, asking for the king to come and speak to him. The king refuses, and the attendant sends back Adamnán's promise to recite fifty psalms until Fínnachta relents and agrees to speak with him. This is repeated two more times, with the number of psalms increasing by fifty until the full repertoire of the psalter has been recited, over a period of three days. While it differs considerably from the list of two psalms previously prescribed in *Cáin Adamnáin* and the poem from MS Rawl. B 512, it is highly reminiscent of the legal procedures, in that there is verbal notice given, a period of delay marked in days, then the final outcome of a full curse.

There are also divergences in the tale which appear to be significant. For instance, the performance of bells and bachaill executed publicly and in the vicinity of the subject has been removed, and the maledictory psalms have been replaced by the full psalter. Additionally, we are told that within each fifty of psalms there will be one maledictory psalm that is hidden. The attendant that delivers the message does not specify which psalm contains the curse, meaning that that information is also hidden to the audience, which in this case is reduced from the local population to the reader of the text. The curse itself also takes the form of three separate punishments, each one

---

[49] John O'Donovan, *Annals of Ireland: Three Fragments* (Dublin, 1860), p. 28 accessed December 5 2022, https://celt.ucc.ie/published/T100017/index.html; Wiley, "The Maledictory Psalms", p. 10.

attached to the three hidden psalms: no descendent of Fínnachta will hold the kingship, God will shorten Fínnachta's life, and finally Fínnachta will be barred from entering heaven. It is only when the final curse is threatened that Fínnachta relents and agrees to speak with Adamnán.

The differences between this episode and the others leaves us with some questions. For instance, a number of psalms in the psalter were already considered maledictory in nature, so by reciting the full one hundred and fifty Adamnán would already be reciting the full number of maledictory psalms over the course of the three days. The increasing threats all appear to have taken place over the course of three games of fidchell, but we are not told if each game takes place on three consecutive days, or over the course of a single day. Additionally, at no stage is Adamnán described as actually carrying out the recitation of psalms or the cumulative curses: we are simply told that this is the action he will take if Fínnachta refuses to speak to him. The similarity with this and the legal procedures, however, with definite verbal notice being given, and the three subsequent stages of recitation, is clear. At the end of each fifty, time is given to Fínnachta to agree to come to terms by meeting with Adamnán, and halt the ritual before it ends.

The accounts of cursing recorded in the Annals of Tigernach and the Annals of the Four Masters follow the model laid out in the hagiographies. In 1043, the Annals of Tigernach record the following entry: "The fasting of the Community of Cíaran, at Tulach Garba, upon Aodh Ó Confhiachla, the king of Teffa, and the *Bernán Ciaráin* was struck against him with the end of the *Bachall Íssu*. Now, in that place at which he turned his back on the Clerics, in that place, his head was cut off before the month's end."[50] An entry in the Four Masters from 1233 is described as follows:

> There were also slain, on this occasion, Raghallagh
> O'Flanagan; Thomas Biris, Constable of Ireland; and
> his brother John; John Guer; and many other
> Englishmen; after they had been cursed and
> excommunicated by the clergy of Connaught, by the

---

[50] Stokes, "The Annals of Tigernach", *Revue Celtique 16,* p. 383. Accessed December 5, https://celt.ucc.ie/published/T100002A/index.html.

> ringing of bells with croziers and the extinguishing of
> candles; for Hugh Muimhneach had violated and
> plundered Tibohine, and many other churches, so that
> he and his party fell in revenge of the saints whose
> churches they had violated.[51]

As with the literary depictions, bells and bachaill were used to cause noise and invite onlookers.

Whether or not apad was given verbally, or the ritual was announced through the clamor raised by religious objects and relics, it appears that a public performance was a key element in providing both authority and efficacy. As Stacey notes, "it is probably the emphasis on shared action and belief, the embeddedness in the community practice and perception that most clearly stands out from the Irish sources, as key to the efficacy of [legal] ritual."[52] While that statement may have been written about the various public legal procedures, it can also be true for cursing and exorcism when the similarities between them and the legal rituals are taken into consideration. Without the audience, drawn by the noise to witness the ritual, there can be no outside interpretation to transform it from simple noise and psalms into a curse or exorcism.

Rituals, at their heart, are a series of actions and behavior, usually perceived as normal, which are exaggerated and combined to transform them into the abnormal. Bells ringing can call a community to work, food or prayer, but in these rituals they act as an auditory warning. The bachall, a symbol of a shepherd safeguarding his flock, is now used in conjunction with the bell to create that warning. Psalms, as Christian prayers, are expressions of faith and devotion, but here they are changed and become threats. Taken together, they become a performance that can affect the audience in a profound way, influencing their judgement and persuading them that the subject of the curse is worthy of the censure being levelled at them.

Clerics, audience and sound combine, transforming the ritual being performed. The clerics remain clerics, and are performing a

---

[51] John O'Donovan, *Annals of the Kingdom of Ireland by the Four Masters* (Dublin, 1990), pp. 268-269. Accessed December 5 2022, https://celt.ucc.ie/published/T100005C/index.html.
[52] Stacey, *Dark Speech,* pp. 48-49.

ritual reserved for clerics, but in the eyes of the audience they are now powerful agents of change. The subject of the curse is going to lose something: he may lose face before his subjects, or even status if he refuses to address the clerics. In extreme cases he may lose his life. The audience is also transformed. Through the simple act of witnessing, their belief in the ritual and the effectiveness of curses allows them to see affirming evidence: any bad luck that befalls the subject will now be ascribed to the curse. This type of confirmation bias produces a mostly coherent, although illogical, narrative that supports the veracity of the curse, and in a time period such as the medieval age, with high mortality rates, disease, and warfare, eventually the curse would come true, and the power of God and his clerics would be affirmed.

As others don't see us–Re-telling history in Scottish Gaelic theatre

Michelle Macleod

Since the first plays were staged in Gaelic at the start of the twentieth century, one of the most common themes or subjects has been the retelling of historical events pertaining to the lives of the Gaelic people. These representations have often challenged the established portrayal of events or brought to light overlooked incidents. This paper will discuss a selection of 'historical plays'[1] and will consider how they challenge the received portrayal of historic events with a version which brings forward a Gaelic perspective. The plays under discussion are: Dòmhnall Mac na Ceàrdaich's *Fearann a Shinnsir* ("The Land of his Forebears", 1913); Tormod Calum Dòmhnallach's *Aimhreit Aignis* (The Aignish Riots, 1988) and *An Ceistear, Am Bàrd 's na Boirionnaich* (The Catechist, The Bard and the Women, 1974), and two historical plays from the last decade: Màiri Nic'IlleMhoire's *Bana-Ghaisgich* (Heroines, 2018) and Muireann Kelly with Frances Poet's *Scotties* (2018).

With few notable exceptions, of bilingual theatre in the eighteenth century[2], the play in Gaelic really originates at the start of the twentieth century. There are undeniably many aspects of 'drama' in Gaelic culture earlier than this and Michael Newton makes a good case for the concept of 'folk drama' in Gaelic,[3] though it is certainly

---

[1] I have chosen to use the term 'historical play' rather than 'history play' or 'historical drama' throughout this discussion: all of these terms are in use by theatre scholars and by and large, there is significant overlap in their meaning. Later in the discussion, I show how some of the plays under discussion might differ to the expectations of a history play as expressed by one critic and it is for this reason that I have chosen the term 'historical play'.

[2] See Archibald Maclaren, *The Humours of Greenock Fair* or *The Taylor Made a Man* (Paisley: John Neilson, 1790) and *The Highland Drover or Domhnul Dubh M'Na-Beinn*, at Carlisle (Greenock: T. Murray, 1790).

[3] Michael Newton, "Folk Drama in Gaelic Scotland," in *Edinburgh Companion to Scottish Drama*, ed. Ian Brown (Edinburgh: Edinburgh University Press, 2011), 41-46.

nowhere near as developed a genre as in the languages of neighbouring countries. Other genres where drama-like tendencies can be found include the Gaelic *còmhraidhean* (conversations);[4] traditional tales with the *seanchaidh* (storyteller) playing the roles of actors and director; dramatic aspect of rituals of social customs and even sermons. The stage play is by and large an artificial and intentional product of the change to the social demographic of Gaelic speakers in the nineteenth and early twentieth centuries when significant numbers of them began settling in the urban areas of Scotland. In these new situations, which did not lend themselves well to facilitating traditional ways of cultural expression, such as via the cèilidh house or communal working tasks, Gaels needed to organise themselves differently in order to deliver and enjoy culturally and artistically enriching experiences. At the same time, many Gaelic societies were established in the cities from as early as the later eighteenth century and Gaelic publishing was also enjoying a boom providing new platforms for experimental writing and it is in this environment that the Gaelic play begins to flourish.[5]

Of course, demographic changes were not the only catalysts for the new art form: among the leaders of the Gaelic societies, there were some who believed that drama and theatre could play an important role in their shared aims of preserving language and culture and sought actively to encourage the writing and production of plays. Early enthusiasts for the development of Gaelic drama as a means of preserving and promoting Gaelic language and culture include the Rt. Hon. Ruaraidh Erskine of Marr (1869-1960) who was one of Gaelic drama's first advocates. Erskine, a staunch Scottish nationalist, was inspired by what he saw happening in Ireland; his vision of an independent Scotland was as a place where Gaelic language and

---

[4] For a discussion of the Gaelic còmhradh / conversation genre see, for example, Sheila Kidd, *Còmhraidhean nan Cnoc: the Nineteenth-Century Gaelic Prose Dialogue* (Glasgow: Scottish Gaelic Texts Society, 2016).
[5] For discussions on the origins of Gaelic theatre see Michelle Macleod, *Ceud Bliadhna air an Àrd-Ùrlar: A Century of Gaelic Drama* (Glasgow: Association for Scottish Literary Studies, 2020) and Michelle Macleod, "Gaelic Drama: The Forgotten Genre in Gaelic Literary Studies," in *Lainnir a' Bhùirn*, eds. E.Dymock and W. McLeod (Edinburgh: Dunedin Academic Press, 2011), 55-70.

culture, including a healthy drama movement thrived. He formed the successful periodical *Guth na Bliadhna* (Voice of the Year) in 1904 and began publishing plays in it as early as 1912, the first being *Domhnull nan Trioblaid* ("Donald of the Troubles") by Dòmhnall Mac na Ceàrdaich (Donald Sinclair, 1885-1932).[6] In addition to publishing plays, Erskine also wrote several articles discussing why he considered Gaelic drama to be an important instrument in the language revival.[7]

Although Erskine was initially critical of the sluggishness of the leading Gaelic organisation of the time, An Comunn Gàidhealach, at getting involved in supporting Gaelic drama, it has played an important role since the early 1900s in supporting it. An early drama advocate within An Comunn was its President and editor of its magazine *An Gaidheal*, Rev. Dr. Neil Ross, who, during the 1920s and 1930s, wrote about the importance of Gaelic theatre. Ross's vision, like Erskine's, emphasised the promotion of this art form not only for art's sake, but also as a vehicle for language maintenance: 'a Gaelic theatre could combine healthy entertainment with the fulfilment of a noble patriotic object . . . the preservation of the language, music and traditions of the race'.[8]

At least some early playwrights also appeared to share the belief that Gaelic drama should be about more than just entertainment and that it should be used within the community as a platform for discussion and for exploring pertinent issues which might then possibly impact on society. One early playwright Iain N. MacLeòid (John MacLeod, 1880-1954), a Skye man who was a teacher, an editor (of the impressive Lewis poem book *Bàrdachd Leòdhais*[9]) and writer,

---

[6] Dòmhnall Mac na Ceàrdaich, "Domhnall nan Trioblaid," in *Guth na Bliadhna*, 9 (1912): 151-94.

[7] The Hon. Ruaraidh Erskine of Marr, "Gaelic Drama," in *Guth na Bliadhna*, 10 (1913): 294-300, 452-62; 11 (1914): 80-90, 206-19; For more detailed discussion on Erskine's views on Gaelic theatre see Petra Poncarová, "'A Fitting Offering to the Gaelic Thalia or Melpomene': Ruaraidh Erskine of Mar and Drama in Scottish Gaelic", in *Litteraria Pragensia*, 2020: 30-59.

[8] Neil Ross, "A Gaelic Theatre," in *An Gaidheal*, 27, 92-3, at 92.

[9] Iain MacLeòid, *Bàrdachd Leòdhais* (Glasgow: A. MacLaren & Son, 1916).

wrote this in the introduction to his short play *Rèiteach Mòraig* ("Morag's Betrothal") which is essentially a simulation of the Gaelic betrothal tradition:

> *Tha ar càirdean an Èirinn a' dèanamh mòran sna bliadhnaichean seo airson chuspairean a bhuineas don Ghàidhlig a chur ann an cruth deilbh-chluich. Tha soirbheachadh mòr gan leantainn san obair sin. Tha mòran aig nach eil suim idir don chànain air an tarraing don ionnsaigh airson beachd a ghabhail air an dòigh anns a bheil an dealbh-chluich air a h-iomairt, agus 'n uair a tha gluasad agus snas nan cleasaichean a' taitinn riutha, tha iad a' dol dhachaigh le beachd na b' fheàrr na bh'aca roimhe air a' chànain, agus bhon àm sin tha iad a' gabhail suime dhith, agus 's dòcha a' fàs mu dheireadh glè fhileanta ann a bhith ga labhairt.*[10]

> Our friends in Ireland are doing much these years to produce topics which relate to Gaelic in the form of plays. They are succeeding in that matter. There are many who are not at all interested in the language who are drawn towards them to consider the way in which the play is directed, and when they enjoy the movement and polish of the actors, they go home with a better opinion than they had before of the language, and from that time they have an interest in it, and perhaps eventually grow very fluent in speaking it.[11]

While the opinions of these individuals could not be said to form a collective philosophical ethos which deliberately shaped the content of all Gaelic drama, there is undoubtedly a shared vision of using theatre to retell issues relating to Gaelic culture and history and this vision has pervaded a significant proportion of the Gaelic play corpus.

---

[10] Iain MacLeòid, *Rèiteach Mòraig* in Macleod, *Ceud Bliadhna air an Àrd-Ùrlar: A Century of Gaelic Drama*, 2.

[11] John MacLeod, "Morag's Betrothal" in Macleod, *Ceud Bliadhna air an Àrd-Ùrlar: A Century of Gaelic Drama*, 12.

That Gaelic theatre should have history as a focus is not of itself remarkable: after all, 'history' is one of the three classical genres of theatre, alongside (though appearing later than) comedy and tragedy. And while the Gaelic plays here share much in common with plays which take history as their focus in other languages, there are some features in the Gaelic plays which are noteworthy. To begin with, we find in Gaelic drama that its focus is uniquely on the impact of history on the 'ordinary' and hitherto anonymous person (discussed below), and this contrasts with, at least, one definition which suggests that a history play should normally have some recognisable characters;[12] the Gaelic plays, as shown here, generally do not have known historical figures. Additionally, history plays are normally based around real events:[13] at least two of the plays under consideration here use simulated, yet commonplace, events as the focus of their action. Another generalisation about the history play genre challenged by some of the plays considered here is that they do not follow a logical narrative sequence on stage; three of the plays under discussion here experiment with time sequences, allowing for action in the modern and historical era to be shown on stage in a single play. In spite of the differences, these Gaelic plays share many features of the history play genre. Clearly, the plays under consideration here present a version of events that took place in the past on stage; the events are by and large 'public' and can be verified independently; and finally, they can be judged to have considerable value as educational tools.[14]

What the plays under consideration here also share in common with each other is that they criticise, albeit obliquely, the power structures which facilitated the weakening of their communities. In the same way that the play *The Cheviot, the Stag and the Black, Black Oil*,[15] about the economics of land ownership from the Clearances to

---

[12] Tom Stern, "History Plays As History," *Philosophy and Literature*; 36:2, (Oct 2012): 285-300.

[13] Ibid.

[14] Ibid.

[15] John McGrath, *The Cheviot, the Stag and the Black, Black Oil* (Kyleakin: West Highland Pub., 1974). This is by and large an English-language play but with some Gaelic dialogue and Gaelic song. For a discussion on this see e.g., Ian Brown and Sìm Innes, "The use of some Gaelic songs and poetry

the oil boom in the Highlands, has been credited with "displaying a grassroots anticolonial discourse on colonial history,"[16] these plays can be considered as bringing forward a version history of the Gaelic people which had hitherto often been dehumanised or trivialised. This, of course, is not unique to Gaelic theatre, Rokem has identified similar in Israeli theatre and French theatre of the Revolution:

> Theatrical performances of and about history reflect complex ideological issues concerning deeply rooted national identities and subjectivities and power structures and can in some cases be seen as a wilful resistance to and critique of the established or hegemonic, sometimes even stereotypical, perceptions of the past.[17]

Even at the start of the twentieth century when, for the most part, the early plays in Gaelic tended to be light-hearted,[18] there are examples which challenged established perceptions of the recent past and criticised the authorities. It is likely that most early plays were created with cèilidh performance in mind. Commonly they included recreations of Gaelic customs, such as Iain N. MacLeòid *Rèiteach Mòraig* (Mòrag's Betrothal), 1911,[19] and *Pòsadh Mòraig* (Morag's Wedding), 1916,[20] or comedy sketches, sometime dealing with serious issues of the day such as land and language loss, as in Iain MacCormaig's (John MacCormick, 1860–1947) *Am Fear a Chaill a*

---

in The Cheviot, the Stag and the Black, Black Oil", *International Journal of Scottish Theatre and Screen* Volume 5 Number 2 (2012).

[16] Silke Stroh, *Uneasy Subjects: Postcolonialism and Scottish Gaelic Poetry* (Amsterdam: Rodopi, 2011), 197.

[17] Freddie Rokem, *Performing history : Theatrical representations of the past in contemporary theatre* (Iowa: University of Iowa Press, 2000), 8.

[18] Macleod, *Ceud Bliadhna air an Àrd-Ùrlar: A Century of Gaelic Drama* and Macleod, "Gaelic Drama: The Forgotten Genre in Gaelic Literary Studies".

[19] Iain N. MacLeòid, *Rèiteach Mòraig* (Glaschu: Gilleasbuig Macnaceardadh, 1911).

[20] Iain N. MacLeòid, *Pòsadh Móraig* (Glaschu: A. MacLabhruinn, 1916).

Ghàidhlig (The Man who Lost his Gaelic), 1925.[21] They very often included song, especially towards the end, perhaps with audience participation in mind. But not all the early plays are light-hearted; Ross has written about how we can find in a number of the early plays a sense of 'othering': of the positioning of Gael against Lowlander.[22] And, as noted by A. MacLeòid, there were several efforts to produce serious drama, including two historical plays by Dòmhnall Mac na Ceàrdaich (Donald Sinclair, 1885–1932).[23] One of these, *Fearann a Shinnsir"* (The Land of his Forebears, 1913), is a four-act play concerning the common problem of eviction and the connection to place felt so strongly by the Gael. The play follows the plight of Alasdair, who was originally forced to emigrate to Canada with his aging parents but returns to his native island, after their death, to be reunited with his love, Mòrag.

Unlike the other plays considered here, both the setting and the characters are fictional, though representative of the lived experiences of many of the era represented; the playwright probably based the unnamed island in his play on his native island of Barra. What makes this play special is, as noted by MacLeòid, "the scrutiny it affords to issues of class and the clearances ensure that it is an important piece of political drama emerging from the early 20th Century Gaelic community".[24] It is, in fact, an important piece of political criticism in any genre and unusually strong for this time period. Rarely would we see such criticism of the landed classes as from Domhnull and his son Alasdair when they are being forced from their land. Domhnull wails to his wife about the inhumanity of their situation being forced from their home by a greedy landlord:

---

[21] Iain MacCormaig, *Am Fear a Chaill a Ghàidhlig* (Glaschu: An Comunn Gàidhealach, 1925).

[22] Susan Ross, "Identity in Gaelic Drama 1900-1949," *International Journal of Scottish Theatre and Screen* 9, (2016): https://ijosts.glasgow.ac.uk/volume-9/identity-in-gaelic-drama-1900-1949/–accessed 15 December 2022.

[23] Aonghas MacLeòid, "The Historical Plays of Donald Sinclair," *International Journal of Scottish Theatre and Screen* 9, (2016) https://ijosts.glasgow.ac.uk/volume-9/the-historical-plays-of-donald-sinclair/ - accessed 15 December 2022.

[24] Ibid.

Tha 'n t-olc air a dhol as a riochd aithnichte agus Ceartas Dhè air a saltairt fo na casan. Mar eun fo spàig na h-iolaire tha gach Crìostuidh 'san dùthaich so fo bhinn nan uachdaran. O, daoine gun iochd! Daoine gun chridhe, gun tlus, gun fhaireachdainn daonna! Tròcaire!– tròcaire cha do thiomaich riamh an cridheachan; ach–ach cha'n fhaigh iadsan fhathast, tha eagal orm, tròcaire.[25]

The devil has changed from his recognisable form and God's Justice has been trampled under their feet. Like a bird under the talon of the eagle, every Christian in this country is under the sentence of the landlords. Oh men without mercy. Men without heart, without compassion, without the feeling of men. Mercy!– mercy never softened their hearts; but–but they will never get mercy, I am afraid. (my own translation)

And at the point when his family is being forced to join the ship that will take them to Canada, Alasdair rages about the unfairness of the situation and the false authority of the landlord:

Ach co bhuaidhe an do ghabh thusa an t-ughdarras so leis a bheil thu gu d' chur féin an riochd an daoifhir? Co a thug dhuit-sa còir air beatha an t-sluaigh no air tiolaicean a chaidh fhàgail aca? An tusa, a tha 'n diugh, ar leat féin, uile-chumhachdach ad ghniomh 's ad fhacal: an tusa, tha mi faighneachd, a tha gabhail de dhànadas agus de ladarnas gu'n canadh tu: "le m' fhacal-sa théid na ceudan a sgiursadh bho thìr an dùchais. . . . "[26]

But from whom did you get this authority that you can turn yourself into a retrobate? Who gave you the right to the lives of the people or the gifts they had been left? Are you, today, do you think, omnipotent in your

---

[25] Dòmhnall Mac na Ceàrdaich. *D.M.N.C.: Sgrìobhaidhean Dhòmhnaill Mhic na Ceàrdaich* (Inverness: Clàr, 2014), 201.
[26] Ibid., 206.

word and action: do you, I ask, have so much audacity and impertinance that you would say: "by my command hundreds will be driven from their homeland. . . . " (my own translation)

There is an interesting twist at the end of the play when Alasdair unexpectedly returns to his native island. The sick landlord, who has seen the error of his ways, begs Alasdair for forgiveness and to take his family's land back. This scenario is surely much more of a wish than representative of the experiences of real people.

Some of Sinclair's generation would certainly have known first-hand the impact of the clearances but in recording their impact on stage and paper, he was bringing that experience of loss and betrayal to a wider audience. The development of Gaelic drama was impacted, of course, by the second world war and following the innovation of the start of the century, there was really a lull in dramatic production until the 1960s or so. The question of land ownership is revisited again in the modern period.

One playwright who began writing in the 1970s and for whom the question of Gaelic authenticity and identity was crucial to his work was Tormod Calum Dòmhnallach (Norman Malcolm MacDonald, born in Thunder Bay, Canada in 1927 of Lewis parents; he died in Lewis in 2000).[27] Dòmhnallach was acutely aware that drama, more than any other modern artistic form, had the capacity, even obligation, to re-tell Gaelic history from an internal gaze. Like Mac na Ceàrdaich, who preceded him by seventy or so years, Dòmhnallach also wrote about the land issue. Unlike Mac na Ceàrdaich, whose play was set on a loosely fictitious island, the two Dòmhnallach plays discussed here which have land ownership as a theme are set in the Isle of Lewis.

Aimhreit Aignis (The Agnish Riot), although focussing on one local episode in the land agitation uprising in 1888, [28] depicts events commonly occurring elsewhere in the Highlands and islands at that time. It focusses on the injustices around land ownership which caused

---

[27] Michelle NicLeòid, *An Fhìrinn agus A' Bhreug: Deich Dealbhan-cluiche le Tormod Calum Dòmhnallach* (Aberdeen: Aberdeen University Press, 2016).

[28] For a discussion on this see e.g., Joni Buchanan, *The Lewis Land Struggle* (Stornoway: Acair, 1996).

much hardship for the ordinary people. Where Dòmhnallach is more successful, perhaps, than his predecessor is in showing the truly human impact of these events which he does immediately by a mother speaking directly to the audience about how she has no food for her child.

> *BOIREANNACH Cha robh talamh againn idir.*
> *Cha robh. Dìreach pìos a fhuair an duine agam bho*
> *m' athair. Blòigh feannag airson buntàta. 'S e*
> *iasgair a bh' anns an duine agam. O cha*
> *diochuimhnich mise an latha ud. An latha a thàinig*
> *iad dhachaigh falamh agus iad air na lìn a chall.*
> *Ruith an leanabh gu athair.*
> *A bhobain, a bhobain.*
> *Dè a ghràidh, ars athair agus e ga thogail.*
> *A bhobain, tha an t-acras orm.*
> *A bhobain, tha an t-acras orm.*
> *A bhoireannaich, ars an duine agam, cuir biadh air*
> *a' bhòrd.*
> *Cha chuir, ars mise, biadh air a' bhòrd. Chan*
> *urrainn sin dhomh. Chan eil biadh ann.*[29]

WOMAN We didn't have any land at all. No. Just a piece my husband got from my father. A strip of land for potatos. My husband was a fisherman. Oh, I will never forget that day. The day they came home with nothing and they had lost the nets. My child ran to his father.
Daddy, daddy.
What my dear, said his father picking him up.
Daddy, I am hungry.
Daddy, I am hungry.
Woman, said my husband, put food on the table.
I won't, I said, put food on the table. I can't do that. There is no food.'[30]

---

[29] NicLeòid, *An Fhìrinn agus A' Bhreug*, 140.
[30] My own translation.

This is nearly immediately followed by a statement, in English, from the farmer in the court-house:

> TUATHANACH I am joint tenant of the farm of Aignish. The stock consists principally of sheep but there are some cattle. There are a large number of crofters and squatters in the neighbourhood of Aignish and sheep belonging to them get over the fence and trespass upon my farm. I send the trespassers back to their own ground and the owners are displeased at me. I am a stranger in the place and as I do not know Gaelic, which the crofters speak, I have little or no intercourse with any of them.[31]

And so, the opposition between local and incomer, land-owner and crofter, law-breaker and law-keeper is established. Dòmhnallach cleverly uses a mix of regular asides to the audience, interactions between representatives of the different sides in the dispute (including crofters, landowners, police and soldiers) and stagecraft, for example sound effects to replicate the noise of British army marching in to remove people from their protest, to create a powerful reimagination of a real event. This and one other play discussed in this paper were written for centenary commemorations of important events in the Isle of Lewis which had traditionally been overlooked by established history. The retelling on stage (and on page), particularly of the human impact of these events, goes some way to balancing gaps in the social history of the Highlands which were not really addressed until the works of historians like James Hunter who began important work on the crofting and Highland community from the 1970s.[32] Dòmhnallach's stage portrayals of the impact of major events on ordinary people and Hunter's histories of the Highland people were part of broader trends to represent the 'ordinary' person 'in intersecting ways within newspapers, popular culture, political debate,

---

[31] Ibid.
[32] See for example James Hunter, *The Making of the Crofting Community* (Edinburgh: Donald, 1976).

scholarly studies'[33] and as part of a revision of social history which took place in the 1960s, sometimes referred to as 'history from below':

> . . . history from below concentrates on the unorganized and the marginal who have been least visible in the historical record. Seeing history from the bottom up does not just mean recreating the rhythms of everyday life. It means seeing the past from the point of view of ordinary people and identifying with their politics. Above all, history from below contests the passivity to which ordinary people have been consigned by so many historians.[34]

One of the transcendent aspirations of Dòmhnallach's plays is his determination to represent what he perceived to be an authentic version of Gaelic history with 'ordinary' people at the focus. In an interview, Dòmhnallach emphasised:

> We have to find the true history underlying our race before we go ahead and come to terms with the present and the future. It's an on-going process and it's not to do with nostalgia. I would hope that, particularly in my plays, I am far from being nostalgic.[35]

Dòmhnallach's statement clearly implies that the version he will present is from an internal perspective and will challenge versions given previsouly by 'outsiders'.

An Ceistear, Am Bàrd 's na Boirionnaich ("The Catechist, The Bard and the Women", 1974) is a powerful and witty portrayal of how stories, and history, can be manipulated through their telling and re-telling and that any version of events should be carefully interrogated paying particular attention to the source of the information. Here, there

---

[33] Claire Langhamer, "'Who The Hell Are Ordinary People?' Ordinariness As A Category Of Historical Analysis" *Transactions of the Royal Historical Society* 28 (2018), 175-195.

[34] John Tosh, *The Pursuit of History : Aims, Methods and New Directions in the Study of History* (London: Routledge, 2015) 57.

[35] Francis Thompson, "A Gael in the Modern World: Norman Malcolm MacDonald", *Books in Scotland* (1978), 27-28, at 28.

are four main characters The Catechist, The Bard and two women: during the play, however, each of the characters also play other parts including in the scene discussed here. Once again, the land issue comes to the fore as one scene is set in a land court in Stornoway in Lewis where a Sherriff, a legal agent of the Crown, obviously brought in to hear a trial about land tenancy involving a crofter, asks about the history and culture of the place he is visiting. To highlight the Sherriff's otherness, Dòmhnallach has him speaking in English to begin with and an interpreter helps to facilitate the conversation between the Sherriff and the Crofter as the Crofter maintains that he does not speak English. To begin with the interpreter carefully moves between the two languages:

> CROITEAR (CROFTER) *Thoir an talamh do na daoine: an talamh tha nise bàn!*
>
> EADAR-THEANGAIR *(TRANSLATOR)* Give the land to the people: the land that is now waste!
>
> CROITEAR *Is ann leinn fhèin a tha an talamh.*
>
> EADAR- THEANGAIR The land was ours by right.[36]

Shortly after this, we see the interpreter both editing and adding to the evidence the Crofter is giving; he even asks additional questions to those of the Sherriff.

> CROITEAR *Chuir an Seumarlan Màiri-Floraidh a-mach às an taigh nuair a chaidh an duine aice chun an iasgaich.*
>
> EADAR-THEANGAIR The Chamberlain put Mary Flora out of the house when her husband went to the fishing. *Carson a chuir e a-mach i?* (Why did he evict her?) [37]
>
> CROITEAR *Dhiùlt i na còig notaichean dha.* (She refused to give him the five pounds.)

---

[36] NicLeòid, *An Fhìrinn agus A' Bhreug*, 34.
[37] Unpublished translations in italics my own.

EADAR-THEANGAIR She refused to give the five pounds to the Chamberlain? *Na dh'iarr e càil tuilleadh oirre?* (Did he ask her for any more?)[38]

But when the Sherriff asks about Gaelic culture, the crofter begins to speak in English and the Sherriff in Gaelic.

SIORRAM *(SHERRIFF)* Any folk tales? History?

CROITEAR Plenty history here, Your Worship!

SIORRAM *Siuthad. Innis dhomh pìos eachdraidh. Thoir dhomh sgeul a bheir mi leam.* (Go on. Tell me a piece of history. Give me a story I can take away with me.)

EADAR-THEANGAIR *Sgeul fìor?* (A true story?)

SIORRAM *Cò dh'aithnicheas an fhìrinn bhon bhreug?* Who can tell the truth from fiction? *Chan eil e gu diofar leamsa.* (It doesn't matter to me.)

CROITEAR *Ta, tha e gu diofar leamsa! Chan fhiach càil ach an Fhìrinn!* (Well, it matters to me! Only the Truth matters!)

EADAR- THEANGAIR *Gabhaidh thusa rud a gheibh thu!* (You will take what you are given!)[39]

It is significant that it is the translator, who is supposed to offer an unbiased retelling of the story and who should be in a position to move comfortably between two languages and cultures, who tells the crofter that he has no control over how his story is told. According to translation theory, this is clearly linked to ideological devices around steering power and control over a subject or speech.[40] The translator becomes aware of his power in this conversation: it is he who shapes

---

[38] NicLeòid, *An Fhìrinn agus A' Bhreug*, 34-5.

[39] Ibid., 35-6.

[40] For discussions on power in translation theory see e.g., Theo Hermans, *The Manipulation of Literature: Studies in Literary Translation* (London: Croom Helm, 1985) or e.g, Mona Baker and Gabriela Saldhana, *Routledge Encyclopedia of Translation Studies* (London: Routledge, 2011).

the story, and it is he who has the power to provide an interpretation of Gaelic culture and the crofter remains powerless and dumb. The crofter can only accept the other's version in spite of his desire for truth.

Even in the modern era, Gaelic writers take episodes of over-looked historic events as the focus of their plays. Màiri Nic'IlleMhoire's (Mairi Morrison) play *Bana-Ghaisgich* (Heroines, 2018) deals with the topic of what history is kept hidden and what is revealed. *Bana-Ghaisgich* is very much a work of remembrance commemorating those who lost their lives in the sinking of HMY Iolaire on New Year's night just metres from the coast of Lewis with the devastating loss of 201 service men out of 283 who were returning after war; it is one of the worst maritime disasters in UK waters in the modern era and had a huge impact on the island.[41] The play is set in two eras and comfortably negotiates different timelines to explore women's experiences of love and loss.

In the modern era we meet two women (both played by the same actress in the staging of the play); the two women are former school classmates who catch up on events in their lives over the last twenty years or so; they reveal that however superficially their lives might appear ordered and full; they have suffered loss and are both seeking ways to heal themselves. As part of their interaction Maggie speaks about the preparations happening in Lewis to commemorate the loss of the Iolaire and reveals her intense anger that until 100 years later, the loss of the Iolaire had hardly appeared on the national conscience:

> *Bho chionn* twenty years[42]
> *chaidh mi a' choimhead air an leabhar-sa*
> *ann an* Waterstone's
> 'Historic Shipwrecks of Scotland'
> There was no mention of the Iolaire
> I was raging!
> *is gun fhiosda dhomh thuirt mi*
> 'Fuck you!'

---

[41] For an account of the loss of HMY Iolaire, see e.g., John MacLeod, *When I Heard the Bell* (Edinburgh: Birlinn, 2010).
[42] The text in Nic'IlleMhoire's play is set out in this format: short lines with no punctuation.

ann am meadhan a bhùth
Cha d' fhuair iad an urram[43] sin fhèin
Whatever a noble death is.[44]

Twenty years ago
I went to look at this book
in Waterstone's
'Historic Shipwrecks of Scotland'
and there was no mention of the Iolaire
I was raging!
and accidentally I said out loud
'Fuck you!'
in the middle of the shop.
They even didn't get that respect.
Whatever a noble death is.[45]

The action alternates between the experiences of Elaine and Maggie and particularly Coleen and Peigi, in war-time Lewis at various points before and after the sinking of the ship.

We first of all meet Peigi as she prepares her son for war in 1914; she is a proud mother sending her son to sea: pleased that he has escaped the attentions of Coleen. We also meet Coleen at this time as she says her farewell to Iain. When next the action in the play returns to this period we learn that Coleen has had a child out of wedlock and is shunned as a result with Peigi being adamant the child is nothing to do with her or Iain. She only relents on this hard-line position when Iain is lost in the disaster: only then is she desperate to acknowledge Coleen's child as her grandchild.

Coleen and Peigi are obviously distraught by their shared loss (Peigi's son Iain who is the father of Coleen's child). Coleen, however, is incandescent with rage at the public inquiry into the ship's sinking as she believed that no-one cared about the huge loss of life or impact to the island.

---

[43] Normally an t-urram, but this spelling reflects Lewis pronunciation.
[44] Màiri Nic'Ille Mhoire, "Bana-Ghaisgich" in Macleod, *Ceud Bliadhna air an Àrd-Ùrlar: A Century of Gaelic Drama*, 297.
[45] Ibid., 328.

It was an unfortunate situation, but I am glad that, for the sake of the officers' relatives, rumours of drunkenness have been dispelled.

Duhduh? Tha thu toilichte? Ach dè mu ar deidhinn-sa? Nam biodh seo air tachairt air ar stairsneach fhèin ann an Westminster bhiodh buaireadh is còmhstri ann an uair sin. Bhiodh ceistean le freagairtean ann. An robh càil as fhiach annainn idir ach airson Cannon Fodder dhuibhse? Tha mi 'n dòchas gun tig breitheanas oirbh![46]

What? You are glad? What about our sake? What if this had happened on your own doorstep in Westminster? There would be plenty grievance and strife then! Questions would be answered. Were we only cannon fodder to you? May judgement fall upon you![47]

Nic'IlleMhoire's play, which was previewed in London and performed in Stornoway, is a poignant act of remembrance. At the end, the names of the villages and the losses they suffered are fully recounted and the honour call is accompanied by the singing of psalm 46; this is used to very powerfully express the immense loss to the island.

Leòdhas. Còrr is ceud baile san eilean-sa, is cha mhòr gin nach do dh'fhulang an latha sin.
Taobh an Ear, Seisiadar. Tè an dùil ri a mac agus an duine. Deichnear marbh. Chaidh am baile a bhàthadh.
Air an tuath, Nis. 23 bàthte. Dà bhràthair, uile nàbaidhean.
An taobh siar, Bràdhagair, sia tiodhlacaidhean san aon latha. Gu deas, Na Hearadh, chaidh seachdnar a chal. . .[48]

---

[46] Ibid., 294.
[47] Ibid., 324.
[48] Ibid., 294.

Lewis. Over a hundred villages in this island and very
few left untouched by this day.
On the east, Sheshader, a woman was waiting for her
husband and son. 10 dead. A whole village drowned.
Ness in the north.   23 lost.   Two brothers, all
neighbours.
The west side, Bragar, six funerals in one day.
Isle of Harris, in the south, 7 dead. . . [49]

While the story of the play is common, love and loss, its setting
with the Iolaire disaster as the background heightens the emotions. For
a long time, the loss of this ship was little known outside of the Isle of
Lewis. Nic'IlleMhoire's play was her contribution to raising
awareness and ensuring the events lived on in people's memories.

One final example of a historical play to be discussed here is
Muireann Kelly's and Francis Poet's *Scotties* (2018). This play, like
Bana-Ghaisgich, has a character who becomes deeply affected by his
study of local history. Though not strictly about the history of Scottish
Gaels, the play is included here as it addresses issues of Gaelic identity
and its relationship with language and how this can be strengthened in
the present through a deeper understanding of the past.

The history this play shares is about an incident in Kirkintilloch
in Central Scotland in 1934 with Irish Gaels as the protagonists. The
action in the play moves between the interactions of a modern-day
family in Glasgow to a dream-like experience in early twentieth
century Scotland with a group of Irish farm laborers. The Glasgow
family consist of a Gaelic-speaking mother, Morag; her husband
Aonghas, who is learning Gaelic; Morag's mother Grace, whose
carefully guarded Irish identity is not revealed until the end of the play;
and Gaelic-speaking teenager Michael, who is the link between the
two eras of the play. Michael's local history school project leads him
to find out about a fire which happened on a farm in which ten Irish
migrant workers from Achill Island, Co. Mayo lose their lives.
Michael finds himself at various points in the play transported back to
witness the lives of the Irish workers: he interacts with Molly, a farm
girl who only speaks Irish. Through Molly he learns of the hard lives
of the itinerant workers: their long working days and how they were

<hr>

[49] Ibid., 324.

segregated from locals, and he eventually learns through her of the terrible loss of the ten young men. *Scotties* is a wonderful mix of Gaelic, Irish, English and Scots with most, but not all, characters competent in at least two of the languages.

The 'Scotties' of the title are the migrant workers from Achill Island. In the scenes which focus on their lives we sense their anxiety as traveling Irish (Catholic) labourers. The Gaffer cautions his squad: "Kirkintilloch looks a pretty green place but it's Orange to the core and don't you forget it."[50] Molly and her "tribe", as she calls them, were right to be frightened as she implies the men were trapped deliberately in the barn they used for sleeping and left to burn when a fire started. While the loss clearly relates to a specific incident, the question of how immigrant workers are treated is equally topical today, as noted by Michael and his father:

> MICHAEL Why are people like that? Even the bit I read for my project I could see that nobody cared enough about them, nobody asked the right questions.

> AONGHAS nods. Why? Feagal 's gràin. [Fear and hate.] Fear and hate. People on boats, coming over the sea, speaking a different tongue from our own, outsiders, wanting to work, it scares the life out of us. Always has, always will. Gran knows that better than any of us.[51]

Aonghas refers to language as one means of expressing both belonging and difference and the theme of language loyalty and language shift is present across this multilingual play. In Michael's family alone, we see how efforts have been made to learn and to forget languages to perform identity. Michael's mother Morag learned Gaelic from her father and as a person who identifies as an island Gael living in Glasgow, she has gone to great lengths to try and ensure that Michael becomes a Gaelic speaker; she is supported in this by her husband who is seen to be learning the language. In conversation about language use and identity with Molly, the Irish itinerant worker, he

---

[50] Muireann Kelly with Frances Poet, "Scotties," in Macleod, *Ceud Bliadhna air an Àrd-Ùrlar: A Century of Gaelic Drama*, 231.
[51] Ibid., 261.

says: "You sound like my Mum. Got to know who my people are, got to speak Gaelic like my people. Seems to think the world will end if I don't speak it."[52] We see later how Molly as a mature woman tells her daughter Grace, Michael's grandmother, that they should abandon Irish when they leave Achill for Scotland permanently in order to fit in: "We'll not speak Irish anymore, Gracie. We'll use their words for it is their world."[53] But Morag, Michael's mother, tells him that is never possible to abandon one's language: that it is an inherent part of a person's identity:

> MORAG *'Fhios agad? Tha Gàidhlig àlainn agad.*
> [You know you have beautiful Gaelic.] Gaelic is in
> you, Michael. You can't give it back. You can try to
> forget it, but it'll be just like that song stuck in your
> head, *bidh e fhathast ann.* [It'll still be there.] Look at
> your Gran, all this never left her, the language, the
> people, the Island, even when she buried it deep
> inside her, *bha iad fhathast ann.* [They were still
> there.][54]

Scotties, like the other plays discussed here, contains a reimagination of a little-known historic event; at the end of the play the modern-day characters demonstrate how understanding the past can help them interpret the present. Moe et al. notes that making this realisation happen should not just be a secondary consideration of a historical drama, it is an obligation for it to do so:

> Historical drama can often remind communities and
> their audiences of what is often forgotten or
> unrealized: the injustices, intolerances, and atrocities
> of history, the mistreatment and disenfranchisement
> of people, the failure of the law ... The historical

---

[52] Ibid., 228.
[53] Ibid., 263.
[54] Ibid., 266.

dramatist has the obligation of reminding people what
should be not forgotten or, in many cases, repeated.[55]

Through portraying parts of the accumulated memories, history
and traditions of Gaelic people on stage, these examples of Gaelic
theatre emphasise a shared identity which can be understood as
manifestations of an effort at reclaiming power and ownership of how
history is retold. The playwrights were clearly aware that their
representations of Gaelic history and culture presented an alternative
position to that which was given by outsiders. Drama offers a unique
way to interpret and tell complex stories through spoken word and
physically staged metaphors. Stern claims that drama can make
history the focus of a play whereas, for example, "the historical novel
uses historical events, or simply a certain historical context, as the
backdrop to the story it wants to tell".[56] Highland historian James
Hunter has acknowledged the contribution of Gaelic poetry in terms
of recounting social history in the nineteenth century.[57] Gaelic theatre,
perhaps, speaks to a community in the same way that oral literature
and the performance and proliferation of verse, so firmly embedded in
Gaelic society, traditionally has and in a way that written literature
does not, necessarily. When we watch a play, we are active
participants; we are asked to share in the experiences on stage and we
often pause at the end to talk to the people around us about what we
have just witnessed. Since its inception to the modern-day, Gaelic
drama has always been very well received with large audiences at both
local and national levels. Gaelic drama allows its audiences to
experience an impactful Gaelic interpretation of the Gael's world
which seeks to be challenging and authentic and succeeds in this in no
small measure.

---

[55] Christian H. Moe, Scott J. Parker, George McCalmon & Romulus Linney. *Creating Historical Drama: A Guide for Communities, Theatre Groups, and Playwrights* (Southern Illinois University Press 2005), 8.
[56] Stern, "History Plays as History", 290.
[57] James Hunter, *The Making of the Crofting Community*, 4.

"Tréig do ghruaim an uair-se, a Shára": A seventeenth-century poem for Sara Nig Uidhir

Ciara Ní Mhurchú

Toireamh Shara Nig Uidhir ("Sara Maguire's Lament"), beginning *Tréig do ghruaim an uair-se, a Shára* (Abandon your gloom this time, Sara) is a seventeenth century Irish language poem in stress-timed (i.e. accentual) metre. This poem is credited to an Andrias Guidhir (presumably Mág Uidhir) in one of the six surviving manuscript copies, and it is addressed to a Sara Nig Uidhir (Maguire), the daughter of Brian Ruadh (†1633) and Róise Ní Néill. Many of Sara's relations were central figures in the Irish Confederate Wars of 1641–1653. The poem was composed after the execution of her brother Lord Conor Maguire, a conspirator of the 1641 rebellion, in 1645. It is rich in references to contemporary Irish placenames and other illustrious families, and places emphasis on interfamily alliances. The poet also addresses the hardship inflicted by oppression and the loss of Gaelic land and of Gaelic leaders through forced migration. Sara is depicted as a Gaelic queen who will relieve the men of Ireland of this hardship. The poem is not only invaluable as an example of a stress-timed poem, it also offers insight into the political and cultural identity of Gaelic noble women and the poet of mid-seventeenth century Ireland. This paper will discuss the surviving manuscripts first, then examine the historical and political context of the poem and highlight some of the imagery and poetic language of consolation. Extracts from the poem will be presented and analysed here for the first time, based on the oldest surviving manuscript, British Library manuscript Egerton 128. I have normalised orthography and provided punctuation in these extracts, and translations given are my own.[1] I aim to publish a complete critical edition of the poem in the future.

Manuscripts

This poem survives in the following six manuscripts:

---

[1] I am responsible for any errors.

POEM FOR SARA NIG UIDHIR

E: British Library, Egerton 128, f. 147v–149r: This manuscript was written by Muiris Ó Gormáin from 1748 to 1749. Ó Gormáin was one of the most prolific scribes of the eighteenth century.[2] The manuscript contains some romantic tales, moral precepts, and religious poems, along with a Finn Cycle tale, and a variety of poems towards the end, some of which are composed in *amhrán* metre, and which also appear in TCD manuscript 1291 (see below). Our poem is the last piece in this manuscript and the poet is not named. The extracts from the poem given in this paper are based on this manuscript as it is the oldest surviving copy.[3]

T: TCD H.1.17, (1291), f. 163b–f. 165: This manuscript is the only surviving copy which names a poet, "Andrias Guidhir". It was written in the years 1755–1757 by Aodh Ó Dálaigh, who states at the end of the manuscript that the work was done for a "Dr. O' Sullivan", presumably Francis Stoughton Sullivan, a Fellow of Trinity College Dublin who employed Aodh from 1742 to 1758.[4] Aodh was one of the twenty six scribes of the Ó Neachtain circle, mentioned in Tadhg Ó Neachtain's poem *Sloinfead scothadh na Gaoidhilge grinn*, a poem on scribes and scholars active in Dublin in the early eighteenth century.[5] According to Abbott and Gwynn, much of this manuscript is copied from TCD manuscripts 1378 and 1381, but the poems towards the back,

---

[2] For further reading on Ó Gormáin's life, work, and collections, see Lesa Ní Mhunghaile, "An eighteenth-century Gaelic scribe's private library: Muiris Ó Gormáin's books," *Proceedings of the Royal Irish Academy: Archaeology, Culture, History, Literature* 110C (2010): 239-276.

[3] It appears that the text was originally presented in **E** as a continuous text, and someone later added horizontal lines throughout the passage to divide the poem into quatrains. The extracts I present in this paper are presented as continuous passages.

[4] See Nessa Ní Shéaghdha, "Irish Scholars and Scribes in Eighteenth-Century Dublin," *Eighteenth-Century Ireland / Iris an dá chultúr* 4 (1989): 41-54, at 45.

[5] See T. F. O'Rahilly, "Irish Scholars in Dublin in the Early Eighteenth Century," *Gadelica: A Journal of Modern Irish Studies* 1, no. 3 (1913): 156-162, at 160.

many of which are also in E, do not appear in either of these TCD manuscripts and seem to have come from another manuscript which does not survive.[6]

G: National Library of Ireland G 482, 19–25: This is another manuscript in the hand of Muiris Ó Gormáin. The only date referred to in the manuscript is on page 81, Ó Gormáin gives songs in English which he states were popular in Dublin in the year 1788.

M: Maynooth C 87a (2 G 13), 22–23: The section of the manuscript containing our poem was written by Peadar Dubh Ó Dálaigh, who added "air na sgriobha re Peadar A Dalaidh" and the date the 3rd of February 1806, on page 23, following our poem. Ó Dálaigh was a schoolmaster and poet of County Meath.[7]

R: RIA 165 (23 O 18), 86–98: The scribe of this manuscript is not named. The paper bears the watermarks 'Kent' and '1821'. It was in the collection of James Hardiman. The

---

[6] T. K. Abbott and E. J. Gwynn, *Catalogue of the Irish manuscripts in the Library of Trinity College, Dublin* (Dublin: Hodges, Figgis & Co, 1921), 233. This manuscript also contains two poems by Toirdhealbhach Ó Conchobhair who composed a *crosántacht* regarding Sara Nig Uidhir's wedding. It does not, however, contain the wedding poem itself. On the wedding crosántacht, see Margo Griffin–Wilson, *The Wedding Poems of Dáibhí Ó Bruadair* (Dublin: Dublin Institute for Advanced Studies, 2010), 412-56.

[7] For further reading on Ó Dálaigh's life, see Lesa Ní Mhunghaile, "The Irish language in County Meath, 1700-1900," in *Meath. History and Society. Interdisciplinary essays on the History of an Irish County*, eds. Francis Ludlow and Arlene Crampsie (Dublin: Geography Publications, 2015), 547-572, at 562-4. See also Máire Ní Mhurchú and Diarmuid Breathnach "Ó Dálaigh, Peadar Dubh (c.1800–1861)," *ainm.ie An Bunachar Náisiúnta Beathaisnéisí Gaeilge*, accessed December 6, 2022, https://www.ainm.ie/Bio.aspx?ID=1192, and Tomás Ua Brádaigh "Peadar Dubh Ó Dálaigh, fear léinn agus scríobhaí," *Ríocht na Midhe: records of Meath Archaeological and Historical Society* II, no. 2 (1960): 47-53.

contents page at the beginning of the manuscript is signed by him.[8]

R1: RIA 1202 (24 E 26), 79–83: There is an existing English translation of the poem in this nineteenth century manuscript. It contains a selection of translations of Irish language poems. The scribe is not named but the initials J.S. appear. The manuscript was in James Hardiman's collection also and on the contents page the translation of our poem "Elegy of Sarah ny Gwyer" is provided with reference to our other RIA manuscript, RIA 23 O 18, as the original.[9]

Poet

The poem is ascribed to an A[i]ndrias [Má]g Uidhir in **T**. We do not know much about this poet. I am aware of one other poem which is ascribed to an Aindrias Mág Uidhir, *Gabh mo chomhairle a chara*, or *Gabh mo theagosg a chara* as it appears in one manuscript. It was composed in *rannaíocht bheag* (*ógláchas*), a loose syllabic metre. This poem was first edited by Tomás Ó Rathile in his *Measgra Dánta* from RIA MS 571 (23 Q 2).[10] He gives nine verses in rannaíocht bheag with two more in his notes. A second edition was published by Joseph Vendryès in *Irish Texts*, edited from the British Museum manuscript Egerton 192 and Rouen manuscript 1678.[11] Vendryès provides twenty-three verses in rannaíocht bheag followed by one quatrain in the stress-timed amhrán metre.[12]

---

[8] See T.F. O'Rahilly *et al.*, *Catalogue of Irish manuscripts in the Royal Irish Academy*, fasc. IV (Dublin and London, 1926–70), 476-77.

[9] See T.F. O'Rahilly *et al.*, *Catalogue of Irish manuscripts in the Royal Irish Academy*, fasc. XXVI (Dublin and London, 1926–70), 3249-54.

[10] Tomás Ó Rathile, *Measgra Dánta I* (Cork: Cork University Press, 1927; reprint 1970), 47-8.

[11] Joseph Vendryès, "Deux Poèmes moraux du XVIIᵉ siècle," in *Irish Texts Fasc IV*, eds. J. Fraser, P. Grosjean, S. J. and J.G. O'Keeffe (London: Sheed and Ward, 1934), 100-6.

[12] The poem appears to be a response to the poem which precedes it in the British Museum manuscript, and follows it in the Rouen manuscript, *A dhrong ga bhfuil an saidhbhrios,* by Diarmuid Mac Muireadhaigh. See Robin Flower (ed), *Catalogue of Irish manuscripts in the [British Library, formerly the] British Museum*, vol. 2 (London: British Museum, 1926), 165.

CIARA NÍ MHURCHÚ

Sara Nig Uidhir

Sara was the daughter of Brian Ruadh Mág Uidhir (†1633), son of Conchubhar Ruadh Mág Uidhir (†1625).[13] This Conchubhar of Magherstephane, nicknamed 'the Queen's Maguire' was knighted in 1585 and received a pardon from the king in 1608.[14] After the plantation of Ulster, he received a land re-grant from James I of 6,500 acres in Fermanagh, with a yearly rent of 20 pounds sterling. His son Brian was also knighted and created Lord Maguire, first baron of Enniskillen by King Charles I on the 21st of January 1627.[15] Brian Ruadh financially supported the four masters in their production of a new edition of *Leabhar Gabhála* (Book of Invasions) in 1631.[16]

Sara's mother was Róise Ní Néill, the daughter of Art Ó Néill, son of the first baron of Dungannon. Róise was the sister of Eoghan Ruadh Ó Néill, a prominent figure of the early seventeenth century who served in the Spanish army during the Eight Years' War and then led the Ulster Army on returning to Ireland during the Confederate wars of the 1640s. The identity of Róise and Eoghan Ruadh's mother is uncertain, but it has been suggested that Eoghan Ruadh's mother was Art Ó Néill's third wife, a daughter of Aodh Conallach Ó Raghallaigh of Bréifne.[17]

---

[13] See pedigree in the National Library of Ireland's Genealogical Office Manuscript Collection *Registered Pedigrees* Vol. 17 at https://catalogue.nli.ie/Record/vtls000530453, 59-60.

[14] His great great grandfather was Tomás Óg Mág Uidhir, brother of Philip Mág Uidhir, from whom the Maguires of Tempo descend. See reference above.

[15] John Thomas Gilbert (ed), *A Contemporary History of Affairs in Ireland from 1641 to 1652* I, (Dublin: For the Irish archaeological and Celtic Society, 1879) 342-3.

[16] P. Ó Gallachair, "The First Maguire of Tempo," *Clogher Record* 2, No. 3 (1959): 469-489, at 475.

[17] Mícheál Ó Siochrú, "O'Neill, Owen Roe (Ó Néill, Eoghan Rua)," *Dictionary of Irish Biography*, Royal Irish Academy, last revised October 2009, accessed December 6, 2022, https://www.dib.ie/biography/oneill-owen-roe-o-neill-eoghan-rua-a6936.

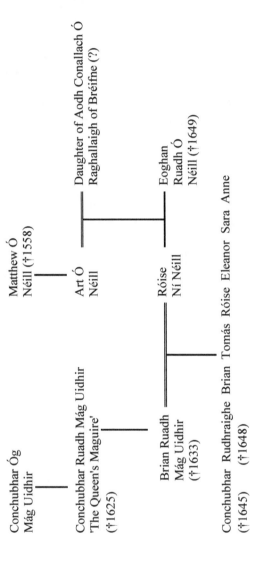

This poem supports this suggestion as the poet states in line 36 that Sara is a Bréifne O'Reilly on her mother's side: *Raegh'llaigh Bréifne thaobh do mháthar*. Róise was also active in the rebellion of 1641, as "Rose ny Neale mother to the lord Magwire" (Sara's brother) is listed as one of the rebells accused of robbing the property of a settler in county Armagh in 1642.[18] Róise and Brian had eight children. Brian died on the 15th of December 1633 and his funeral entry states:

> Sr Bryan McGwyer, Knight, baron of Enniskillyn, he deceased the xv[th] of December 1633. He had to wife Rose, daughter of Arte Mac Avernan O'Neile, of Carickestikin, in the County of Armagh, Esqre, by whom he had issue Connor, now Lord mcGwyer, Baron of Inniskillyn, married Mary, daughter of Thomas Fleming of Castle Fleming, in the County of Cavan; Rory, Bryan, Thomas, Rose, Elanor, Sarah, and Anne. His Lo[p] is buried in Aughive, in the County of Fermanagh, the xxii[th] of December.[19]

Ó Cadhla's *Geinealaighe Fearmanach* names only three sons: "Clann Bhriain .i. Tighearna Inisceillionn .i. Conchubhar, Rughraighe agus Tomás óg'."[20] This Conchubhar, Lord Conor Maguire, was the well-known figure of the Confederate wars. He was born in 1616 and assumed the title of second baron of Enniskillen on his father's death in 1633. He had spent time in Magdalen College, Oxford, and entered the Irish House of Lords in 1634.[21] He played a central role in the beginning of the 1641 rebellion. That year, Ruairí Ó Mórdha came to Mág Uidhir about starting a Catholic rebellion and in August they started to make plans to seize Dublin Castle that October. However,

---

[18] Aidan Clarke *et al.* (eds), *1641 Depositions, Volume I: Armagh, Louth & Monaghan* (Dublin: Irish Manuscripts Commission, 2014), 53.

[19] W. Copeland Trimble, *The History of Enniskillen* I (Enniskillen: William Trimble, 1919), 91-2. See the National Library of Ireland's Genealogical Office Manuscript Collection *Funeral Entries* Vol. 6 (1633), 16.

[20] This is a collection of pedigrees of Fermanagh families from manuscript CF 6, Maynooth. See Ó Cadhla, "Geinealaighe Fearmanach," *Analecta Hibernica* 3 (1931), 100 §517.

[21] Gilbert, *A Contemporary History* I, xxi.

their plans were betrayed and Mág Uidhir was captured and sent to the Tower of London. His trial was an important show trial, during which it was declared that many men, women, and children had lost their lives as a result of this bloody war "plotted and begun in Ireland by this Lord Maguire".[22] He was hanged, drawn and quartered at Tyburn in February 1645. The beginning of this poem confirms that he has died and so allows us to date it after this time.

The second eldest of the family, Rudhraighe, also played a role in the 1641 rebellion and is mentioned in the 1641 depositions.[23] He was a colonel in his uncle Eoghan Ruadh Ó Néill's Ulster army and was killed at Cora Droma Rúisc (Carrick-on-Shannon) in 1648. Line 18 of our poem, *Rudhraighe Ruadh [rug] bua gach báire* (Rudhraighe Ruadh who won every battle) presumably refers to this brother. Brian's fourth and youngest son Thomas is probably the Tomás Óg referred to in line 19, suggesting that he went to Spain: *is Tomás Óg do chóidh chum Spáinne.*

Sara married Domhnall Óg Mág Aonghusa (Magennis) of County Down. A wedding crosántacht regarding their marriage survives: *Slán ma do phósadh a Dhomhnuill Mhég Nósa*, in which the poet, Toirdhealbhach Ó Conchobhair, urges Domhnall to consummate the marriage, in celebration of the union of the two distinguished families, and in anticipation of the reputable couple producing offspring. The poet also includes other members of Sara's family in the celebration, mentioning Sara's brother, "Coronéal Rughruighe ruadh", and her mother, "Róisi Ní Néill", in the poem. An edition of this poem has been published by Margo Griffin-Wilson.[24]

---

[22] See *The Whole Triall of Connor Lord Macguire with the Perfect Copies of the Indictment, and all the Evidences Against Him* (London 1645), accessed December 6, 2022, https://elib.tcd.ie/login?url=https://www.proquest.com/books/vvhole-triall-connor-lord-macguire-with-perfect/docview/2240952175/se-2, 4.

[23] See for example Aidan Clarke *et al.* (eds), *1641 Depositions, Volume II: Cavan & Fermanagh* (Dublin: Irish Manuscripts Commission, 2014), 64, 479, and 370.

[24] Margo Griffin-Wilson, *The Wedding Poems of Dáibhí Ó Bruadair* (Dublin: School of Celtic Studies, Dublin Institute for Advanced Studies, 2010), 412-457. In this poem, the poet calls our patroness Sorcha.

Domhnall was the son of Art Mág Aonghusa (†1629) who received a grant of lands in Upper Iveagh in County Down in 1611 and was given the title of viscount Magennis of Iveagh by James I. Domhnall's mother was Sarah Ní Néill, a daughter of Aodh Ó Néill, Earl of Tyrone.[25] Domhnall's eldest brother Aodh (†1639) was second viscount of Iveagh and his son Art Mág Aonghusa (c. 1623–84), whose regiment defended Wexford against Cromwell in October 1649, was third viscount Magennis of Iveagh. Domhnall was also involved with the 1641 insurgents. "Donald oge Magennuis of Glasscorr Esquire" is mentioned frequently in the 1641 depositions as a rebel. A "Colonell Daniell oge Magenis Esquire of Glascoe" is accused of having "expelled robbd and dispoyled" a Thomas Richardson of Newry in the "Countie of Downe" along with his brother Conn Magennis in 1641.[26] He is mentioned in *Cin Lae Ó Mealláin* along with his brother in law "Ruraidhe MáGuidhir" as a participant in the burning of Downpatrick, Saul, Bishops Court, and other areas in June 1646.[27] Domhnall is stated to be in prison in Carrickfergus in June 1653 and died in 1658.[28]

Metre

Tréig do ghruaim an uair-se, a Shára is composed in the stress-timed (i.e. accentual) *amhrán* metre. Unlike the classical syllable-timed (i.e. syllabic) poetry (*dán díreach*) of the school-trained

---

[25] Henry S. Guinness, "Magennis of Iveagh," *The Journal of the Royal Society of Antiquaries of Ireland* seventh series, 2, no. 1 (June 1932): 96-102 at 97.

[26] Aidan Clarke et al. (eds), *1641 Depositions, Volume III: Antrim, Derry, Donegal, Down & Tyrone* (Dublin: Irish Manuscripts Commission, 2014), 271.

[27] Tadhg Ó Donnchadha, "Cín Lae Ó Mealláin," *Analecta Hibernica*, no. 3 (1931): 1-61 at 43.

[28] See Aidan Clarke *et al.* (eds), *1641 Depositions, Volume III: Antrim, Derry, Donegal, Down & Tyrone* (Dublin: Irish Manuscripts Commission, 2014), 358-359. This deposition is not dated but was likely made in 1653. See also Thomas Fitzpatrick, "The Fall of Down, 1642," *Ulster Journal of Archaeology* second series, 12, no. 1 (January 1906): 1-10 at 3. The date of his death, along with a wife, "Eliza Magennis", possibly a second wife after Sara Nig Uidhir, is given in John O' Hart, *Irish Pedigrees, or, the Origin and Stem of the Irish Nation* (Dublin: M. H. Gill & Son, 1881), 157.

poets, the rhythm of this poem is based on the stress of the vowels in each line.[29] We know that stress-timed metres existed for centuries before the composition of this poem, as stress-timed metres were a feature of some early Irish poetry.[30] Later, we have references specifically to an amhrán in the fourteenth century Book of Magauran: one of the earliest surviving family poem books. The poet Giolla na Naomh Ó hUiginn references an amhrán as an inferior metre with which the trained poets of the classical and intricate dán díreach metre competed.[31] We cannot know exactly what is meant by the amhrán in this case as we have no written example of an amhrán from before the late sixteenth century, but it seems to have existed alongside the syllable-timed poetry for centuries. Tadhg Dall Ó hUiginn, who died in 1591, composed a poem in amhrán metre for a patron who died in 1579, which is noteworthy as Tadhg Dall was a distinguished classically trained poet.[32] It is in the seventeenth century then, and pre-eminently in the eighteenth century, that stress-timed metres come to light and gain traction, eventually out-competing the classical syllabic verse altogether. This poem is valuable, therefore, as an example of a stress-timed poem from this period of what seems to be a change in

---

[29] For further discussion on 'stress-timed' and 'syllable-timed' languages and verse, see V. S. Blankenhorn *Irish Song-Craft and Metrical Practice since 1600* (Lampeter: Edwin Mellen Press, 2003), 56-60.

[30] See for example James Carney, "Three Old Irish Accentual Poems," *Ériu* 22 (1971): 23-80.

[31] See Lambert McKenna, *The Book of Magauran: Leabhar Méig Shamhradháin* (Dublin: Dublin Institute for Advanced Studies, 1947), poem 27: *Tánag d'Fhánaid an einigh*, quatrain 3:
Is é an t-abhrán ro fhalaigh
a n-éadáil a n-ealadhain;
do sgar an daghdhán re a dhath
abhrán ban agus bhachlach.
'Tis abhrán which has made to disappear their (i.e. the poets') profit and science; the abhrán of women and churls has robbed genuine poetry of its colour (McKenna's translation).

[32] *Searc mná Ír dhuit, Aoidh, ná léig a bhfaill*, see Seán Mac Airt, *Leabhar Branach: The Book of the O'Byrnes* (Dublin: Dublin Institute for Advanced Studies, 1944), poem 16, and Eleanor Knott, *The bardic poems of Tadhg Dall Ó hUiginn* (London: Irish Texts Society, 1922 and 1926), poem 35.

attitude towards the stressed metre and a movement away from syllabic verse. The fact that it was recorded in a manuscript indicates that it was perceived as a composition of value.

The form of this poem is quite loose; most lines have four stresses, some have three, with an irregular syllable count between each stress. The pattern is as follows:

$$(-)\,(-)\,y\,(-)\,|\,(-)\,z\,(-)\,|\,(-)\,z\,(-)\,|\,(-)\,á\,-$$

The y and z stressed vowels vary throughout the poem but the $á$ stress followed by a monosyllable at the end of each line is consistent throughout.[33] Some lines contain only three stresses, however, in which case the y stress at the beginning of the line is omitted. For example, in the first three lines of the poem, there are four stresses:

> *Tréig do ghruaim an **uair**-se, a Shára,* [34]
> *is cuir dhíot do bhrón is tóig an smál-sa,*
> *'s an brat ciaich 'tá ndiaigh ar mbáthadh ...*

Abandon your gloom this time, Sara, and give over your sorrow, and lift this cloud, and the wave of grief that is after drowning us.

However, lines 7 and 8, for example, contain only three stresses. Speaking about Conchubhar Mág Uidhir, the poet says he was:

---

[33] See also another mid-seventeenth century Ulster stress-timed poem *Tuireamh Philip meic Aodha Uí Raghallaigh*, which is in a very similar metre, with lines of three or four stresses, mostly finishing with *á* followed by a monosyllable, in James Carney *Poems on the O'Reilly's* (Dublin: Dublin Institute for Advanced Studies, 1950), poem XXVII. In *Prosóid Gaedhilge*, Tadhg Ó Donnchadha calls this style of stress-timed metre "caoineadh", see Tadhg Ó Donnchadha *Prosóid Gaedhilge* (Dublin: Brún agus Ó Nualláin, 1937), 48-51.

[34] It is clear from the metre that the poet intended Sara's name to be pronounced as *Sára* with a long *a* vowel here, as in the manuscript.

(. . .)
*a Lonndoinn gan **O**lltaibh 'na ghárda,*
dá chosnamh ar dhochar a námhad
(. . .)

(. . .)
in London without Ulster men as his guard, defending
him against the harm of his enemies
(. . .)

This pattern continues for 105 lines of the poem, a new pattern is introduced in the concluding quatrain, called the *ceangal* (conclusion). Generally, the ceangal presents a summary of the thoughts put forward in the main body of the poem, and the poet may offer advice to the patron in conclusion.[35] This quatrain is also in stress-timed amhrán metre but follows a stricter pattern of stresses than the rest of the poem. Each of the four lines conform to this pattern:

(–) (–) é (–) | í – (–) | í – (–) | o – | ua (–) | ó

Tréig do mhaoithe, a naoi na gcorcair gcuach
    n-óir,
cé gur cloíte saoithe is socharshluagh an fhóid
beid choíche fá dhaoirse san dochar buan ód
nó go n-éirghidh dhíbh-se faoidh do thocht
    a-nuas dóibh.

Abandon your grief, o young woman of the golden red curls, although the wise men (i.e. the leaders) of the country and the host who do it good are defeated, they will be oppressed forever in that everlasting hardship, until a cry (?)[36] comes from you down to them.

The language of the poems in stress-timed metre generally represents the vernacular as opposed to the formal and intricate

---

[35] On ceangal, see V. S. Blankenhorn *Irish Song-Craft and Metrical Practice since 1600* (Lampeter: Edwin Mellen Press, 2003), 295-301.
[36] The final line in **T** has *faoisedh* in place of *faoidh*, in which case the line may be translated: until relief comes from you down to them.

language of classical verse. Some words, for example, have a more modern pronunciation which departs from the classical standard. For example, the classical disyllabic verbal noun ending *-ughadh* in *sárughadh* appears in our poem as a monosyllabic ending *-adh*. The metre confirms this monosyllabic termination as short, as it is at the end of the line and, as we have seen, the poet follows the end rhyme pattern of the *á* stress followed by an unstressed short syllable, as can be seen in the final words of the lines preceding and following *sáradh*: *bhádar, táinte, rá-sin*:

> (. . .)
> *gach glanord anallód mar a **bhádar**,*
> *an fhréimh is aithre i n-aice a **dtáinte**,*
> *gan neart Gall san rann dár **sáradh**;*
> *och, a Rí, go mba fíor an **rá-sin**.*

> Every pure [religious] order as it was before, the [ancestral] stock and fathers beside their cattle, without the power of foreigners in the district thwarting us, o God, if that were true.

O'Rahilly notes in *Irish Dialects Past and Present* that the verbal noun endings *-adh* and *-aghadh* fell together in northern Irish, and he notes that *-aghadh, -eaghadh* or *(i)ughadh* and *-adh* give both the long *-ú* and short *-u* in Ulster.[37] These modifications are valuable in showing that the likes of *sáradh* with a short monosyllabic verbal noun ending were heard by and available to the poet at the time in his own or in other dialects.[38]

Text

The poem, including the ceangal, is 109 lines long. It begins as a lament for Sara's brother Conchubhar, who we are told was sent to

---

[37] T.F. O'Rahilly *Irish Dialects Past and Present* (Dublin: Browne and Nolan, 1932) 678, and 223.
[38] Another example of this shortened verbal noun ending is fásughadh which must be pronounced as though written 'fásadh' in conformity with the metre in *Tuireamh Philip meic Aodha*. See James Carney *Poems on the O'Reilly's* (Dublin: Dublin Institute for Advanced Studies, line 3242). The discussion of the language of the poem will be extended in the future along with the full edition of the poem.

London. The poet describes him as a strong lion, Noah of the Ark, and a warrior, and states that this loss is a great cause for grief.[39] As noted above, by confirming that Conchubhar has died, the beginning of the poem allows us to date it after his death in February 1645.

(...)
Conchubhar Óg budh chródha i ngábha,
ar bhfachain bróin 's ar mór-ábhar,
ar réalt eólais beó nach dtárlaigh
(...)

(...)
Young Conor who was most brave in times of danger,
our cause for sorrow, indeed our great cause; our
guiding star who is no longer alive.
(...)

The poet states that Sara must now be protected by others. She is presented as a person of significance in society as she is of the renowned Mág Uidhir family, a powerful family with many important familial connections which the poet highlights. Of the other members of her family, the poet says that the King of the elements must keep them safe, and protect Sara:

Rí na ndúl dá gcumhdach slán dúinn,
is dod chumhdach-sa . . .

May the King of the elements keep them safe for us,
and protect you . . .

Addressing Sara, he pleads that she abandon her grief after the death of Conchubhar and think of the roots of her family and the number of warriors around Ireland to whom she is related. He lists

---

[39] Katherine Simms has discussed some examples of poems of lamentation in the classical syllabic metre addressed to women, some of which are addressed to sisters of the deceased. She has noted that most of such examples from the surviving corpus of bardic poetry were composed in the first half of the seventeenth century. See "Bardic poems of consolation to bereaved Irish ladies" in Conor Kostick (ed) *Medieval Italy, Medieval and Early Modern Women* (Dublin: Four Courts Press, 2010), 220-30.

several placenames where these warriors can be found, which offers
us an insight into contemporary geographical points of significance
and indicates that this poet was learned and well-versed in Irish
topography. He goes first from South to North, from the Beara
peninsula to Fanad in Co. Donegal; he then names a place in each
province, beginning in Dublin, and then proceeding to the Assaroe
falls in Donegal, to Croagh Patrick in the West, to Doonainy in Co.
Limerick. Finally, he goes in a near perfect straight line eastward from
Erris to Newry:

> (. . .)
> *dearc ar mhéid do ghaoil 's do pháirte,*
> *ar a liacht tréanfhlaith ó Bhéarra go Fánaid,*
> *ó Dhuibhlinn na dtreas go hEas Rámha,*
> *thart máguairt go Cruaich Phádraig,*
> *as sin a rún go Dún Áine,*
> *ó chuan Iorrais go hIobhar Chionn Trágha,*
> *re bhfuil do ghaol, a chraobh an ágha* (. . .)[40]

> . . . look at the extent of your family and your
> supporters, how many strong lords you are related to,
> from Beara to Fanad, from Dublin of the battles to
> Assaroe, around to Croagh Patrick, from there, my
> darling, to Doonainy, from Erris harbour to Newry, o
> branch of good fortune– . . .[41]

He lists several illustrious Gaelic families of the period as her
relations, beginning with the family with the highest status
traditionally, the Ó Néills, to whom she is directly related on her
mother's paternal side, and he then lists the Ó Briain, Mág

---

[40] Note the similarity between these lines and lines in a poem which appears
before this poem in E, "Tuireadh Phegidh Déin" beginning "Lá dá rabhas a
gcath*air* na Gailbhe': 'air a liacht flaith ó Bhanna go Bean*n*chuir,/ o Dhoire
na long go Gonn na Teamhrach,/ gcrích fódhla is fós a nAlbain,/ a
sacsanaigh mbreatain*n* 's a bhFrancaibh,/ re bhfuil do pháirt a bhlathnaid
sheanghlan . . ." I will discuss this further in my future edition.
[41] I have taken *Eas Rámha* as a reference to *Eas Ruadh,* the Assaroe Falls of
the River Erne. I have not seen them referred to as Eas Rámha in any other
poem, but I am not aware of any other placename to which it could be
referring.

Mathghamhna, Ó Domhnaill and many other families of the north-west and west of Ireland. He names other nobles who also played important roles in the 1641 rebellion, such as "Tighearna Mhúsgraidhe", presumably Donnchadh Mac Cárthaigh, a prominent Gaelic leader in the Confederate Wars. This extensive listing of Gaelic nobles in the poem is significant as it suggests an attempt to demonstrate that such interfamily alliances should still be perceived as important and powerful in society, despite the decline of the Gaelic tradition. The poet is re-asserting the importance of these families at a time of resurgence. He emphasises the fact that Sara will still be protected, despite the loss of her brother, as there are so many powerful warriors who will rise in her defence.

> *Do ghaol, ní furas a thoireadh nó áireamh,*
> *Ó Néill daoineach faoileach fáilteach,*
> *Ó Briain ó ríoghfhuil fhíochmhar ághmhar,*
> *Mac Mathghamhna catharmach cráifeach,*
> *Ó Domhnaill Doire budh hurra le dámhaibh,*
> *Ó Conchubhair Donn mar Gholl ar thánaibh,*
> *Ó Conchubhair Sligigh, an cuinge nár cáineadh,*
> *Ó Ruairc, Ó Ceallaigh, Ó Seachnasaigh,*
>   *Ó Máille (. . .)*[42]

It is not easy to recount or enumerate your pedigree; well-attended pleasant hospitable O'Neill, O'Brien from a ferocious battle-like bloodline, battle-equipped devout MacMahon, O'Donnell of Derry, guarantor for poets, O'Conor Don like Goll on plundering expeditions, O'Conor Sligo, the champion who has never been criticised, O'Rourke, O'Kelly, O'Shaughnessy, O'Malley (. . .)

---

[42] A similar listing of relations appears in another seventeenth century stress-timed poem addressed to a woman composed by Caitlín Dubh entitled "'Sí Máire inghean an iarla mo sgrúda". See Marie-Louise Coolahan, "Caitlín Dubh's keens: literary negotiations in early modern Ireland", in Victoria E. Burke, and Jonathan Gibson (eds), *Early modern women's manuscript writing: selected papers from the Trinity/Trent Colloquium* (Aldershot: Ashgate, 2004), 91-110 at 101-102.

CIARA NÍ MHURCHÚ

The poet also alludes to the impact of the transformation of society in Ireland in the seventeenth century on the Gaelic world, referring to the oppression of the Gaelic families and lamenting the effects that this repression had on Gaelic culture, stating that the Irish had been deprived of their power and exiled abroad and that their people, their poets, and their religious order had been restrained by the control of these enemies. This section of the poem adds to the contemporary account of the political anguish and response of the Gaelic nobility to the social turbulence and upheaval of the seventeenth century. Since the plantation of Ulster, their place in society had been taken by foreign settlers:

(. . .)
mun' mbeith neart do ghabh an státa,
lér díbreadh ar saoithe tar sáile,
ar ndaoinibh treóin, mo sgeól cráite,
ar n-ollamhain eólcha, 's ar n-ord bráthar,
go déarach faoi ghéarsmacht a námhad,
dá ruagadh insna cuantaibh gan ábhar.

(. . .)
were it not for the power assumed by the state, by which our wise men were banished abroad, our strong people, my torment, our learned poets, and our order of brothers, tearful under the strict control of their enemies, herded into the harbours without cause.

In stark contrast, however, Sara is portrayed as a powerful leader who could reverse the current state of affairs and guide the Irish to power again. The poet describes a prophecy that Sara will be proclaimed the Queen of Ireland and that under her rule, the culture, identity, and power of Gaelic society will be restored; the Catholic clergy will regain their position in society and the Gaelic family lines will regain their power without the intrusion of foreigners.

(. . .)
's go ngoirfear dhíot, más fíor na fáidhe,
ríoguin na ríoghacht' Fáil-se,
go gcuirfear arís do ríoghacht 'na n-áitibh,

285

gach glanord anallód mar a bhádar,
an fhréimh is aithre i n-aice a dtáinte,
gan neart Gall san rann dár sáradh
(. . .)

(. . .)
that you will be proclaimed, if the prophets speak
truly, queen of this kingdom of Ireland, that [the
people] of your kingdom will be restored to their
places: every pure [religious] order as it was before,
the [ancestral] stock and fathers beside their cattle,
without the power of foreigners in the district
thwarting us.
(. . .)

The poet also introduces imagery of nature and music to depict
the joy that would be felt not only by the people but by their
surroundings if this were to become true, referencing the sweet music
of birds, the ringing of bells, and the weeping voice of the harp. The
imagery here evokes the concept of *fír flathemon* (ruler's truth) which
was traditionally associated with kingship ideology but is employed
here in relation to a female ruler. The concept of nature acting in
harmony with the rightful ruler is a commonplace in Gaelic poetry
addressed to male patrons. The male patron is understood to be
married to the land, which is depicted as a female sovereignty figure.[43]
As Proinsias Mac Cana has observed, if the king was a just ruler, "the
land responded with an increase in its fertility and general prosperity;
if he was an unjust or illegitimate ruler, or blemished in his person, it
became barren and strife-torn".[44]

Describing a scene of ceremonial parading, the poet asserts that
many coaches will follow and precede Sara, and that beautiful women,
young queens (like the mythological goddess Diana), warriors, and

---

[43] See Damian McManus "'The smallest man in Ireland can reach the tops
of her trees': Images of the King's Peace and Bounty in Bardic Poetry," in
Joseph Falaky Nagy (ed) *Memory and the modern in Celtic literatures,*
Celtic Studies Association of North America Yearbook V (2006): 61-117.
[44] Proinsias Mac Cana, "Women in Irish Mythology," *The Crane Bag* 4, no.
1 (1980): 7-11 at 8.

great poets will come to her from afar with fistfuls of gold, admiring her fashion.

> *Budh hiomdha maighdean bhráide báine,*
> *is ríoguin óg ar nós Diána,*
> *de do bhantracht-sa, mallrosgach, bláithcheart,*
> *ag gabháil dhíbh tríd na sráidibh.*
> *Budh hiomdha cóiste rómhaibh 's in bhur*
> *ndeáidh-se,*
> *ag féachaint t'fhaisiúin 'na seasamh ar ardaibh*
> (. . .)

There will be many pale-necked maidens, and young queens like Diana, of your womenfolk, so noble-eyed and beautiful, going from you throughout the streets. There will be many coaches before you and after you, looking at your fashions, standing on heights (. . .)

The picture given here draws on the perceived feminine ideal and virtues of the time. The poet references Sara's 'fashions', which will draw the attention of her followers; Diana, the goddess of virginity; and the significance of the physical features of Sara's women-followers who are 'pale-necked', 'noble-eyed' and 'beautiful', like Sara who is earlier (in lines 26 and 27) addressed as *a bhé gheal mhuirneach shoilbhir fháilteach, / a ghéis an chuain go mbuaidh n-áilne* (o fair, loving, well-spoken, hospitable woman, o swan of the harbour of surpassing beauty). As is to be expected of a poem of its time, the main attributes assigned to the men of Sara's world at the beginning of the poem are more politically charged than those assigned to the women. However, the poet finishes with an appeal to Sara to cast aside her grief and to come to the aid of her people, depicting her as a leader, and as a person of influence in her own right, who could relieve the Gaelic society.

Conclusions

Not only is this piece valuable as an example of a composition in stress-timed metre from a time in which classical verse was being displaced by accentual verse, but it is also important as a historical political pamphlet from a time of struggle which attempts to emphasise Gaelic interfamily connections as still relevant, to validate the power of the poet's patron, and to express a contemporary account of the political anguish of the Gaelic sphere and their need for the restoration of their tradition. The poem is also of great importance as an address to a woman and adds to our understanding of the relationship between the male poet and the female patron. Sara Nig Uidhir, overshadowed by her esteemed brother at the beginning of the poem, is brought into the light in what can be imagined as a performance designed to honour her, by referencing her feminine virtues and features, and equally by depicting her as a powerful leader in her own right.

Acknowledgements

I am very grateful to the anonymous reviewer for generous suggestions and insightful comments, and to Eoin Mac Cárthaigh and Deirdre Nic Chárthaigh for their valuable feedback. Any remaining errors are my own. I would also like to thank the organising committee of the forty-first Harvard Celtic Colloquium.

From Marged Dafydd to Rebecca Williams: Bardic Identity in Welsh Women's Poetry of the Eighteenth Century

Shannon Rose Parker

This paper traces the development of bardic identity in Welsh-language women's poetry from Marged Dafydd, (*c*.1700–1785?), to Rebecca Williams, (fl.1810–1820). I aim to place their poetry in the context of bardic identity expressed in men's poetry in order to examine the extent to which female poets also subscribed to a bardic identity and whether, as a result, their canon differs from their male counterparts. Poetry written by women before 1800 is an understudied area and Anglophone literature has tended to attract mainstream research.[1] I hope that a study of this kind can illuminate a fresh area of inquiry and add to our understanding of how bardic identity manifested in a wider context, giving voice to poets hitherto excluded from the male poet dominated discourse.

The formation of Great Britain and Britishness

Following the 1707 Act of Union of England (and Wales, in union with England since the sixteenth century) with Scotland, a new state was formed: the United Kingdom of Great Britain. According to Linda Colley in her influential *Britons: Forging the Nation, 1707–1837* (1992), most British subjects considered themselves to be (modern) "Britons" by the end of the eighteenth century, united by their common Protestantism and attitudes towards wars with France. This thesis, however, is criticized by modern scholars of Welsh and Scottish history as "an Anglocentric one, with eccentric peripheries

---

[1] With the exception of Cathryn A. Charnell-White's work and the Leverhulme project, *Women's Poetry from Scotland, Ireland, and Wales: 1400-1800*, the accompanying anthology which is soon to be published. See also J. Stevenson and P. Davidson, eds., *Early Modern Women Poets* (Oxford: Oxford University Press, 2001) which represents poetry composed in all languages used in the British Isles between 1500 and 1800.

needing to be cajoled, humored or bribed into cooperation."[2] An archipelagic response is more desirable in the case of analyzing British poetry from largely isolated Celtic-language communities. Murray Pittock for example, is critical of Colley's "fashionable" views and favors a "four nations" literary history of Britain and Ireland in *Inventing and Resisting Britain: Cultural Identities in Britain and Ireland, 1685-1789* (1997), analyzing identity in all four nations of the archipelago and including Ireland and Scottish Gaels, something which Colley did not do. Katie Trumpener's *Bardic Nationalism: The Romantic Novel and the British Empire* (1997) is also critical of Colley's integrationist approach, and Rosemary Sweet argues that the version of eighteenth-century identity put forward by Colley only works on a political and rhetorical level in *Antiquaries: The Discovery of the Past in Eighteenth-Century Britain* (2004).

In literature, the "four nations" approach is known mostly as 'archipelagic theory' and was most fully applied by John Kerrigan in his seminal work, *Archipelagic English* (2008); a book which focuses on interactivity to encompass the reciprocity and tension of considering the four nations (England, Wales, Scotland, and Ireland) together. When it comes to language, Kerrigan acknowledges that "discussion can only be complete when fully polyglot because important controls, perspectives, and elements of inter-ethnic dialogue lie in the Celtic tongues."[3] Yet, understandably he recognizes that it would be a heroic task to acquire all the languages used in the archipelago and suggests even that this would likely sacrifice specificity and particularity in studies. Kerrigan hoped for a collective future, populated with studies like his, authored by scholars of different language competencies. It is my belief that only an archipelagic approach to literature of this period can produce any secure findings into identity formation and, after all, as Prescott questions: "if this comparative cross-national and multilinguistic context is not taken into account, on what terms do we decide which poems are especially fine, worthy of editorial scrutiny or further

---

[2] Bethan M. Jenkins, *Between Wales and England: Anglophone Welsh Writing of the Eighteenth Century* (Cardiff: University of Wales Press, 2017), 16.

[3] John Kerrigan, *Archipelagic English: Literature, History, and Politics 1603–1707* (Oxford: Oxford University Press, 2006), 60.

study?"[4] It is my hope that studies of this kind, dealing with previously understudied literature in the Welsh language, can add to a more archipelagic understanding of not just Welsh literary activity in the eighteenth century but a wider British one.

"Anglo-British" is the hyphenated term used by Sarah Prescott and Bethan M. Jenkins to describe the Anglocentric version of Britishness in the eighteenth century that had its core in London. There are many other hyphenated identities from this period: Cambro-Briton, North Briton, Hiberno-Briton, Scoto-Briton, and Anglo-Welsh which was from the outset pejorative.[5] It is undeniable that an Anglo-British identity glued the new state together but in Wales's case, "the truth of the matter was that in order to be accepted as a modern Briton [the Briton of Colley's study] and not be ridiculed as a backward Taffy, a person had to adopt the trappings of metropolitan Englishness such that they could pass as English."[6] Jenkins goes on: "an eighteenth-century Anglophone Welsh writer is a Puncinello–he might choose to display one side, or another, or he may choose to face the front and show his particoloring to the world."[7] The unfortunate truth is that, as Sarah Prescott writes, writers from Ireland, Scotland, and Wales "are absorbed by an often unconscious Anglo-British bias or treated separately with regard to their native linguistic and literary traditions."[8]

The new hyphenated identity that I propose is Celto-Briton–a hybrid identity that merges the obsession with Celticity and bardic identity. Celto-Britons are those (Welsh, English, Irish, Scots, or Gaels) who consider themselves to be of a common Celtic origin in the face of the Anglocentricity emanating out of London and

---

[4] Sarah Prescott, "Archipelagic Literary History: Eighteenth-Century Poetry from Ireland, Scotland, and Wales" in *Women's Writing, 160–1830* eds. J. Batchelor and G. Dow (London: Palgrave Macmillan, 2016), 169-191, 169-87.

[5] For more on identity formation and literature in the eighteenth century, see Murray G. H. Pittock, "Orc and the Primitives" in *Inventing and Resisting Britain: Cultural Identities in Britain and Ireland, 1685–1789* (London: Macmillan Press Ltd., 1997), 153-178.

[6] Jenkins, *Between Wales and England*, 6.

[7] Ibid.,15.

[8] Prescott, "Archipelagic Literary History", 169-170.

permeating all corners of the islands. Edward Williams (Iolo Morganwg, 1747–1826), James Macpherson, and Thomas Gray would be Celto-Britons, for example. Bardic identity grew out of the idea that the Welsh and Gaelic bardic traditions in the eighteenth century had been handed down throughout the centuries as an invaluable and unchanged cultural product and the rediscovery by antiquarians of medieval manuscripts (real or imagined) containing ancient literature proved this. According to Charnell-White, the allegiance to bardic identity in Wales, was "the response of patriotic antiquarianism to the ambivalent attitudes towards the Celts which characterized the Celtic revival of the Romantic period and the increasingly contested ideas of Britishness witnessed during the closing decades of the eighteenth century."[9] Bardic identity served as the basis for a new type of nationalism: one which was defined by a shared native literary culture of age-old historical duration, not dynasty, religion, laws, political boundaries, or sovereignty.

Bardic and Celto-British identity

Bardic identity was mostly exhibited during Marged Dafydd and Rebecca William's lifetimes by male, Welsh poets. Cathryn Charnell-White, in the introduction to her anthology of Welsh poetry from the French Revolution, writes of the poets (all men) anthologized:

> Their status as poets was fundamental to the self-image, social persona, and national identity of most of the poets anthologized here, albeit to differing degrees, not least because bardic identity was so crucial to the construction of Welsh cultural identity in eighteenth-century Britain, both within Wales and without. Bardic identity provided a ready cultural frame and a set of generic conventions which enabled poets to engage with current events – whether local, Welsh, British or European in significance- whilst simultaneously negotiating the fault-lines of Welshness and Britishness. Their responses to the French Revolution and the Revolutionary wars may be construed as peculiarly bardic, since, by and large,

[9] Cathryn Charnell-White, *Bardic Circles* (Cardiff: University of Wales Press, 2007), 3.

the poems anthologized here were performed or transmitted in what was (thanks to the intersection of poetic and correspondence networks) a relatively well-defined bardic sphere.[10]

We see from this quotation that bardic identity relied to a large degree on belonging to "bardic spheres" or network of poets, meeting and corresponding to share poetry and ideas.

Lewis Morris (Llewelyn Ddu o Fôn; 1701-1765), antiquary and poet, and renowned patriot belonged to a network of architects in Welsh cultural identity and bardic identity. The bardic tradition, as summarized here by Rosemary Sweet, "was believed to stand in a line of unbroken continuity from the earliest inhabitants until the massacre of the bards by Edward I. It appeared to offer a direct link to the time of the Roman invasions when the influence of the Druids was at its height."[11] Although bards and druids are reported as separate entities during Caesar's time, because Caesar also writes in *De Bello Gallico*, a text that was widely read in Latin by British schoolboys, that druids were responsible for "matters of religion" and held "supreme authority," spending their time memorizing "a large number of lines of poetry," the eighteenth-century poet began thinking of their own bardic art as one of Druidical claim.[12] Continuing the idea of Welsh Druidical succession, the use of British to refer to the Welsh language "continued to validate contemporary Welsh culture by means of a created past which centered on the antiquity and continuing purity of both language and culture."[13] The past is used to create a kind of centeredness for Wales, a nation on the periphery of a much larger and culturally imposing neighbor.

During his lifetime, Lewis Morris published poems in only one volume, *Diddanwch Teuluaidd* ("A Seemly Diversion"), edited by Huw Jones of Llangwm and printed in 1763. In the introduction to the

---

[10] Cathryn Charnell-White, introduction to *Welsh Poetry of the French Revolution, 1789-1805* (Cardiff: University of Wales Press, 2012), 2.

[11] Rosemary Sweet, *Antiquaries: The Discovery of the Past in Eighteenth-Century Britain*, (London: Hambledon and London, 2004), 139.

[12] Carolyn Hammond, trans., *Caesar: The Gallic War*, (Oxford: Oxford University Press, 1996), 126-7.

[13] Juliette Wood, "Perceptions of the Past in Welsh Folklore Studies", *Folklore*, 108 (1997): 93-102, 97.

work, Huw Jones, echoing the sentiments of Lewis's poetry, introduces the Welsh language as an ancient curiosity to English readers:

> It may not be improper to introduce this work in English, for the encouragement of Englishmen, or others, who might be inclined to dip into this curious ancient language: the principal remains of the Celtic tongue . . .[14]

Such an introduction to Anglophone readers both exoticizes the Welsh language and establishes it as the 'original' language of Britain. What is curious is that very few Englishmen would in fact have been able to appreciate the poetry contained in the volume as no translations were provided. One wonders what purpose this English-facing introduction serves if not to push an agenda—Welsh poetry is truly bardic, being the oldest in Britain. Huw continues: "[a]mong the ancient Britons, (a main branch of the Celtae) the Bards managed a considerable part of the Druidical religion, who sang their verses to the harp."[15] These passages show that many of the proponents of bardic identity had one foot in the world of English literature and produced poetry at least in part to educate the English as to what bardic identity meant to them. In the words of Bethan M. Jenkins, "whilst proselytizing on the genius and antiquity of the Welsh language and manuscripts, he [Morris] was also imbibing English influences and incorporating them into his Welsh- and English-language productions."[16]

For Evan Evans (Ieuan Fardd or Ieuan Brydydd Hir; 1731-1788), the bardic tradition in Wales, again, is a Druidic one; an ancient order that far predates any English literary customs. Evan Evans was another antiquarian giant of the eighteenth century, and he writes in English in answer to Thomas Gray's influential poem *The Bard: A Pindaric Ode*

---

[14] Huw Jones, ed., *Diddanwch Teuluaidd; Y Llyfr Cyntaf: Yn cynnwys Gwaith y Parchedig Mr. Goronwy Owen, Lewis Moris, Esq.; a Mr. Huw Huws, &c, Beirdd Mon, Mam-Gymru, Ac Aelodau o Gymdeithas y Cymmrodorion.* (London: William Roberts, 1763), iii.

[15] Ibid., v.

[16] Jenkins, *Between Wales and England*, 34.

(1757) in "A Paraphrase of the 137th Psalm, Alluding to the Captivity and Treatment of the Welsh Bards by King Edward I":

> What!–shall the Saxons hear us sing,
> Or their dull vales with Cambrian music ring?
> Thou God of vengeance, dost thou sleep,
> When the insulted Druids weep,
> The victor's jest the Saxon's scorn,
> Unheard, unpitied, and forlorn?[17]

The Saxons Evans refers to here are the English under the rule of Edward I, the king who, in legend as much as in reality, sought to destroy the bardic tradition in Wales in 1282. Katie Trumpener interprets the poem in terms of political sovereignty: "To play for their Saxon captors, as they have been ordered, would be to surrender their nation's last cultural treasures along with its political sovereignty".[18] Here we see again that Bardic identity served the Welsh patriot's agenda. Evans was responsible for producing an anthology (including editions and translations) of medieval Welsh poetry, *Specimens of the Poetry of the Antient Welsh Bards* (1764); a work which left an enduring mark on scholarship and antiquarianism and allowed, for truly the first time, a glimpse into the world of Welsh literature for Anglophone readers. Evans, through proving the antiquity of Welsh poetry, sought "a place not only in the history of a specifically "British" literature, but also among the ancient expressions of vernacular literary genius for which all of Europe was hungering in the second half of the century."[19]

Referring to the Welsh as "Britons"; for this read 'the indigenous inhabitants of the island' rather than Colley's Britons, became commonplace throughout the eighteenth century in both Anglophone and Welsh-language poetry, especially during the time of the French

---

[17] Evan Evans, "A Paraphrase of the 137th Psalm, Alluding to the Captivity and Treatment of the Welsh Bards by King Edward I" in *The Cambro-Briton,* 2, no. 14. (Oct. 1820): 87-89.

[18] Katie Trumpener, *Bardic Nationalism: The Romantic Novel and the British Empire*, (Princeton: Princeton University Press, 1997), 3.

[19] Catherine McKenna, "Aspects of Tradition Formation in Eighteenth-Century Wales", in *CSANA Yearbook 5*, ed. Joseph Falaky Nagy (Dublin: Four Courts Press, 2006), 37-60, 38.

Revolution. Dafydd Ddu Eryri equates the Britons with Celts in *Awdl ar ryddid* ("An awdl on liberty"):

> *O'i phlaid yr hen Geltiaid gynt*
> *Diddwl, anorfod oeddynt*
> *A'u harfau yn gwae mewn gwynt,*
> *A dynion marwol danynt*

> The Old Celts long ago were in favor of liberty
> with their weapons darting about on the wind,
> and dead men under their feet,
> they were wise and unconquerable.[20]

Allegiance to a personified Britannia also became commonplace as Jonathan Hughes writes in *Cerdd o anogaeth i lanciau chwe sir Gwynedd, am godi yn glau ym mhlaid Britannia, pan oedd y deyrnas mewn perygl o gael ei gorthrechu gan y gelynion* ("A poem of encouragement to the lads of Gwynedd's six counties for rising quickly in the cause of Britannia when the kingdom was in danger of being overcome by the enemies"):

> *Mae achos mawr yn awr i ni*
> *Godi'n gad hoff rad a ffri*
> *Ym mhlaid Britannia brafia' ei bri,*
> *Fun heini, fwyn henedd.*

> there is now a great cause for us
> rise up in a blessed and fearless army
> on Britannia's side, the most lovely in prestige,
> ancient, gentle and vigorous maiden.[21]

Cathryn Charnell-White, the editor of the anthology (*Welsh Poetry of the French Revolution*) from which these two examples come, explains of the poets' poetic identity: "What marks out the

---

[20] David Thomas, "Awdl ar ryddid" in *Welsh Poetry of the French Revolution, 1789-1805* ed. and trans. Cathryn Charnell-White (Cardiff: University of Wales Press, 2012), 230-249 at 236-7.
[21] Jonathan Hughes, "Cerdd o anogaeth i lanciau chwe sir Gwynedd, am godi yn glau ym mhlaid Britannia, pan oedd y deyrnas mewn perygl o gael ei gorthrechu gan y gelynion" in *Welsh Poetry of the French Revolution*, 88-93 at 88-9.

chorus of conservative and radical voices in this anthology as Welsh is the way in which they fulfil the prescribed role of poet and subscribe to the genres and conventions of their native poetic traditions, both strict- and free-meter."[22]

As Celto-Britishness grew in the eighteenth century, we see the growth of Welsh male-dominated patriotic societies based in London such as the *Gwyneddigion*, or 'the Gwynedd men' and The Honourable Society of *Cymmrodorion*, literally translated 'the aboriginals'; the insignia for which contains depictions of a druid and a bard, both donning robes and headdresses much like the modern *Derwyddion* (Druids) wear at the national *Eisteddfod* festival. Both figures are, of course, men. The bard became a powerful symbol of the cultural self-identity of the Welsh and the insignia suggests the connection the modern Welsh 'race' has to the most ancient people of Britain, ensuring their dominance over British pedigree. No women were admitted to these societies and, increasingly throughout the eighteenth century, there was no place for women within bardic spheres. Edward Williams was the catalyst for the explosion of bardic identity during the turn of the nineteenth century and is no secret that he was a great believer in the bardic majesty of the Druids. In fact, he wrote to the *Gentlemen's Magazine* in 1792 concerning the autumn equinox celebration on Primrose Hill where he founded the *Gorsedd*:

> [T]he Bardic Institution of the Ancient Britons, which is the same as the Druidic, has been from the earliest times, through all the ages, to the present day, retained by the Welsh . . . is now exactly the same as it was two thousand years ago.[23]

The celebration was set according to what Edward claimed were ancient "Druidic rites". He was a self-proclaimed "bard" (the last one, indeed) and antiquarian and, again, much of Edward's work, although he did write a great deal in Welsh, was English-facing and he had an agenda to push that included proving the legitimacy of the Welsh

---

[22] Charnell-White, introduction to *Welsh Poetry of the French Revolution, 1789-1805*, 2.
[23] Quoted in Trevor Herbert and Gareth E. Jones, eds., *The Remaking of Wales in the Eighteenth Century*, (Capel Garmon: Gwasg Carreg Gwalch, 1988), 161-2.

literary tradition, the legitimacy of the Welsh as descendants of the Britons, and his own legitimacy as a bardic authority.[24]

Marged Dafydd: strict-meter poetry and Bardic Identity

The flurry of antiquarian interest in Welsh-language material, as evidenced above, was a male-dominated endeavor. Marged Dafydd (or, Margaret Davies), however, was recognized by Lewis Morris as being one of two female collectors and transcribers of manuscripts in eighteenth-century Wales, the other being Angharad James. Lewis Morris named her, along with Angharad, in the list of people who were in possession of collections of Welsh-language manuscript, NLW 604D. In terms of manuscripts, Marged wrote the following: Cwrtmawr 128 (*Llyfr Ofergerddi Margaret Davies*/ "Marged Dafydd's Book of Worthless Poems") (1738), Cwrtmawr 129 (*c*.1760-2), Cwrtmawr 448 (1725), Minor Dep. 56 (1738), Card. 4.156 (1736-7) and Add. 14996 part (ii). She also made contributions or additions to: Cwrtmawr 27, Cwrtmawr 244, Minor Dep. 1206 (*c*.1767-8), NLW 1746, NLW 5241, NLW 12732, Pen. 244, Pen. 245 (1730), Pen. 327iii, Aber. UL D/M7/22, Card. 2.201, Card. 2.202 and Card. 5.30 (*c*.1737).[25] With 25 or more surviving poems, all published posthumously, Marged's body of work is the second largest we have before 1800 (the largest belonging to the medieval woman poet Gwerful Mechain). She not only wrote poetry but showed an allegiance to manuscript culture, collecting and transcribing manuscripts–an unusual activity for women of the period. The subjects of these were women's poetry from the Middle Ages to the modern day with some manuscripts preserving work by Welsh-language women poets that would otherwise be lost to us today, namely in *Llyfr Ofergerddi Margaret Davies* (Cwrtmawr 128): Frances Parry and Margaret Rowland whose work appears in NLW Cwrtmawr 128, 129, 483, and 485; and Jane James whose work

---

[24] For an exploration of his work in English, see Jeff Strabone, "The Fall and Rise of the Welsh Bards, or, How the English Became British" in *Poetry and British Nationalisms in the Bardic Eighteenth Century: Imagined Antiquities* (Cham, Switzerland: Palgrave Macmillan, 2018), 230-245.

[25] Daniel Huws, *A Repertory of Welsh Manuscripts and Scribes, c.800-c.1800,* vol. II (Aberystwyth: National Library of Wales and University of Wales Centre for Advanced Welsh and Celtic Studies, 2022), 18.

appears in NLW, Dep. 56B, 391. Marged's manuscripts are also the only known source for one of the englynion written by Gwerful Mechain. It seems that Marged was attempting, in her own way, to present the women's canon in Welsh as was being done parallel in men's poetry by Evan Evans in his *Specimens*.

It is suggested in the *marwnad* (elegy) to Marged's mother, that it was from her that she learnt the basics of *Cerdd Dant* (String Music: the art of improvising the melody to a poetic text over harp music) and *Cerdd Dafod* (Tongue Craft: poetic meters requiring strict observance of the rules of cynghanedd). It is also certain that she had some instruction from her aunt, Margaret Rowland and John Davies, Bronwion. By 1728, Marged Dafydd was corresponding with Michael Prichard (1709-33) and instructing him in cynghanedd and the strict meters. *Cynghanedd* is an incredibly important and complex skill of internal rhyme, consonance and assonance and is essential to the eighteenth-century idea of a trained poet–the poets of 'old' composed in cynghanedd. It is unsurprisingly a skill that takes years of learning and practicing and was a skill not often passed to women. Michael Prichard took pride in this instruction, and in a letter to Marged Dafydd that was published in Cymru xxv (1903), 93-8, he differentiated between "poets" who knew cynghanedd and "clumsy poets": oral poets who did not practice cynghanedd like his own father, William Prichard, sexton of Llanllyfni. Clearly, poetic networks were important to Marged Dafydd and poetic relationships grew with several significant figures around her locality and beyond: Dafydd Jones from Trefriw, Rhys Jones from y Blaenau and the copyist Dafydd Ellis from Cricieth. We cannot prove J. H. Davies' assertion that Marged Dafydd and Angharad James (mentioned as the other female manuscript copyist by Lewis Morris) were corresponding with each other, but it is significant that one copy of Angharad's *marwnadau* (elegies) to her son is written in Marged Dafydd's hand. One could say these poetic connections and correspondences created a bardic sphere around Marged–a sphere of which Lewis Morris was aware.

Marged Dafydd was daughter to Dafydd Evan (d. 1729), Coedgae-du, Trawsfynydd, and his wife Ann Dafydd (d. 1726). Her home was in Coedgae-du and she spent periods visiting relatives in y Brithdir, Llanelltyd and Dolgellau, where she had the opportunity to collect and copy poems. Marged was unmarried and free to travel as she pleased, being untethered to home and family and she was also the executor of her father's will when he died in 1729. A remarkable amount of her poetry survives (25 poems), and the majority of these are in strict meters. According to G. J. Williams in his entry on Marged in the *Dictionary of Welsh Biography*, however, "they do not display much merit".[26] Literary expressions of Welsh culture were important to Marged and, as such, she subscribed to the literary anthologies *Dewisol Ganiadau yr Oes hon* ("Selected Songs of this Age") (1759), *Y Nefawl Ganllaw* ("The Nefawl Guide") (1740) and *Diddanwch Teuluaidd* ("A Seemly Diversion") (1763). In letters to Dafydd Jones of Trefriw and Michael Prichard, she complained about the ignorance in her area regarding the poetic tradition. Because of her varied activity–composing, copying, collecting and transcribing–it can be said that she partook in the literary renaissance of the eighteenth century.[27]

As mentioned above, Marged was aware of native strict- and free-meter poetic traditions and wrote many poems in the strict meters, on which she tutored Michael Pritchard. This was not without insecurity, however, and in one *ymryson*, (poetic conversation) with him she apologizes:

> *Un wyf i o awen feth*
> *Mawr ei brys mewn dyrys daith*
> *A thebyga-i bara byth,*
> *Di a bardyni, o mynni maeth.*[28]

> I am one of failing poetic inspiration,
> whose haste is great on a difficult journey,

[26] G. J. Williams. "Davies, Margaret (c. 1700-1785?), transcriber of many of the manuscripts preserved in our public collections." In *Dictionary of Welsh Biography*. 1959; Accessed 16 May 2023. https://biography.wales/article/s-DAVI-MAR-1700

[27] This biographical information is taken from Cathryn A. Charnell-White, ed., *Beirdd Ceridwen: Blodeugerdd Barddas o Ganu Menywod hyd tua 1800* (Llandybïe: Cyhoeddiadau Barddas, 2005), 389-392.

[28] Marged Dafydd, "I ofyn pymtheg bai cerdd gan ferch ieuanc o sir Feirionnydd" in *Beirdd Ceridwen*, 180-183, lines 69-72.

and, I believe, will last forever,
pardon me if you desire sustenance.[29]

Apologias are not uncommon amongst amateur and free-meter poets of the eighteenth century in general but for female poets we see them often, signalling the depths of the poets' insecurities.[30] Nevertheless, Marged was versed in cynghanedd, as shown in the opening line of a *marwnad*, (elegy) to her mother: "Och! Gan hiraeth, maith methiant."[31] Women of this period, including Marged, mostly saw their poetry as an individual pursuit–indeed, none of Marged's poems were published during her lifetime–and perhaps this is the impetus behind Marged apologia as she fears to make her work public through correspondence.

Marged was also aware of the medieval poetic convention of *llatai* or 'messenger poems'–popular with Dafydd ap Gwilym but also employed by and for the female poet Gwerful Mechain–in which an animal or natural element is sent to convey love to the recipient. In Marged's case she sends a swallow to her friend as a display of platonic love:

> *Y wennol fain, annwyl fach,*
> *Luniaidd, pa un lanach?*
> *Yn d'wyneb, y mae donie,*
> *Aderyn wyd, Duw o'r ne'.*[32]

The dear small, graceful, slender swallow,
who is more pure?
In your face, there are talents,
You are a bird, God from heaven.[33]

---

[29] My own translation.
[30] For more on female poetic authority, see Cathryn A. Charnell-White, "'Megis Archoll yw Ngholled': Marwnadau Mamau i'w plant" in *Ysgrifau Beirniadol XXVIII*, ed. Gerwyn Williams (Llandysul: Gwasg Gee, 2009), 21-46, 30-31.
[31] Marged Dafydd, "Cwyn colled ar ô lei mam, 1726" in *Beirdd Ceridwen*, 171-5, line 1.
[32] Marged Dafydd, "Cywydd i anfon y wennol yn gennad i annerch merch ifanc oddi wrth ei ffrindiau fain" in *Beirdd Ceridwen*, 188-191.
[33] My own translation.

There is also a reference in Marged's body of work to a character from Welsh legend, Ceridwen; an enchantress who owns a cauldron containing the *awen* (poetic inspiration). Ceridwen is first textually attested in a sixteenth-century manuscript in Elis Gruffydd's hand but he claimed that the story was well-known in Wales in both written versions and lore. Marged Dafydd writes in this englyn to Michael Prichard:

> *At brydydd â'r awenydd wen,–dywedaf*
> *Nid ydwyf i'w adwen;*
> *Ond credaf mai bardd Caridwen,*
> *Sŵn y pair sydd yn y pen.*[34]

> I say to the bard who has the bright muse,
> I am not one to follow;
> But I believe the sound of the cauldron which is in the
>   mind
> is Ceridwen's poet.[35]

It is striking that while poets such as Lewis Morris, Evan Evans and Edward Williams were looking towards Aneirin and Taliesin as the fathers of their cherished poetic tradition and lineage, Marged looks to Ceridwen and sees not Ceridwen's work (there is none attributed) but the birthplace of all poetic inspiration. Marged Dafydd can, I would argue, even by her own trepidation, be considered a bardic poet as she demonstrates competency in and knowledge of the ancient traditions of the bardic orders, valued and worked to preserve the poetic tradition of women, and worked within a bardic sphere. It is also clear that this was her aim. It can be suggested, even, that Marged Dafydd displays a similar sense of Celto-Britishness to Lewis Morris, Evan Evans, and Edward Williams in that she situates her ouvre within a bardic past and present, albeit on a much smaller local and Welsh level, rather than a British or European one.

Rebecca Williams and free-meter poetry

Why then, do we see nothing of Celto-British identity in Rebecca Williams' work when she inhabited the same space in time as Edward

---

[34] Marged Dafydd, "Nodiadau" in *Beirdd Ceridwen*, 390.
[35] My own translation.

Williams (d. 1826), a man responsible for the bardic revolution in Wales? We have also seen from Marged Dafydd's work and life that it is possible for women to identify with bardic identity. Little is known of Rebecca Williams (*fl.*1810-1820) and the details we can glean come from her ballads themselves. She published her songs in ballad pamphlets and wrote a Christmas *plygain* carol. She writes of the earthquake in London in 1755, a murder in her area, the sinking of a ship in the Menai Straits and a eulogy to a local man, Sir Robert Williams. What links her poetry is a keen and deep sense of religiosity and the only sense of obvious Britishness we find is that she is a supporter of the Hanoverian succession in a common, formulaic passage:

> *Duw fendithio George y trydydd*
> *Pen llywydd ae ei lle,*
> *A'i holl frenhinol deulu*
> *Yn gyfan gydag ef;*
> *A'i swyddogion dano*
> *Hyd y gwaela' ddyn,*
> *Amen, mai felly byddo*
> *Yn nyfodiad Mab y Dyn.*

> God bless George the third
> Head ruler of this place,
> and his whole royal family
> With him;
> And his officials under him
> To the poorest man,
> Amen, that so
> he be in the advent of God's Son.[36]

All of Rebecca's poems are in free meters. There is no doubt that her recounts of local narrative and eulogistic writing, strict-meter or not, perform a poetic function within her community. The Christmas plygain would also have been written for local performance. Surely, Rebecca's poetry operated to some degree at a local level but does nothing to intentionally situate itself within a wider historical Welsh

---

[36] Rebecca Williams, "Cân Newydd, sef cwynfan Prydain am Arian…" in *Beirdd Ceridwen*, 326-333, lines 209-214.

or British tradition like Marged Dafydd's work did. According to Nia Powell, "there is no evidence of a further flowering of the strict meters amongst women during the eighteenth century" after Marged's death.[37] We do find examples of *englynion* and *cywyddau*–specific historical poetic meters–in several places but none of them display the quality or innovativeness of Marged's work and certainly there is none in Rebecca William's hand. Of course, 'bardic' poets like Edward Williams and Lewis Morris also composed in free meters but they make pains to connect themselves to the bardic tradition by also knowing and composing the older cynhanedd meters, meters which they held in much higher esteem. To examine the loss of bardic identity in women's poetry in greater detail, I will trace what we do see in terms of Celto-British identities between the oeuvres of Marged and Rebecca.

Firstly, we see an engagement with the British military and a personification of Britannia, making sure to label the king as England's monarch alone. Lowri Parry (*fl.*1738-60) writes in "*Ymddiddan rhwng gŵr ifanc a'i gariad ar 'Fenra Gwen'*" ("A conversation between a young man and his love on the tune 'Fentra Gwen'"):

> Mi â'n f'union dros y dyfnder, yn was i frenin
> Lloegr,
> I rodio i Gibralter, er i ti gael dy bleser, . . . [38]
>
> *I will go directly over the deep, a servant to England's king,*
> *to walk in Gibraltar, for you to have your pleasure,*
> . . .[39]

Later in the same poem we find:

---

[37] Nia Powell, "5: Women and Strict-Metre Poetry in Wales" in *Women and Gender in Early Modern Wales,* ed. Michael Roberts and Simone Clarke (Cardiff: University of Wales Press, 2000), 129-58, 145.

[38] Lowri Parry, "Ymddiddan rhwn gŵr ifanc a'i gariad ar 'Fenra Gwen' in *Beirdd Ceridwen,* 267-269, lines 23-24.

[39] My own translation

Oni chaech chwi, lliw'r eira, trwy gennad Duw'r
    gorucha'
I nofio'r dyfnion donnau ffarwél i dir Britannia[40]

Unless I get you, the color of snow, through God's
    consent,
I will swim the deep waves, farewell to Britannia.[41]

Secondly, we find harsh judgements on those who have left
Britain to find riches in America, as in Mrs Parry from Plas yn y
Faerdre's (*fl. c.*1777) words in *Carol plygen i'w ganu ar 'Susanna'"*
("A plygain carol to sing to 'Susanna'"):

Mae yn America dinistrio, o achos pechod, Duw
    sy'n blino,
Nyni sy'n tynny llid i'n pobol, am ein bod ni'n byw'n
    annuwiol[42]

In America there is destruction as a result of sin; God
    is tired,
we attract wrath for our people, because of our
    ungodly lives"[43]

And in Mary Rhys from Penygeulan, Llanbryn-mair's (*c.*1747-
1842) poem, *Carol haf gan Mary Rhys, 1825* ("A summer carol by
Mary Rhys, 1825"):

Rhai'n ffoi i wledydd health
Cael cywaeth yn America.
Petaem ni yn byw yn dduwiolion,
Danfone Duw i'n fendithion
Ar diroedd Brydain dirion,
A ffrwythlon hinon ha'.[44]

---

[40] Lowri Parry, "Ymddiddan rhwn gŵr ifanc a'i gariad ar 'Fenra Gwen' in *Beirdd Ceridwen*, 267-269, lines 33-34.
[41] My own translation.
[42] Mrs Parry o Blas yn y Fa[e]rdre, "Canu Plygain i'w ganu ar 'Susanna'" in *Beirdd Ceridwen*, 298-301, lines 7-8.
[43] My own translation.
[44] Mary Rhys o Benygeulan, Llanbryn-mair, "Carol Haf gan Mary Rhys, 1825" in *Beirdd Ceridwen*, 277-279, lines 27-32.

Some fleeing to plentiful lands
To find riches in America.
If we were to live as godly people,
God would send blessings to us,
on Britain's pleasant land,
And a fair, fruitful summer."[45]

It is common, when referring to military pursuits or overseas wars, to refer to Britain rather than the smaller nations or identities and this mirrors Rosemary Sweet's argument that identifying as a (modern) "Briton" works on a political and rhetorical level.

This is all the engagement with Britishness, Celto-Britishness, or bardic identity that I can find between or around Marged Dafydd and Rebecca Williams. The reason for the move away from bardic identity is not easy to pinpoint but as Nia Powell suggests: "Changes in behavioral expectations in polite society, in England as much as in Wales, encouraged an amusing frivolity in women and this may have discouraged serious literary endeavor on their part."[46] Marged Dafydd had the luxury of being financially independent and able to devote herself to the study of poetry and the collection of manuscripts. How many other women following her had the same opportunity? Most other female poets have only one poem to their name. Alongside this, we have the growth in bardic identity as seen in Edward Williams's work and activity which excluded rather than included women because of the male-dominated circles it burgeoned within, although personally, Edward was not against corresponding with female poets.[47] Marged Dafydd had a connection to manuscript culture; a culture within which great Welsh antiquarians and poets had a hand and she used it to compile books of her own that contained poetry by women. Rebecca Williams, however, did not have this connection which almost definitely prevented her from having knowledge of the older bardic traditions and strict meters particularly that composed by

---

[45] My own translation.
[46] Powell, "Women and Strict-Metre Poetry in Wales" (2000), 145.
[47] Cathryn Charnell-White, "Women and Gender in the Private and Social Relationships of Iolo Morganwg", in *A Rattleskull Genius: The Many Faces of Iolo Morganwg*. ed. G.H. Jenkins (Cardiff: University of Wales Press, 2005)

women. Of course, we also have the general lack of poetic education for women which was seen as an endeavor, millennia-old, of unbroken male tradition.

Acknowledgements

Diolch o galon i'r adolygydd a wnaeth yr erthygl hon yn llawer well.

Seasonality and the Gnomic Mode: *Kalangaeaf* and the Monthly Englynion

Joseph Shack

Introduction

Kenneth Jackson begins his 1935 edition of the medieval Welsh gnomic corpus with a rebuttal of the view posited by earlier scholars that gnomic poetry, then called 'early Welsh nature-poetry,' consisted of the remnants of true nature poetry.[1] This undiluted verse, the scholarly narrative held, had been corrupted by later sententious poets who used the natural imagery as a frame in which to insert their irrelevant gnomes and maxims. Jackson rebuffs such notions, stating, "I prefer to regard the descriptive element, which is the smaller, as the irrelevant one, and to treat the poems as essentially sententious or "gnomic" verse."[2] While Jackson's desire to redeem the sententious element of the poetry was laudable, his rejection of the "descriptive element" seems a pendulum swing in the opposite direction that preserves the exclusionary attitude of the scholarly narrative he hoped to revise. I contend that the elements of gnomic poetry that describe natural phenomena should not be regarded as inferior additions to more sententious gnomic utterances. Rather, such visions of the natural world constitute an essential aspect of the gnomic mode, and attempting to circumscribe and disentangle them from gnomic poetry ultimately robs the force of expression from such verse.

As a means of investigating the relationship between natural description and gnomic utterance within the corpus of gnomic poetry, in this article I examine a particular sort of 'nature-description' particularly prevalent in the genre: the seasonal image. I argue that the

---

[1] Kenneth Jackson, ed., *Early Welsh Gnomic Poems* (Cardiff: The University of Wales Press Board, 1935), 1. Jackson here cites the work of J. Glyn Davies, specifically, "The Welsh Bard and the Poetry of External Nature: From Llywarch Hen to Dafydd ap Gwilym," *Transactions of the Honourable Society of Cymmrodorion* (1912-13): 81-128. Barry Lewis provides a summary of the search for a "pure" Welsh "nature poetry" in his examination of "Claf Abercuawg" in "*Genre* a Dieithrwch yn y Cynfeirdd: Achos 'Claf Abercuawg'," *Llenyddiaeth mewn Theori* 2 (2007), 1-37.
[2] Jackson, Early Welsh Gnomic Poems, 1.

seasonal imagery that recurs in gnomic poetry reflects and enhances the temporalities implied in verse that assumes a gnomic mode. Such temporalities are conveyed by means of formal features deployed by the composers of gnomic verse that imply habitual occurrence while simultaneously gesturing towards the future. Rather than being an intrusive or unsuitable element of gnomic poetry, the seasonal image is uniquely suited to the genre. The bounties and hardships that accompany seasonal cycles are recurrent and predictable. The 'descriptive elements' found in gnomic poetry render images of the regular, experiential world consonant with the verbal and syntactical expressions that make this form of expression unique.

Definitions and Gnomic Temporality

Prior to examining the poetry itself, it is worth clarifying my own terminology, beginning with the expression for which the poetic genre is named, the gnome. While technical rhetorical use of the term may be traced back to Aristotle, scholarly definitions have shifted since the classical period.[3] I use the term 'gnome' to refer to an ontological statement concerning the natural world or the social structures and values pertaining to the community from which it emerges.[4] The

---

[3] Aristotle defines the gnome as a statement "not . . . concerning particulars" but generalities, though not all generalities "as for instance that the straight is the opposite of the crooked," and which may deal "with the objects of human actions," *Aristotle, Art of Rhetoric*, trans. J.H. Freese, revised by Gisela Striker, Loeb Classical Library 193 (Cambridge, MA: Harvard University Press, 2020), 227.

[4] This deviates from Aristotle's definition, but generally accords with modern scholarly definitions of the term used as a means of describing a sort of poetic expression that appears in various literary traditions. The application of the term to medieval literature may, perhaps, be traced back to John Josias Conybeare's 1826 collection, *Illustrations of Anglo-Saxon Poetry*, ed. William Daniel Conybeare (London: Harding and Lepard, 1826), in which he refers to the Old English poem from the Exeter Book now known as Maxims I as "Gnomic Poem." The term was taken up by later scholars, perhaps most saliently by the Hector and Nora Chadwick in *The Growth of Literature*, which comparatively examines Greek, Welsh, Irish, English, and Scandinavian forms of gnomic poetry, which they view as a precursor of natural science and moral philosophy, see H. Munro

Welsh gnomic sequences known as the *Bidiau* furnish many examples, but representative are statements like *Bit grwm biw a bit lwyt bleid* (let the cattle be hunched and let the wolf be gray) and *Bit lew vnben a bid avwy vryt* (let a leader be a lion and let his spirit be ardent).[5] These are universalizing assertions: cattle are typically hunched over, wolves are typically gray, kings are (or should be) fierce and ardent. Each statement constitutes a singular gnome, the former focusing on nature and the latter on the social world. Essentially, gnomes are *not* prescriptive. Though they may imply an idealized context or course of action, they will never explicitly tell their audience what to do or how to act.[6] Rather, gnomes describe the state of an ordered and idealized world.[7]

Verse gnomes such as those above may be found in different poetic contexts. Gnomic poetry consists mostly or entirely of gnomic statements. In the Welsh tradition, the corpus of gnomic poetry includes the Bidiau, the Gnodiau, the Kalangaeaf stanzas, "Llym awel," and "Eiry mynyd," among others. When gnomes appear in

---

Chadwick and N. Kershaw Chadwick, *The Growth of Literature, Volume I: The Ancient Literatures of Europe* (Cambridge: Cambridge University Press 1932, repr. 1986), 377-403.

[5] Nicolas Jacobs, ed., *Early Welsh Gnomic and Nature Poetry* (London: Modern Humanities Research Association, 2012), 9, ll. 8a, 4a. All quotations from the corpus of Welsh gnomic poetry are taken from Jacobs' edition, translations are my own unless otherwise noted. 4a's *lew* may be mutation of either *glew* 'brave' or *llew* 'lion.'

[6] The literary tradition that expresses something close to the Welsh gnome is that of Old English, as exemplified by the Maxims poems and the Rune Poem. The Irish and Old Norse poetry that the Chadwicks identify as gnomic tends to be much more overtly prescriptive than the Welsh and English material.

[7] Throughout this paragraph, I have referred to the 'genre' of gnomic poetry, and I have imposed my own definitions and classification upon the material. Though there *are* clear, observable features that characterize what I refer to as 'early Welsh gnomic poetry,' there is no evidence that medieval Welsh poets held a concept of 'gnome' or 'gnomic poetry' anything like the modern scholarly conception of those terms. As Barry Lewis points out, though they may use generic techniques, "mae cerddi'n rhy lithrig i'w dal mewn genres," "poems are too slippery to be caught in genres," Lewis, "*Genre* a Dieithrwch," 32.

other genres of verse, the poet (and the poem) may be said to assume a gnomic mode.[8] Poems that have been described as 'elegiac' and 'lyric' seem a common locus for the assumption of this mode A pair of englynion from "Claf Abercuawg" demonstrates this phenomenon:

> *Amlwc golwc gwylyadur*
> *gwnelit syberwyt segur.*
> *crei vym bryt, cleuyt am cur.*
>
> *Alaf yn eil meil am ved.*
> *nyt eidun detwyd dyhed.*
> *amaerwy adnabot amyned.*

> Clear the sight of the watcher,
> the secure one may perform generosity.
> Raw my mind, illness wastes me.
>
> Cattle in a shed, mead in the cup.
> It is not the wish of the fortunate for strife.
> The boundary of knowledge: patience.[9]

Assuming a gnomic mode invites connections between the mind-state of the elegiac speaker and the generalized gnomic statement; though *gwnelit syberwyt segur* is a gnome, its juxtaposition with the following line *crei vym bryt, cleuyt am cur,* a personal statement, affects our reading. The state of the *claf* 'sick person' is far from secure. Is he looking back at a past in which his position or that of his patron was more stable and thus facilitated the sort of generosity expected in an aristocratic warrior society? The operative genre, elegy, guides audience interpretation in such instances, given that the situation of the speaker provides a secure platform from which to

---

[8] Perhaps the most familiar instances of an assumption of the gnomic mode occur in the Old English elegiac poems such as "The Wanderer", "The Seafarer," and "The Wife's Lament." In each, the poem contrasts the mournful, persona plaints of the speakers with broad, impersonal gnomes. *Beowulf* also frequently slips into the gnomic mode, for which see Catherine Karkov and Robert Farrell, "The Gnomic Passages of *Beowulf*," *Neuphilologische Mitteilungen* 3 (1990). 295-310.

[9] Jenny Rowland, *Early Welsh Saga Poetry: A Study and Edition of the* Englynion (Cambridge: D.S. Brewer, 1990), p. 450, ll. 21-22, translations my own.

construe the universal expressions of the gnomes. Gnomic poetry, consisting only or predominantly of gnomes, lacks the sense of a 'center' afforded by the position of the elegiac speaker.

Gnomes, whether they appear in gnomic poetry or other poems that shift into a gnomic mode, convey an ambiguous temporality by means of their lexicon and other formal features. For example, the englynion of the Bidiau are characterized by their reliance on the verb *bit*, the third-person singular consuetudinal/future and imperative form of the copula *bod*.[10] The precise sense of this verb form, however, varies in the context of the verses, supporting readings such as 'is characteristic,' 'is by nature,' 'must be,' or, with imperative force, 'let [subject] be.'[11] A similar valence may be found in another tag in the corpus, *gnawt,* an adjective meaning 'usual,' 'customary,' 'natural,' 'characteristic,' or 'known,' present in many of the gnomic poems but most concentrated in a series of englynion known as the Gnodiau (due to the *cymeriad* repeating the adjective at the beginning of each englyn).[12] The use of a vocabulary that implies regularity imbues gnomic statements with an sense of permanence that allow them to convey how things are now and how they will be in the future. Gnomes place their subjects in a sort of immanent ever-present. Though temporally ambiguous and hazy, they nevertheless impress a stability upon the structure of the world.

Supporting the murky temporalities expressed by the gnomic lexicon are several syntactic constructions typical of gnomic poetry. Middle Welsh accommodates clauses in which the finite verb is dropped and the sentence order is left unclear, which requires the assumptions of an audience to fill in the blanks. Within the gnomic englynion the most typical of these constructions is the 'pure nominal sentence,' in which the predicate consists only of a complement that

---

[10] For the forms see D. Simon Evans, *A Grammar of Middle Welsh* (Dublin: Dublin Institute for Advanced Studies, 1964), pp. 136-141, §144-146.

[11] For Jackson's take on the semantic ambiguity of the verb, see Jackson, *Early Welsh Gnomic Poetry*, 62. Jacobs treats the same subject in Jacobs, *Early Welsh Gnomic and Nature Poetry*, xxxvii, 43.

[12] *GPC*, s.v. gnawd, accessed October 1, 2022, http://welsh-dictionary.ac.uk/gpc/gpc.html. Jacobs edits the poem, "Gnawt gwynt" in *Early Welsh Gnomic and Nature Poetry*, 11-12.

precedes the subject and any explicit verbal form is absent.[13] The initial englynion of the sequence known as Baglawc Bydin furnish numerous examples (pure nominals are underlined):

> Baglawc bydin, bagwy onn;
> hwyeit yn llynn, graenwynn tonn;
> trech no chant kyssul callon.
>
> Hir nos, gordyar morua;
> gnawt teruysc ygkymanua;
> ny chytuyd diryeit a da.

Arrayed (is) the host, budding (is) the ash
ducks in a lake, white-capped (is) the wave;
stronger than a hundred (is) the counsel of the
   heart.
Long (is) the night, resounding the salt-marsh;
usual (is) trouble in an assembly;
the ill-starred one and the good one will not
   agree.[14]

In these short 'pure nominal' constructions, the copula is there by implication alone. How an audience might have construed this lack is not immediately clear. The default assumption was likely *ys*, the third person singular present indicative form of *bod*, but its absence creates some ambiguity.[15] Perhaps an audience familiar with a series like the

---

[13] Jacobs provides an overview of the form in *Early Welsh Gnomic and Nature Poetry*, xxxvi. This linguistic phenomenon may be more commonly known as the 'zero copula,' in which subject and predicate are joined without an explicit marking of the relationship. This phenomenon is present in many languages, perhaps most pertinent in this instance is Irish, for which see Rudolf Thurneysen, *A Grammar of Old Irish*, revised and enlarged editions, trans. D.A. Binchy and Osborn Bergin (Dublin: Dublin Institute for Advanced Studies, 2010), p. 494, § 818.

[14] Jacobs, *Early Welsh Gnomic and Nature Poetry*, 16-17. The parenthetical "is" translates the absent copula, though present indicative "is" is only one possibility.

[15] This is indeed the case in Irish, in which the omitted copula is often a form of the third person indicative, see Thurneysen, *A Grammar of Old Irish*, § 818. Such ambiguity is not only limited to the form of the copula,

Bidiau would assume the imperative or consuetudinal/future form of *bod*. Could another form of the copula, such as the imperfect, also apply here? These are speculative questions, but in the context of gnomic poetry, lacking an overt copula seems to imply the same sort of timelessness as other gnomic verbs and tags. All of these features work in tandem with the imagery and sentiments conveyed by gnomic poetry to construct an ambiguous sense of time suggesting the ever-presence of nature and asserting the permanence of the wisdom offered.

The Jacksonian Taxonomy

In clarifying my own terminology, I have attempted to resist taxonomizing the gnomes themselves. The history of scholarship examining gnomic material abounds in categorizations and attempts to circumscribe certain types of gnomes, as exemplified by the Chadwicks' 1932 analysis of the subject, in which they detail two primary gnomic types, the second of which has three sub-types.[16] Jackson constructed his own taxonomy for the Welsh material, which remains influential; Sarah Lynn Higley, for example, extensively discusses the difference between gnome and description, and Nicolas Jacobs adopts the system in his recent edition of the gnomic poems.[17] In such verse, according to this scheme, one may find "human-gnomes" and "nature-gnomes," universal statements about societal affairs and external nature, respectively. These account for gnomes, but there is also a "nature-description," what Jackson describes as an "intrusive element" derived from "nature-poetry" proper, which is a

---

but also the relationship between subject and predicate complement. Since initial mutations are not always marked in Middle Welsh, a pair such as *graenwynn tonn* above, could conceivably be read (in modern orthography) as *graenwyn don*, 'a white-capped wave.'

[16] The Chadwicks' Type I includes gnomes that conform to Aristotle's definition and Type II all those gnomes excluded by the Aristotelian form, see *The Growth of Literature*, 377-80.

[17] Sarah Lynn Higley, *Between Languages: The Uncooperative Text in Early Welsh and Old English Nature Poetry* (University Park, PA: Pennsylvania University Press, 1993), particularly 108-18, wherein Higley adopts the view originally posited by Thomas Parry that a gnome makes a statement that always true, while the description makes a statement "that is true only in a particular circumstance" (at 109).

descriptive statement relating to particulars.[18] Jacobs takes the following englyn from "Claf Abercuawg" as representative of the Jacksonian taxonomy:

> *Gordyar adar; gwlyb gro.*
> *Deil cwydit; divryt divro.*
> *Ny wadaf, wyf claf heno.*

> Clamorous are the birds; wet is the gravel.
> Leaves fall; disconsolate is the man with no
> homeland.
> I do not deny it, I am sick tonight.[19]

According to Jacobs, the first line contains two natural descriptions, the second includes one "nature-gnome" and one "human-gnome," the third is not treated, but exemplifies the sort of elegiac subjectivity typically found in saga englynion or the lyric poems. Semantically, not much distinguishes the natural images in the first line from that of the second–birds make noise, gravel gets wet, and leaves fall. None of these statements is operative all the time, so the distinction between the descriptive and the gnomic breaks down in terms of meaning. There are syntactical distinctions, in that the 'descriptive' statements in line one are pure nominal sentences, whereas the "nature-gnome" in line two includes a subject noun and finite verb. Yet even that formal discrepancy begins to collapse if considered closely, given that the "human-gnome" in line two, *divryt divro*, is also a pure nominal sentence, matching those 'non-gnomes' in the first line. Why should scholars construct and adhere to these categories, then? What is the utility in differentiating the statements in the first line of the englyn from those of the second, except to render them arbitrarily intrusive or irrelevant to the larger work? And if the

---

[18] Most clearly outlined in Jackson, *Early Welsh Gnomic Poems*, 1-2, though Jackson also discusses the intrusion of natural descriptions in Kenneth Jackson, *Studies in Early Celtic Nature Poetry* (Cambridge: The University Press, 1935), 127. Jacobs discusses the relationship between gnomic poetry and natural description in *Early Welsh Gnomic and Nature Poetry*, xxi-xxv.

[19] Here, the edition and translation is that provided by Jacobs in his introduction for illustrative purposes, *Early Welsh Gnomic and Nature Poetry*, xxvii.

suitability of such images within gnomic poetry is asserted, what function do they perform? What work are they doing? Why are they *gnomic*?

Welsh Seasonal/Gnomic Material

Examining the seasonal imagery that appears in gnomic poetry and other genres that assume a gnomic mode may provide some answers. Perhaps the most salient seasonal image that occurs in gnomic poetry, given that an entire sequence relies upon cymeriad of the term, is *Kalangaeaf,* literally 'the first day of winter.'[20] The series appears as part of the cluster of gnomic poetry found in both the Red Book of Hergest of about 1400 as well as Jesus College, Oxford MS 20 of the first half of the fifteenth century, though linguistic evidence points to possible composition dates as early as the eleventh or twelfth centuries.[21] Following the kalangaeaf at the beginning of each englyn, the stanzas include gnomic statements concerning nature, redolent of

---

[20] Jackson takes the sequence as demonstrating the influence of a genre of nature poetry written to mourn the passing of summer, *Early Celtic Nature Poetry*, 159-60. This is Hollantide, a festival celebrated on the first of November, a counterpart to Irish *Samain* and Cornish Allantide, typically construed as the beginning of the winter season, James MacKillop, "Hollantide," in *A Dictionary of Celtic Mythology* (Oxford: Oxford University Press, 2004). The term contains the elements *kalan*, derived from Late Latin *calandae* 'calends,' and *gaeaf,* the Welsh seasonal term denoting winter. This appears to be an ancient word rather than a learned ecclesiastical derivation, as Jackson argues, "The use of the of the word *Kalan* in the Welsh poems is no argument for derivation from learned calendars, for the word was borrowed into Welsh in the Romano-British period, just as in the continental May songs where *Kalendas Mayas* and *Chalenda Maia* come from the popular Latin of Roman Gaul," *Early Celtic Nature Poetry*, 170.

[21] For an overview of the Red Book *englynion*, see Jenny Rowland, "The Manuscript Tradition of the Red Book *Englynion*," *Studia Celtica* 18 (1983): 79-95. For a reconsideration of the sequencing of the englynion, see David Callander, "Trefn Canu Llywarch Hen yn Llyfr Coch Hergest," *Llên Cymru* 38 (2015), 1-11. For more on the manuscripts, see Daniel Huws, *A Repertory of Welsh Manuscripts and Scribes, c. 800-1800*, Vol. I: Manuscripts (Aberystwyth: National Library of Wales and University of Wales Centre for Advanced Welsh and Celtic Studies, 2022), 738-9 (Jesus College, Oxford MS 20) and 741-2 (Red Book of Hergest).

the winter season, alongside social mores. A few englynion from the middle of the sequence are representative:

> *Kalangayaf, kalet cras;*
> *purdu bran, buan [e]vras;*
> *am gwymp hen chwerddit gwen gwas.*

> *Kalangaeaf, cul kerwyt;*
> *gwae wann pan syrr; byrr vyd byt;*
> *gwir, gwell hegarwch no phryt.*

> *Kalangayaf, llwm godeith;*
> *aradyr yn rych, ych yg gweith;*
> *or kant odit kedymdeith.*

> First day of winter, hard (is) the dry vegetation;
> jet-black (is) the raven, swift (is) the one in their
>   prime;
> at the fall of an old one, the smile of a youth
>   turns to laughter.

> First day of winter, thin (are) the stags;
> woe when the weak one takes offense; the world
>   will be ephemeral;
> true, better (is) graciousness than comeliness.

> First day of winter, bare (is) the ground
>   for burning;
> plough in the furrow, the ox at work;
> out of one hundred a companion is a rare thing.[22]

Following the logic that an utterance or observation about a specific day or period is disqualified from being a gnome, a sequence that continually evokes a specific day, Calan Gaeaf, the first of November, would fall squarely into the category of 'nature-description.' However, the form of the poem pushes against that assumption. The recurring cymeriad of the term and the accretion, over time, of images redolent of the winter season–the thin stag, a common appearance in gnomic poetry, the dried vegetation, the bare

---

[22] Jacobs, *Early Welsh Gnomic and Nature Poetry*, 13, st. 7-9.

ground–convey precisely the opposite sense.[23] This is not the image of a singular first day of winter, but the general state of that season, the hardships that it brings and the way that it affects the landscape and its inhabitants. This sense, borne out in the imagery of the poem, is also reinforced by the persistence of the pure nominal construction that recurs throughout these verses. The lack of an overt copula separates these expressions from the sort of descriptive definitiveness ascribed to nature imagery and imbues them with a sense of gnomic timelessness. The conceptual space between discrete englynion fosters this feeling of temporal recurrence. From one stanza to the next, a whole year may progress conceptually in the mind of a reader or listener, taking them from spring to summer and then back again to the first day of winter with the arrival of each kalangaeaf. By mingling all of these formal and imagistic details, the poem constructs its own seasonality. Just as in lived experience, Kalangaeaf and the season it inaugurates consistently come again as part of the yearly cycle, always immanent and anticipated no matter when, in the year, one might consider it.

This sense of recurrence infuses what might be classified as 'nature-descriptions' with gnomic force, affording them the same broad applicability as the truism in 9c, that a good friend is a rare thing. It is in such juxtapositions that gnomic poetry finds its most generative expression. Next to a gnome regarding the appearance of ravens, *purdu bran*, is a gnome about the ability and vitality of youth and then, in the following line, a statement that speaks to the nature of youth; adjacent to the formulaic winter image of the thin stags are a number of gnomes related to human society, underscored by the word beginning 8c, *gwir*, 'true' or 'truth'; and one may find similar statements abutting one another throughout the verses of the sequence. No matter the type or the referent, each gnome reinforces the other: just as winter must come again, bringing thin stags, dry vegetation, and bare ground, the comments on youth, graciousness, and friendship are presented as equally true and apparent. Likewise, the traditions and mores of the social world are as immanent and graspable as the

---

[23] The image of the thin stag, for example, appears throughout "Llym Awel" and "Eiry Mynyd," such that this evocative representation of the winter season may be regarded as a trope characteristic of the Welsh gnomic material.

experience of interacting with external nature. Each sort of statement might be said to activate the other, awakening them to their gnomic quality: take away the social statements, and the only thing remaining is straightforward natural description; excise the nature gnomes and the audience is left with a list of trite axioms unsupported by the force of seasonal recurrence.

"Kalangaeaf", then, exemplifies the generative relationship between gnomes that describe natural phenomena and those that reflect the values and wisdom of the early Welsh poet. The interplay of these aspects *creates* gnomic poetry, with the sense of seasonal recurrence reflecting and reinforcing the temporal ever-present conveyed by the formal characteristics of the verse. A variant of "Kalangaeaf", called by Jacobs "Calan Gaef a'r Misoedd," that appears in the collection known as Englynion Duad seems to confirm such an interpretation.[24] Despite the early modern manuscript provenance of the sequence, both Jacobs and Jenny Rowland, in her work on the sequence, point out that the text may be older than the sequence in the Red Book due to some linguistic archaisms and conservative verse features.[25] This sequence presents a valuable point of comparison given the composition of these stanzas. They begin with verses redolent of the series found in the Red Book:

> *Kulan gauaf yw henoeth;*
> *cul ewig, elwig rhygoeth;*
> *daiar ffrwd, <ac> eir[wn]g pob noeth.*
>
> *Calan gauaf, <c>alaf clyd;*
> *t[w]n to das, rhyfelfawr rhyd;*
> *rhybudd i ddrwch, ni weryd.*

---

[24] Englynion Duad is a diverse collection including gnomic poetry and more moralistic, prescriptive verse found in two early modern manuscripts, NLW MS Peniarth 102 and BL Add MS 31055, for more on which see Jenny Rowland, "Englynion Duad," *Journal of Celtic Studies* 3 (1981-2): 51-87; Jacobs treats the Kalangaeaf variant, which he calls "Calan Gaeaf a'r Misoedd", in his edition of the gnomic poetry (*Early Welsh Gnomic and Nature Poetry*, 13-6), as well as in an earlier article, "Englynion Calan Gaeaf a'r Misoedd o 'Englynion Duad,'" *Studia Celtica* 36 (2002), 73-88.
[25] Rowland, "Englynion Duad," 64-5; Jacobs, *Early Welsh Gnomic and Nature Poetry*, 52.

The first day of winter is tonight;
thin (is) the hind, prosperous (is) the
  excellent one;
solid (is) the stream, and every destitute one
  is deserving.

The first day of winter, sheltered reeds;
broken (is) the roof's thatch, turbulent (is)
  the ford;
a warning to the incorrigible, it does not avail.[26]

However, as the englynion progress, a sudden shift occurs from the general seasonality rooted in the idea of the first day of winter to more specific monthly expressions. A number of stanzas replace the repeated term kalangaeaf with a new formula: *calan*, ultimately from Latin *kalendae*, the first day of the month in Roman temporal reckoning, followed by the name of a particular month. The eighth and ninth stanzas of the sequence exemplify the shift:

> *Calan Tachwedd, twym\<n\> ennaint;*
> *ni nawd difenwir cywraint;*
> *ni bydd dyvn (duun) hun a haint.*

> *Calan Ionawr, pesgitawr gorwydd;*
> *gnawd awel i golofn;*
> *ni bydd dialwr diofn.*

The first day of November, hot (is) the bath;
it is not usual for a skillful one to be slandered;
there will not be sleep and sickness together.

The first day of January, a horse is fed;
Typical (is) the wind on the peak;
an avenger will not be without fear.[27]

Beyond the substitution of the initial term, here exchanged for notices of the arrivals of November and January, the verses proceed in a manner expected of such sequences, as the poet provided gnomic natural images associated with the specific month juxtaposed with social observances.

---

[26] Jacobs, *Early Welsh Gnomic and Nature Poetry*, 13-4, stt. 1-2.
[27] Ibid., 14, st. 8-9.

Rather than readings of any individual gnomes, more pertinent to the matter at hand is the appearance of a nearly complete set of monthly stanzas in the middle of a Kalangaeaf sequence. My own assertion here assumes an order of operations that is far from secure given that nothing can be said for certain regarding the development of these stanzas, especially their precise dates of composition. However, as has been postulated by Rowland, this does appear to be a composite sequence.[28] Within Englynion Duad, the collection in which this series appears, a series of seven Calan gaeaf stanzas occurs, followed by eleven stanzas dedicated to all of the months, in order, with the exception of December, and then an additional Calan gaeaf englyn. It appears that the monthly stanzas have been dropped right into the middle of an already-circulating gnomic sequence.[29] Such a chronology seems to be supported by the appearance of three Calan gaeaf stanzas with direct analogues from the collection in the Red Book:

(P 102) 3.
Calan gauaf, cal[et] cras;
du plu bran, gnawd buan bras;
am gwymp hen chwerddid gwen gwas.

(RH) 7.
Kalangayaf, kalet cras;
purdu bran, buan [e]vras;
am gwymp hen chwerdit gwen gwas.

(P 102) 4.
Calan gauaf, llwm goddaith;
aradr yn rhych, ych yngwaith;
odid o'r cant cydymddaith.

---

[28] Rowland, "Englynion Duad," 67-9.
[29] Indeed, this seems to be the case with other gnomic sequences. For example, it has been observed that the survival of various redactions of the Bidiau (including a potential version of the poem in the hand of Gutun Owain, for more on which see Ben Guy, "A Lost Medieval Manuscript from North Wales: Hengwrt 33, The *Hanesyn Hên*," *Studia Celtica* 40 (2016): 69-105) point to a period of oral circulation of various versions before they were ultimately copied.

(RH) 9.
Kalangayaf, llwm godeith;
aradyr yn rych, ych yg gweith;
or kant odit kedymdeith.

(P 102) 19.
Calan gauaf, llwm blaen gwrysg;
gnawd o ben diriaid terfysg;
yn y bo dawn y bydd dysg.

(RH) 4.
Kalangayaf, crwm blaen gwrysc;
gnawt o benn dirieit teruysc;
lle ny bo dawn ny byd dysc.[30]

Jacobs points out that it is impossible to say which series might precede the other.[31] Yet this consonance attests to the possibility of various gnomic englynion associated with Kalangaeaf circulating in medieval Wales, perhaps orally, some of which were copied into the Red Book and some of which were copied into the manuscript source for Peniarth 102, with some overlap and reordering.

Issues of influence and precedence deserve additional attention, but in considerations of the ways that the seasonal image constructs meaning in the gnomic englynion, the insertion of an almost complete accounting of the months of the year into an Kalangaeaf series in much the same gnomic styleis particularly significant. This act of accretion may provide valuable insight into how the gnomic sequences were received and understood by contemporary poets. In this case, perhaps whoever inserted the monthly englynion understood the sequence as a meditation on recurrent seasonality rather than a corrupted amalgamation of descriptions of external nature and sententious remarks. This seems particularly apparent in the sequencing of the stanzas: the first monthly englyn begins Calan Tachwedd, the same date of Kalangaeaf, and then proceeds through all of the months (with the exception of December), so they may slot in between any two

---

[30] The editions are taken from Jacobs, *Early Welsh Gnomic and Nature Poetry*, 11-16, though they have been rearranged in order to illustrate the various resonances.
[31] Jacobs, *Early Welsh Gnomic and Nature Poetry*, 52.

kalangaeaf englynion. In doing so, this later poet rendered the cyclicality and recurrence that was implicit in the verse–the gaps between stanzas, the repetitive winter images, the gnomic temporalities–explicit by inserting an unbroken procession through the months of year between two Calan Gaeaf occurrences. In this expansion of the material, the poet underscores the core seasonal and gnomic message; that sense of being locked in the endless, immanent cycle of time, while also expanding and re-inscribing it: not only may an audience look forward to an endless cycle of winters, but also an infinite concatenation of Novembers, Aprils, and Augusts, as well.

A short poem found in a sixteenth-century manuscript, NLW, Peniarth 182 may represent another contemporary path that such poetry took.[32] The work consists of only three eight-line stanzas, which begin Neud Kalan Ionawr, Neud Kalan Mehevin, and Neud Kalan Tachwedd. The unique composition of the verse may be apprehended with attention to its first stanza.

Neud Kalan Ionawr iaenuawr kras
Neud amdud llynniav lliuvawr gwyrddlas
Grandines ymber super terras
Neud tremyn aper inter siluas
Pericklid homo per pecunias
Nid ydyw yn bryd man y mae addas
A chennym oes bresswyl pwyllad yn vas
Mor vychod vydd in oes mors rydadlas.

It is the first of January, hard and large (is) the
   ice-sheet,
covered (are) the lakes, many-hued, bluish-green;
a shower of hail upon the lands.
A wild boar wanders among the woods.
Man was brought into danger on account of wealth;
Our intent is not where it is fitting;

---

[32] The poem was brought to light by the short study and edition of Graham Thomas, "An Early Welsh Seasonal Poem," *Bulletin of the Board of Celtic Studies* 34 (1987): 61-5. Jacobs added it to the corpus of gnomic poetry edited as *Neud Kalan Ionawr* in *Early Welsh Gnomic and Nature Poetry*, 25-6.

and we shall have eternal life, it is basely thought,
death has determined how short our life will be.[33]

The set has its own formal peculiarities and ambiguities that make translation difficult, as is apparent above. First, and perhaps most obviously, these lines are not written in the typical three- or four-line englyn meters associated with gnomic poetry. Rather, each stanza consists of eight lines of nine syllables, all of which share a single end-rhyme. These eight lines are also rigidly structured, divided in half formally and conceptually, with the initial set rendering natural imagery related to the relevant month and the second providing a few lines of moralizing, didactic wisdom at odds with the more descriptive ontological 'wisdom' proffered by the gnomic englynion. Additionally, and rather distinctively, the poem is macaronic, interposing Welsh and Latin in various lines, though words from each language participate in the sort of metrical ornamentation typical of Welsh poetic composition.

Yet even in this distinctive sequence, as we move further away from gnomic poetry into a more hybrid form, the relationship between the natural image and the sententious statement remains integral. If this fragment represents some separate reflex of the gnomic tradition represented by the Kalangaeaf sequence, these stanzas may reflect the reaction of another medieval person to that tradition. Based on orthography, the editor of the poem, Graham Thomas, supposes that an early twelfth-century composition date for the poem would not be unreasonable.[34] If so, these stanzas would be roughly contemporary with the Red Book's Kalangaeaf verses as well as the series included in Englynion Duad. There is nothing to be said for certain about which of these three poems may have come first or the relationship of these texts with one another. Yet we might imagine a similar origin for these stanzas as for "Calan Gaeaf a'r Misoedd": perhaps a poet familiar with some Kalangaeaf sequence wrote these monthly stanzas, possibly in

---

[33] Jacobs, *Early Welsh Gnomic and Nature Poetry*, 25-6.
[34] Thomas, "An Early Welsh Seasonal Poem," 60-1, given that he identifies orthographical features consistent with the Black Book of Camarthen as well as Welsh texts in earlier manuscripts like the Juvencus englynion.

an ecclesiastical context given the presence of Latin in the verses.[35] In the modulation between descriptions of the individual month and the didactic/moralistic statements–here formally embedded in the structure of the stanza–it seems that the poet did not deem it appropriate to separate entirely the cyclical processes of nature from human wisdom. The relationship between these elements, however drastically transformed, remains integral.

Conclusion

Each of these seasonal or monthly poems insists upon the integral connection between states of nature and social norms and customs. The seasonal image represents an overt expression of the sorts of temporalities and references to habitual occurrence integral to the form of gnomic poetry. Examining possible contemporary reactions to the Kalangaeaf sequence demonstrates that medieval audiences of such poetry understood this relationship and re-inscribed it, rendering it more overt in their own work. Their readings echo across the centuries and tell modern scholars that neither natural image nor social gnome is irrelevant or intrusive. Rather, they coexist in a generative relationship necessary in the sort of expressions posited by gnomic poetry.

---

[35] If an ecclesiastical context is assumed, perhaps versified liturgical calendars were an influence as well.

The Juvencus Englynion: Text, Co-text, Intertext

Fay Slakey

Introduction

The Juvencus Englynion are best known as a linguistic object, being among the very first still extant witnesses to the Welsh language. Prior to the ninth century, Welsh is materially a paratextual tongue or a contextual one, whose cultural wealth we can only theorize about, and painstakingly reconstruct from precious marginal crumbs and inscriptions. The englynion found bordering Juvencus' *Evangeliorum Libri Quattuor* are the first traces of Welsh that carry the substance of self-contained meaning: neither glosses nor proper names, neither funerary nor boundary markers, but two poems. However, as they are both short pieces, apparently truncated and difficult to decipher due to the physical degradation of the manuscript, they have most often been read either for linguistic information and examples, or with a comparative approach seeking to highlight potential intertexts in the tradition of Irish poetry, Insular theology, and Christian liturgy.[1] Reading with an eye for intertextual links between our poems and other extant medieval pieces is clearly of great import in cases such as that of the Juvencus manuscript: if a connection can be proved, or even convincingly suggested, some light may be cast on difficult or obscure verses and expressions. However, this kind of reading has an obvious pitfall, in that historicization is rarely a straightforward endeavour in this early period. Contact between Ireland and Wales in the ninth century may be an accepted fact, but in the granular matters of textual interaction, little can ever be proved with certainty, and it is generally possible to dispute a potential link by pointing out that a contradictory element might well have existed in the massive body of lost manuscripts. In the case of the Juvencus Englynion, there is one intertext whose connection to the poems cannot be disputed, very simply because it exists within the same manuscript, as the Englynion's co-text.

---

[1] Patrick Sims-Williams, *Irish Influence on Medieval Welsh Literature* (Oxford, 2011), pp. 30-39.

The following study reads the Juvencus Englynion as a part of their material environment, taking methodological inspiration from Patrick K. Ford's work on Irish marginal poems from the same period.[2] By considering the physical object and the many sedimented layers of text it offers us, the tension between the page's centre and its margins may help to sharpen our understanding of difficult poems, written in a densely polysemic language that says much in few words. To co-text and possible intertexts we turn, and seek to understand what is the link, if any, between the englynion and the text they came to border. Progression through the object's many layers must be methodical, but in the interest of time and space, the greater part of this article will focus on the longer chain of englynion, as it has more to tell us of the modalities of its inscription than its shorter companion, the Juvencus Three.

The manuscript

Cambridge University Library Ms Ff.4.42 was copied in the ninth century and glossed over the following two centuries by up to thirteen scribes. It was recently digitized and is entirely available online.[3] The manuscript's parchment is of poor quality, bearing several holes that must have been there from the calf, and a number of stains caused in part by the humidity it was exposed to in the intervening centuries. A first set of seven scribes, named A to G, was described by Henry Bradshaw in the nineteenth century.[4] The authority of his codicological analysis holds to this day, having for the most part been only expanded, not fundamentally questioned.[5] The chronology of

---

[2] Patrick K. Ford, "Blackbirds, Cuckoos and Infixed Pronouns, Another Context for Early Irish Nature Poetry," in *Celtic Connections: Proceedings of the Tenth International Congress of Celtic Studies, volume 1, Language, Literature, History, Culture*, ed. Ronald Black, William Gillies and Roibeard Ó Maolalaigh (East Linton, 1999), pp. 162-70.

[3] Cambridge, Cambridge University Library MS Ff.4.42 "Christian Works: Cambridge Juvencus," University of Cambridge Digital Library, accessed 05/25/2023, https://cudl.lib.cam.ac.uk/view/MS-FF-00004-00042/6.

[4] Henry Bradshaw, *Collected Papers* (Cambridge: 1889).

[5] Michael Lapidge is the first to have suggested there may be more scribes than the initial seven, based solely on the examination of the Latin language glosses. Michael Lapidge, "The Study of Latin Texts in Late Anglo-Saxon

scribal additions indicates that glossing happened from the ninth century, as early as the copying of the main text, and until the eleventh century. There were at least as many phases of glossing as there were scribes, and it is probable that each scribe's campaign can be split into several smaller phases. The scribe Bradshaw called A, the earliest and main scribe responsible for copying the manuscript's principal textual layer, signed his name at the end of the text. The colophon in question reads *araut dinuadu*, which is Old Welsh for "a prayer for Núadu".[6] McKee describes Núadu's hand as "set minuscule of an unusually monumental form", quite distinct from most examples of insular script of the same period.[7] It is unusual even within the narrower scope of early Welsh script to which it has been related.[8]

The manuscript's heavy trilingual glossing (in Latin, Old Irish, and Old Welsh) registers a slightly higher frequency of miscopied Welsh words than Irish words, which indicates that the manuscript was likely copied by some Irish scribes, like A, E and G, as well as some Welsh scribes, like B, who were all working in the same place

---

England. I. The Evidence of Latin Glosses," in *Latin and the Vernacular Languages in Early Medieval Britain,* ed. Nicholas Brooks (Leicester: Leicester University Press, 1982), 99-140.

[6] This Irish name signed in Old Welsh points to monastic migrations from Ireland to Wales in this period. Nancy Edwards, "Early Medieval Wales: material evidence and identity," *Studia Celtica,* 51 (2017): 65-87. https://doi.org/10.16922/SC.51.2. See "Irish Identities," 16-24. It is worth pointing out, however, that there are other possible explanations for this colophon than that of an Irish person working in Wales. It might have been a case of adoption in Wales of Irish naming practises or the nickname of a Welsh scribe familiar with Irish tales. See, Helen McKee, *The Cambridge Juvencus manuscript glossed in Latin, Old Welsh, and Old Irish: text and commentary* (Aberystwyth: CMCS Publications, 2000), 20, 21. The most probable explanation remains the most straightforward: that of an Irish scribe working in Wales.

[7] McKee, *Cambridge Juvencus manuscript,* 9.

[8] McKee, *Cambridge Juvencus manuscript,* 1. "Although it is almost unanimously agreed to that the Cambridge Juvencus was written by an Irishman, its script seems often to have been viewed as generically Welsh."

during the tenth century.[9] In light of this Harvey suggests that the everyday language used in this monastery would have been Latin:

> A monastery located in Wales, but in which the everyday tongue was Latin, would seem to fit the bill. On this view one can see how guest monks could come to participate fully in the life and work of the house, and to be trained in the scriptorium there, while remaining ignorant of the language of the country.[10]

The Cambridge Juvencus manuscript is therefore a witness to the frequency of interactions between monasteries in Britain and Ireland in this period, that would have made Latin a living tongue of necessity. It must not however have been a pristine *lingua franca*, and instead intermingled with those words of Irish or Welsh that were recognizable in the other vernacular or made familiar by the frequency of their use. It is therefore apparent from the detail of its pages that this manuscript was produced in a multilingual context, marked by a

---

[9] McKee, *Cambridge Juvencus manuscript*, 68-70. She cites Anthony Harvey's study in "The Cambridge Juvencus Glosses" (see below): "His [n.b. : Scribe E] gloss reads conabula .i. mapbrith .i. onnou. The vernacular portion of this may be compared with a gloss in the Oxford Ovid: in cunis: mapbrethinnou. Mapbrethinnou must be the word that *mapbrith .i. onnou* is meant to represent: a compound consisting of *map* 'child' plus the plural of *brethyn* 'cloth'. Scribe E would appear to have become confused while copying his gloss: perhaps he wrote mapbrith thinking of *brith* 'speckled', and was then left with *innou*, to be interpreted as *.i. onnou* (a plural of *onn* 'ash-tree'?). This scenario would certainly suggest that he knew Welsh, although it is of course possible that his exemplar already contained the mistake." McKee points out however that both E and G made mistakes in their Irish and Latin glossing work, and that it is therefore quite possible that they could have made mistakes in their own native tongues, whatever they may be, meaning the miscopied words cannot be certainly attributed to lack of familiarity with Welsh.

[10] Anthony Harvey, "The Cambridge Juvencus Glosses–Evidence of Hiberno-Welsh Literary Interaction?," in *Language Contact in the British Isles, Proceedings of the Eighth International Symposium on Language Contact in Europe*, Douglas, Isle of Man, 1988, ed. P. Sture Ureland and George Broderick (Tübingen: Niemeyer, 1991), 194.

plurality of lived, everyday tongues that included Latin. Multiple idioms coexisted at every level of the linguistic experience, in what appears to be a symbiotic environment rather than a strictly competitive one. There could be nothing more natural in such a polyglot space than for the barriers between an oral tradition and a written one to begin to break down, little by little, each acquiring traits of the other. Latin, a language of written literature, might serve for everyday concerns, and Welsh literature, primarily oral, might become clothed in the materiality of text.

The Main Text: Juvencus' biblical epic

The main textual layer in this manuscript is *Evangeliorum Libri Quattuor* (hereafter *ELQ*) composed in the fourth century by a little-known figure named Gaius Vettius Aquilinus Juvencus. Jerome makes at least five direct references to him, informing us that he was a priest of Spanish nationality, born to a very noble family, who wrote under the emperor Constantine.[11] His seminal and sole extant work consists in a rendering of the life of Jesus in dactylic hexameter, the meter of epic, and in a style very reminiscent of the *Aeneid*. Jerome describes Juvencus's work by saying that "he did not fear to subject the majesty of the Gospel to the laws of metre."[12] This suggests that there was some question in this period as to whether the enterprise of telling

---

[11] Juvencus himself makes a topical reference to Constantine in his epilogue, praising him as merciful ruler. Gregory of Tours, in a historiographical comment on Jerome's comments on Juvencus, further specifies that *ELQ* was composed at the explicit request of Constantine, but there is no mention of this in Jerome's works, and a sufficient temporal gap between Gregory and Juvencus that we ought not take this to be certain. See Gregory of Tours, *Historia Francorum, I, 36,* in *Scriptores Rerum Merovingicarum*, vol. 1, ed. W. Arndt (Hanover: Hahn, 1884), 51. "From the twenty-first year of his reign, the priest Jerome made an entry, mentioning that the priest Juvencus wrote the Gospels in verse, at the request of the aforesaid Emperor." Quoted in M. A. Norton, "Prosopography of Juvencus," in *Leaders of Iberian Christianity (50–650 AD),* ed J.M.F. Marique (Boston: St. Paul editions, 1950), 115.

[12] Jerome, "Epistola LXX ad Magnum Oratorem Urbis Romae, ch. 5," in *Corpus Scriptorum Ecclesiasticorum Latinorum (CSEL)*, vol. 54, ed. J. Hilberg (Vienna: F. Tempsky and Leipzig: G. Freytag, 1910): 707. Quoted in Norton, "Prosopography," 115.

FAY SLAKEY

Christ's story in the style of a pre-Christian text was entirely appropriate, as Jerome implies that to do it would naturally incur in most people some amount of fear. On the other hand, Lactantius had raised the problem, some years before the composition of *ELQ*, that scripture was not being read by the powerful because of its plain style and suggested that a solution would be to give the story of Christ the advantage of classical *ornamenta*.[13] This opinion evidently had a direct impact on Juvencus, as shown by Green and Sandnes, while it is possible that Jerome's more nuanced position on the matter might not even have occurred to him.[14]

The genre of the biblical epic, which *ELQ* inaugurates, bears traits that mark it out as intrinsically medieval in a fascinating way. It has faded out of the common canon of medieval texts because it answers endogenous, period-specific concerns that have not resonated with readers since the Renaissance. Its ties to the literature of Antiquity make it a striking example of classical reception in the medieval period, when the imperative to learn good Latin ran up against the necessity of avoiding pagan morals.[15] The biblical epic solved this contradiction by combining holy history with proper language. Juvencus' text is replete with the style and expressions of pagan classics, containing numerous direct references to various classical masterpieces such as those of Ovid, Lucian and most importantly Vergil. Indeed, approximately ninety-five percent of *ELQ*

---

[13] Lactantius, *L. Caeli Firmiani Lactanti Opera Omnia*, in *CSEL* 19, ed. S. Brandt and G. Laubmann (Prague: Vienna, and Leipzig, 1890) and Lactantius. *L. Caeli Firmiani Lactanti Opera Omnia I-II*, in *CSEL* 27 ed. S. Brandt and G. Laubmann (Prague: F. Tempsky, Vienna: F. Tempsky, and Leipzig: G. Freytag, 1927). See sections 5.1.15 and 1.1.10. Quoted in McGill, *Evangeliorum,* 23.
[14] R.P.H. Green, *Latin Epics of the New Testament: Juvencus Sedulius Arator* (Oxford: Oxford University Press, 2006) and K. O. Sandnes, *The Gospel "According to Homer and Virgil": Cento and Canon* (Leiden and Boston: Brill, 2007). Quoted in McGill, Evangeliorum, 23.
[15] J. M. Ziolkowski, "Epic", in *Medieval Latin. An Introduction and Bibliographical Guide*, ed. Mantello (Washington D.C.: Catholic University of America Press, 1996), 547-555.

Book 1's vocabulary is Vergilian in origin, and beyond lexical influence, there are also many stylistic borrowings.[16]

Juvencus' text stands at the cusp of Antiquity and the Middle Ages: it is the direct descendant of foundational works of the Ancient World and was considered of their number by later authors.[17] For ninth and tenth century scribes and scholars, it would have embodied comfort, ease and the fortunate alliance of good Latin and acceptable textual material. The Cambridge Juvencus manuscript with its utilitarian qualities, having been a space of direct and unhindered textual encounter for more than a dozen scribes, represents this aspect of its main textual layer. Of this layer, only the Preface will be discussed further in the following pages, as it provides the readiest point of comparison from which to analyse the Old Welsh poems in its margins.[18]

The Englynion

The two poems, inscribed in the margins of this text and which constitute the earliest witnesses of Welsh literary tradition, are named the Juvencus Nine and the Juvencus Three by a process of metonymy. They are so called because they take the form of chains of *englynion*, a poetic form consisting of short stanzas called *englyn* in the singular. In its first incarnations, the englyn counts three lines for a total of

---

[16] McBrine cites the storm on the sea of Galilee, described in much the same way as Vergil tends to describe tempests, and a speech where Jesus warns the people against Hell that is very reminiscent of Aeneas' descent into Tartarus. Patrick McBrine, "Juvencus' Euangeliorum Libri Quattuor (c. 330 CE)," in *Biblical Epics in Late Antiquity and Anglo-Saxon England: Divina in Laude Voluntas* (Toronto: University of Toronto Press, 2017), 22-56.

[17] Braulio, bishop of Saragossa from 631 to 651, introduces a quote from *ELQ* in the following words: "In the very elegant words of one of the ancient poets." See Braulio, *Vita Sancti Aemiliani*, in *Patrologiae Cursus Completus*, Series Latina, ed. J. P. Migne (Paris: Jacques-Paul Migne, 1844, 1864), vol. 50, col. 702. Quoted in Norton, "Prosopography," 116. Similarly, Eulogius of Toledo, in the first half of the 9th century, refers to Juvencus as "the philosopher," which rings more of classical texts than medieval, and multiple references to him as one of "the poets" produce a similar effect. See Norton, "Prosopography," 114-120.

[18] Full text of the Preface and translation in Annex I.

twenty-one syllables, but in the eleventh century four-line englynion become more popular and begin to replace the three-line poem, which allows for their dating, to a degree.[19] As three lines is a very short space in which to build narrative or argument, poets chained englynion to one another, building chains that could span full sagas.[20] It is perhaps not quite accurate to refer to each englyn in a chain as a stanza, as there can be metrical variation from one englyn to the next even when they share an overarching plotline or topic. They are individual poems that have a symbiotic relationship with each other. Thus, it is possible that the two chains extant in the manuscript are not complete.

The two poems are written in one hand, that of the scribe referred to as C by Bradshaw. They are also responsible for some Latin glosses mainly restricted to f. 2r-v, as well as at least one Latin poem in dactylic hexameter on f. 55v. This last poem has provided some clues as to the possible dating of Scribe C's work, being generally concerned with a person named Féthgna who was saved by Christ from a dreadful plague.[21] The mention in the Annals of Ulster of a bishop by the same name who died in CE874 has led scholars to settle on dating Scribe C's work to the end of the ninth or the beginning of the tenth century. This coincides elegantly with the palaeographic features of C's hand, which are on occasion archaic and at other times rather more fitting of

<hr/>

[19] Jenny Rowland, *Early Welsh Saga Poetry, a study and edition of the englynion* (Cambridge: D.S. Brewer, 1990).
[20] Rowland, *Saga*. See also Patrick K. Ford, *The Poetry of Llywarch Hen, Introduction, Text and Translation* (Berkeley, Los Angeles, London: University of California Press, 1974).
[21] The rarity of the name Féthgna, which only appears elsewhere in the Annals of Ulster (the entry for AD 874 records the death of a bishop of Armagh named Féthgna), has been used to suggest that the two occurrences refer to the same person. Further supporting this theory is the mention in the Annals of Ulster of a great pestilence recorded about fifty years before the bishop's death. S. Mac Airt and G. Mac Niocaill, *The Annals of Ulster (to A.D. 1131)* (Dublin: Dublin Institute for Advanced Studies, 1983).

tenth century practices.[22] C's abbreviations, furthermore, generally tend to be more conservative.[23]

As concerns the manuscript's internal chronology, C is one of the earliest glossators to have annotated the Cambridge Juvencus. This is clear at least from the organisation of the hexameters on f. 55v, where another Latin poem composed by Scribe D is organized in such a way that it was clearly written at a later date. As for scribe C's origin, the act of copying Old Welsh poems could suggest a Welsh origin, but by that logic, the act of copying a Latin poem on a person bearing an Irish name who might have been an important Irish bishop, could also suggest an Irish one. McKee makes an interesting remark on the habits of C:

> (C seems to have felt most at ease writing in a margin, as on ff. 25v-26v: where one was not available, he may be observed to have written at the very top of the page, as on f. 1r, or on one side of the page, as on f. 55v.)[24]

This parenthetical remark highlights C's taste for the manuscript's marginal spaces and must be connected to the fact that although the scribe interacted with the whole manuscript, inscribing a poem on f. 55v., the vast majority of C's work is limited to the folio bearing the preface to *ELQ*. This supports our own attempt to think of the Juvencus Englynion as resulting from a dynamic interaction with the manuscript, shaped by the various habits and idiosyncrasies a

---

[22] Where Bradshaw considered that their hand is probably no later in date than the second half of the 9th century, T. A. M. Bishop describes it as being "a square minuscule," a characteristic that points to the 10th century. See T. A. M. Bishop, "The Corpus Martianus Capella," *Transactions of the Cambridge Bibliographical Society* 4, (1967): 258.

[23] McKee, *Cambridge*, 17. "Finally we may note that C's script (unlike B's) displays Late Celtic features–his suspension for -um contains a 'bird-silhouette' u (*merobiliorum* f. 2r17, and we also see one on f. 55v)–but his abbreviations are not all modern, for he favoured Insular rather than Continental *per* (appearing independently on f. 2r16 and in the old Insular abbreviation for *propter* on f. 2r19)."

[24] McKee, *Cambridge*, 18.

scribe would develop into something we might call a *style of encounter*.

The Juvencus Three

The Juvencus Three appear on folios 25v to 26v, in three single lines along the top of each page. They were cut out of the manuscript by the antiquarian Edward Lhuyd (1660-1709), in a fit of excitement at having found Old Welsh poems (he labels them "Hen Vrithonaeg", Old British, in pencil along the top of the page). This was a matter of understandable consternation to many scholars until the second half of the twentieth century, when the strips were restored to their original place. The poem's subject matter is profane and reads as the following:

Niguorcosam nemheunaur henoid Mitelu nit gurmaur Mi am (franc) dam ancalaur.	I shall not talk even for one hour tonight, My retinue is not very large, I and my Frank, round our cauldron.
Nicananiguardam nicusam henoid Cet iben med nouel Mi amfranc dam anpatel.	I shall not sing, I shall not laugh, I shall not jest to-night, Though we drank clear mead, I and my Frank, round our bowl.
Namercit mi nep leguenid henoid Is discirr micoueidid Dou nam riceus unguetid.[25]	Let no-one ask me for merriment tonight; Mean is my company. Two lords can talk: one speaks. [26]

Table 1: transcription and translation of the Juvencus Three.

---

[25] Ifor Williams, *The Beginnings of Welsh Poetry*, ed. R. Bromwich (Cardiff: University of Wales Press, 1980), 90.
[26] Ibid.

This poem's meter is mainly *englyn penfyr*, meaning that it consists of a *toddaid byr*, which refers to a specific organisation of the first two lines in which generally the second line contains six syllables and has at its cesura the previous line's final word, followed in final position by a seven syllable line and containing the same rhyme in each line.[27] It bears little relation to the epic meter of *ELQ*, although as established, englynion can be used to recount full sagas.[28] This description is not intended to serve as solid ground for analysis, as there appears to be little overlap between the Latin dactylic hexameter of *ELQ* and the above-described Welsh meter. The detailing of the chain's metrical specificities does, however, give a sense of how complex Welsh poetic meters already were in this early period. Although we may doubt that there exists a direct relationship between the meters of the main textual layer and that of the poems, such a degree of complexity in the first attestations of Welsh literature points to an extensive prior tradition, and a probable longevity of the Welsh vernacular tradition. These englynion, far from being the first act of creation in the vernacular language, are more probably an early witness of scribes intuiting the written word's potential, demonstrated presumably by the routine act of copying classical texts. The Juvencus Englynion are probably not the first instance of this new consciousness either, but their fragmentary nature does suggest that they are close to the first.

The profane subject-matter of the Juvencus Three distinguishes itself by departing from the manuscript's principal religious text. This, combined with its short format, the use of an omnipresent lyrical first person, and oblique references to a specific context all contribute to making it an enticing literary object. The speaker has plainly fallen on hard times and feels the loss of what must have been a larger company of people. The present bad fortune is not absolute, since the two still possess some clear mead to drink, but that is clearly only a consolation, and not something that can compensate for the sorrowful situation the speaker is in.

In essence, the Juvencus Three are most reminiscent of early poems such as those of the Heledd cycle, like *Stafell Cynddylan* which

---

[27] Meic Stephens, *The New Companion to the Literature of Wales* (Cardiff: University of Wales Press, 1998), 219.
[28] See Rowland, *Early Welsh Saga Poetry*.

carries similar themes of grief, loss, and loneliness, conveyed also in a mournful first person.[29] These are generally accepted to be among the earliest Welsh poems, dated around the ninth or tenth centuries although they are only preserved in fourteenth-century manuscripts. They tend to carry obscure references to a context that is obviously political in nature, much like the Juvencus Three. As such, they have been used on occasion to formulate theories about what was happening in Wales during the so-called Dark Ages. Of course, extrapolating historical fact from literary material is methodologically dubious. What these texts do provide is a sense of their authors' preoccupations and these are certainly quite political.

The Juvencus Three's immediate co-text is of questionable relevance to the content of the Old Welsh poems. It recounts the part of Christ's story that begins when he is travelling to spread the news of imminent salvation. He meets fishermen Simon and Andrew, and later James and John, and then travels around the Middle East performing miracles, leading to the sermon on the mount. The first englyn along the top of folio 25v has for its immediate context the following passage, which quotes the prophet Isaiah's words:

> Zebulun and the land called Naphtali,
> The way far past the sea through Galilee:
> The tribes and peoples past the Jordan held
> By dark will see a great and sudden light.
> For those residing in the shadow of death,
> Joy rises gleaming with the light of faith.[30]

The clearest link between these lines and the Juvencus Three is the reference to darkness and the shadow of death. The Juvencus Three's first englyn does indeed refer to a mysterious context that may be reminiscent of the tribes and peoples' situation before Christ's coming. However, assuming the impressionistic thought-processes of a scribe who lived a thousand years ago can make for little more than

---

[29] Published in Ifor Williams, *Canu Llywarch Hen* (Cardiff: University of Wales Press, 1935), 35-37. See also Jenny Rowland, *A Selection of Early Welsh Saga Poems* (London: Modern Humanities Research Association, 2014), 7-8.

[30] McGill, *Evangeliorum*, 45.

fanciful interpretations, and these are therefore merely potential intertexts.

Overall, the englynion of the Juvencus Three resist interpretation. They might have some relation to the manuscript's context of production, but nothing can be definitively advanced on that side either. They retain much of their mystery, and as such will certainly continue to be the topic of much speculation. One thing that we can note with a modicum of certainty is the poem's obvious fragmentary nature, suggesting that it was part of a longer chain. This is further supported by the fact that it does not seem to have been composed in these margins, merely copied. It might have been pulled from a still-extant cycle, but considering the heavy losses suffered by high medieval Welsh literature in intervening centuries, it could also be from an entirely distinct cycle of vernacular poetry. Either way, the chain coheres, both in tone and style, with the extant corpus of Welsh poetry from this period. Whatever the reason for their inclusion in Cambridge Juvencus, these short poems in the margin of a classical text are part of a tradition perhaps just as rich as that of Antiquity. We must now turn to the longer chain, which has a greater degree of thematic coherence with the main textual layer of Cambridge Juvencus.

The Juvencus Nine

The Juvencus Nine are so-called because they are a chain of nine englynion, religious in subject, written on the very first folio before the text begins in earnest. They bear little relation to their immediate co-text. The first folio of the Cambridge Juvencus is mainly concerned with recounting the genealogy of the Gospels, leading up to *ELQ* itself, in a style that has little literary merit but does hold a certain fascination. The text on the first folio is a commonplace example of Hiberno-Latin exegesis.[31] It traces the history of the gospels from their composition by each Evangelist and makes certain specific claims about each, for example associating them with specific liquids. This almost synesthetic affiliation is also found elsewhere in such texts as

---

[31] McKee, *Cambridge,* 81.

pseudo-Jerome's *Expositio IV euangeliorum* and the Gospels of Mael Brigte.[32]

Further complicating matters, this first folio of the manuscript appears to be a palimpsest.[33] The ghost of a lower text is evident under the Juvencus Nine, although it is unfortunately unreadable on the digitized manuscript. There are other places in the manuscript that also appear to have undergone at least a partial process of effacement, which is to be expected as it would have been most economical for scribes to reuse what they had on hand as much as possible, especially when it came to classroom texts such as *ELQ*.

For the sake of simplicity, Ifor Williams' transcription and translation have been chosen as the basis for the following analysis, but it must be noted that both Helen McKee and Marged Haycock have produced their own versions of the text.[34] Significant deviations from Williams' text will be noted, but for the most part these do not materially alter the analysis, although due to the text's poor state, it is worth pointing out the difficulty of reaching a full consensus on many readings. Apart from a few interruptions rendered typographically, the Nine read as follows:

Omnipotens auctor tidicones Adiam*r**....	Almighty Creator Thou hast made . . . .
Nit arcup betid hicouid canlou Cet treidin guel haguid T**e – rdutou ti guird****	The world cannot express in song bright and melodious Even though the grass and trees should sing

[32] See Lapidge, "Latin learning", 101, or Robert McNally, "Two Hiberno-Latin Texts", *Traditio* 15 (1959): 387-420. Quoted in McGill, *Evangeliorum*, 2016.
[33] Williams, *Poetry*, 101. "By examining the manuscript under a microscope I came to the conclusion that it was a palimpsest; that there had been earlier writing on the page, and that it was only by rubbing this out that room had been found for the Welsh englynion (. . .)." McKee suggests however that the marks Williams identifies as a palimpsest could just be faint pen trials. See McKee, *Cambridge Juvencus*, 81.
[34] Marged Haycock, "Y Creawdwr Hollalluog," in *Blodeugerdd Barddas o Ganu Crefyddol Cynnar* (Swansea: Cyhoeddiadau Barddas, 1994), 3-16.

	All thy glories (miracles, riches), O true Lord!
Dicones pater harimed presen Isabruid icinimer Nisacup nis arcup leder	The Father has wrought [such a multitude] of wonders in this world That it is difficult to find an equal number Letters cannot contain it, letters cannot express it.
Dicones ihesu dielimlu pbetid Aguirdou pan dibu Guotiapaur[35] oimer[36] didu	Jesus wrought on behalf of the hosts of Christendom [such a multitude] of miracles when he came (? like the grass is the number of them).
Gut dicones remedaut elbid Anguorit anguoraut Ni guor[37] gnim molim trintaut.	He who made the wonder of the world, will save us, has saved us. It is not too great toil to praise the Trinity.
It cluis (it) diban[38] iciman guorsed Ceinmicun ucnou ran Ueatiutaut[39] beantrident.	Purely, without blemish In the great assembly, Let us extol . . .

---

[35] McKee gives "guotcapar". Haycock gives "Guoti a<t>paur," and reads it as "atgyfodiad" in Modern Welsh, meaning "resurrection". See McKee, *Cambridge Juvencus*, 81 and Haycock, *Blodeugerdd*, 8.

[36] McKee gives "dimer". Haycock gives "oimer" and does not translate it.

[37] McKee gives "niguru". Haycock concurs with Williams.

[38] McKee and Haycock prefer "[in]ba*m*". Haycock translates rather differently than Williams, but concurs in the idea that it is concerned with audible praise of divine subjects.

[39] McKee gives "ucatritaut" and Haycock "Ucatriutaut," and does not offer a translation.

It cluis it humil inhared celmed Rit pucsaun mi ditrintaut Gurd meint icomoid imolaut.	Purely, humbly, in skilful verse I should give praise to the Trinity, According to the greatness of his power.
Rit ercis d**raut inadaut presen Piouboi int groisauc Inungued guoled trintaut.	He has required of the host in this world that belong to him That they should at all times All together fear the Trinity.
Un hamed hapuil haper Uuc nem isnem intcouer Nitguorgnim molim map meir.[40]	The one who has both wisdom and dominion above heaven, Below heaven, completely; It is not too great toil to praise the son of Mary.[41]

Table 2: transcription and translation of the Juvencus Nine.

The main meter used from englyn 2 to 8 is that of englyn penfyr, described above, with the final englyn being *englyn milwr*, a metrical change serving to mark the end of the poem that indicates it is not fragmentary but whole. Marged Haycock suggests that the inclusion of three different meters is an additional nod to the Trinity, which would then permeate the very structure of this poem intended to praise the glory of God.[42] However, as with the Juvencus Three, metrical comparison with the Preface does not help interpretation greatly, and we turn instead to noteworthy literary features and thematic echoes between the Juvencus Nine and the Preface to *ELQ*.[43] Considering that these Nine do not occur on the same folio as the Preface, a justification for this comparison must be offered. It is a simple one: the hand responsible for copying the Nine is that of scribe C, whose main glossing work is restricted to the Preface, tapering off after folio 2v and finishing on folio 3r, only seventeen lines into Book 1 of *ELQ*.[44] After these glosses, scribe C is a purely marginal and very infrequent

---

[40] Williams, *Poetry*, 101.
[41] *Ibid.* 102.
[42] Marged Haycock, "Y Creawdwr Hollalluog," 7.
[43] Again, see Annex 1 for full text and translation of the preface.
[44] McKee, *Cambridge*, 104.

presence. The fact that C's glossing work is focused on the Preface forms the basis of this study into the tension between main text and marginal poems, a tension embodied by the hand of C.

The Nine open with an address to God himself in Latin, but the first person, the necessary partner in enunciation of a vocative, comes in quite late. The seventh englyn gives us its only occurrence, seven lines before the end. This line, however, seems to carry the poem's core message: the poet's function is to praise the Trinity humbly, yet in a way that befits its greatness. The expression "pucsaun mi" on line 19 indicates both will and duty, highlighting that the poet's activity in this regard is not simply artistic play, the result of a whim or inspiration, but something more akin to righteous labour.[45] This is a strong statement on the merits of poetry, and the fact that it is included in Welsh, not Latin, indicates that the vernacular was, in the time of the poem's composition and in that of its copying, becoming an acceptable part of spiritual life. It was evidently a linguistic medium pure enough by this point to give God praise appropriate to the measure of his greatness.

The Nine	The Preface
Line 1: *Omnipotens auctor* Almighty creator	Lines 25 – 26: *Ergo age sanctificus assit mihi carminis auctor/Spiritus (. . .)* So Come! Be near o Sanctifying Spirit, Source of my poem (. . .)
Line 19: *Rit pucsaun **mi** ditrintaut* I should give praise to the Trinity	Line 19: *Nam **mihi** carmen erit Christi vitalia gesta* For I will sing of Christ's life-giving deeds

Table 3: comparing vocative addresses and first person in the Nine and the Preface.

As shown in the comparative table above, the Preface to *ELQ* also contains these elements, although they are organized slightly differently. The first person is similarly slow to make an appearance,

---

[45] Williams, *Poetry*, 115.

coming in only at line 19 with a possessive pronoun. This can perhaps be read as a mark of humility on the part of both poets. The vocative address to the Holy Spirit occurs at the very end of the Preface rather than at its beginning, although in purely structural terms this is not a very strong difference. The first and the final lines of any poem, forming the extremities of a textual whole, bear a similar weight and responsibility in regard to the rest of the verse. Emphasised by this positioning, the Preface's address conveys a similar sense of duty as that found in the Nine. The fact that the earlier text ends with the vocative and the later text opens with it supports the idea that the Nine could have been copied as the result of C's work on the Preface.

The poet Juvencus, who is able to extend great men's lives by praising their deeds, can extend his own by combining *"hos celsi cantus,"* "high-flown verse," and *"nobis certa fides,"* "steadfast faith," to speak *"ut Christo Digna loquamur,"* "as Christ deserves." These three expressions find direct echoes throughout the Nine, and are particularly condensed in the seventh englyn. Furthermore, we find throughout the same topical references to God as the creator, the maker of all things. The preface opens with the universe, and the Nine very quickly turn to the world, in a similar amount of detail.

The Nine	The Preface
Lines 3-5:	Lines 1-3:
Nit arcup betid hicouid canlou	*Immortale nihil mundi*
Cet treidin guel haguid	*compage tenetur*
T**e – rdutou ti guird****	*Non orbis, non regna hominum,*
	non aurea Roma,
	Non mare, non tellus, non
	ignea sidera caeli.
The world cannot express in	The universe has nothing
song bright and melodious	without end -
Even though the grass and trees	Not earth, not realms of men,
should sing	not golden Rome,
All thy glories (miracles,	Not seas, not land, not stars that
riches), O true Lord!	burn above.

Table 4: comparison of references to the whole of creation.

Both of these excerpts, occurring early on in each poem, serve to name elements of God's creation. In doing so, both highlight limitations through negative opening verses: in the Nine nothing can praise the creator as he deserves, and in *ELQ* nothing can endure beyond the time that has been preordained. While distinct in meaning, these mechanisms of limitation express a similar relationship between the omnipotent, unknowable force at the source of all things, and the one who is distinguished by taking on the duty of divine praise. In the Preface to *ELQ* nothing in the world can endure beyond the time that God has ordained, however the poet's present work will ensure not merely his immortality but also, more importantly, his salvation. In this way he will endure, because poetry has set him apart from the rest of God's creation.

In the Nine, it is the poet's privilege to give praise in "skilful verse" to the Trinity that marks them out from the rest of the world. Interestingly, the third englyn indicates that such poetry is too potent for writing, with the final verse "Nisacup nis arcup leder," telling us that letters cannot contain or express the glory of God's creation. This is a strange statement in a poem that does proceed to claim that its verse is skilful enough to praise God. But perhaps the Nine's author does not consider verse itself to be inapt to contain the magnitude of God's wonders, but rather writing specifically. The poem, copied on the manuscript's opening folio, could serve as a warning to students reading it not to get so wrapped up in the literary quality of the text that they forget the unknowable and inexpressible majesty of God's power. This could also explain the intricate meters chosen to structure the poem, that may have been considered in all their complexity the most well-suited for this encomiastic purpose. This line suggests that the growing consciousness of the merits of writing we pointed to earlier might not have been a completely smooth process, and supports the idea that this poem existed as an oral composition prior to being copied in this manuscript.

Both poems also introduce a degree of complexity in their references to God, as they both skilfully balance the role of Maker with that of Unmaker. God is not merely the world's source, but also its end.

The Nine	The Preface
Line 1: *Omnipotens auctor* Almighty creator	Line 4: *Nam statuit genitor rerum* *irreuocabile tempus*

	The Father of all things set a fixed time
Line 6: *Dicones pater harimed presen* The Father has wrought such a multitude of wonders	Line 19: *Nam mihi carmen erit Christi vitalia gesta* For I will sing of Christ's life-giving deeds
Line 13: *Anguorit anguoraut* Will save us, has saved us	Line 5: *Quo cunctum torrens rapiat flamma ultima mundum.* When final scorching fire will seize the world.
Line 23: *Inungued guoled trintaut* All together fear the Trinity	Line 21: *Nec metus, ut mundi rapiant incendia secum* Nor do I fear world-wasting flames will seize

Table 5: comparison of God as maker and unmaker of the world.

Both poems refer to God in similar ways, as simultaneously "omnipotens auctor" and "coruscans iudex." The Nine put the emphasis on creation, but the last judgement is present in oblique references to salvation and fear of the Trinity. The Englynion poet is thus reversing the equilibrium of the Preface, where the last judgement is emphasized and God's role as Creator is more subtle, folded into words like 'genitor' and terse references to "life-giving deeds". The Preface is much more openly eschatological. The Nine, on the other hand, speak very little of any such concerns for the future. This indicates a fixed temporality, built around a solid past and a diffuse sense of the poem's own self-referential, self-contained present. The only hint we may find of any future considerations is in the two lines cited above, which refer to God's requirement that we fear him, and forthcoming salvation. The Nine therefore do not echo the Preface perfectly, but appear to deliberately introduce reversals on themes laid out by Juvencus at the opening of his epic. Indeed, for Juvencus, the Last Judgment is the foremost reason to praise God, whereas the Englynion poet holds God's acts of creation as the highest, most-praiseworthy sign of His power. This introduces a sense of something like a poetic debate between scribe C and the text they were glossing.

Although these differences indicate that the correspondence between both poems is not absolute, there are deeper underlying convergences, which are most evident in those verses concerned with the function assigned to poetry.

The Nine	The Preface
Lines 12 – 14: *Gut dicones remedaut elbid* *Anguorit anguoraut* *Ni guor gnim molim trintaut.* He who made the wonder of the world, will save us, has saved us. It is not too great toil to praise the Trinity.	Lines 6 – 8: *Sed tamen innumeros homines* *sublimia facta* *Et virtutis honos in tempora* *longa frequentant* *Adcumulant quorum famam* *laudesque poetae.* Still, lofty deeds and honor paid to virtue Exalt throughout the ages countless men Whose fame and praise the poets amplify.

Table 6: comparison of the purpose of poetry.

Both texts agree: praise of God is the *telos* of poetry. This theme is more developed in the Preface to *ELQ*, where Juvencus, in accordance with principles of ancient rhetoric, takes a very roundabout way of making the same point laid out very straightforwardly in the Nine. If the poets of antiquity were able to write such beautiful praise of various noble men and pagan heroes that their works survived and will live on till the end of days, then a similar work of praise untainted by impious lies will necessarily be much more powerful and long-lasting. Juvencus does not simply propose to praise God in an unprecedented style; instead, it seems that he has chosen the genre of epic precisely because he perceives it as fundamentally encomiastic. This serves to nuance the moral dimension of Juvencus' claim that earlier epics are false narratives. They may contain lies, and in that Juvencus is automatically superior to them, but they are still worthy of being read because of their stylistic and generic qualities. McGill points this out as a necessary rhetorical device to justify his own use of the genre.[46] And indeed, were Juvencus to consign pagan authors to irredeemable sinfulness, he could not in good consciousness write an epic according to the genre's conventions, nor could he reasonably make as many direct references to the *Aeneid* as he does. Thus, the complexity of the Preface's argument serves as a topical justification preceding the text of *ELQ*, such as can be found throughout medieval literature. It bolsters the sense that poetry is the best medium by which to praise God, although it departs from the plain style of the Gospels.

In the Nine, we find that although it is impossible to fully express the wonders of God, toiling towards that purpose is a reward unto itself. Poetry must always fall short of the Creator's ineffable greatness, but it can never cease to try, as that is its highest purpose. In essentials, therefore, the Preface and the Nine convey the same message, telling us that there is nothing more natural and nothing better than to compose poems and sing songs that praise the glory of God.

The Nine	The Preface
Line 14: *Ni guor gnim molim trintaut.* It is not too great toil to praise the Trinity. Lines 18 – 19: *It cluis it humil inhared celmed* *Rit pucsaun mi ditrintaut* Purely, humbly, in skilful verse I should give praise to the Trinity Line 26: *Nitguorgnim molim map meir.* It is not too great toil to praise the son of Mary.	Lines 25 – 27: *Ergo age sanctificus assit mihi carminis* *auctor* *Spiritus et puro mentem riget amne* *canentis* *Dulcis Iordanis ut Christo digna* *loquamur.* So come! Be near o Sanctifying Spirit, Source of my poem, and you, sweet Jordan, flood Me with pure drafts, to speak as Christ deserves.

Table 7: comparison of the poet's highest duty.

---

[46] McGill, *Evangeliorum*, 9.

Praise, the central function of poetry for both texts, brings this reading back to the poets themselves. The very core of each poem holds that, while making verse fit to praise the glory of God is difficult, it is justified in and of itself, and sets the poet apart. It is not simply a matter of duty or salvation. Work and song are sublimated in the act that marks the poet out from the rest of creation. Juvencus and the Englynion poet do not just make verse, but they make verse for the highest purpose, that of praising the son of Mary and speaking as Christ deserves.

Conclusion

The Juvencus Nine appear to have a direct relationship with their co-text. This is evident in physical traces, as they were copied in the same hand that made annotations on the Preface to *ELQ*. It is also evident, on close reading, in the thematic links between both texts. There are a certain number of similarities between the Nine and the Preface, which both revolve around the topic of poetry and its relation to God. Both texts hold that the encomiastic function of poetry makes it the most appropriate medium through which to praise God's glory, and there is also a similar distinction established in both texts between the poet and the world. There are also interesting points of divergence that are best explained by C's work on the Preface. Beginning with a similar address as that which closes out the Preface, and subtly highlighting a different reason for which to praise God are two elements that suggest a critical approach to the text they were glossing. Although it is impossible to know whether the poem was composed or just copied by its scribe, there is an evident connection between both layers of the manuscript, and it seems that the classical text in this instance is directly responsible for the presence of the vernacular poem in its margin. The inclusion of the poem on a folio reserved for exegesis further supports this idea, although its situation at the very top of the page does set it more on the level of annotation than that of main text.

That the poems can partly be tied to their co-text suggests precisely the symbiotic environment described in the earlier part of this paper, and indicates that the classical text might very well have had a direct influence on the emergence of written vernacular literature. The margins of the Cambridge Juvencus manuscript evidently offered some of its scribes a degree of creative freedom that allowed one, at least, to reflect on what they were glossing. A process that was not simply one of copying or glossing occurred, a process by which the rich literary tradition of Wales found itself put to paper for what might have been the first time. The vernacular emerged, encouraged by the classical text its speakers copied, not as a fledgling language finding its poetic power, but as an already sophisticated medium for verbal art. In the margins of Cambridge Juvencus, we see the relation to *text* shifting. The function of the written word as a translator of ancient knowledge becomes applicable to other forms of knowledge and art, including those native to the scribe's environment.

THE JUVENCUS ENGLYNION

Appendix: The Preface to the *Evangeliorum Libri Quattuor*
Translation by Scott McGill (2016)

Immortale nihil mundi compage tenetur	The universe has nothing without end -
Non orbis, non regna hominum, non aurea Roma,	Not earth, not realms of men, not golden Rome,
Non mare, non tellus, non ignea sidera caeli.	Not seas, not land, not stars that burn above.
Nam statuit genitor rerum irreuocabile tempus	The Father of all things set a fixed time
Quo cunctum torrens rapiat flamma ultima mundum.	When final scorching fire will seize the world.
Sed tamen innumeros homines sublimia facta	Still, lofty deeds and honor paid to virtue
Et virtutis honos in tempora longa frequentant	Exalt throughout the ages countless men
Adcumulant quorum famam laudesque poetae.	Whose fame and praise the poets amplify.
Hos celsi cantus, Smyrnae de fonte fluentes,	The high-flown verse that flows from Smyrna's spring
Illos Miniciadae celebrat dulcedo Maronis.	Lifts some, the charm of Mincian Virgil others.
Nec minor ipsorum discurrit gloria vatum,	The poets' glory ranges just as far,
Quae manet aeternae similis, dum saecla volabunt	Almost eternal, lasting long as time,
Et vertigo poli terras atqua aequora circum	Abiding while the spinning axis turns
Aethera sidereum iusso moderamine volvet.	The starry sky on its determined path.
Quot si tam longam meruerunt carmina famam,	And yet if poems that weave together lies
Quae veterum gestis hominum mendacia nectunt	With ancient acts have earned such long repute,
Nobis certa fides aeternae in saecula laudis	My steadfast faith will grant the deathless glow
Immortale decus tribuet meritumque rependet	Of endless praise to me, my due reward.

Nam mihi carmen erit Christi vitalia gesta,	For I will sing of Christ's life-giving deeds -
Divinum populis falsi sine crimine donum.	A gift to nations, cleared of lies, divine.
Nec metus, ut mundi rapiant incendia secum,	Nor do I fear world-wasting flames will seize
Hoc opus; hoc etenim forsan me subtrahet igni	My work: this might, in fact, deliver me
Tunc, cum flammivoma discendet nube coruscans	When Christ the gleaming judge, his high-throned Father's
Iudex altithroni genitoris gloria, Christus.	Glory, descends with a blazing cloud.
Ergo age sanctificus assit mihi carminis auctor	So come! Be near o Sanctifying Spirit,
Spiritus et puro mentem riget amne canentis	Source of my poem, and you, sweet Jordan, flood
Dulcis Iordanis ut Christo digna loquamur.	Me with pure drafts, to speak as Christ deserves.

Back to the Sources: Re-translations from the Latin in Two Middle Irish Saints' Lives

Nicholas Thyr

Scattered across many late-medieval and early-modern manuscripts is a body of homiletic Lives of Irish saints.[1] These Lives all have a similar structure: they begin with an interpretation of a passage from the Bible (the *exordium*). Following this, the Lives proper begin, presenting a largely biographical narrative; they conclude with a short *peroratio* addressed directly to the audience.[2] There is general agreement that, based on certain features of their language, these homiletic Lives are Middle Irish, in the sense that their language, by and large, reflects a date of composition between about 900 and 1200, but their precise dating (as well as most other contextual

---

[1] That is, accounts of the deeds and miracles of a particular holy man or woman, worked into the form of a homily though the homiletic material and the Life itself are often only loosely connected: Máire Herbert, "Latin and Vernacular Hagiography of Ireland from the Origins to the Sixteenth Century," in *Hagiographies: Histoire internationale de la littérature hagiographique latine et vernaculaire en Occident des origines à 1550*, vol. 3, ed. Guy Philippart (Turnhout: Brepols, 2001), 327-60, at 344. The most complete account of medieval Irish homiletic Lives is Martin McNamara, "Irish Homilies A.D. 600–1100," in *Via Crucis: Essays on Early Medieval Sources and Ideas, in Memory of J. E. Cross*, ed. Thomas Hall, with assistance from Thomas Hill and Charles Wright (Morgantown: West Virginia University Press, 2002), 235-85, at 273-4; see too Frederic Mac Donncha, "Medieval Irish Homilies," in *Biblical Studies: The Medieval Irish Contribution*, ed. Martin McNamara (Dublin: Dominican Publications, 1976), 59-71, at 61. Neither list is complete: see Caoimhín Breatnach, "An Irish Homily on the Life of the Virgin Mary," *Ériu* 51 (2000), 23-58.

[2] See Mac Donncha, "Homilies," 61-5; also Martin McNamara, "Téacs agus Tuiscint an Bhíobla i Seanmóirí Gaeilge, AD 600–1200," in *Saltair Saíochta, Sanasaíochta agus Seanchais*, eds. Dónall Ó Baoill, Donncha Ó hAodha, and Nollaig Ó Muraíle (Dublin: Four Courts Press, 2013), 124-43.

information about them) generally remains a matter for informed speculation.[3]

In this paper, I will discuss two of these homiletic Lives, both unedited, and preserved only in seventeenth-century manuscripts. One is a version of the Middle Irish Life of St. Patrick; the other is a version of the Middle Irish Life of St. Brigit. The Life of Patrick survives in full only in Dublin, Royal Irish Academy (RIA) MS C iv 3 (1192), ff. 233r–242v ('G'), written by Dáibhidh Ó Duibhgheannáin in the later seventeenth century (several paragraphs also survive as interpolations into the Life of Patrick in the Book of Lismore, a late fifteenth-century manuscript).[4] Brigit's Life is preserved in two Mícheál Ó Cléirigh manuscripts from the years around 1630, Brussels, Bibliothèque

---

[3] Mac Donncha, in "Homilies," 67-71, sought to identify a core of homilies compiled in the late eleventh century, an assertion that has been broadly accepted, though with numerous caveats: see e.g. Gearóid Mac Eoin, "Observations on Some Middle-Irish Homilies," in *Irland und Europa im früheren Mittelalter*, eds. Próinséas Ní Chatháin and Michael Richter (Stuttgart: Klett-Cotta, 1996), 195-211; and Máire Herbert, "Representation of Gregory the Great in Irish Sources of the Pre-Viking Era," in *Listen, O Isles, Unto Me: Studies in Medieval Word and Image in Honour of Jennifer O'Reilly*, eds. Elizabeth Mullins and Diarmuid Scully (Cork: Cork University Press, 2011), 181-90, at 185.

[4] Available on the Dublin Institute for Advanced Studies' Irish Script on Screen database (ISOS) (https://www.isos.dias.ie/RIA/RIA_MS_C_iv_3. html; accessed December 13, 2022), with catalogue entry by Kathleen Mulchrone, *Catalogue of Irish Manuscripts in the Royal Irish Academy*, fasc. 26 (Dublin, Hodges and Figgis, 1942), 3221-33. For more on Dáibhidh and his family, see Paul Walsh, "The Learned Family of O Duigenan," in Paul Walsh, ed., *Irish Men of Learning* (Dublin: Three Candles, 1947), 1-12. For the shared passages, see Ludwig Bieler, "*Bethu Phátraic*: Versuch einer Grundlegung des Verhältnisses der irischen Patriciusviten zu den lateinischen," *Anzeiger der Österreichische Akademie der Wissenschaften, Philosophisch-Historische Klasse* 111 (1974): 253-73, at 258; for the date of Book of Lismore, see Brian Ó Cuív, "Observations on the Book of Lismore," *Proceedings of the Royal Irish Academy* 83C (1983): 269-92. This manuscript is also available on ISOS: https://www.isos.dias.ie/UCC/ UCC_TheBookOfLismore.html (accessed August 21 2023).

royale de Belgique/Koninklijke Bibliotheek van België (KBR), MS 2324-40, ff. 24r–30v ('B1') and MS 4190-200, ff. 6r–30v ('B2').[5]

These Lives stand out from the mass of other Middle Irish homiletic Lives because they incorporate passages freshly translated from the Latin Lives of those two saints into the pre-existing Middle Irish texts. As I will demonstrate, a significant percentage of the Brussels Life of Brigit is a new translation from the so-called *Vita prima*, the "first life" of Brigit, as dubbed by the Bollandists ('V1'), a Latin work potentially datable to the seventh century, or maybe the eighth; much of the RIA Life of Patrick, meanwhile, appears to be translated from the *Vita tertia*–that is, John Colgan's "third life" of that saint ('V3'), which came together at some point between the eighth and early twelfth century.[6]

There has been, to date, no general overview of the transmission of these homiletic Lives. Máire Herbert, in her studies of the Middle Irish Lives of Colmcille and Martin of Tours, drew attention to a

---

[5] Catalogue by Pádraig Breatnach, *Catalogue of Manuscripts in the Irish Language in the Bibliothèque royale de Belgique / Koninklijke Bibliotheek van België*, on ISOS (Dublin Institute for Advanced Studies, 2019), accessed December 13, 2022, https://www.isos.dias.ie/RLB/RLB_MS_2324 _40.html; https://www.isos.dias.ie/RLB/RLB_MS_4190_4200.html.

[6] "*Vita I S. Brigidae auctore anonymo* [. . .]," in *Acta sanctorum quotquot toto orbe continet* [. . .], Feb. I (Antwerp, Société des Bollandistes, 1658), cols. 119-35 (= Bibliotheca Hagiographica Latina [BHL] no. 1455). See Richard Sharpe, "*Vitae S. Brigitae*: The Oldest Texts," *Peritia* 1 (1982), 81-106; Kim McCone, "Brigit in the Seventh Century: A Saint with Three Lives," *Peritia* 1 (1982), 107-45; Seán Connolly, "*Vita prima Sanctae Brigitae*: Background and Historical Value," *Journal of the Royal Society of Antiquaries of Ireland* 119 (1989), 5-49. Ludwig Bieler, ed., *Vita tertia sancti Patricii, in Four Latin Lives of St. Patrick: Colgan's Vita secunda, quarta, tertia, and quinta* (Dublin: Dublin Institute for Advanced Studies, 1971), 115-90, date at 26 (BHL nos. 6506–7); see also David Dumville, "St. Patrick in Cornwall? The Origin and Transmission of *Vita tertia S. Patricii*," in *A Celtic Florilegium: Studies in Memory of Brendan O Hehir*, eds. Kathryn Klar, Eve Sweetser, and Claire Thomas (Lawrence, MA: Celtic Studies Publications, 1996), 1-7.

shared pattern of transmission for those two works.[7] The bulk of the manuscripts–including the Book of Lismore (now in the collection of University College Cork); Paris, Bibliothèque Nationale de France, Fonds Basques et Celtiques MS 1 ('P'); and London, British Library, Egerton MS 91–form one branch of transmission, which can be identified with what Ludwig Bieler, following Kathleen Mulchrone, dubbed the "*p* branch" in their respective studies of the transmission of the Irish Lives of St. Patrick.[8] From my own research, I have been able to establish that many of the Middle Irish homiletic Lives, such as those of Brendan, Senán, and Mochua, are found only in manuscripts from this branch.[9] For the 'Big Three' Irish saints (Columcille, Brigit, and Patrick), as well as a few other homilies of non-Irish saints (including Gregory the Great and Martin of Tours), there are a handful of other witnesses independent from the *p* branch, the most important of which are the fifteenth-century manuscript Dublin, King's Inns MS 10 ('K'), and the Leabhar Breac (RIA, MS 23 P 16 [1230]), written shortly after 1400 ('Lb').[10] Based on her study

---

[7] Herbert, *Iona, Kells, and Derry*, 211-16; Herbert, "The Life of Martin of Tours: A View from Twelfth-Century Ireland," in *Ogma: Essays in Celtic Studies in Honour of Próinséas Ní Chatháin*, eds. Michael Richter and Jean Michel Picard (Dublin, 2002), 76-84, at 79.

[8] Bieler, *"Bethu Phátraic*," 258; Kathleen Mulchrone, "Die Abfassungszeit und Überlieferung der Vita Tripartita," *Zeitschrift für Celtische Philologie* 16 (1927), 1-94, at 24-6.

[9] These findings will be outlined in more detail in my forthcoming doctoral thesis.

[10] See, respectively, Pádraig de Brún, *Catalogue of Irish Manuscripts in King's Inns Library, Dublin* (Dublin: Dublin Institute for Advanced Study, 1972), 20-24; Kathleen Mulchrone and Elizabeth Fitzpatrick, *Catalogue of Irish Manuscripts in the Royal Irish Academy*, fasc. 27 (Dublin, Royal Irish Academy, 1943), 3379-3404. These manuscripts are both available on ISOS: https://www.isos.dias.ie/RIA/RIA_MS_23_P_16.html; https://www.isos.dias.ie/KINGS/KINGS_MS_10.html (accessed August 21 2023). The Life of Patrick, at least, can be dated precisely to 1411: Tomás Ó Concheannain, "The Scribe of the Leabhar Breac," *Ériu* 24 (1973), 64-79, at 72.

of the textual evidence, Herbert associated K with *p* in the Lives of Martin and Colmcille, a relationship that can be sketched as follows:[11]

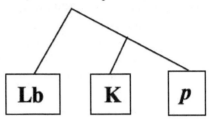

Fig. 1: Relationship of LB and K to *p*

The Lives of Patrick and Brigit, however, do not appear to conform to this pattern. The *p* branch remains a coherent unit, but the relationship between K, Lb, and *p* is less consistent.

In the Life of Brigit, K and Lb, along with the two manuscripts mentioned above (B1 and B2), form a separate branch against *p*. Below are two sets of readings: first, two representatives of *p*, the Paris manuscript and the Book of Lismore; then the Leabhar Breac, King's Inns MS 10, and the two Brussels manuscripts (there is a guide to sigla in the appendix). In text from printed editions, I have respected the editors' practices of punctuation and expansion of abbreviations. In text drawn from my transcriptions from manuscripts, I have marked all expansions (including lenition marks) with italics. Punctuation, capitalization, and spacing are editorial. I have included length marks only if clearly present in the manuscript.

1. Good news for Dubthach

A: **P f. 77rb, ll. 28–9**: Ba buide*ch* da*no* Dub*th*ach don aith*h*escc si*n ar* ní r*u*cad i*ngen* dó co si*n*.

L l. 1172: Ba buide*ch* Dub*thach* don aithi*u*sc-sein, ár ni rug*a*d i*ngen* dó cosin.[12]

---

[11] Diagram simplified from Herbert, *Iona, Kells, and Derry*, 213, where 'B' stands for my 'Lb' and *z* for my *p*.

[12] This and all further citations from the Book of Lismore from Whitley Stokes, ed. and tr., *Lives of Saints from the Book of Lismore* (Oxford: Clarendon Press, 1890), albeit with my own translations.

"Dubthach was grateful for that response, as no daughter had yet been born to him." (L: my translation)[13]

B: **Lb p. 62a ll. 29–31 (p. 54)**: Ro f*h*ailtnig D*ub*t*h*ach ₇ *in* chum*al* de sin. At b*er*t D*ub*t*h*ach, "u*air* tec*h*taim-sea m*a*ccu, ropad maith lea*m*m di*diu co m*beth i*n*gen occu*m*."[14]

  K: [acephalous]

  B2 f. 7r, ll. 2–3: Ro failtnig*h* Dubt*h*ach ₇ an cum*h*al de sin ₇ adub*a*irt, "Tectaim maca ₇ ro bad*h* mait*h* lem d*a*no co mbeit*h* ingen occom."

  B1 f. 25r, ll. 2–4: Ro ba faoili*dh* trá Dubtac*h* ₇ an c*h*umal de si*n* & atbert Dub*h*tac*h*, "Atá meic liomsa ₇ noc*h*an f*h*uil ingena," ar se.

"Dubthach and the slavewoman were gladdened by that, and he said, 'I have sons; I would like, now, to have a daughter.'" (B2: my translation)

2. Easter draws near

  A: **P f. 78vb, l. 2**: Fe*ch*t an*n* o ro coi*m*foicsig soll*a*main na Casc–[*line skip*]

  L l. 1355: Feacht o rochomfhoicsigh sollam*a*n na casc duthracair . . .

"Once, when the feast of Easter had drawn near, [Brigit] wished that . . . " (L: my translation)[15]

---

[13] Cf. Stokes, *Lives*, 183.

[14] Whitley Stokes' 1877 edition of Lb is useful, but flawed; for the Life of Brigit, I have referred to the manuscript. Here, the second page number in parentheses refers to Whitley Stokes, ed. and tr., *Three Middle Irish Homilies on the Lives of Saints Patrick, Brigit, and Columba* (Calcutta: Private press, 1877). For the Life of Patrick from Lb, I have, however, cited from the Stokes edition, as presented on the CELT site ("Betha Phatraic," compiled by Beatrix Färber, Elva Johnston, and Ruth Murphy, *Corpus of Electronic Texts*, 2012, accessed December 13, 2022, celt.ucc.ie/published/G201009/).

[15] Cf. Stokes, *Lives*, 188.

B: **Lb p. 64a ll. 62–4 (p. 66)**[16]: Ba do fe*r*taib Bríg*t*e: o ra c*h*om*a*csig soll*a*main na Casc, gabais B*r*igit i *n*-araile locc i com*fh*acraib do eps*c*op Mél gar ria Caplait. Rop' ail do B*r*igit . . .

K f. 20ra, ll. 14–16: Ba do fertaib Brig*h*ti: ro boi Brig*it* i n-*ar*oile inud com*fh*occ*us* do eps*c*op Mel gairit ria Caplait ₇ rop' ail do Brig*it* . . .

B2 f. 13r, ll. 1–2: Ba dia fertaib B*r*ig*h*de: gab*h*ais Brig*h*it araile locc i cco*mh*fochraibh d'esp*occ* Mel g*ar* ria Caplait. Rob' ail do Brig*it* . . .

(**B1 f. 28v, l. 7**: Rob' áil do B*h*rigitt aims*er* air*i*d*h*e i*ar*sin, i n-at*h*focc*us* Cásg do s*h*un*n*rad . . .)

"[It] was one of Brigit's miracles: Brigit was in a certain place near to Bishop Mél, shortly before Maundy Thursday, and Brigit wanted to . . . " (K: my translation)

In both passages, where they are extant, B2, K, and Lb agree against the two witnesses of *p* on most points. B1 tends to hew less closely to the shared text; still, the first passage suffices to show its affiliation with the group.[17]

It is possible to further refine the relationships between the non–*p*-branch texts. B1 and B2 form a closely-related pair that lies somewhat nearer to K than Lb, as detailed below. Each, however, has their own unique characteristics. B1 is imperfect, missing perhaps half of the Life; and, though B2 is complete, the scribe, Mícheál Ó Cléirigh, wrote that he had stitched the Life together from two sources: "an ced cuid don beth*aidh* as leab*ur* meg niallg*us*a do sgrio*badh*. Et an cuid ele as leab*ur* memraim do sgriobhat*ur* muint*ir* cianain, do sgrio*badh* g*ach* a ffuil sunn" ("The first portion of the Life was written from the book of [Brian] Mac Niallgusa, and the second part from a

---

[16] Stokes here rearranged the order of passages in the text for his edition; there is no explanation, but, as he accurately reports the page, column, and line numbers of the passages in question, it was certainly intentional.

[17] One manuscript of the *p*-branch Life, London, British Library, Egerton MS 91, uses the text of a K-Lb-B1-B2 Life for approximately three columns of text (ff. 57ra l. 35-57vb l. 36), perhaps as a result of a missing or defaced folio in the chain of transmission; this includes the passage in question here, and so its evidence cannot be used to reconstruct the *p*-branch text.

parchment book that the *muintir Chianáin* wrote, all that is here was written").[18]

The extent of each of the two sections is not explicitly marked in the text. There are two plausible candidates for the dividing line between them. The first comes between folios 22 and 23, where the handwriting and orthography shift substantially. Before the split, 'Brigit', when spelled in full, is typically *Brighit, Brighitt,* or *Brigit*; afterwards, it is generally *Bricchitt* or *Bricchit* (similarly with *Laighen*/*Laicchen*, etc.). Abbreviations shift as well, from *im̄* to *v⁰* for the common adverb and conjunction *immorro*. The handwriting is now somewhat cramped, and becomes more so over the remaining folios; where f. 6v has 22 lines and approximately 260 words (depending on one's definition of a 'word'), f. 26v has 23 lines and 330 words or so, and, near the end, f. 30r has 29 lines and roughly 440 words; the final page (f. 30v) has over 600 words. Letter shapes change; for instance, the *br-* of 'Brigit', typically separate letters before f. 23, is afterwards generally written as a digraph, with *b* followed by an *r* rotunda (shaped like the Arabic numeral '2'). In a note incorporated into the text block on the bottom of 12v, Ó Cléirigh notes he was writing on April 11, 1629, 'Cedaine M*hair*nti Iosa' (i.e. Spy Wednesday); no similar note exists for ff. 23–30, but the change in the presentation of the text could suggest a change in sources, perhaps after an interval of time.

Against this hypothesis, there are no clear signs that the content–as opposed to the presentation–of the Life is any way different after the shift in handwriting; Ó Cléirigh's regular handwriting and orthography regularly appear in the margins of the later folios (e.g. 23v), and a single sentence spans 22v and 23r (. . . an d*ara* // clam*h* altucc*adh* . . .). It seems more plausible, then, that we are only

---

[18] Upper and right margins on f. 6r; quoted from Donncha Ó hAodha, ed. and trans., *Bethu Brigte* (Dublin: Dublin Institute for Advanced Study, 1978), xxviii (my translation). 'Brian' is added above *meg Niallgusa* in an interlinear gloss. For the *muintir Chianáin*, see Michael O Mainnin, "Muintir Chianáin Ard Mhacha, agus Borradh na dTeaghlach Léannta," in Jurgen Uhlich and Eoin Mac Cárthaigh, eds., *Féilscríbhinn do Chathal Ó Háinle* (Indreabhán: An Clóchomhar, 2012), 697-719. For the little we know about Brian mac Niallghusa, see Ó hAodha, *Bethu Brigte*, xxviii, n. 96.

confronted here with a decision to save space and time, as Ó Cléirigh shifts from his standard book hand into a smaller, more rapid near-cursive script.[19]

The other option for the dividing line comes at f. 6v l. 19, not quite a full folio into the Life. At this point, the text of B2 switches from a *p*-branch text very closely related to that found in the Book of Lismore to following the K-Lb-B1 version of the Life.[20] Perhaps, then, Ó Cléirigh's copy of the Life from the *muintir Chianáin* lacked the opening section, and was supplemented with Brian mac Niallghusa's version of the Life. This hypothesis is reinforced by the fact that there is a later passage from the *p* branch present, written in the margin of f. 7v (= L ll. 1186–8), not found in either Lb or B1 (the relevant folios in K do not survive).

The most probable scenario, it would appear, is that Brian mac Niallghusa's book provided only a limited portion of the entire life. B2 contains much extra material not present in its sister text, B1, such as a long string of passages that are derived from, or at least closely related to, the marginal notes preserved in a copy of the *Liber Hymnorum* written *circa* 1100 (the hymn *Brigit bé bithmaith* appears, with accompanying glosses, on f. 27r); furthermore, two passages with close parallels to the ninth-century Irish translation of the Life of Brigit, *Bethu Brigte*, are incorporated as well, as Donncha Ó hAodha suggested in his edition of that text.[21] Donncha Ó hAodha has already

---

[19] Both hands are Ó Cléirigh's, as can be seen in the elaborate double-loop abbreviation for *-air* and the use of a short tick mark under the Tironian *et* symbol, 7. See Pádraig Breatnach, *The Four Masters and Their Manuscripts* (Dublin: Dublin Institute for Advanced Studies, 2013), 133-62. My thanks to Professor Breatnach for confirming this for me (pers. comm., April 11, 2023).

[20] See Appendix B.

[21] The string of passages drawing on the Liber Hymnorum is §§49–62 in Ó Cléirigh's numbering (ff. 25r l. 13 – 30v l. 5), though the influence is not limited to that portion. The Life draws from both *Brigit bé bithmaith* and Broccán's Hymn (*Ní car Brigit*): see J. H. Bernard and Richard Atkinson, eds. and trans., *The Irish Liber Hymnorum*, 2 vols. (London: Henry Bradshaw Society, 1898), 107-28. The origins and transmission of the prefaces and *scholia* in the two copies of the Liber Hymnorum are

discussed the potential relationship of B2 to *Bethu Brigte*; he concluded, cautiously, that these two passages, along with a few other details scattered through B2, "may indicate acquaintance with a text such as ours [i.e., *Bethu Brigte*]."[22]

The material from the *Liber Hymnorum* was added in with some care; often, bits and pieces from the scholia are stitched into the transmitted text of the Irish Life, as in the following passage, where the underlined text in B2 appears to be derived from the scholia to the *Liber Hymnorum* (text from B1 included below for purposes of comparison):

B2 f. 12v, ll. 2–17

O't *connairc* tra Easp*occ* Mél an*n*sin Brig*i*t, ro f*h*iarf*aigh* hi [*sic*]. As b*e*rt M*a*c Caille, 'As í so,' *ar* sé, 'an c*h*aill*ech* erd*e*rc a Laig*h*nib .i. Brig*i*t.' 'Mocen di,' ol Esp*occ* Mel, 'as me ro t*h*airngir hi ₇ as me do b*h*era grad*h*a fuirre,' & as b*e*rt epsc*op* Mel, 'T*a*rr, a naemh Brig*h*it, go ro sént*ar* caille for do c*h*end ríasna hog*h*aibh ele atá ag gab*h*ail g*r*ad*h* aniú.'

Atre Brig*i*t c*h*uicce, ₇ is *edh* do rala don esp*occ* tre rath an Sp*iora*t Naoi*m*h, grad*h* n-epscoip do erleg*h*ad*h* for Brig*h*it gerbo grad*h* aitr*i*cc*he* n*a*111a 1ob áil do B*h*rigit [. . .]

In oc*h*tm*adh* uath*aidh* ro gen*air* Brig*h*it [. . .]

When Bishop Mél, then, saw Brigit there, he asked, "[Who is] she?" Mac Caille said, "This," he said, "is

understudied, but portions, at least, were very likely composed at Armagh c. 1000: Máire Herbert, "Crossing Historical and Literary Boundaries: Irish Written Culture Around the Year 1000," *CMCS* 53–4 (2007), 87-101, at 89-91. Most of the relevant scholia are found, however, only in the Franciscan copy (Dublin, University College Dublin, MS A. 2, which was written, according to Ludwig Bieler, in the early twelfth century, or maybe somewhat before: Ludwig Bieler, "The Irish Book of Hymns: A Palaeographical Study," *Scriptorium* 2.2 [1948], 177-94, at 177). The two chapters from *Bethu Brigte* are §§15–16 (ff. 11v l. 11 – 12r l. 13); see Ó hAodha, xxviii-xxix, and ll. 136-63.
[22] Ó hAodha, *Bethu Brigte*, xxviii.

the well-known nun (*caillech*) from Leinster, Brigit."
"She is welcome," said Bishop Mél; "it is I who
foretold her, and I shall give her orders," and Mél
said, "Come, holy Brigit, so a veil may be blessed
upon your head before the other virgins who are
taking orders today."

Brigit rose [and came] to him, and this is what
Bishop Mél did, by grace of the Holy Spirit: he
bestowed a bishop's orders on Brigit, though Brigit
wanted only a penitent's orders [. . .]

On the eighth [day of the moon] Brigit was born
[. . .]

Lib. Hymn., p. 117:23

Atcondairc tra epscop Mél sen, ocus ro·iarfaig,
"caiche na caillecha?" ar se. Asbert Mac Caille fris,
"is hí sen," ar se, "in caillech airdirc a Laignib, co
Brigit." "Mocen di," ol epscop Mel, "is me-se
do·s·rairgert in tan bói i mbroind am-mathar [. . .]
"Dober-sa on [na gráda]," ar epscop Mél. Iar-sein tra
ro·eirlegait grada fuirri, ocus is grad epscuip do·rala
do epscop Mél do thabairt for Brigit, ciarbo grad
athrige nama rop ail disi féin [. . .]

Then Bishop Mél saw a sign, and he asked, "Who are
these nuns?" he said. Mac Caille said to him, "She,"
he said, "is the well-known nun from Leinster,
Brigit." "She is welcome," said Bishop Mél; "I am the
one who foretold her when she was in her mother's
womb" [. . .] "I shall give out, then, [the orders],"
said Bishop Mél. Then he bestowed orders on her, and
it is a bishop's orders that Mél happened to give her,
even though she only wanted a penitent's orders
[. . .]

---

[23] Bernard and Atkinson, *Liber Hymnorum*, 117; translation my own,
though based on theirs (vol. 2, p. 192).

Cf. B1 ff. 28r, l. 20 – 28v, l. 6

Ro f*h*iarf*aigh* Esp*occ* Mél, "Cía hog*h* súd?" *ar* sé. Ro f*h*reg*air* Easp*occ* M*a*c Caille é, "Brig*h*it sin," ar se. At b*er*t Easp*occ* Mel, "Tairr, a naomh Brig*h*itt, go ro séntar caille finn fort' *ch*ion*n* ríasna hog*h*a eile." As ed*h* do rala an*n* tria rat*h* an Spiorait Naoim*h*, grad*h*a uaisle espuicc do uirléig*h*en*n* for B*h*rig*h*itt. [. . .]
    In octmad*h* úath*aidh* u*m*orr*o* ro genair B*r ighitt* [. . .]

Bishop Mél asked, "Who is that virgin (*ógh*)?" he said. Bishop Mac Caille answered him: "That is Brigit," he said. Bishop Mél said, "Come, holy Brigit, so a white veil may be blessed upon your head before the other virgins." This is what happened then through the grace of the Holy Spirit: the noble order of a bishop was bestowed upon Brigit [. . .]
    On the eighth [day of the moon], moreover, Brigit was born [. . .]

The *Liber Hymnorum* and *Bethu Brigte* material appear in B2 alone. Both B2 and B1, however, supplement the Middle Irish Life of Brigit with a substantial block of passages derived from the Latin *Vita prima* ('V1') of Brigit. Unfortunately, B1 cuts off in the middle of the retranslated passages, but of B2's 25 folios, six of them–from §20 (f. 13r l. 20) to §33 (f. 19r l. 20)–are derived from V1.
    B1 and B2, despite numerous minor differences in wording and detail, derive from the same translation of V1; this translation is quite faithful to the Latin original, as can be seen in the passage below:

V1 §21

Duæ Virgines de genere S. Brigidæ, quæ paralyticæ erant, & in proximo habitabant loco, miserunt ad eam, vt veniens curaret eas. Exiit ergo ad eas, & benedixit salem & aquam: quæ sumentes sanatæ sunt.

Two virgins of St. Brigit's kin, who were paralytic, and lived nearby, sent to her, so that she would come and cure them [lit. 'coming, she would cure them'].

She set off, therefore, to them, and blessed salt and water: they drank this, and were cured.

B1 f. 28v, ll. 20–4:

Ro bad*ar* da*no* dá oig*h* do muin*n*tir Brig*h*de a ffain*n*e ₇ a laige galair a n-éccmais Brig*h*de go ro f*h*aoid*h*seat teac*h*taire uat*h*a go Brig*h*itt go ttíosad*h* dia n-íoc. Do c*h*uaid*h* Brig*h*itt dia n-ion*n*saig*h*id*h* ₇ ro b*h*ennac*h* salan*n* ₇ uisge doib*h* ₇ o ro ib*h*sett an t-uiscce robtar slána foc*h*edóir iad.

There were, then, two virgins of Brigit's community, weak and enfeebled by disease in the absence of Brigit, so they sent out a messenger to Brigit so that she would come to heal them. Brigit came to them, and blessed salt and water for them, and as soon they had drunk the water they became healthy at once.

B2 ff. 13r, l. 20–13v, l. 3:

Ferta ele do rin*n*e Bricc*it* an*n* so .i. dí óig*h* do c*h*enél mB*r*ig*h*de [*sic*] ro b*h*attar i n-anbrac*h*taig*h*e ₇ i ffain*n*e coro faid*h*set t*e*c*h*tair*e* uait*h*ib*h* go Brig*h*it co tísed*h* dia n-íc. Ó do c*h*u*aidh* Brig*it* dia saig*i*d*h*-siu*m*h, ro bennac*h* salan*n* & uiscce doibh & tormaltat*ar* na hog*h*a in ní sin. Ro híct*h*a fo céttoir iatt & ro b*h*att*ar* a ccom*h*aitteac*h*t Brig*h*de ag fognamh do D*h*ía & disi ₇rl.

Here are other miracles Brigit did: [there were] two virgins of Brigit's kindred [cf. V1 *de genere*] who were wasting away[24] and weak, so they sent a messenger to Brigit so that she would come to heal them. When Brigit came for them, she blessed salt and water for them, and the virgins consumed that. They were healed at once, and were in Brigit's company, serving her and God, etc.

---

[24] Or perhaps 'paralytic': see *Electronic Dictionary of the Irish Language* (*eDIL*) s.v. anfabrachta, accessed December 13, 2022, https://dil.ie/3542

There are, as I mentioned, some minor variations between the two Irish Lives. B2 tends, for instance, to expand on the translated narrative: the clause about how the two healed virgins "attended on Brigit, serving her and God" (*ro bhattar a ccomhaitteacht Brighde ag fognamh do Dhía & disi*) is not present in either B1 or V1. These variations are secondary, however; close comparison reveals that B1 and B2 are ultimately derived from the same translation. For instance, where V1 has *miserunt ad eam*, "they sent [word] to her . . . ", both B1 and B2 make the action more explicit: they send a messenger (*techtaire*) to Brigit.

The translated passages, moreover, hew closely not only in wording, but in order, to the Latin original. The series runs as follows, according to the section numbers in the *Acta sanctorum* edition: §§21, 17, 20, 23, 24, 28, 33, part of 34, 35, 36, 38, 39, 40, 42, 49, 90, 93, and 94.[25]

This orderly progression suggests the reviser went through a copy of the *Vita prima* methodically. Why these passages, and not others, were chosen is best understood in reference to the text of K. That version of the Life has been heavily abbreviated; for instance, the entire section equivalent to L ll. 1431–96, in which Brigit travels to a synod convened by Patrick and rescues Brón, a bishop, from a false charge of having fathered a child, is absent. In B1-B2, this passage has been translated from V1 §35; the entire string of translated passages, moreover, comes between two anecdotes in K f. 20ra, and the ensuing text of B2 follows the order of passages in K.[26] It appears, therefore, that these passages were translated and added to an ancestor of the text

---

[25] Note, however, that B2 lacks §§24 and 28, and B1 cuts off after §38.
[26] In B2, the last passage before the string of V1-derived text is the story of the leper who would rather be cured of his leprosy than be king of the world (= K f. 20ra ll. 29-37); the passage after the string of V1 passages tells of two blind Britons and a young boy that Brigit cured (K f. 20ra ll. 37-47). Ensuing passages in B2 are Brigit's trip to Ard Achadh (not in K, but in Lb: p. 72 [Stokes]), then a trip to Brigit *ingen* Chongaile (K ff. 20ra l. 47 – 20rb l. 27), a trip to Patrick at Mag Léna (K ff. 20rb l. 27 – 20va l. 11), and then a trip to Ard Macha (K f. 20va ll. 11–20). Setting aside the missing passage on Ard Achadh, K is the only surviving Life of Brigit that preserves these passages in this precise order.

now preserved in King's Inns 10.[27] The relationship of the Irish Lives of Brigit can thus be sketched as follows ('BB' = *Bethu Brigte*; 'LH' = *Liber Hymnorum*):

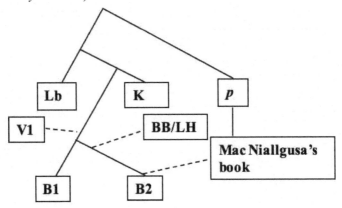

Fig. 2: Irish lives of Brigit

The Life of Brigit in B1-B2 is not the only surviving Middle Irish Life to have augmented an earlier Irish text with a largely faithful translation from a Latin Life. Another case is the Life of Patrick in RIA C iv 3 ('G'), which, worked, in part, it appears, from the Latin "Third Life" (*Vita tertia*, 'V3') of that saint.[28] This text has rarely been analyzed before; the only scholar to examine it in detail is Ludwig Bieler, who, throughout his career, made careful study of the relationships of Latin and Irish Lives of Patrick. His conclusions regarding the Irish Lives can be illustrated schematically as follows:[29]

---

[27] They cannot derive from K itself, since, as noted, B2 §35, the story of Ard Achadh, (ff. 19v, l. 10-20r, l. 7) is present in Lb, but not in K.

[28] Preliminary evidence for this claim is provided below. A full argument is contained within my doctoral dissertation, due to be completed in 2024.

[29] Bieler, "Bethu Phátraic," 265, 273. This diagram is considerably simplified.

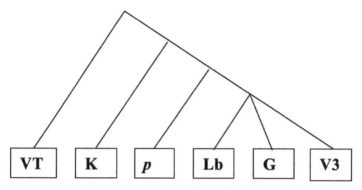

Fig. 3: Lives of Patrick

This diagram works best as a description of similarities. On the left, there is the Irish-Latin Tripartite Life of St. Patrick, or the *Vita Tripartita* ('VT'), a sprawling account over three thousand lines long in Kathleen Mulchrone's edition, compiled, it seems, over several centuries, from the ninth down to the eleventh.[30] The rest, save V3, are various shorter Irish abridgments of the Life. The copy in K preserves a version very close to VT in many of its readings, as this diagram suggests; it is, however, heavily abbreviated.[31] The *p*-branch texts share some readings with K against all other branches, but they also share readings with G, Lb, and V3 against K and VT.[32] On the right, the three boxes hanging from a single node share a major innovation in the plot of the Life: all these texts narrate Patrick's stay on Cruachán Aigle, or Croagh Patrick, as one of the last things Patrick does before he dies in Saul, as opposed to other Lives, where this scene comes towards the middle of the Life.[33]

---

[30] Mulchrone, *Bethu Phátraic*; for the date, see Jackson, "The Date," and David Dumville, "The Dating of the Tripartite Life of St Patrick," in *Saint Patrick, A.D. 493–1993*, ed. Dumville (Woodbridge: Boydell, 1993), 255-8.

[31] Edited by R. I. Best in *Anecdota from Irish Manuscripts*, vol. 3, eds. O. J. Bergin, R. I. Best, Kuno Meyer, and J. G. O'Keeffe (Halle a. S.: Max Niemeyer, 1910), 29-42.

[32] As noted by Mulchrone, "Die Abfassungszeit," 22-33.

[33] See further Ludwig Bieler, "Anecdotum Patricianum: Fragments of a Life of St. Patrick from MSS. Cotton Vitellius E. vii and Rawlinson B 479," in *Measgra i gCuimhne Mhichíl Uí Chléirigh*, ed. Sylvester O'Brien (Dublin: Assisi Press, 1944), 220-37, at 234-6.

While a useful tool, however, this picture is an imperfect summary of many different cross-currents of textual relationships. For instance, it is unlikely that G and Lb actually share a single common ancestor with V3, *pace* Bieler. Rather, I believe, we should instead see Lb and G as separate revisions of older Patrician Lives, which have each drawn on V3 to varying degrees. Lb sometimes appears to translate V3 closely; at others, it paraphrases, and it often weaves passages of V3 in with those drawn from other Lives.[34] G, in general, follows V3 far more closely.[35]

There is not sufficient space here to lay out my argument for this in full, though it is possible to sketch out the reasoning using the gifts Patrick receives on Cruachán Aigle, where G follows V3 in having only three gifts, while Lb presents a text intermediate between V3 and the full list of seven found in VT. The list of gifts, as found in VT, can be paraphrased as follows:

1. A number of souls freed from torment equivalent to the number of birds flocking around Cruachán

2. Seven souls freed from torment every Thursday, and twelve every Saturday

3. That the sea will cover Ireland seven years before Doom

4. That the Saxons (*Saxain*) will not dwell in Ireland "as long as I [Patrick] am in Heaven" (*céin mbéo-sa for nim*)

5. That anyone who sings part of Sechnall's hymn in honor of Patrick, or gives something in his name, or does penance in Ireland, will not go to Hell

6. That seven people for every thread in his cloak will be freed from Hell on Doomsday

---

[34] In addition to the example below, see also the passage where Patrick receives the Staff of Jesus (Lb pp. 14-16 [Stokes]), which draws on both VT ll. 276-82 and V3 §§23–5 (even leaving one phrase, *super ripam maris Tyrreni*, untranslated).

[35] It is possible that Lb and G both drew on the same translation of V3, though I regard this as doubtful; I plan to explore the connections between Lb, G, and V3 in more detail in my doctoral dissertation.

7. That Patrick will be the judge of the men of Ireland on Doomsday.[36]

V3, for its part, has Patrick make only three requests.[37] These are replicated nearly word-for-word in G; Lb, as mentioned, splits the difference: it includes all three requests from V3, then adds four from VT—in order—to fill out the complete roster of seven gifts:

V3 §85:

> *In ipso monte tres peticiones rogauit. [A] Prima, ut omnes habitatores huius insule, si quis ex ipsis una hora penitentiam egerit, infernus non claudatur super eum. [B] Secunda, ut alienigene in hac insula non habitarent usque in diem iudicii. [C] Tercia, ut septem annis ante diem iudicii insulam istam mare operiat.*

> On the mountain he made three requests: [A] First, that every inhabitant of this island, if any of them do even a single hour of penance, that Hell not close over him. [B] Second, that foreigners not dwell in this island until Doomsday. [C] Third, that the sea cover the island seven years before Doomsday.

G f. 240v, ll. 22–6:

> Is annsin tra ro thothlaigh Patraic tri hitche for Dhía. [A] As í an ceadna hitche nabdís iffreanaigh fir Erenn, acht conos tairset aithraighe bheg ría mbás. [B] As í an itche thánaisi na ro aittreabhtais echtrainn

---

[36] VT ll. 1323-64. K reproduces the same requests, in the same order; so does *p*, save that there, no. 4 has been lost, presumably because someone, at some point after 1169, recognized that the fact that 'Saxons' (or, rather, Normans) were actually dwelling in Ireland would lead to the awkward conclusion that Patrick was no longer in Heaven. K in Best, "Betha Pátraic," 37-9. For *p*, see RIA MS 24 P 25 (475), pp. 98a l. 42 – 98b l. 44 (L is missing text here).

[37] These are based off the account appended to Tírechán's *Collectanea de sancto Patricio*, in *The Patrician Texts in the Book of Armagh*, ed. and trans. Ludwig Bieler (Dublin: Dublin Institute for Advanced Studies, 1979), 122-66, at 164 (§52).

in in*n*si-se co brát*h*. [C] As í da*no* in *t*reas itc*h*e co
ttios*adh* muir t*ar* Eri*nn* sec*ht* mbl*iadh*na ria mbrát*h*.

That is when Patrick made three requests of God. [A]
The first request is that the men of Ireland not be
damned, so long as they perform a little penance
before death. [B] The second request is that foreigners
not dwell in this island till Doomsday. [C] The third
request is that the sea come over Ireland seven years
before Doomsday.

Lb pp. 36–8 [Stokes]

Dixit Patricius: "Ni rág [. . .] co tartar dam .uii.
nidche on Chomdid .i. [A] cipe do feraib Erenn do-
gne aithrigi re m-bas, cid fri re envaire na
ro h-iatta iffernd fair i m-brath ocus [B] co na ro
aittrebat echtraind in indsi, & [C] co ti muir tarsi
.uii. m-bliadna ria m-brath. & [2] co ra sœrur-sa
mor-fessiur cecha dardain & .xii. cecha sathairnd ar
phianuib iffirnd. & [5] cipe gebus m' imund h-i l-lou
a etsechta co rub nemidach amal do-rarngert-sa do
sechnall. & [6] co tucar-sa a pianaib iffirnd i l-lou
bratha mor-fessiur cecha brodhirne dom chassul do
neoch no
do n-aidlife & [7] corup me fen bus brithem
i m-brath do feraib Erenn." "Do-bertar duit indsin
uli," ar in t-aingel[.]

Patrick said, "I won't go [. . .] until I am given seven
requests from the Lord: that is, [A] any of the men of
Ireland who does penance before death, even if for a
single hour, that Hell not close upon him on
Doomsday, and [B] that foreigners not dwell on the
island, and [C] that the sea cover it seven years before
Doomsday, and [2] that I might save seven people
every Thursday and twelve every Saturday from the
torments of Hell, and [5] whoever recites my hymn
on the day of his death, that he be guaranteed Heaven
(as I promised to Sechnall), and [6] that I might bring

370

seven people for each thread on my cloak from the
torments of Hell on Judgment Day for everyone who
touches it, and [7] that I myself might be [the] judge
for the men of Ireland on Doomsday." "That shall all
be given to you," said the angel.

The first three petitions are clearly those of V3 (and G); the next four
proceed in order of those in VT, which were, apparently, used to arrive
at the full complement of seven. This contrast in use is present
throughout Lb and G: Lb usually attempts to follow both the Tripartite
Life and the Vita tertia, while G, by and large, hews to V3's text quite
closely in passages it shares with that text.

The bulk of G, however, derives from a short Life of Patrick
probably related to the *p* branch, and the reviser(s) of G had access to
other materials as well, some of which cannot be traced.[38] For
instance, G draws on a legend found in the Middle Irish Life of Senán,
in which Patrick baptizes the Corca Baischinn from a nearby hill, and
foresees the birth of Senán.[39] It also contains at least one story found
elsewhere, to my knowledge, only in the seventh-century account by
Tírechán, where Erc mac Dego, judge to Laogaire, the King of Tara,
perceives a stream of fire transmitted from Patrick to himself.[40] The
form of the story is different enough, however, that direct transmission
is unlikely: in Tírechán, Patrick asks Erc why he stood in his honor; in

---

[38] The relationship to the *p* branch can be seen in the following passages:
"Ba Cothraige a ainm in tan sin iarsan ní fo ghní dona ceithre muinnteraibh,
7 ro bháoi do dhiochradhus ind fhoghnamha do ghnídh Patraic co
ccoimhleadh gath [*sic*] muinnter dona *ceithre* muinteraibh ba dí [*sic*] namá
no fhoghmadh. Céd sléchtain leis dano gacha maitne, 7 ced ele gacha
fescuir lá taobh a fhoghnamha cheana, 7 longadh dano leis o trath go tráth"
(G f. 235r ll. 4-9), vs. "Ba de tra ro lil-sium in t-ainm as Cothruighi ar
foghnum do cethrar muinntire. Bai tra do dhichracht in fhoghnuma i mbai
Pátraic co toimniudh cechae dona cetheora muinteruib dia bhfoghnad
cumad do a oenar foighneth, et bai gidh in anmcairdine ele fairsium .i. cét
slectain matan 7 cét fescor 7 oenproind on trath co araili" (L ll. 141-6).
Versions of this passage can be found in other Lives of Patrick, Irish and
Latin, but *p* and G are the only texts to mention 'diochradhas'/'diochracht',
as well as the '(single) meal' (*oenproind/longad*).
[39] G f. 239v ll. 16–31 = L ll. 1799–1821, 1845–50, 1864–8 (approximately).
[40] Tírechán, *Collectanea*, 133 (§13). A version–without many of the
identifying details–is present in V3 §92.

G, one of Laogaire's druids asks Erc why he rose, though it meant a grave insult to the king.[41]

With the evidence of the three Lives discussed above–the two related Lives of Brigit in B1 and B2, and that of Patrick in G–it is possible to draw a sketch of the wider picture of hagiographical composition and transmission underlying these texts. It is clear, for instance, that their revisers had Latin accounts of their saints' deeds to hand, and were able to translate them with a high degree of accuracy and merge them into pre-existing Middle Irish accounts.

The reviser of Brigit's Life preserved in B1 and B2 had ready access to the *Vita prima*, as well as an earlier form of what is now K. Furthermore, how V1 was used seems to signal a wider familiarity with how the Life of Brigit should go–that is, when it came time to copy the Irish Life of Brigit from the exemplar, the reviser may have felt that something was missing from the narrative, and therefore supplied relevant passages from an available copy of the *Vita prima*. The actual process of revising appears to have been relatively simple. The passages from the Life were used to fill a gap in the text of the Irish Life as it came down to the reviser; there was no need to synthesize competing traditions, and did not draw upon sources beyond the Vita Prima or the Middle Irish Life.[42]

The Life of Patrick in G, however, presents a different picture. If the text as we have it was largely the work of a single compiler-translator (which I think likely), it is clear they were familiar with at least two Lives of Patrick and various shorter legends, and had the

---

[41] G f. 238r ll. 8–12: "Ro *conghradh* Patraic *chu*ca, 7 atr*aracht* Earc m*a*c Deagh*adh* mic Brain roi*mh*e ar i*n* ion*adh* i mbói 7 is b*ert* an dráoi fri hEarc, 'C*idh ar*a n-eirea*cht* ria bPatraic d*ar* s*á*r*ughadh* in ríog*h*?' 'Ni caom*h*nagur-sa b*heith* i tt*air*isio*mh ar* a cion*n gan* eirg*h*e roi*mh*e, *ar* do d*h*each*aigh* colom*ha* t*h*eint*idh*e as a *gh*ion im' *gh*ion-sa.'"

[42] A possible exception is a passage about Ninnidh, a scholar (*mac léiginn*) who gave Brigit her last rites. This passage is present, in part, in Lb p. 76, V1 §77, L ll. 1759–65, and K f. 20vb ll. 17–30. B2 ff. 22r l. 18 – 22v, l. 19 expands on this passage, however, with a text that closely parallels the Latin *Vita quarta* ("Fourth Life") of Brigit (BHL 1460: *Acta Sanctorum, Vita IV bipartita auctore anonymo*, Feb. I, cols. 156–72, at col. 168 [§II.9]). There is additional material in B2 not present in the *Vita quarta*, however, so it may be that each shares a common source.

ability to synthesize these into an impressively lively account (in one scene, Patrick doesn't merely revive a dead cow, as he does in most surviving Lives, Latin and Irish, but stuffs its innards back into it with his bare hands).[43] Even if the various sources were added in over a lengthy period of time, by various revisers, the difference in the texts used in the Life of Brigit and in the Life of Patrick would still be striking: every passage in both Lives of Brigit discussed above, B1 and B2, can be accounted for in some other source, Latin or Irish; this is not the case in the Life of Patrick in G.

What might explain this? To a degree, this may be attributable to the varying literary skills and interests of the respective revisers. Other explanations are possible, however. One would consider the vibrancy of the traditions surrounding each saint: when it came time to revise each Life, perhaps there was simply more material about Patrick than there was for Brigit–a situation that has survived until the present day, when a biographer of Patrick can give an approximate outline of his *actual* life, while anyone who writes about the historical Brigit must first confront the question of whether or not she existed.[44] Another potential explanation would look at the place where these Lives were composed: fifty years ago, Frederic Mac Donncha suggested that many of the homilies found in the Leabhar Breac, including Lives of Brigit and Patrick, had their origins in a collection put together in the late eleventh century at Armagh.[45] Scholars there would, of course, have been rather more familiar with material about Patrick than about Brigit.

These explanations are not mutually exclusive, and it will take more research to come to a firm conclusion on the origins and composition of these Lives, and their relation to the wider intellectual and cultural environment in which they were composed. Still, I hope this brief discussion of two relatively neglected Irish Lives of saints shows the promise they offer: since they were translated from known

---

[43] G f. 234r, ll. 14–15 ("do b*eir* [Patrick] a hionat*h*ar in*n*te co*n*a m*éa*raib*h*"). Cf. L ll. 99–100, V3 §9.

[44] Compare, for instance, Roy Flechner, *Saint Patrick Retold: The Legend and History of Ireland's Patron Saint* (Princeton: Princeton University Press, 2019) to Noel Kissane, *Saint Brigid of Kildare: Life, Legend, Cult* (Dublin: Four Courts Press, 2017).

[45] Mac Donncha, "Homilies," 67-70.

Latin sources, we can, in certain cases, describe the style and usage of individual writers; they help to clarify the relationship of other surviving Lives of the saints; and finally, they may help us to understand how Irish hagiographical texts were composed, revised, preserved, and transmitted in the central and later Middle Ages.

Appendix A: Sigla

Lb: Dublin, RIA MS 23 P 16 (1230/"An Leabhar Breac"), ff. 24b-29b (Patrick); 61b-66a (Brigit)
    Ed. and trans. Whitley Stokes, *Three Middle Irish Homilies* (1877), 1–47; 49–87

p: L: Cork, University College Cork, Book of Lismore, ff. 1a-7b (Pat.); ff. 11b-17a (Brig.)
      Ed. and trans. Stokes, *Book of Lismore* (1890), 1–19, 149–67; 34–53, 182–200
    P: Paris, Bibliothèque Nationale de France, Fonds Basques et Celtiques MS 1, ff. 74–6 (Pat., acephalous); 76–81 (Brig.; 77ra badly stained)
    Others (Brigit: London, British Library, Egerton MS 91 ff. 57–60; Patrick: see Bieler, *"Bethu Phátraic"*)

K: Dublin King's Inns MS 10, ff. 17–20 (Pat., acephalous, imperfect); 20–1 (Brig., acephalous)

G: Dublin, RIA MS C iv 3 (1192), ff. 233-43 (Patrick)

B1: Brussels, KBR MS 2324–40, ff. 24a-30b (Brigit, imperfect)
B2: Brussels, KBR MS 4190–200, ff. 6a-30b (Brigit)

V1: *Vita prima s. Brigidae* (AASS, Feb. I, cols. 119–35)

V3: *Vita tertia sancti Patricii,* in *Four Latin Lives of St Patrick: Colgan's Vita secunda, quarta, tertia, and quinta*, ed. Ludwig Bieler (Dublin: Dublin Institute for Advanced Studies, 1971), 115–90

VT: *Bethu Phátraic: The Tripartite Life of Patrick*, ed. Kathleen Mulchrone (Dublin: Hodges and Figgis, 1939)

Appendix B: B2 and the *p* branch

The following passages show the point where B2 switches from following the *p* branch (represented by L) to sharing readings with the remainder of the Lives (as represented by B1). See further Lb p. 62a ll. 22–9 (pp. 52–4 Stokes) and P f. 77rb ll. 19–27. Apparent moment of switch marked by //.

B2 ff. 6v l. 17– 7r l. 2

Fiarf*aigh*is an d*r*ai cía órbó torr*ach* an cum*h*al. "Uaimsi," ar Dub*h*tach. Adub*air*t an d*r*ai, "Bid*h* am*h*ra an g*h*ein fil ina b*r*oin*n*, & ní bia a cosmail for talm*ain*." Adub*air*t Dub*h*tach, 'Ni léicc mo s*h*eit*igh* dam*h*sa gan reic na cum*h*aile-si.' // Adubairt an drai t*r*ia rath faitsine, "Foig*h*enait síl do mna-sa do s*h*iol na cum*h*aile, & taitnebaid*h* **an g*h*ein uasal oirm*h*idne*ch* fil ina broin*n* fiad*h* daoinib*h* an talm*an*** am*h*ail taitnes g*r*ian et*ir* ren*n*aib*h* nim*h*e."

B1 ff. 24v l. 21 – 25r l. 2

Ro fi*ar*faigh an draoi cia órbh*á* halac*h*ta an c*h*umh*a*l. "**Ó Dh*u*pt*h*ach,**" *ar* an c*h*umh*a*l. "Bid*h* am*h*ra i fiad*h*naisi Dé an gein fil it' brú," ar Dub*h*t*h*ach an draoi, "*7* ni bía a cosm*h*ailes isna talman*n*aib*h*." Atb*er*t Dub*h*tach, "Ní léig mo s*h*eitigh dam*h* gan a **creic** na cum*h*aile-si." Atb*er*t an draoi tre rat*h* faitsine, "Foigen*aidh*," *ar* se, "síol do m*h*ná-sa do siol na cum*h*aile, óir béraid*h* an c*h*umal **an g*h*ein b*ús* uaisle** *7* **b*ús* airm*h*idnig*h*e** fíad*h* dáoinib*h* an talman, *ar* am*h*ail t*h*aitnes grían idir rennaib*h* nim*h*e, as am*h*laid*h* sin t*h*aitnes gniom*h*a na hingine si*n* **fil ina broin*n* fíad*h* d*h*aoinib*h* an talm*h*an uile**[.]"

L ll. 1166–72

Imcomaircidh in d*r*ai in rob al*ach*ta o neoch? 'Is al*ach*ta uaimsi,' ol Dub*th*ach. Asbert in d*r*ai: 'Bidh amhra in gein fil ina broinn, ni bhia a cosmuil isna talm*an*daib.' 'Ni leig dhamhsa mu shetig,' ar Dub*th*ach, 'gan a reic na cumaili-si.' Adub*air*t an d*r*ai t*r*ia rath faitsine: 'Foighen*a* sil do mhna-sa do sil na cumuili, áir ber*aid* in cum*al* ingin reil teitnem*aich* thaitnighfes am*ail* g*r*ein itir renna nimhe.'

The Female Critic in *Feasta*, 1948-1988

Katie Whelan

Introduction

There is no specific method or approach in literary criticism from the female reviewer that is not also used by non-feminist critics.[1] However, what literary criticism from the female perspective does provide is an "acute and impassioned awareness to the ways in which primarily male structures are inscribed (or encoded) within our literary inheritance".[2] This approach provides a comprehensive criticism of the female voice as character, reader and as writer. The analysis of the journalistic practice of literature reviews, within the context of post-revival Irish language media, allows one to assess theories and methodologies relating to the media's role in the redefinition of the public role of women. The press allowed both communicator and reader to interact with one another. Ideas could be shared and the female journalist could engage with political and linguistic writings offering their own interpretations and perspectives. Through journalistic practice in the post-revival period of the 1940s and 50s, the female journalist began to realise her identity and value, in the world and in a national context. Building on Benedict Anderson's theory of an imagined community, female Irish language journalists began to recognise themselves as a group unto themselves, with their own cultural and political aspirations, set within the wider Irish language community.[3]

Feasta

Feasta is a monthly literary magazine, established by Conradh na Gaeilge/The Gaelic League in 1948, via the publishing house Clódhanna Teoranta. *Feasta* provided–and continues to provide–an

---

[1] Toril Moi, 'Sexual/Textual Politics' in Mary Eagleton (Ed.) *Feminist Literary Theory: A Reader*. (New York: Basil Blackwell, 1986).
[2] Annette Kolodny, 'Dancing between Left and Right: Feminism and the Academic Minefield in the 1980s', *Feminist Studies* Vol. 14, No. 3. (Autumn 1988): 462
[3] See Benedict Anderson, *Imagined Communities: Reflections on the Origin and Spread of Nationalism*. (London & New York: Verso, 2016).

important public forum for Irish language literature, political commentary and current affairs discussion. The title of the journal, translating to 'henceforth' or 'hereafter, reflects the sentiment of the journal to project the Irish language into the future, in the landscape of the Irish Free State founded in 1922, rather than aligning it with the past tense. The journal's aims were many, amongst them to provide a public platform for Irish language poets, writers and even visual artists through which to showcase their work in the public sphere. *Feasta's* objectives were laid out clearly in the first issue in April 1948, and it's apparent that the journal's loyalties laid with furthering the case of the Irish language rather than that of the female journalistic voice:

> *Seasaímíd leis an nGaelachas: seasaímíd lenár náisiúntacht ina hiomláine . . . Is mór againn gach foirm trína gcuireann ár náisiúntacht í féin in iúl; ceol, ealaíon, rinncí, cluichí srl . . . ach ní tábhachtaí linn aon fhoirm acu ná an mháthair-fhoirm–an teanga féin. Í sin agus a mbaineann léi ár bpríomh-chúram.*[4]

> We stand with Gaelicism; we stand with our nationhood in its entirety . . . We value form through which our nationhood is expressed; music, art, dance, games etc. . . . but more importantly than the form is the native form–our language. It is our language and all that relates to her, which is our primary concern.

This sentiment is also reflective of Conradh na Gaeilge's stance on women at the time, as the organisation, although welcoming of women as members, was primarily concerned with the promotion, conservation and revival of the Irish language, rather than developing the role of women as citizen. As Maryann Valiulis has stated "The Gaelic League needed women to keep an Irish home, to teach Irish to the children". [5] This stance is exemplified in the official pamphlet Conradh na Gaeilge published on the topic in 1900. Entitled *Irish Women and the Home Language,* it suggested women assume a central

---

[4] Editorial, *Feasta.* (April 1948): 8. All translations are my own.
[5] Maryann Gialanell Valiulis, 'Power, Gender and Identity in the Free State' *Journal of Women's History* (Winter/Spring 1995): 129.

role in the domestic sphere, and focus on their role as mother of the next generation of Irish speakers and patriots, rather than on their possibilities outside the home:

> The power is in the hands of the whole people of Ireland, it is true, but it is an especial manner in the hands of the women of Ireland. Why? Because the language movement is not an academic one. It is a living one. What is wanted is to make the language living in the land; to do this it is necessary to make it the home language; and to make it the home language it is necessary to enlist the co-operation of woman–the home maker.[6]

This juxtaposition of the woman's high status in the home, and low visibility on the public sphere was evident again in the drafting of the 1937 Constitution of Ireland.

Feasta's manifesto echoes the famous speech of Irish language activist and later first President of Ireland, Dubhghlas de hÍde (1860-1949), given in November 1892 before the Irish National Literary Society in Dublin. This pivotal address encouraged the development of Irish culture and society in the founding of an independent State. De hÍde lamented "how one of the most reading and literary peoples [had] become one of the least studious and most un-literary" and called for the Irish language and all elements of Ireland's culture, including journalism and literary practices, to assume a central role in arousing "some spark of patriotic inspiration" amongst the people.[7] This ethos was further emphasised by D. P. Moran in his book *The Philosophy of Irish Ireland,* published in 1905, in which the author encouraged "a native colour in arts, industries, literature, social habits, points of view, music, amusements and so on, throughout all phases of human activity".[8]

---

[6] Mary E.L. Butler, *Irishwomen and the Home Language.*(Conradh na Gaeilge. Oifig an tSoláthair: 1900).
[7] Douglas Hyde,"The Necessity for De-Anglicizing Ireland". *Irish Literary Society,* (25.11.1892): 120.
[8] David Patrick Moran, Preface, *The Philosophy of Irish Ireland* (Dublin: James Duffy & Company, 1905), 9.

Feasta succeeded in playing a instrumental role in the development of Irish language writing in the post-revival period. This is evident in the hundreds of poems, stories and many dramas that populated the pages of *Feasta* throughout the first 40 years of its publication, a catalytic time in Irish history as during this period Ireland matured from a Free State to an independent country, the Irish language gained further prominence on the public stage and Ireland's national broadcaster, and Telefís Éireann (later Raidió Teilifís Éireann) was founded. *Feasta* joined the ranks of other publications such as *An tUltach* (founded in 1924) and *Comhar* (1942) as pivotal public platforms in Irish language post-revival print media. All three publications, *Feasta, An tUltach* and *Comhar* have been credited amongst scholars with modernising the language and making it more accessible to a post-revival, independent readership.

Women in mid twentieth century Ireland

Feasta would provide a valuable public forum for female literary reviewers at a time in Irish history when the female voice was largely marginalised. This marginalisation had been the norm within Irish language writing since the beginning of the literary tradition. Although women had played a central role in the earliest forms of Irish language journalism, such as the tradition of an caoineadh/the keen and sean-nós singing, this had not translated to the practice of print journalism. The keen is a traditional expression of sorrow in the form of vocal lament to those who have died, or have emigrated. Eibhlín Dhubh Ní Chonaill's 1773 *Caoineadh Airt Uí Laoghaire* (The lament of Art O'Leary), is perhaps the most well-known keen, which Nuala Ní Dhomhnaill has alleged was proof that a perfect piece of literature could be written by a female.[9] The keen is seen as an early form of sean-nós singing, an unaccompanied vocal music, the music of human reactions to events in their lives.

The birth of journals *Shan Van Vocht* and *Bean na hÉireann* in 1896 and 1909 respectively, marked the first time a publication was aimed purely at the female reader. Both these journals, although they featured Irish language pieces and were sympathetic to the cause of an

---

[9] "Is féidir saothar foirfe ealaíne a chur ar fáil agus fós fanacht i do bhean". Nuala Ní Dhomhnaill, "Caoineadh Airt Uí Laoghaire", *Comhar* (January 1986): 25.

independent Ireland and the voting rights of women, were written in English.

Regina Uí Chollatáin has argued that the emergence of *Feasta* in 1948, as well as its contemporary, Irish language journal *Comhar* six years previously in 1942, marked a turning of the tide in the context of Irish language literary criticism saying: "Very few newspaper articles address the poetry genre and although much poetry was published, the treaties on the criticism of it is scant until the emergence of the periodicals *Comhar* (1942) and *Feasta* (1948)".[10] *Feasta* wasn't as cataclysmic for Irish language female writers however, in the sense that the ratio of male and female journalists remained largely disproportionate, with only one work by a female writer being reviewed by either of the female critics examined in this chapter. *Feasta* did, however, provide them a public platform upon which to write, discuss, debate and communicate.

The founding of *Feasta* coincided with an era in which Irish language print media came of age and further developed as a medium independent of the influence of the English language. Although young women in the 1940s had more educational opportunities than the generation that preceded them, their opportunities to participate in public life were hindered by restrictive legislation introduced from the 1920s onwards, specifically the introduction of the Marriage Bar in 1932 and the mention of the role of women in the 1937 Constitution of Ireland under article 41 which some have described as confining.[11] This led to Irish women organising a campaign to oppose the draft constitution and prompted a lively debate between Éamon de Valera, President of the Executive Council, and the Joint Committee of

---

[10]Regina Uí Chollatáin, "Twentieth Century Irish Literature: A Journalistic Criticism" in Mark O'Brien and Felix M. Larkin (Eds). *Periodicals and Journalism in Twentieth-Century Ireland.* (Dublin: Four Courts Press. 2015), 300.

[11] "[T]he State recognises that by her life within the home, woman gives to the State a support without which the common good cannot be achieved". Constitution of Ireland, 1937. Article 41.2, 'The Family'. https://www.irishstatutebook.ie/eli/cons/en/html#article41

Women's Societies and Social Workers in regards to "women's constitutional and economic condition".[12]
The Irish language revival moment of the late-nineteenth and early-twentieth century had been well-known for its willingness to accept women on a par with men, and what this resulted in was a small cohort of university-educated women who actively embraced public engagement through the medium of an Irish language platform.[13] This trend would continue into the mid-twentieth century, and *Feasta*–true to the ethos of the Gaelic League and the theory of D. P. Moran's 'Irish-Ireland'–provided a platform for several highly educated Irish-speaking women to develop their own literary voice. The relationship between women and the literary tradition is a complicated one, as women are both included and excluded. Montefori described this juxtaposition: "as readers and writers, we belong to it [literary tradition], but as women we are excluded".[14] This chapter will situate *Feasta* within the context of Irish-language journalism and will provide an insight into some of the early examples of women journalists reviewing literary works through the medium of Irish. While there is a growing body of scholarship on Irish-language women writers and poets in twentieth century Ireland, this does not yet extend to Irish language female journalists.

Cultural and Educational Context

Feasta emerged in a decade of renewed energy within the Irish language movement, in spite of the impact of World War II.[15] The decade of the 1940s was a highlight in terms of the teaching of Irish in schools.[16] It was from this context that *Feasta* was born, and this

[12] Maria Luddy, "A 'Sinister and Retrogressive' Proposal: Irish Women's Opposition to the 1937 Draft Constitution," *Transactions of the Royal Historical Society.* Vol. 15. (UK: Cambridge University Press. 2005) 177.
[13] See Ríona Nic Congáil, and Máirín Nic Eoin, "Women's Writing in Irish, 1900-2013", in Heather Ingman and Clíona Ó Gallchóir (Eds), *A History of Irish Women's Writing,* (Cambridge: Cambridge University Press, 2018).
[14] Janet Montefiore, *Feminism and Poetry.* (London, 1987), 26.
[15] For example an tOireachtas in 1939, and Comhdháil Náisiúnta na Gaeilge 1942.
[16] P. Ó Riagáin, "Bilingualism in Ireland 1973-1983: An overview of national sociolinguistic surveys," *International Journal of the Sociology of Language* Issue 70 (1988): 31.

literary magazine proved instrumental in adapting Irish language literature to the requirements of a post-revival Irish reading public, and helped to promote the course and further development of Irish language writing. *Feasta* aimed to build on the legacy of the Irish language Revival, a time when the creation and promotion of an Irish language reading republic was the main objective. *Feasta* adopted the Gaelic script in the earliest editions of its publication as a way of ensuring continuity with the revolutionary revival. The need to modernise the language was a key element of print media, with ideas of religion, communications and education assuming a central role.[17] The post-revival period focused more on the most basic element of journalistic practice, the creation and continuance of an Irish-language public, that would provide material for teaching and for leisure enjoyment of Irish. In his forward to *Feasta: Innéacs 1948-2000* (a work compiled by Liam Mac Peaircín), scholar Nollaig Mac Congáil further stressed the importance of *Feasta* in Irish language publishing and writing:

> *Chuidigh na foilseacháin sin [An tUltach, Comhar agus Feasta] ach go háirithe leis an Ghaeilge a thabhairt isteach sa nuaré agus dúshraith bhuan a leagan dár tharla i gcinniúint fhoilsitheoireacht agus scríbhneoireacht na Gaeilge ó shin.[18]*

> Those publications [*An tUltach, Comhar* and *Feasta*] aided especially in bringing the Irish language into a new era and laying a permanent foundation which has been fateful in the realm of Irish language publishing and writing.

Women and Feasta

There have been many editors of *Feasta* but only one woman, Íte Ní Chionnaith, who was also the first woman elected as president of Conradh na Gaeilge (1985-1989), and held the position of editor

---

[17] See Marie-Louise Legg, *Newspapers and Nationalism: The Irish Provincial Press 1850-1892.* (Dublin: Four Courts Press, 1998).
[18] Nollaig Mac Congáil, "Réamhrá/Introduction", in Liam Mac Peaircín (ed.) *Feasta: Innéacs 1948-2000,* ed. (Cork & Dublin: Clódhanna Teoranta, 2003).

between February 1979 and April 1980. However, the literary works of female writers and journalists have proven a regular feature on the pages of *Feasta* from the beginning of the publication in 1948, with contributions from accomplished Irish language writers, such as: poet Mairéad Ní Ghráda[19] (1896-1971); dramatist Siobhán Ní Shuilleabháin[20] (1928-2013); and writer and academic, Úna Bean Uí Dhiosca[21] (1880-1958). Creating a public forum upon which literary review was crucial to the vision of the Irish language revival, and as such it featured regularly on the page of *Feasta*. Literary reviews assumed a central role in *Feasta* and there were two primary female literary critics in the journal, Máire Mhac an tSaoi (1922-2021) and Máirín Ní Mhuiríosa (1906-1982), both accomplished poets and writers in their own right, who contributed literary reviews to the magazine on a fairly regular basis between 1948 and 1988. Although the journal featured a regular review column 'Léirmheasta' for a period in the 1950s, which many male reviewers contributed to, it is the reviews from Mhac an tSaoi and Ní Mhuiríosa that shall provide the focus of an analysis of literary reviews from the female journalist in *Feasta*.

Máire Mhac an tSaoi (1922-2021)

Born in 1922, the same year as the foundation of the Irish Free State, Máire Mhac an tSaoi is widely regarded as one of the most prolific poets in the Irish language. Mhac an tSaoi has seven published literary works attributed to her, comprising of poetry collections, biographies and an autobiography: *Margadh na Saoire* (1956), *Codladh an Ghaiscigh* (1973), *An Galar Dubhach* (1980), *An Cion go dtí Seo* (1987), *The Same Age as the State* (2003), *Cérbh í Meg Russell?* (2008) and *Scéal Ghearóid Iarla* (2010). Mhac an tSaoi is also credited in 1972 as co-author, under her married name of Máire McEntee O'Brien with her husband, Conor Cruise O'Brien, politician, writer and historian, of *A Concise History of Ireland*. Cló Iar-Chonnacht, a publishing house based in the Irish speaking district of Connemara, Galway published Mhac an tSaoi's German to Irish

---

[19] Máiréad Ní Ghráda, "D'fhile nach maireann, GMH", *Feasta* (October 1959): 15.
[20] Siobhán Ní Shuilleabháin, "Bean ar bhean", *Feasta* (November 1968): 5.
[21] Una Uí Dhiosca, "Cad is litríocht ann?", *Feasta*. (March 1950).

translation, *Marbhnaí Duino,* of Rainer Maria Rilke's *Dunieser Elegien* in 2013. No study of twentieth century Irish language literature would be complete without analysis of her works and influence included. Mhac an tSaoi has been identified by scholar and poet Louis de Paor, alongside Máirtín Ó Direáin[22] and Seán Ó Ríordáin[23], as one of a "trinity of poets who revolutionised Irish language in the 1940s and 50s", [24] the same period as the earliest years of *Feasta.* De Paor gives this title to the trio for their instrumental role in developing the Irish language literary tradition, and in the case of Mhac an tSaoi, for introducing topics into the public sphere which hadn't been addressed, especially not by a female, at the time–such as adoption, sexual desire, and racism. Although best known for her poetry, Mhac an tSaoi was also a journalist, translator and reviewer, with *Feasta* providing a public platform upon which to publish these works.

It's worth noting that when signing off on each piece in *Feasta* Mhac an tSaoi included her full name, Máire Mhac an tSaoi. This is at odds with her practice in *Comhar,* a predecessor of *Feasta* first published in 1942, in which she usually signed with the initial M in the earliest editions of the magazine.[25] Coming from a well-known political family, with her father Seán McEntee being a recognised Fianna Fáil politician, who served in various ministries of government, including Tánaiste, deputy prime minister, between the years 1959-1965. It could be argued that Mhac an tSaoi's adaptation of her journalistic signature was a way in which she could forge her own way as an independent figure, especially when including highly controversial subject matter in her works, as she often did. However, by the year 1947, Mhac an tSaoi had chosen to sign all her pieces in *Comhar* with her full name. This practice was fully honed by the time

---

[22] Máirtín Ó Direáin (1910-1988) was an Irish poet from the Aran Islands, a Gaeltacht area off the West Coast of Ireland.
[23] Seán Ó Ríordáin (1916-1977) was an Irish language poet and newspaper columnist from Baile Mhúirne, County Cork, a Gaeltacht area in the South West of Ireland.
[24] Louis De Paor, "Réamhrá/Introduction," *Máire Mhac an tSaoi: An Paróiste Míorúilteach.* (Inverin: Cló Iar-Chonnacht, 2014).
[25] For example, see Máire Mhac an tSaoi, "An tSeantóir", *Comhar.* (December 1944): 2.

she turned to *Feasta* when it first emerged in 1948, and the writer never deviated from signing all works featured in the literary magazine with her full name. It can be presumed therefore that it was on the pages of *Comhar* that Mhac an tSaoi first practiced her journalistic voice, and by the time *Feasta* emerged she was confident in her identity as journalist, writer, essayist and translator.

Liam Mac Peaircín's *Feasta: Innéacs 1948-2000,* reflects Mhac an tSaoi's active role in the journal's publishing as she's named as the author of 13 pieces, between the years 1953 and 1988, with seven of those pieces consisting of literary reviews. The works reviewed by Mhac an tSaoi were all written by male writers, thereby reflecting the fact that during the mid-twentieth century, most Irish language writers were men. See the index at the end of this chapter for a full list of reviews conducted by Mhac an tSaoi in *Feasta.*

In *Feasta's* October 1953 edition, Máire Mhac an tSaoi contributed to the column "Rogha an Chlub Leabhair"(Book Club Choice) by penning a review on Liam Ó Flaithearta's collection of short stories, *Dúil* first published in 1953. This is Ó Flaithearta's only published collection of stories in Irish, with many critical reviews written after its publication. The negative reception to the collection discouraged Ó Flaithearta from publishing again, however *Dúil* has been reprinted many times since the 1950s, with the publishing house Cló Iar-Chonnacht asserting that the public demand on the book shows that contemporary readers of Irish don't share in the views of the collection's critics. Mhac an tSaoi's review of *Dúil* opens with praise of Ó Flaithearta's "gift of fluid expression", [26] and goes on to say that the 18 short stories in the collection show what can be achieved when "heritage, a gift of storytelling and the commandment of a trade" come together in one writer.[27] In light of Mhac an tSaoi's glowing review, it can be claimed that the reviewer was one of few who recognised the merit within this collection of work upon its publication, and, was

[26] "I ngach teangain tá scríbhneoirí a bhfuil bua saoráide acu". Máire Mhac an tSaoi, "Rogha an Chlub Leabhar", *Feasta* (Deireadh Fómhair 1953): 7.
[27] "Is leor go fairsing iad chun a chur ar ár súile an feabhas is féidir a thuar nuair a thagann dúchas, féith na scéalaíochta agus aithne na ceirde le chéile san aon scríbhneoir amháin" Máire Mhac an tSaoi, "Rogha an Chlub Leabhar", *Feasta* (Deireadh Fómhair 1953): 7.

ahead of her time in regards to her appreciation of the work–an appreciation which, it appears, became more prominent in the years that followed.

Perhaps the most controversial of Mhac an tSaoi's pieces for *Feasta,* however was the first review she wrote, which featured in the March 1953 edition of the journal, on the first poetry collection *Eireaball Spideoige* from Seán Ó Ríordáin, contemporary Irish language poet and newspaper columnist, and one third of the trinity of poets mentioned earlier. First published in 1952, *Eireaball Spideoige* provoked heated debate in English and in Irish, that extended beyond the usual literary and language journals to the letters pages of national newspapers, such as *The Irish Times.*[28] Mhac an tSaoi didn't mince her words when analysing the collection, describing reading some of the lines as like *ag fáscadh ghainmhe fét'fhiacla* (crunching sand through your teeth).[29] Mhac an tSaoi took particular issue with Ó Riordáin's lack of deference to the spoken language of the Gaeltacht in his collection, and accused the poet of a lack of proficiency: *easpa máistríochta ar an dteangain agus easpa tuisceana do scop meadaireachta na Gaeilge* (a lack of mastery of the language and lack of understanding of the metrical range of Irish). Mhac an tSaoi argued that as the Irish language is a living, spoken language one could not take too many liberties without compromising the meaning of the language itself. Mhac an tSaoi accused Ó Ríordáin of creating a barrier between the reader and the language, and leaving the former ill-equipped to access the language:

Sé toradh a bhíonn ar a leithéid ná comharthaí nach féidir a léamh gan eochair.

The result of this kind of approach is a series of signs that one cannot read without a key.[30]

---

[28] Louis De Paor, "Adhlacadh mo mháthar" by Seán Ó Riordáin, in Peter Denman (Ed.). *Irish University Review: A Journal of Irish Studies* (Sept 2009): 172.
[29] Máire Mhac an tSaoi, M. "Filíocht Sheáin Uí Ríordáin", *Feasta.* March 1953: 17.
[30] Máire Mhac an tSaoi, M. "Filíocht Sheáin Uí Ríordáin", *Feasta.* March 1953: 17.

Although quite critical of Ó Ríordáin's use of Irish language that Mhac an tSaoi alleged made his poetry inaccessible to the native Irish speaker, there were aspects of the collection that she commended in this review, which would take centre stage in Ó Ríordáin's later works–primarily his ability to express in words the most human, and often indescribable, experiences. Mhac an tSaoi notes Ó Ríordáin's *misneach agus macántacht* (courage and honesty) in this collection, and identifies the glimmers of poetic practice that Ó Ríordáin would master in his later works: *"Fiú ins na dréachta is tuirsiúla acu abairtí aonaracha is geall le clocha scáil* (Even in the most mundane drafts, occasional gems of sentences can be found)".[31]

Mhac an tSaoi's praise of Ó Ríordáin's poetic prowess is reiterated in a review she wrote in 1996, of a collection of essays by Irish writer Seán Ó Tuama. Mhac an tSaoi draws comparison between Ó Tuama and Ó Ríordáin, who was by this time one of the literary giants in the Irish language community. Mhac an tSaoi claimed that whatever talent he had as a writer was evident, however scant, in his earliest collection, *Eireaball Spideoige.* Mhac an tSaoi again refrained from commending the quality of Irish used in the collection, but did praise Ó Ríordáin's more mature poetry as "astringent, profound, serious, original and witty". She claimed that "although not popular", Ó Ríordáin's poetry has merit and asserted that "it stands comparison with the later Yeats or with Ó Bruadair".[32]

Mhac an tSaoi's review of the work is distinguished by the gender of the reviewer and her candid assessment, especially in terms of the language used in the collection. Surely what is important here is that this is the first woman in the Irish language coming out publicly and having the audacity to criticise the work of an emerging male poet at the time. This was unheard of. One can therefore gather that Mhac an tSaoi didn't subscribe to the opinion held by Ó Ríordáin, that woman is 'poetry not poet' (*"Ní file ach filíocht an bhean"*), a claim he made, in jest, in his poem *"Banfhile"*, composed in 1971 for Dámhscoil

---

[31] Máire Mhac an tSaoi, "Filíocht Sheáin Uí Ríordáin", *Feasta.* (March 1953): 17.

[32] Máire Mhac an tSaoi, "Review of Repossessions: Selected essays on the Irish literary heritage by Seán Ó Tuama", *from Poetry Ireland Review.* Vol. 49 (1996).

Mhúscraí.[33] Although the line was clearly satire to those in attendance, and received with good humour, this line gives life to a long founded conception of the feminine sex as the inspiration for poetry, as an image or a mythological character, rather than as an active writer or poet. Although one cannot assume this line captures Ó Ríordáin's outlook on women in general, one can argue that a writer as prolific, evocative and, at times, controversial as Máire Mhac an tSaoi serves as the antithesis to this claim.

Mhac an tSaoi dared to step outside of the restrictive boundaries based on the female writer by the patriarchal structure in terms of 'appropriate' traditional literary topics for women to explore in their works. Mhac an tSaoi's *Ceathrúintí Mháire Ní Ógáin* for example, went against women's place in literary life–"a place from which men grant her leave to write about either love or religion".[34] In both her own poetry, and her critical reviews, Mhac an tSaoi tackled such ground-breaking topics as sexual desire, adoption and religious guilt.

Feasta, under the editorship of Seosamh Ó Duibhginn (1914-1994), published Mhac an tSaoi's *Ceathrúintí Mháire Ní Ógáin* in its entirety, after the poem was awarded a literary prize at the 1956 Oireachtas na Gaeilge awards. The Oireachtas festival was founded in 1897 as an annual arts event that celebrates and promotes all aspects of the Irish language. *Ceathrúintí* was a radical piece of literature as it explored the most intimate desires of a woman. Mhac an tSaoi used the written word to go against the restrictive beliefs of the Catholic Church towards women, and the juxtaposition between the female authority in the home and their concurrent invisibility in the public sphere.

Ceathrúintí Mháire Ní Ógáin explored sexual love in its most intimate form, while using religious terminology to both describe sex and, perhaps, to empower the poet, and even the reader, to use religious terminology in a purely sexual sense, free of its religious connotations or 'prohibitions.' Mhac an tSaoi likened her sexual love to *Comaoine is éisteacht Aifrinn,*[35] (taking Communion and hearing

---

[33] Seán Ó Ríordáin, *Banfhile* (Dámhscoil Mhúscraí, 1971).
[34] Louise Bernikow, *The World Split Open–Women Poets 1551-1950.* (London: 1984), 6.
[35] Máire Mhac an tSaoi, 1956. "Ceathrúintí Mháire Ní Ógáin". *Feasta* (November 1956): 4.

Mass). She expressed a disregard for the oppression of society and the religious condemnation of the Church, describing the blinding capability of sexual attraction to all other aspects of life:

> *Beagbheann ar amhras daoine,*
> *Beaghbheann ar chros na sagart,*
> *Ar gach ní ach bheith sínte*
> *Idir tú agus falla–*

> I care little for people's suspicions,
> I care little for priests' prohibitions,
> For anything save to lie stretched
> Between you and the wall–

Mhac an tSaoi's admission, through the character of Máire Ní Ógáin, epitomises the birth of the new woman in Irish society after the founding of the Free State, and sequentially the emergence of an independent Nation in 1937. Kevin O'Higgins described this woman in a debate in Dáil Éireann in 1926, four years after the founding of the Irish Free State: He spoke of "an extremely able woman, an extremely strong-minded woman, a woman of highly developed public spirit and civic sense".[36] All of these trailblazing traits are clearly shown in *Ceathrúintí Mháire Ní Ógáin*.

It is important to note that Mhac an tSaoi employed the persona of Máire Ní Ógáin in this piece of literature, as a way of providing the writer the freedom with which to explore controversial material without hindrance, fundamental especially in the exploration of the female sexual desire. This is as she had done in her earliest pieces for *Comhar* under the alias M.. Poet Aifric Mac Aodha analysed *Ceathrúintí Mháire Ní Ógáin* in depth for the commemorative edition of *Comhar* in October 2022, to mark the first anniversary of Mhac an tSaoi's death. *Ceathrúintí* was a central piece of Mhac an tSaoi's collection of poetry *Margadh na Saoire*, published in 1956. *The Irish Times* has named *Margadh na Saoire* amongst one of the most valuable literary works in Ireland, again emphasising the point that the use of her native tongue, further granted the poet freedom to probe contentious topics: "The Irish language provided her with access to

---

[36] Kevin Ó Higgins, *Dáil Debates,* Vol. 1, Col. 1678, October 18 1922.

powerful precedents for the forthright expression of female desire".[37] Mhac an tSaoi's *Margadh na Saoire* featured itself as reviewed material in *Feasta's* contemporary, *Comhar*. Seán Mac Réamoinn reviewed the collection in 1957 and predicted a literary heritage for Mhac an tSaoi whose writings would further develop the field of Irish language literature:

> *Má mhaireann an Ghaeilge, agus saíocht na Gaeilge,*
> *tá mé ag ceapadh go mairfidh cuid mhaith de fhilíocht*
> *Mháire Mhac an tSaoi, de bharr an fhiúntais atá ann*
> *agus mar léiriú ar an bhforbairt nádúrtha a tháinig*
> *ar dhúchas ár n-éigse san aimsir seo.[38]*

> If the Irish language and all the wisdom contained in it is to survive, I think that the majority of Máire Mhac an tSaoi's poetry will survive too, because of its merit and its portrayal of the natural progression of our poetic heritage during this period.

When reflecting on *Ceathrúintí Mháire Ní Ógáin* and its longevity and lasting effect on the portrayal of the female voice in Irish language literature, one must conclude that Mac Réamoinn's prediction was accurate.

Máire Mhac an tSaoi was a ground-breaking force in Irish language writing, and her works in *Feasta* reflect her journalistic and critical strengths also. As a woman who came of age at the same age as the State, Mhac an tSaoi endeavoured to widen the 'woman's place', whatever that was, in Irish language literature. She dared to challenge the status quo by taking a stand in her literary reviews, especially when reviewing the works of male writers.

Máirín Ní Mhuiríosa (1906-1982)

Máirín Ní Mhuiríosa was an Irish scholar, poet and journalist, and although not as influential as trailblazer Mhac an tSaoi, Ní Mhuiríosa was a journalistic voice frequently featured in the pages of *Feasta* with

[37] Máirín Nic Eoin and Fintan O'Toole, "Modern Ireland in 100 Artworks: 1956–Margadh na Saoire, by Máire Mhac an tSaoi" *The Irish Times* (22 August 2015).
[38] Sheán Mac Réamoinn, "Filíocht Mháire Mhac an tSaoi", *Comhar* (April 1957): 5.

a substantial 55 pieces written by her between the years 1948 and 1980. 23 of these pieces were literary reviews, while the other 32 pieces attributed to Ní Mhuiríosa consisted of poems, reflective essays and letters. A full list of reviews Ní Mhuiríosa wrote for *Feasta* is given in the appendix following this article.

Máirín Ní Mhuiríosa is credited in *Feasta* under two spellings, Ní Mhuiríosa and Ní Mhuirgheasa, with the common theme in all of her literary reviews in the journal being the Irish speaker's and Irish society's perspective. For example in August 1958, *Feasta* published a review Ní Mhuiríosa wrote of *Aiséirí Flóndrais* by Albert Folens, a book which discussed the rise of Flanders, a Flemish speaking northern territory of Belgium, with reference made in Ní Mhuiríosa's review to the state of the Irish language at the time. Reflecting on the lessons of both Flanders and Ireland, Ní Mhuiríosa claimed that such a literary source as Folens' manuscript, would benefit both Irish language and Flemish communities, as both possessed something the other aspired to:

> *Nuair a chuirtear scéal na hÉireann agus scéal an Fhlóndrais i gcomórtas le chéile, seo mar a shamhlaítear do dhuine iad: gur éirigh le hÉirinn stát neamhspleách a dhéanamh di féin ach gur dhóbair di an teanga bheith caillte aici roimhe sin, agus ar an taobh eile de, cé nach stát é Flóndras fós, go bhfuil an teanga sábháilte aige ar chuma nach baol di inniu. Mar sin ba bhuntáiste don dá dhream, d'Éireannaigh agus do Phléimeannaigh, eolas ar scéal a chéile.*[39]

When one compares the story of Ireland with the story of Flanders, this is how one imagines it: Ireland succeeded in forming an independent state for herself, but had nearly lost her language beforehand, whereas Fanders, though not yet an independent state, has managed to save its language to the point that it's no longer in danger today. Therefore, it's of benefit for both parties, Irish and Flemish, to be aware of each other's story.

---

[39] Máirín Ní Mhuiríosa, "Críoch Chorraithe", *Feasta* (August 1958): 14.

Ní Mhuiríosa's assessment in the context of the Irish language movement on Folen's offering, allowed the *Feasta* reader to connect personally to the story of Flanders, and aided in situating the Irish language in an international setting. It also allowed the reader to understand the concept of the Revival in an international context, as it didn't apply only to Ireland and to the case of the Irish language.

The only work from a female writer reviewed by either Mhac an tSaoi or Ní Mhuiríosa, was the novel *Triúr Againn* by Siobhán Ní Shúilleabháin. Ní Shuilleabháin was a respected author of Irish-language novels, short stories, poems and play, but she also wrote for children. *Triúr Againn,* published in 1955, is a novel about three teenage girls as they solve a mystery. In her review, Ní Mhuiríosa praised the author's decision to place the story in her native West Kerry Gaeltacht, with the fictional school, Coláiste Ghobnatan based upon Coláiste Íde, where Ní Shuilleabháin herself lived and studied during her teenage years.[40] Ní Mhuiríosa commended Ní Shuilleabháin's *Triúr Againn* for providing a learning resource to young female learners of the Irish language.

Ní Mhuiríosa often wrote on the topic of education, not only for *Feasta* but also for *Comhar,* and for newspaper *The Irish Press,* the nationalist paper that favoured the political party Fianna Fáil. Ní Mhuiríosa appears to have understood the educational value of journalism and how it should provide a valuable resource for Irish language teaching and learning. Writing for *The Irish Press* in 1937 in an article entitled *"An Nuachtán mar Choir Oideachais"* (The newspaper as an educational tool), Ní Mhuiríosa claims that the Irish language must be modernized in order to survive, and that a resource such as journalism can prove invaluable to achieving this:

> *Samhlaítear dom, áfach, go bhféadfaí feidhm níos iomláine do bhaint as an bpáipéar nuachta chun cuidiú le hoideachas na bpáirtí agus le múineadh na Gaeilge ag an am céanna. Foilsítear ar an bpáipéar seo gach lá colún beag i nGaeilge ina mbíonn beachtaíocht ar scéal an lae. Nár chóir go bhféadfadh na múinteoirí–sa mheánscoil ar aon chuma–úsáid a*

---

[40] Máirín Ní Mhuiríosa, "Triúr Againn le Siobhán Ní Shuilleabháin", *Feasta.* (March 1956).

bhaint as an gcolún sin chun eolas éigin do thabhairt
do na scoláirí ar chúrsaí a linne féin.[41]

I imagine, however, that a greater use could be made of newspapers to help with the education of the parties and the teaching of Irish language at the same time. There is a small column in Irish posted in this paper [*The Irish Press*] each day giving an accurate account of the stories of the day. Shouldn't teachers– at second level at least–be able to use this column as a way of giving their students some insights into current affairs.

From this article, coupled with Ní Mhuiríosa's piece on *Triúr Againn* by Ní Shuilleabháin, we can gather that the inclusion of the female journalistic voice in print media was important to Ní Mhuiríosa in an educational context.

The March 1964 issue of *Feasta* was *Eagrán na Leabhar* (The Book Issue), and focused solely on analysing the impact of the Oireachtas an Gaeilge festival on Irish language literature. Máirín Ní Mhuiríosa's image was visible on the cover page, under the alternate spelling of Máirín Ní Mhuirgheasa, along with 37 other recognisable *Feasta* writers. Ní Mhuiríosa was one of only two women featured, Mairéad Ní Ghráda, short story writer and poet being the other. Most notable however, in its absence, was Máire Mhac an tSaoi's image. It's unclear why Mhac an tSaoi wasn't included in the cover art, or in the edition at all–as she had penned all seven pieces for *Feasta* by this time.[42]

---

[41] Máirín Ní Mhuiríosa, M. "An Nuachtán mar Choir Oideachais", *The Irish Press* (09.04.1937).
[42] "Eagrán na Leabhar", *Feasta.* (March 1964): 1. Courtesy of the National Library of Ireland.

March 1964 cover page

THE FEMALE CRITIC

Ní Mhuiríosa emphasised the importance of literature competitions in her regular additions to the journal, not only in regards to further developing the Irish language reading public, a topic that was discussed at length in a two-part essay *"An Léirmheastóireacht"* (Reviewing) published in the August and September editions of 1948, but also to provide learners the opportunity to engage with meaningful material, that inspired them to learn what they understood to be a vibrant and living language. Ní Mhuiríosa also spoke of the influence of the Oireachtas literary competitions on the growth of Irish language literature, one of which Mhac an tSaoi won for *Ceathrúintí Mháire Ní Ógáin* in 1956. She spoke of the opportunities afforded by the competitions for Irish speakers and learners of all levels, and capabilities:

> *Thug siad deis do Ghaeilgeoir na Galltachta eolas níos fearr a chur ar theanga bheo na Gaeltachta agus ar an tsaíocht atá ag gabháil léi.*

> They [Oireachtas literature competitions] provided Irish speakers of the English speaking districts the opportunity to improve their knowledge of the living language of the Gaeltacht and the thought behind it. [43]

Unlike Máire Mhac an tSaoi, Ní Mhuiríosa embraced her full name on this public platform, using it without hesitation or fear of retaliation from readers who were against a public role of women– such as in the essay *Deir Mairín Ní Mhuirgheasa* ("Máirín Ní Mhuirgheasa Says") in the May 1964 edition of the journal in which she gave her opinions on the affairs of the day.

Conclusion

The number of literature reviews in *Feasta* is a testament to the significant role it played as a minority language literary journal in promoting Irish language and literature. It was also, as Uí Chollatáin has asserted the first time Irish language literature reviews assessed content and material, rather than language alone, an aspect that is

---

[43] Máirín Ni Mhuirgheasa, "Na Comórtais Liteartha: Tionchar an Oireachtais ar an Litríocht", *Feasta.* (March 1964): 14.

crucial to the development of any print culture.[44] However, when the reviews of Máire Mhac an tSaoi and Máirín Ní Mhuiríosa are analysed, *Feasta* was not as cataclysmic in terms of furthering the cause of women in Irish language print media. The majority of contributors and editors of *Feasta* in its first forty years of publication were men, and it was substantially aimed toward the male reader. However, it was reflective of the time in which it spawned and when we consider Declan Kiberd's 1993 theory that literature must mirror the mind of the people and the era in which it is created,[45] the importance of *Feasta* as an important source in contributing to the understanding of the modern day reader in reviewing literature of the post-Revival period through the scope of the female voice cannot be overlooked. Mhac an tSaoi and Ní Mhuiríosa asserted women's educational, economic and political rights in the public sphere by providing a regular literary outlet for the female perspective. They also didn't shy away from reviewing all kinds of literary works—poetry, novels, translated works and performative pieces, such as plays and dramas. Although not a seismic shift in the journalistic practice of female writers, through their work in *Feasta*, both Mhac an tSaoi and Ní Mhuiríosa helped to broaden the woman's place in the public sphere and to further the case for the importance of the female perspective, at a time when both the Irish woman and the Irish public sphere were simultaneously coming of age.

Acknowledgements

My thanks to the Irish Research Council for funding this research under the Government of Ireland Postgraduate Programme. I am also very grateful to my supervisor Aoife Whelan and to my colleague Ríona Nic Congáil for their comments and suggestions.

---

[44] Uí Chollatáin, R. "Twentieth Century Irish Literature: A Journalistic Criticism" in *Periodicals and Journalism in Twentieth-Century Ireland.* Mark O'Brien and Felix M. Larkin (Eds). (Dublin: Four Courts Press, 2015) 300.

[45] See Declan Kiberd, *Idir Dhá Chultúr.* (Dublin: Coiscéim, 1993).

Reviewed works by Máire Mhac an tSaoi in *Feasta*

Poetry collections

- *Eireaball Spideoige* by Seán Ó Ríordáin, a collection of poetry (March 1953)

Journals/magazines

- *Irisleabhar Muighe Nuadhat,* a literary magazine (August 1953)

Song collections

- *Early Irish Lyrics,* a collection of early Irish songs, compiled and edited by Gerard Murphy (October 1956)
- *Dónall Óg: Taighde ar an Amhrán,* a book on the history of sean-nós songs by Seosamh Ó Duibhginn, second editor of *Feasta* from August 1949-June 1963 (March 1961)

Novels

- *Dúil,* by Liam Ó Flaithearta (October 1953)
- *Gearrcaigh na hOíche* by Seán Mac Fheorais (August 1954)
- A comparative piece on *Trí Ghluine Gaedheal* by Pádraig Ó Mileadha and *Amhráin ó Dheireadh an Domhain* by Fionán Mac Cártha (September 1954)

Reviewed works by Máirín Ní Mhuiríosa in *Feasta*

Biography

- *Eoghan Ó Gramhnaigh,* biography written by Seán Ó Ceallaigh (April 1970)

Children's books

- Children's book, *Bambi* by Felix Salten, translated by Mícheál Ó Cléirigh (July 1951)
- *Rí na gCat,* children's book by Eileen Ó Faoláin, translated by Brighid Ní Loinsigh (July 1950)

Poetry collections

- *Cnuasach 1966,* collection of prose and poetry compiled by Breandán S. Mac Aodha (ed.) (February 1967)
- *Dánta agus Duanta 1941-1947,* poetry and prose collection by L.S. Gógan (March 1953)
- *Dánta do Pháistí,* a compilation of short stories for young children by Séamus Ó Néill (February 1950)
- *An Dáin-leabhar* by Seán Mac Fheorais (October 1951)

Journals/magazines

- *Irisleabhar Muighe Nuadhat,* a literary magazine (June 1960)

Song collections

- *Seán de Hóra* a biography edited by Brian Mac Cumhghaill (September 1956) and *Coillte an Cheoil* by Séamas Ó Céileachair (September 1956)
- *An Grá in Amhrán* [sic] *na nDaoine,* collection of songs compiled by Seán Ó Tuama (September 1960)
- Collection of the literary works of Seán Ó Gadhra, *Dánta is Amhráin Sheáin Uí Ghadhra,* by Fr. Mac Domhnaill (ed) (July 1956)

Translated works

- *Immortale Dei* a book by Pope Leo XIII, translated by Ard-Deochan Mac Gionna Cheara (June 1958) as well as *Dhá Choinneal do Mhuire* by Henry B. Zimmerman, translated to Irish by Niall Ó Domhnaill (June 1958)
- Analysis on translation in the following works: *Eadarbhaile* by Peadar O'Donnell, Seosamh Mac Grianna who translated; *Thall is Abhus* by Tadhg ó Scanaill; *Teine fá Cheilt* by Partholón Ó Deasúna and *Páistidheacht* by Dr. Séamus Ó Beirn (April 1954)

THE FEMALE CRITIC

- *Ó Neamh go hÁrainn* by Máire, literary pseudonym of Séamus Ó Grianna; *Soineann 's Doineann* by Mícheál Ó Siochfhradha; *Is Truagh ná fanann an óige* by Mícheál Ó Gaoithín; Eoghan Ó Domhnaill's *Na Laetha a bhí; Mar Mhaireas é* by Peadar ó hAnnracháin; *The Priests Hunters, Sealgairí Sagart* written by James Murphy and translated by Conchubhar Ó Muimhneacháin; Charles Kickham's *Tales of Tipperary, Scéalta ó Thiobraid Árann*, translated by Conchubhar Ó Muimhneacháin (June 1954)
- Máirtín Ó Cadhain's translation of Saunders Lewis' *Bás nó Beatha* (November 1963).

Novels

- *Aiséirí Flóndrais* by Albert Folens (August 1958)
- *Glaotar ar Ridirí,* book by Críostóir Ó Floinn (May 1955)
- *Éigse na Máighe,* a book by Risteárd Ó Foghludha on literary history (June 1953)
- *Mar Mhaireas É II* prisoner story by Peadar Ó hAnnracháin (May 1956)
- *Fiadhach is Tóir is Scéalta Eile* by Amhlaoibh Ó Suilleabháin, compiled by Fr. Mícheál Mac Craith; *Thiar i nGleann Ceo* by Tadhg Ó Rabhartaigh; and *Cinneamhna Dé agus Scéalta eile* from the pen of Seán Ó Ciarghusa (July 1954)
- Novel *Bláth an Bhaile* written by Séamas Ó Céileachair and published by An Gúm (May 1952)
- The only work from a female writer reviewed by Ní Mhuiríosa, *Triúr Againn* by Siobhán Ní Shúilleabhán (March 1956)
- Fr. Pádraig Ó Fiannachta's book *An Chomharsa Choimhthíoch* (November 1957)

400

Abstracts of HCC 41 Presenters

'Amhail a-deir an file': Verifying Verse. Poetry and Historical 'Truth' in Medieval and Early Modern Ireland

Emmet de Barra

This paper seeks to investigate the relationship between Irish poetry and historical 'truth' as found in prose texts from medieval and early modern Ireland. As Keating famously wrote, "poems are the bone and marrow of the ancient record', and ancient authors 'framed the entire historical compilation in poems, in order that thereby the less change should be made in the record".

Keating was not alone in his use of poetry as evidence for his historical writings. Alongside the Four Masters, he was developing upon an inherited tradition central to Gaelic texts. Keating, aware of historiographical developments, references heavily from medieval writers such as Bede but, for Gaelic sources, poetry is used as a 'footnote' to prose commonly prefaced by some form of *amhail a-deir an file* or 'as the poet says'. These metrically-fixed references appear across multiple genres, such as annals, genealogies, (pseudo-)histories, and dinnseanchas. Poetry was held to contain a universal truth within medieval and early modern Ireland. While modern eyes might not perceive these poems as evidence of 'the truth', it must be recognised as containing 'a truth', a 'truth' which held inherent value within its own cultural milieu.

Building on an exploration of the use of poetry within prose texts, this paper will examine the impact that the understanding of poetry as evidence of historical 'truth' has on wider perceptions and uses of poetry, and the role of poets as 'truthmakers' and propagandists within the political culture of medieval and early modern Ireland.

Mutations and their non-standard usages in modern Breton

Myrzinn Boucher-Durand

Modern Breton is a minority language in France, and though unrelated to French, it is heavily influenced by this majority language. The linguistic situation also makes the majority of Modern Breton speakers second-language speakers. Because of that situation, and the

ABSTRACTS

low numbers of native speakers, we can observe the language in its evolution.

In this paper, I propose to look at this linguistic evolution from the point of view of mutations. Indeed, initial consonant mutations are an integral part of the Breton language, and, not existing in French, tend to pose problems to learners. I therefore propose to study the way in which mutations are used by a wide sample of speakers, learners and natives, to determine if their usage shows signs of an evolution in usage, between these two sample populations and the spectrum in between.

Verses in the scholia to the *Amrae Coluimb Chille*: some stemmatic considerations

Christina Cleary

The Middle Irish scholia to the *Amrae Coluimb Chille* contain over 150 verses, some of which make up poems and some of which have been extracted from prosimetrum texts or poems that no longer survive. In this paper, I will examine the date and language of a selection of verses in the later recension that deviate from the core scholia shared by all manuscripts. I will focus mostly on the relationship between the manuscripts BL MS Egerton 1782, RIA MS C iii 2 and NLI MS G 50 but their relationship with the Yellow Book of Lecan (TCD MS 1318), An Leabhar Breac (RIA MS 23 P 16) and NLI MS G 466 will also be taken into consideration. The purpose of this examination is to gain a better insight into the system of accretion in the later recension of scholia regarding the verses in the hopes of constructing a stemma.

Putting the 'English' back into Sasanach: religion and identity in the revival of Irish

Aidan Doyle

In the period between the imposition of the Penal Laws and the disestablishment of the Church of Ireland (c.1700-c.1870), the focus of conflict in Ireland narrowed to that of religion. Because of the sectarian nature of society, which was enshrined in law, religion became the defining force in people's lives. This was reflected in the

402

semantics of words which originally denoted members of ethnic groups. Because a Protestant was the descendant of a *Sasanach* 'Englishman' or *Albanach* 'Scot', the word *Sasanach* became shorthand for Anglican (Episcopalian), while *Albanach* came to represent a Calvinist. Furthermore, *Gall* 'foreigner' also became a term for a Protestant, with the adjective *Gallda* meaning Protestant (adj.). In parts of Ireland, *Gael* 'Irishman' became synonymous with Catholic.

This terminology presented language revivalists with a dilemma, particularly since the leading member of the Gaelic League, Douglas Hyde, was the son of a Church of Ireland clergyman, and hence a *Sasanach / Gall* for speakers of Irish. This paper examines how Hyde and others managed to sanitize the form of Irish which was taught in the education system of the new Free State after 1922, and which found its way into dictionaries and teaching materials. It is argued that this conscious manipulation of language was largely successful, although the older associations persisted in the Gaeltacht regions. The paper shows that while language reflects the nature of society, it can also be harnessed to bring about changes in how a given society views itself.

'This is our battle': John Rowlands' Arch ym Mhrâg, and a Welsh perspective on the end of the Prague Spring

Elis Dafydd

As Russian forces invaded Ukraine on 24 February 2022, it was a scene reminiscent of the USSR and other Warsaw Pact countries' invasion of Czechoslovakia in 1968. Now, Russia under Putin is concerned about Ukraine's interest in joining NATO, and in 1968, the Soviet Union under Leonid Brezhnev was concerned about Czechoslovak President Alexander Dubček's liberalizing reforms, and his attempt to steer away from Soviet Communism and create what was dubbed 'Socialism with a human face'.

One who was present in Prague on that night in 1968 was Welsh lecturer, novelist, and literary critic John Rowlands. The experience had a significant effect on him, and he published *Arch ym Mhrâg* ['A Coffin in Prague'], a novel exploring the event, in 1972. It is a step away from his previous psychological, Angry Young Man-esque

ABSTRACTS

novels, as it is a political, documentary novel, with extensive quotations from contemporary poems and political documents included in the text.

This paper will give a brief overview of the novel and its contexts before analysing closely the novel's criticism of Welsh nationalists' eagerness to draw parallels between Wales' and other nations' struggles. Czechoslovakia was a beacon of hope for Welsh patriots during the 20th century as a small European nation who had gained its independence from a greater power, but the interaction between Welsh and Czech characters in *Arch ym Mhrâg* emphasizes the differences between the two countries' situations, and asserts that Welsh solutions must be found for Welsh political problems.

Epigraphic and linguistic observations on the inscription at the so-called Mur d'Hannibal (Liddes, Valais, Switzerland)

Joseph F. Eska / Charlene M. Eska

This paper argues that the Celtic inscription engraved in the Alphabet of Lugano in sinistrograde ductus at the so-called Mur d'Hannibal (Liddes, Valais, Switzerland) should be read as Poenino | ieur{e}u 'he dedicated to P.' The first form is a thematic dative singular. The desinence may well be Latin, but a case is made that it could be a Celtic desinence that displays a regional phonological development. The fourth character of the second form is a reversed Roman open *R*, well attested in Cisalpine and Transalpine Celtic epigraphy. This form also displays a token of dittography, a phenomenon attested elsewhere in the Continental Celtic epigraphic corpus.

Byd Anafus - Staging Anarchy: Folk Culture and Popular Drama in early-modern Wales

Jerry Hunter

It is generally agreed that most surviving eighteenth-century anterliwt texts contain two layers, the 'original' or 'authored' part of the play and an older layer adapted from Welsh folk tradition. However, the traditional aspects of these plays remain under-studied and under-appreciated. Focusing on the work of Huw Jones of

404

Llangwm (d. 1782), this paper will examine his use of traditional material and themes and suggest that he was particularly adept at staging anarchic comedy well suited to the carnivalesque contexts in which anterliwtiau were often performed. The definitions of contrasting and overlapping spheres and modes–folk, popular and professional–will be discussed. The analysis will be inflected by a consideration of the social status of the performers, the religious tensions of the period, and the relationship between festive disorder and political status quo. Finally, the methodological challenges inherent in studying texts used in performances which are now lost to us will be examined.

Ymddiddan, Performance, and Mutual Entertainment in Aberystwyth, National Library of Wales MS Peniarth 65

Morgan E. Moore

Examining the manuscript Aberystwyth, National Library of Wales MS Peniarth 65 permits a clearer, more nuanced understanding of how the Welsh word *ymddiddan* (lit. "conversation" or "dialogue") was used in the early modern period. In this paper, I will present a summary of my codicological investigation of this small, 16th century collection of Welsh verse, which is an important source for medieval Welsh drama. I will then argue that previous attempts to define an ymddiddan as a form of literary "recitation" by a sole performer (c.f. Ford 1975 and Davies 1992) unnecessarily narrow our understanding of this genre and the array of literary and performance qualities which it may have had. I will use the physical and visual characteristics of MS Peniarth 65, its selection and presentation of texts, and the existing literature on Welsh drama and verse performance (e.g. Jones 1918, Campbell 2005, and Klausner 2008 and 2018), to suggest the utility of a broader, more fluid, and more performance-oriented approach to ymddiddanau. This study, though focused on a 16th-century manuscript and deliberately circumspect in its conclusions, nonetheless may prove useful for future examination of earlier medieval ymddiddanau, such as those found in the Black Book of Carmarthen, and the genre's popularity throughout medieval Welsh literature.

ABSTRACTS

The Great Library of Cambria: Investigating the Surprisingly Large Corpus of Welsh Translations from Greek

Alexander Morgan

The Coleg Cymraeg Cenedlaethol , an organisation operating in Welsh universities to promote Welsh-medium teaching and scholarship, launched a corpus of foreign language translations into Welsh in 2014 called Cronfa Cyfieithiadau'r Gymraeg. This corpus covers works published since the twentieth century in Welsh from any language, from short stories to book-length translations. Within this corpus, one of the most striking categories is translations from Greek. There are twenty-two entries, including translations of plays by Aeschylus, Euripides and Sophocles, poetry translations from all kinds of sources, and philosophical texts, including full translations of Plato's Republic and Aristotle's Nichomachean Ethics. This is an extensive corpus for a minority language, particularly as many of the works were produced before Welsh gained legal recognition.

This paper will examine the reasons behind the relative abundance of Greek translations in Welsh compared to most other European minority languages. Through an analysis of the translators, their social contexts and the translations themselves, it will investigate possible motivations for translation in this language pair, including Christian influences, the National Eisteddfod translation competition, and the impact of Welsh-language provision in the University of Wales. This study will show how a combination of diverse institutions led to multiple paths for the creation of translations, creating a corpus larger than would have been likely with the sole use of any of the individual institutions.

'Dord muice ar seachrán': a satire on an incompetent Irish harper

Deirdre Nic Chárthaigh

A handful of satirical poems on harpers are preserved in Irish manuscripts. This paper will focus on one of these compositions, a short poem of seven quatrains beginning *Athraigh gléas a Ghiolla Íosa*. The only known surviving copy of this poem was added in a later hand to the fifteenth-century vellum manuscript A7 in the Franciscan collection (now held in University College Dublin). Although the date of the poem is uncertain, it will be suggested here that it is one of a number of poems on harpers that were composed at the end of the Classical Irish period. Gillespie has interpreted these compositions as evidence "that the harp and its music fitted into the changing fabric of Irish society rather better than its poets did" (Gillespie 2009, 31). This paper will argue that they bear witness, instead, to the marginalization and decline of the harping profession. It will also be argued that certain features of this poem, such as the use of animal imagery and of poorly attested vocabulary, and the identification of the subject with a particular occupation, demonstrate a continuity in Irish satire from the early to the modern Irish period.

Marginal and Interlinear Marks and Symbols in Rome, BAV, Reg. lat. 49 (*s.* X^{ex}, Brittany?)

Jean Rittmueller

Rome, BAV, Reg. lat. 49 is a compilation of 56 Latin texts, a third of which were drawn from Hiberno-Latin sources and named 'catechesis celtica' by A. Wilmart. It has a tentative late tenth-century date and a possible Breton origin. It has been of interest to modern scholars since 1913, but scholars contemporary with the MS added technical signs that show that they also engaged with it in a number of ways. The scribe himself used double sets of interlinear and marginal correction marks to add omitted text. The scribe or another scholar added interlinear construe marks to identify syntactic, grammatical, and logical units. An unidentified scholar added cross-reference symbols and *appels de note*. Another scholar, using a light reddish ink, added marginal technical signs and interlinear transposition marks.

This paper will provide an overview of the technical signs used in this manuscript, referencing the work of P. McGurk, M. B. Parkes, P. Y. Lambert, and E. Steinová. It will describe their forms and categorize their uses, making them available for comparison and to aid in identifying the origin of Reg. lat. 49.

ABSTRACTS

Dynastic Networks and Landscape Mythology

Marie-Luise Theuerkauf

The late Middle Irish prosimetrical corpus *Dindshenchas Érenn* (The History of Ireland's Prominent Places) consists of over 200 topographical legends in prose and in verse about famous places in Ireland. The corpus's episodic structure is not dissimilar from what we find in the Fenian *Acallam na Senórach*. Unlike the *Acallam*, however, the *Dindshenchas* does not have a central cast of characters, nor does it follow a particular plot. Indeed the various placename stories contained in the corpus seem, at first glance, to offer little in terms of literary cohesion, and are seemingly unconnected to one another. This paper will offer a new reading of this fascinating corpus by laying bare the dynastic networks which represent the literary grid on which the text operates.